THE BOOK OF
ULSTER
SURNAMES

ROBERT BELL

THE
BLACKSTAFF
PRESS

BELFAST

First published in 1988 by
The Blackstaff Press Limited
3 Galway Park, Dundonald, Belfast BT16 0AN, Northern Ireland

Reprinted 1990, 1994, 1997

Printed by The Guernsey Press Company Limited

British Library Cataloguing in Publication Data
Bell, Robert, 1953–
The book of Ulster surnames.
I. Northern Irish surnames. Etymology
& distribution
I. Title
929. 4'2'09416

Library of Congress Cataloging-in-Publication Data
Bell, Robert, 1953–
The book of Ulster surnames / Robert Bell.
p. cm.
Bibliography: p.
Includes index.
I. Names, Personal—Ulster (Northern Ireland and Ireland) –
– Dictionaries. 2. Ulster (Northern Ireland and Ireland)—Genealogy.
I. Title.
CS2415.B45   1988   88-7452
929.4'09416—dc19   CIP

ISBN 0-85640-602-3

for

Bob Bell   Nellie Gordon
Jan Bell
Beth Bell
Andrew Bell
and
Melanie Bell

CONTENTS

**APPROXIMATE LOCATIONS OF ANCIENT KINGDOMS
AND TERRITORIES IN IRELAND**

INTRODUCTION

What's your name? What was your mother called? And her mother? What was your father's mother's name? Most of us know at least a few of the surnames that make up the heritage of our own families. But what do these names mean and where did they come from?

The surnames of Ulster stem from many different peoples and many eras and can be difficult to unravel. The Cruthin, the Pictish race that inhabited the province before the invasion of the Gaels, have left virtually no mark on our surnames, not surprisingly, since hereditary surnames only came into being in the province in the tenth century and only became widespread in the eleventh. The arrival of the Vikings, too, predated the rise of a surname system, but they left a legacy of personal names, many of which became popular in Gaelic society and were eventually incorporated into surnames: MacManus, for instance, derives from the Norse personal name Magnus.

From the twelfth century the Anglo-Normans and then the English brought their surnames to Ulster through the Pale and its outposts on the coasts of Down and Antrim. Scottish mercenary families, the famed galloglasses, were brought to the province by the warring 'clans' of Ulster and quickly adapted to and settled in Ulster Gaelic society. Many of their names are well documented – MacCabe, MacDonnell, MacSweeney – but research is still required to unravel the complexities of some (see MacCallion, for instance).

Before the Plantation the galloglass influence is only a part of the Scottish connection in the surnames of Ulster. Many of the Scottish clans claim descent from the same (historical and legendary) figures as their Irish equivalents, and from the time of the creation of the Irish Dalriadic kingdom in Scotland, the two regions and their surnames have been closely related through language, alliance, war, marriage, migration and trade (see MacDonald, particularly).

Add to this the most significant influx of names of all, the Plantation of the early seventeenth century, and the variety and complexity of the problem of Ulster surnames begins to become obvious.

Further, the domination of Ulster by the English from the seventeenth century has meant dramatic changes in the forms of the indigenous Irish names of the province. From the enactment of the Statute of Kilkenny in 1397 the English Crown made attempts to forbid the use of Irish names, but it is thought that such legislation in itself made little impression. After the Plantation, however, English administrative officials, of government and of individual landlords, were unable or unwilling, or both, to accept Irish forms of names, and in the ensuing centuries widespread anglicisation of these names took place. One of the few names to survive virtually unscathed is the one that is most identified with Ulster, O'Neill (in Gaelic Ó Néill).

The prefixes Mac- and particularly O' disappeared, though many families have resumed them since the late nineteenth century. Names were anglicised to a form in English that approximated to the Gaelic sound. Thus Ó Dubhthaigh became O'Duffy, then Duffy. Very many, however, acquired or were given an English or Scottish name that was often only vaguely similar to the sound: thus Mac Cuinneagáin was made Cunningham. Others were translated or half-translated or mistranslated. Exactly the same processes happened in Gaelic Scotland – Mac Thómais (MacThomas), for instance, became Holmes.

The result is that very many people in Ulster with English names who assume that they are of English descent may not be. It is of course quite possible that they are; but to take the most common Ulster name as an example, a majority of those in the province by the name of Smith will be of Scottish or Irish descent and will have been originally O'Gowans, MacGowans and Gows, their name having been translated from the Gaelic *gabha*, meaning 'smith'. Mac Cathmhaoil was once one of the most common names in Tyrone and has now become lost in a variety of anglicised forms. Although its most reasonable anglicisation is rare, I have given MacCawell a separate entry to help to locate the other extant forms of the name.

A very great deal remains to be done to understand more fully the history of surnames in Ulster particularly at a local level. As Peadar Livingstone pointed out in his invaluable studies of Fermanagh and Monaghan, an Irish Gaelic name famous nationally as originating in one county may be of a different derivation in part of another. Even less work has been done on the history of post-Plantation settler names, though the work of such people as Dr Brian Turner has uncovered much in specified areas that was previously forgotten.

In particular, Dr Turner's brilliant insight into the influence in Fermanagh of settlers from the Scottish Borders has deepened our awareness not only of the history of surnames in that county but also of

Fermanagh's political and religious history as well.

In 1603, when James VI of Scotland became also James I of England, he set out to 'pacify' the Borders, now his 'Middle Shires', home of the turbulent and notorious riding clans. The following decade saw a ruthless programme there of executions, banishments, transportations and the seizure of lands by the Crown. The power of these clans and their social system were broken for ever.

Many members of these broken clans opted for a new life in Ulster to escape persecution, the Plantation just getting under way at that time. They settled principally in Fermanagh and by the mid-seventeenth century the names of the riding clans – Johnston, Armstrong, Elliott, Irvine, Nixon, Crozier and so on – had come to predominate in that county, managing to weather the storm of the 1641 rising which had largely destroyed the Plantation settlement in other counties.

For some years Dr Turner has also been building up from the electoral rolls a complete picture of the exact distribution of surnames in present-day Ulster, and I look forward to the publication of his findings. In their absence I have had to rely on earlier studies to find where a particular name is most common. However, surnames are notoriously conservative. Planter names have often been associated with an area for hundreds of years and in the case of Ulster Gaelic names, often for over a thousand.

The main entries constitute an alphabetical listing of over 500 of the most numerous surnames (in their most common forms) in nine-county Ulster. (However, a few names that are rarer have been included because of their intrinsic interest or because of the light they shed on other more numerous names.) Very popular alternative spellings, anglicisations, variants and so on, are also to be found in the alphabetical listing and refer the reader to the main headings under which they are discussed. A very large number of other, less common, names are also mentioned within each entry and can be found via the Index of Surnames. Many distinctively Ulster names, particularly those of Huguenot origin, do not appear because, despite their fame, they were simply not common enough to warrant discussion. Where I state that a name is most common in a particular county or parish, this of course discounts Belfast – the metropolitan district of any country naturally attracting all surnames.

In the text reference is repeatedly made to Gaelic Ulster septs as 'erenaghs'. This term means that the family concerned had control over the church lands of a particular parish in the medieval period. This information is included because it denotes that such septs were very important or powerful in their district and, in the main, that they were based in those particular parishes.

3

One distinct element appears and reappears in the Gaelic names of both Ireland and Scotland: Irish Gaelic *giolla* and Scots Gaelic *gille*. Each can have one of three origins. Both words can mean 'devotee', as in the sense of 'devotee or follower of (a saint)', for example, Mac Giolla Chiaráin (MacElheron), meaning 'son of the devotee of (St) Ciaran'. They can also mean 'servant', a form that survives in the Scots dialect word 'gillie', as in Mac Gill' Easpuig (Gillespie), meaning 'son of the servant of the bishop'. Finally, it can mean 'lad' or 'youth', as in Mac Giolla Rua (MacIlroy), meaning 'son of the red (-haired) youth'. Most of our Gil-, Kil-, MacEl- and MacIl- names derive from these elements.

The spellings I have used in the text cannot be taken as definitive. This applies particularly to the spelling of Mac- names. Throughout I have tried to avoid the use of Mc- and of the now rare M' prefixes. Both of these are simply abbreviations of the Gaelic Mac, meaning 'son of', and for the sake of consistency all such names, except those of historical characters or of certain names quoted from specific documents, have been given the full Mac- spelling. The resumption of the O' prefix in the nineteenth and twentieth centuries has affected only a fraction of those names that in the original Gaelic would have been so rendered. None the less, in some names the O' form is now more common – O'Hagan, for instance – and these will be found listed under O. The myth that Mac-names are Scottish and O' names Irish has no foundation. They are Gaelic elements in both countries, though it must be said that in Scotland O' is much rarer. The standardisation of Gaelic in both Ireland and Scotland and indeed the much earlier standardisation of English have led to many anomalies in the spellings of names. Further, surnames are often one of our most treasured possessions and individual families have tended to adopt and maintain particular spellings. It would be impossible to list all known forms but I have given the most common variants where appropriate; I apologise if any particular spelling does not appear.

I doubt if this book could have been researched anywhere other than in the Genealogy Collection of the Linen Hall Library in Belfast and so for me this has been something of an inside job. The collection houses hundreds of family histories and thousands of learned articles, many of which I have consulted and which will not appear in the select bibliography. I would like to record the debt I owe to the authors of these. The staff of the Linen Hall have been a great help to me and I thank them all, particularly John Killen, and Maureen Larmour, Mary Hughes and Gerry Healey in the Irish section. I am also grateful to Gregory Toner of the Department of Celtic, Queen's University, Belfast, who helped with the Irish and Scots Gaelic; Roger Dixon of Belfast Central Library;

Lorraine Tennant of the Ulster American Folk Park; Billy Ingram of the University of Ulster at Jordanstown; Dr Brian Turner of the Down Museum; and Kathleen Agnew.

Lastly, I would like to thank Jan, Melanie, Andrew and Beth.

Robert Bell
Linen Hall Library
Belfast, 1988

ALPHABETICAL LIST OF SURNAMES

ACHESON *see* Atkinson

ADAIR (*also* Edgar)

In Ireland these are almost exclusively Ulster names. Both are found mainly in counties Antrim and Down. Though the original name Edgar is English, from the Old English personal name Eadgar, meaning 'happy spear', in Ulster both surnames stem mainly from Scotland. They originate from and are still most common in the province of Galloway, where Edgar was first noted in the thirteenth century.

The Edgars of Nithsdale in Dumfriesshire were of Gaelic origin. The progenitor of the family was Edgar, *c.* 1200, son of Duvenald, son of Dunegal of Stranid (now Strath Nith). He held extensive lands in Nithsdale. His descendants assumed the name of Edgar. Adair appears first in the fourteenth century as an alternative pronunciation of Edzear, itself a local pronunciation of Edgar.

Many of the Galloway Adairs came to Ulster during and after the Plantation. A William Adair of Wigtownshire settled in Ballymena, Co. Antrim, in 1614. Patrick Adair came to Co. Antrim in 1641 and later became famous as the author of *The True Narrative of the Rise and Progress of the Presbyterian Church in Ireland*. In the seventeenth century Adair was particularly common in the barony of Antrim. One of the Co. Antrim Adairs, James, *c.* 1709–*c.* 1783, was a pioneer in America and wrote *The History of the American Indians*. A few Adairs may originally be of the Irish family Ó Dáire.

Other old pronunciations of Edgar were Agar and Eager and both are found in Ulster, Agar particularly on the Ards peninsula in Co. Down. In mid-nineteenth-century Down Edgar was found mainly in the parish of Killaney, barony of Upper Castlereagh.

ADAMS

This name is much more common in Ulster than in the other Irish provinces. It is particularly popular in counties Antrim and Derry and can be of either Scottish or Irish origin.

The name Adam, Hebrew for 'red', was very popular in medieval England where it ranked as third favourite male Christian name. In Scotland, where it was also popular, it gave rise to the pet forms Aidy and Eadie. The Aidies and Adams were septs of Clan Gordon; the MacAidies, a sept of Clan Ferguson; the Adamsons septs of Shaw and Mackintosh; and the MacAdams a sept of the MacGregors.

In Co. Antrim in the nineteenth century the main concentrations of the name were in the baronies of Upper Dunluce and Kilconway, and in Co. Down, in the barony of Ards near Donaghadee.

Adams is also used as an anglicisation of three different Irish Gaelic names. In the Roslea–Clones area of Fermanagh–Monaghan Adams was often originally Ó Cadáin (also anglicised as O'Cadden and Cadden); in Co. Armagh it was anglicised from Mac Cadáin; in Co. Cavan it can be an anglicisation of the Irish Mac Ádhaimh (*see* MacAdam). Not all Adamses in these areas are of Irish origin, of course. One well-documented Co. Cavan family of Scottish origin stems from a Colonel James Adam who first settled in Co. Down in the early seventeenth century and married into the Magennises. He added the 's' during his lifetime. The name in Scotland is common only as Adam but in Ulster it is almost invariably found as Adams.

Around 1900 Adams was recorded as interchangeable with Aidy in the Downpatrick area and with Eadie around Dromore, both in Co. Down.

See also MacAdam.

AGNEW

The Agnews in Ireland, apart from a small number in Dublin, hail almost exclusively from Ulster. Seventy per cent are from Co. Antrim and a further 20 per cent from counties Armagh and Down. The name is of either Gaelic or Norman origin.

The original family of d'Agneaux took their name from the Baronie d'Agneaux in Normandy. They came to England with William the Conqueror. In the twelfth century a branch of the family came to Ulster with John de Courcy and was granted the lordship of Larne, Co. Antrim.

Another branch of the family settled in Scotland and was first recorded there at about the same time. In 1363 in Wigtownshire the Lochnaw branch of this family was appointed hereditary sheriffs of the Scottish province of Galloway and became great landowners there. Coincidentally, a branch of Lochnaw Agnews came to Ulster and was granted lands near Larne by James VI of Scotland in the seventeenth century.

To add to the confusion, the Ulster sept of Ó Gnímh, famous as poets to the O'Neills of Clann Aodha Bhuidhe, or Clandeboy, in Antrim, also acquired

7

the surname Agnew. The sept name was first written in English as O'Gnive. This later became O'Gnyw and then O'Gnew. In northern pronunciation this became a'Gnew and hence Agnew. It is thought that this sept came to Co. Antrim from Scotland in the fourteenth century at roughly the same time as the MacDonald galloglasses but it was not a galloglass family itself. It is presumed they were among the original Irish colonisers of Scotland in the fifth century. But in Co. Antrim they too settled around Larne as well as in the north of the county. The most famous of the Ó Gnímh poets was Fearflatha O'Gnive, c. 1580–c. 1640. Another Irish sept, the MacAneaves, have in some instances anglicised their name to Agnew in parts of Co. Tyrone (see Forde).

The early history of the state of Pennsylvania owes much to Agnews of Ulster ancestry. Sir James Willson Agnew, 1815–1901, who was born in Co. Antrim, became premier of Tasmania.

AIKEN (also Aitken, Eakin, Eakins)

In Ireland common only in Ulster, Aiken is of Scottish origin. It is the Scottish form of the English name Atkin, which comes from Adkin, a pet form of Adam. The name was very common in the parish of Ballantrae in Ayrshire and many of our Aikens may stem from there. There are many variant spellings. It was recorded as being used interchangeably with Eakins in Belfast, Eakin in counties Derry and Donegal, Ekin in Co. Donegal and Egan in Co. Down. Some of the Irish sept of O'Hagan (see O'Hagan) may have further anglicised their name to Aiken.

In Co. Antrim, where it is most popular, it was found to be most concentrated in the area northwest of Ballymena in the mid-nineteenth century.

Dr Joseph Aiken published a contemporary account of the Siege of Derry in verse entitled *Londerias, or, a narrative of the siege of Londonderry* (1699).

AITKEN see Aiken

ALEXANDER (also Saunders)

Although Alexander is a Greek name by origin (meaning 'defender of men') it is nowhere so common as in Scotland. Indeed, the pet form Sandy rivals Donald as the archetypal Scottish name. The name Alexander was brought to Scotland in the eleventh century by Queen Margaret, wife of King Malcolm Ceannmór, from the Hungarian court and quickly became popular. It was gaelicised as Alaxandair which in turn became Alasdair. It was this Christian name that gave rise to the surname MacAllister (see MacAllister). An Elizabethan spelling of the name was Alesaundre and from this and the original, the pet forms Sanders, Saunders, Saunderson and so on, derived.

The surname Alexander was popular on the west coast of Scotland particularly on Kintyre and in Ayrshire. There were Alexander septs of Clan MacAllister, Clan Donald, Clan MacArthur, and Clan MacDonnell of Glengarry.

Many Alexanders came to Ulster during and after the Plantation. One of these, the Revd Andrew Alexander, a Presbyterian minister, settled in 1618 in what was then Coleraine county and began a family business in tanning, later bleaching and eventually trading as merchants.

The name is most common in Co. Antrim and to a lesser extent in Co. Down. In mid-nineteenth-century Antrim the largest concentration of Alexanders was found to be in the barony of Lower Belfast between Carrickfergus and Larne.

Around 1900 a very large number of synonyms were recorded for the name, including Elshinder, Elshander and Kalshander near Lisburn, Co. Antrim; MacAlshender, Esnor and MacCausland near Broughshane, Co. Antrim; Elchinder and MacElshunder around Ballymoney, Co. Antrim; and M'Clatty near Stewartstown, Co. Tyrone. During the twentieth century almost all of these have become rare.

ALLEN (*also* MacAllen)

Allen is among the fifty most common surnames in both England and Scotland, and the Ulster Allens can stem from either country. The English Allen derives from the Old French Alain, Old Breton Alan, and was originally a Germanic tribal name Alemannus, meaning 'all men'. Alan, the name of a Welsh and Breton saint, was brought to England by Bretons in the train of William the Conqueror. Although there were references to the name in Ireland in the medieval period, and it is found in Plantation records, the first important influx of Allens arrived with Cromwell in the mid-seventeenth century.

In Scotland the name has two derivations. Firstly, as in England, it came to Scotland with the Normans. There its popularity as a Christian name with the Stewarts, whose progenitor was Walter FitzAlan, quickly spread outside that family. However, the name was already popular in Scotland from the Gaelic name Ailín, from *ail*, meaning 'rock'. This gave rise to the surname Mac Ailín or MacAllan. There were several different septs of this name belonging to separate clans. Many of them anglicised to Allen or Allan. In Scotland Allens can belong to Clan Allen, Clan MacAllan, Clan Campbell and even Clan Mackay but most stem from either Clan MacFarlane or MacDonald of Clanranald.

The Scottish Allens who first made an impact in Ireland were the Clan Campbell Mac Ailíns who were brought from Argyllshire to Tirconnell by the O'Donnells during the fifteenth century and fought for them as galloglasses. Some Ulster Allens and MacAllens descend from these, many others from subsequent migrations (*see* MacCallion).

Two-thirds of the Allens in Ireland are in Ulster, where the name is particularly associated with counties Antrim and Armagh.

ANDERSON (*also* Andrews)

The Scottish name Anderson, which is among the forty most common names in Ulster, has two principal origins, both of which derive from the Greek name Andrew, meaning 'manly'. In Scotland the name is among the ten most common and the majority of those of the name are Lowlanders. In this case Anderson means 'Andrew's son', as indeed does the name Andrews. As the name of the Scottish patron saint, Andrew was a very popular Christian name and both Andrews and Anderson sprang up, as patronymics, in a wide variety of locations. Most of the Ulster Andersons and Andrewses are of this Lowland stock, their ancestors arriving during and after the Plantation. A family of Andersons was one of the lesser of the riding clans of the Scottish Borders. They lived in Redesdale on the English side of the Middle March.

However, earlier in Scotland the name of the patron saint had been gaelicised as Andreis. There is mention in early records of the name Mac Gille Andrais, meaning 'son of the servant of (St) Andrew' (*see* Ross). This name was anglicised to Anderson, Andrews, MacAndrew and Gillanders. Gillanders is also found frequently in Co. Monaghan, where it is an Irish name of the same Gaelic derivation. The Clan Donald Mac Gille Andrais sept were numerous in the west of Scotland, particularly on Islay and Kintyre. They later anglicised their name to Anderson, and the Andersons of Rathlin Island, off Co. Antrim, and many of those in north Antrim are of this origin. (MacLandish, another anglicisation of the Gaelic name, is also common on Rathlin.)

In the mid-nineteenth century the main Co. Antrim concentration of Andersons was found to be in the barony of Lower Antrim near Broughshane and the main Co. Down centre was in the barony of Ards near Newtownards. The Andersons are also numerous in Co. Derry.

The name Andrews is most popular in counties Antrim and Down. The famous milling family of the name in Comber, Co. Down, had many distinguished members. Of these, the two most famous were brothers. John Miller Andrews, 1871–1956, was prime minister of Northern Ireland after Sir James Craig. He was also Orange Grand Master first of Down, then of Ireland, then of the world. Thomas Andrews, 1871–1912, was managing director of shipbuilders Harland and Wolff. As chief designer and naval architect, he was also responsible for building the *Titanic*. He sailed on the ill-fated maiden voyage as the firm's representative and chose to go down with the ship.

ANDREWS *see* Anderson

ARMOUR *see* Larmour

ARMSTRONG

This name comes from the Scottish Borders, where the two most important families lived in the Debateable Land and Liddesdale, the Ulster Armstrongs stemming mostly from the latter. The derivation of the name is from the Old English *earm*, 'arm', and *strang*, 'strong', and the Armstrongs were a warlike clan famous for centuries for raiding and reiving. Alexander, the first chief, held the seat of Mangerton in the late thirteenth century. It was the most feared and dangerous clan on the whole border and at its height, in the sixteenth century, it could put three thousand men into the saddle. In the decade after 1603 James VI, newly King of England as well as of Scotland, began a ruthless campaign to 'pacify' the Borders, and the great riding clans of Armstrong, Elliot, Johnston and Graham, among others, were broken. After the death of the tenth chief in 1610 the Armstrongs scattered, many coming to Ulster, particularly Fermanagh.

Armstrong is among the fifty most common Ulster surnames. A 1962 survey found it to be the third most numerous name in Fermanagh, where Elliott and Johnston are also in the first five. (All three names have been common there since the early seventeenth century.) It is popular too in Co. Antrim and to a lesser extent in counties Cavan and Tyrone.

In mid-nineteenth-century Co. Antrim the name was found to be most concentrated in Upper Massereene around Crumlin. The bulk of these Armstrongs, however, were not of Scottish origin. The Laverys of that district were so numerous that there were three distinct septs: Baun-Laverys, Roe-Laverys and Trin-Laverys (from Gaelic *bán*, 'white'; *rua*, 'red'; and *tréan*, 'strong'). The Trin-Laverys often mistranslated their name to Armstrong and indeed at the start of the twentieth century Armstrong was still being used interchangeably with Lavery and Trin-lavery in Co. Antrim in Crumlin, Aghalee, Glenavy and Lisburn (*see* Lavery). Armstrong was also adopted as a quasi-translation of the Irish name Trainor, originally Mac Thréinfhir (*tréan*, 'strong' and *fear*, 'man') (*see* Treanor).

Sir Alexander Armstrong FRS, 1818–99, the naval surgeon and Arctic explorer, was born in Co. Fermanagh.

ATKINSON (*also* Acheson)

In Ireland both these names are common only in Ulster and both are most numerous in counties Antrim, Armagh and Down. The form Atkinson is more usually found in England and Acheson more usually found in Scotland.

Atkinson is an English name particularly common in the north of England. It derives from the pet name Adkin, a diminutive of Adam. Several of the name came to Ulster during the Plantation. One in particular, Roger Atkinson, who came to Co. Fermanagh as a servitor in the early seventeenth century, became the first MP for Enniskillen. A family of Quakers, the Atkinsons of Crowhill in Co. Armagh, came there from Newcastle, Northumberland, in 1649, settled in the townland of Money and were active in the formation of the linen industry in the north of Ireland.

Acheson is a variation. In Scotland and the Border country Atkinson was spelt Atzinson. The 'z' was pronounced 'y' (as in 'yet') and 'Atyeson' was gradually smoothed to Acheson. Indeed, even at the start of the twentieth century the two names were recorded as being used interchangeably around Armagh city, Kilkeel, Co. Down, and Lurgan, Co. Armagh. Although Acheson appears occasionally in earlier Irish records, it was not until the Plantation that it became common.

Henry Acheson of Gosford, Haddingtonshire, east of Edinburgh, was one of the fifty Scottish undertakers of the Ulster Plantation and in 1610 he was granted 1000 acres in the northern part of the barony of the Fews in Co. Armagh. A year later he bought chief undertaker Sir James Douglas's 2000 acres in the south of the barony. Markethill grew up close to the fortified bawn he built (later Gosford Castle). Henry's brother, Sir Archibald Acheson, solicitor general of Scotland, later created Lord Gosford, joined him in Armagh. One of his descendants, another Archibald, 2nd Earl of Gosford, 1776–1846, was MP for Armagh before becoming governor general of Canada.

BAILEY *see* Bailie

BAILIE (*also* Bailey)

This name, in both England and Scotland, is of Norman origin and derives from the Old French *bailli*, meaning a 'bailie' or 'bailiff'. In Scotland, from which most of the Ulster Bailies stem, the four most important families were of Lamington and Jerviswood in Lanarkshire, Polkemmet in West Lothian and Dochfour in Inverness-shire.

Counties Antrim and Down are the two main centres. While the -ie spelling is common in both counties, the -ey spelling is more common in Co. Antrim. The Bailies first arrived from Scotland at the time of the Plantation. One of these became an important family in Co. Down, the Bailies of Innishargy. In the mid-nineteenth century by far the greatest concentration of the name was found to be on the Ards peninsula, Co. Down, in the parish of Ardkeen.

William Baillie of Finlayston, Renfrewshire, was one of the fifty undertakers of the Plantation of Ulster and in 1610 he was granted 1000 acres in the barony of Clankee in Co. Cavan. By 1622 he had built Bailie-borough Castle around which the town of Bailieborough grew.

BAIRD

This Co. Antrim and Co. Down name is Scottish in origin and can derive from the Gaelic word *bàrd*, a 'bard' or 'poet'. The Scottish name MacWard, Gaelic Mac a' Bhaird, meaning 'son of the bard', was also largely anglicised to Baird. However, the earliest record of it as a surname is the de Bard family of Lanarkshire in the thirteenth century. De Bard also appears in the following century in Aberdeenshire and the Lothians. In this case the name is territorial in origin, many of the Scottish Bairds descending from Normans who came to Scotland in the train of William the Lion in the twelfth century. These in turn had descended from le seigneur de Barde who came to England with William the Conqueror.

Baird is an old and popular name in Ayrshire, whence stemmed so many of the Plantation settlers. In the mid-nineteenth century it was found to be particularly popular on the Upper Ards around Portaferry, Co. Down.

BARR

This name, most common in counties Down, Antrim, Derry and Donegal, is of predominantly Scottish origin. It is a toponymic taken from Barr in Ayrshire or Barr in Renfrewshire, both placenames deriving from *barr*, Gaelic for 'top' or 'height'. The first recorded person of the name was Atkyn de Barr, who was bailie of Ayr around 1340. It was first noted in Ulster after the Plantation.

BARRON

Of those of this name living in Ireland about half are in Ulster, particularly in counties Antrim and Donegal. Barron can be of Irish, Scottish or English origin.

The MacBarrons, in Gaelic Mac Barúin, were an important branch of the O'Neills in counties Armagh and Louth. They descend from Sir Art

MacBarron O'Neill. The Mac- was dropped by the end of the seventeenth century.

The Scottish name MacBarron, meaning 'son of the baron', did not denote noble blood. It was a Gaelic custom to call small landed proprietors barons. Also, the Frasers of Reelick in Inverness-shire were known as MacBarrons and the name was popular in Angus and Inverness.

In England too the name was not used in a literal sense but most often as a nickname for someone who was proud or haughty.

In the late nineteenth century the main Co. Antrim concentration was in the barony of Upper Belfast.

BAXTER

This Co. Antrim name is of Scottish origin. The MacBaxters, Gaelic Mac an Bhacstair, 'son of the baker', were a branch of the Clan Macmillan. The name derives from the Old English word *bœcestre*, meaning a 'female baker', and was common in Angus. Forfar in Angus was a royal residence and it may be that the first Baxters were bakers to the king. The MacBaxters were also noted on the Highland Border and in the Isles. Baxter came first to Ulster during the Plantation.

BEATTIE (*also* Beatty)

This popular Ulster name is common throughout the province. The -tie spelling is most common in counties Antrim and Down and the -ty spelling in counties Armagh and Tyrone. In Scotland the name derived from the personal name Bate or Baty, pet or diminutive forms of Bartholomew.

It was well known in the Scottish province of Galloway and in the Scottish Borders, where the Beatties or Batys were one of the lesser of the riding clans broken by James VI after 1603. Many members of these broken clans came to Ulster during the Plantation and in particular to Fermanagh. Beatty was noted as the fifteenth most numerous name in Fermanagh in 1962 and was recorded there as being used synonymously with Betty and MacCaffrey (*see* MacCaffrey) around 1900.

It is also suggested that the name can derive from the Gaelic Mac a' Bhiadhtaigh from *biadhtach*, 'one who held land on condition of supplying food (*biad*) to those billeted on him by the chief'. This name was also anglicised to MacVitty, MacWatty and MacWattie (*see* Watson).

Outside Ulster the Irish name Biadhtach (Betagh), which means 'public victualler', was made Beatty.

BEATTY *see* Beattie

BEGGS

This specific form of the name is peculiar to Ireland where, outside of Dublin, it is an exclusively Ulster name. Half of all those of the name live in Co. Antrim. Strangely, the name has two different derivations, each with an opposite meaning, either 'small' or 'large'. In all cases it served originally as a description of the bearer.

Those of Scottish or Irish origin derive their name from the Gaelic *beag*, meaning 'little' or 'small of stature'. And indeed in Ulster, Small and Begg have been noted as synonyms (*see* Small).

However, some at least of the Ulster Beggses are of English origin, and in this case it is a variation of the name Bigge or Biggs, which derives from the Middle English *bigge*, meaning 'large', 'strong' or 'stout'.

In mid-nineteenth-century Co. Antrim the name was found almost exclusively in the barony of Upper Antrim.

BELL

This mainly Scottish name is among the 100 most numerous names in Ireland and among the twenty most numerous in Ulster. About half of all the Bells live in Co. Antrim where it is among the ten most popular names. It is among the fifteen most numerous in Co. Down and is common too in counties Tyrone and Armagh.

There are several possible derivations of the name. The most important are: from the Old French *bel*, meaning 'handsome' or 'beautiful'; or of local origin from the Old English *belle*, a 'bell', denoting either someone who lived by a church or town bell or was employed as a bellringer.

The name was common on the Scottish Borders for centuries and the 'Bellis' of Annandale, Dumfriesshire, were one of the unruly riding clans broken and scattered by James VI in the decade after 1603. Many members of these clans resettled in Ulster at the time of the Plantation. The family descended from one Gilbert le fiz Bel.

Bell is also an anglicisation of the Gaelic Mac Ghille Mhaoil, which was also anglicised as MacGilveil, MacIlveil and Macmillan (*see* Macmillan). As such they were an important branch of the Clan Macmillan and indeed in some parts of Argyllshire the clan itself was known as Na Belich, The Bells. The name is common in the Isles, particularly on Islay.

Although the name first came to Ireland with the Normans, it was not until the Plantation that it became common. In the late nineteenth century the largest Co. Antrim concentration was found to be on the shores of Lough Neagh near Ballinderry. In Co. Down it was most numerous in the Dromore–Magheralin area and around Hilltown.

BENNET

Only slightly more popular in Ulster than in Leinster or Munster, the name is most common in counties Antrim, Armagh and Down. The -et ending is most common in Scotland and Ireland and the -ett ending, in England. It was originally a Christian name, Benet, a diminutive or pet form of Benedict which derives ultimately from the Latin name Benedictus.

Benet was established as a surname in Ireland very early and was later gaelicised as Beinéad. The names MacBennett and Bennett (Mac Beinéid) are common in seventeenth-century Co. Armagh records. Of this connection was Art Bennett or McBennet, the early-nineteenth-century Forkhill Gaelic poet. It has been suggested that these Bennetts do not derive their name ultimately from Benedict but from a more obscure Pictish origin.

The name Benedict was very popular in Scotland because of the fame of St Benedict, 480–503, the patriarch of the monks of the west of Scotland. The surname Bennet too became very popular and many of the Ulster Bennets will be of Scottish descent.

BINGHAM

This name, as such, is rare outside Ulster, although it was formerly associated with Co. Mayo. In Ulster it derives from the Scottish name Bigham or Biggam, which originated from either of the places so named in Ayrshire and Dumfriesshire. There is a suggestion that it may also derive from Bingham in Nottinghamshire. As it was still being used interchangeably with Bigam and Bigham in late-nineteenth-century Ireland, the Scottish derivation is probably more likely. Most of the Binghams are from counties Down and Antrim.

BISHOP *see* Gillespie

BLACK

This popular Ulster name, most common in counties Antrim, Armagh, Tyrone and Down, is mainly of Scottish and English origin. If English, the name derives from either the Old English *blæc*, meaning 'black', or the Old English *blác*, meaning 'white', 'bright' or 'pale'. In theory *blác* should give the name Blake, but a lot of intermingling occurred which it is now impossible to unravel.

However, most Ulster Blacks are of Scottish and distinctly Gaelic origin and can belong to Clan Gregor, Clan Lamont, or Clan Maclean of Duart. Clan Gregor and Clan Lamont were each 'broken' at different times and forbidden to use their clan names. In each case one of the alternative names they chose was Black (*see* Greer *and* Lamont for details). Black was particularly popular with the Lamonts, as one of the main clan septs was the Clann Mhic Gille Dhuibh, 'son of the black lad'.

While many of the Ulster Blacks arrived in the post-Plantation period, many, particularly in north Antrim, on Rathlin Island and in the Glens, arrived earlier from the west and south Highlands. It is thought that these are of the Clan Lamont Mac Gille Dhuibh family.

BLAIR

In Ireland very few of the Blairs live outside Ulster where over half are from Co. Antrim and most of the remainder from counties Derry and Tyrone. It is a Scottish name, common here since the Plantation. It is territorial in origin taken from any one of a number of places in Scotland so named. The placename itself derives from the Gaelic *blar*, meaning 'plain', 'field' or 'battlefield'.

BOAL *see* Boyle

BOGUE see Boyce

BONAR (*also* Bonner *and* Crampsey)

The Ulster names Bonar and Bonner can be of Irish, Scottish or English origin. If English or Scottish it is a descriptive name deriving from the Old French *bonnaire*, meaning 'gentle' or 'courteous'. If a settler family, Bonars are more likely to be of Scottish background.

However, most of the name in Ulster are native Irish and stem from the Co. Donegal sept of Ó Cnáimhsighe. This is one of Ireland's oldest surnames, first recorded in 1095. It derives from the personal name Cnáimhseach, which may have meant 'midwife'. Since this was a female name, Ó Cnáimhsighe may be one of the few Irish matronymic surnames.

It was common in the seventeenth century for English officials to write down either an approximation of what an Irish name sounded like or a mistranslation. In this case both types of anglicisation apply. Although there are some instances on record of O'Cnawsy, which is at least approximate in sound to the original, the name was anglicised generally as Crampsey or Bonar. This latter was a mistranslation that assumed the name had something to do with *cnámh*, which means 'bone'. Another anglicisation was Kneafsey.

The great majority of the Ulster Bonars, Bonners and Crampseys are still to be found in north Donegal and in particular in the Ballybofey district.

BONNER *see* Bonar

BOYCE (*also* Bogue)

Originally Boyce was a Norman name, del Bois, from the French for 'wood', and denoted someone who lived by or near a wood. As such Boyce has been in Ireland since the early thirteenth century. It was also a well-known name in Scotland. The English name Boyes derives from the Old English *boia*, 'young man' or 'servant'.

In Ulster it is most common in counties Donegal and Derry and to a lesser extent Down. In Donegal and Derry it is mainly of Gaelic Irish origin, an anglicisation of the Donegal sept name Ó Buadhaigh, from the Gaelic *buadhach*, meaning 'victorious'. This name was early anglicised as Buie and Bwee, which technically correspond to the Gaelic epithet *buidhe*, meaning 'yellow'. In sixteenth-century Ireland this was generally anglicised as 'boy' (Clandeboy from Clann Aodha Bhuidhe is a case in point — *see* O'Neill). It is interesting therefore to note that both Buie and Bwee were still being used as synonyms for Boyce in Donegal at the start of the twentieth century.

Ó Buadhaigh was also anglicised as Bogue. However, MacLysaght states that the large connection of Fermanagh Bogues are of Scottish Planter stock. George Black, in *The Surnames of Scotland*, says that Bogue was never common in Scotland but that it derived mainly from the place of that name in the parish of Minnigaff in Kirkcudbrightshire. It may well be irrelevant but an R. Bogas from Suffolk was one of the eleven English undertakers of the Plantation in Fermanagh, granted 1000 acres in Cloncarn.

The Donegal-born priest, the Revd John Boyce, 1810–64, became a successful novelist in the USA.

BOYD

This Scottish name is among the thirty most common names in Ulster and among the fifteen most common in both Co. Antrim and Co. Down. It is also popular in Co. Derry. It derives either from the Isle of Bute or from the Gaelic *buidhe*, meaning 'yellow'.

The Gaelic name for Bute is Bod. (The Marquis of Bute's title in Gaelic is Morair Bhoid.) However, Boyd is also a sept name of the royal line of Clan Stewart or Stuart and this family claims that the name derives from *buidhe*.

The first Boyds on record were vassals of the De Morevilles in the regality of Largs in Ayrshire. It is suggested that previous to that the progenitor of the family was Robert, son of Simon, who was one of the two Norman brothers who founded the Stewart dynasty in Scotland (*see* Stewart). He was known as Robert Buidhe because of the colour of his hair. The family was well established in Ayrshire before the reign of Robert the Bruce in the fourteenth century. A branch of this family was related to the Montgomerys and came to the Ards peninsula in Co. Down in the early seventeenth century. The name Boyd is still numerous there. The main Co. Antrim centre of the name was in the Ballycastle area.

Also of Ayrshire was Sir Thomas Boyd of Bedlay, sixth son of Lord Boyd of Kilmarnock. As one of the fifty Scottish undertakers of the Plantation, he was granted 1500 acres around the townland of Seein, barony of Strabane, Co. Tyrone, and settled many of the Boyd clan there.

A Manx name Mac Giolla Bhuidhe was also anglicised as Boyd (but *see also* MacKelvey) and it is known that some of this origin also settled in Ulster.

BOYLAN

This Co. Monaghan sept name is properly O'Boylan, the original Gaelic name being Ó Baoighealláin, probably from the root word *geall*, meaning 'pledge'.

They came originally from the same stock as the O'Flanagans in Co. Fermanagh and took over the kingship of the Dartry area of Monaghan some time between 946 and 1006. At their height at the end of the eleventh century they controlled a territory stretching from Fermanagh to Louth and their chief was King of Fermanagh. By the fourteenth century their power had been reduced by the MacMahons and they were under-kings to them.

The Gaelic poet Seán Ó Dubhagáin in *c.* 1350 praised them for their horsemanship and went on:

> The blue-eyed host of the hostages,
> The red-lipped clan of Boylan,
> Warriors whose deeds have never been ugly,
> Theirs is the brave kingdom of Dartry.

However, not much is known about them during this period because, strangely for such a powerful family, none are recorded in the annals as churchmen. And it was the churchmen who wrote the history.

Boylan was noted as the thirty-fourth most popular name in Co. Monaghan in 1972 (*see also* Boyle). It is also common in Co. Cavan and, outside Ulster, in Co. Meath.

BOYLE (*also* Boal)

Boyle is among the fifty most common names in Ireland, among the fifteen most common in Ulster and is the third most popular name in Co. Donegal, over half of all the Ulster Boyles living in that county. The name is also common in counties Antrim, Tyrone and Armagh.

Boyle is an anglicisation of the Donegal sept name Ó Baoighill. This was a large and powerful family which in medieval times, along with the O'Donnells and the O'Dohertys, controlled the entire northwest. Ballyweel, near Donegal town, was originally Baile Uí Bhaoighill, 'town of the O'Boyles'. The name, like Boylan, is thought to derive from the Gaelic root word *geall*, meaning 'pledge'. The Boyles of Desart, Co. Armagh, are of this connection. The Boyles of Co. Monaghan, however, are thought to be really Boylans (*see* Boylan).

Many of the Ulster Boyles, though, are not of this stock. A family of de Boyville, from Beauville near Caen in France, came to England during the Norman Conquest. A branch of this family came to Scotland at the invitation of David 1 and became very powerful in Galloway and in particular, in Ayrshire (the family seat is still Kelburn Castle at Fairlie). Many Scottish Boyles came to Ulster from the time of the Plantation on. The Boyles of Limavady, Co. Derry, for instance, settled in 1660. The painter Alicia Boyle, born 1908, is of this family.

Another (Welsh) branch of the de Boyvilles were ancestors of Ireland's most famous Boyle family, the Earls of Cork and Shannon, and it is possible that some of the Ulster Boyles may be of this connection.

There are a few different synonyms for the name. Boal or Bole has been used as a synonym in Ulster for both the Donegal sept name and for the English Bowles. Further, since Boyle in Ayrshire and Wigtownshire was until recently pronounced 'Bole' in common speech, it is plain that some Boals are of this Boyle origin. The Donegal O'Boyle has been anglicised as Bohill in Co. Down and it has been suggested that in the northwest many of the name Hill may originally have been O'Boyles (but *see* Hill).

BRADLEY

This popular Ulster name is most common in Co. Derry (where it is the fourth most numerous) and in counties Antrim, Tyrone and Donegal. Though technically an English toponymic taken from one of the many northern English towns and villages of the name, few of the Ulster Bradleys are of English stock. The majority are O'Brallaghans by origin.

The territory of the Ó Brolacháin sept was the area in which the present-day borders of counties Derry, Donegal and Tyrone meet. The Ó

Brolacháins were a prolific and adventurous race and a branch of the family, the O'Brologhans, was early established in the Western Highlands of Scotland via their connections with the monastery on Iona, where Domhnall Ua Brolcháin, prior of Derry, was abbot in the twelfth century. Here too the name was anglicised to Bradley and also Brodie. This latter is distinct from the ancient Pictish Clan Brodie who took their name from the barony of Brodie, Gaelic Brothach, in Morayshire. Those Ulster Bradleys who can verify a Scottish origin outside the Highlands probably take their name from the lands of Braidlie in the barony of Hawick in Roxburghshire.

Another branch of the Derry family early migrated to Co. Cork and the numerous Bradleys of that area descend from them. Some of the Brollaghans of Co. Cavan assumed the Norman name Brabazon.

BRADY

Brady is among the sixty most common names in Ireland, among the forty most common in Ulster, among the twenty most common in Monaghan and ranks third in Co. Cavan, the homeland of the sept. The name is properly MacBrady from the Gaelic Mac Brádaigh, the derivation of which is uncertain. The Mac- has only rarely been resumed.

The MacBradys were a very powerful Breffny sept controlling a large territory from their headquarters east of Cavan town. There are many references to them in the Irish annals, and Cavan Bradys and MacBradys became famous in many different fields. General Thomas Brady, 1752–1827, who was the son of a Cootehill farmer, became a field marshall in the Austrian army and governor of Dalmatia. James Bernard MacBrady of Loughtee, 1732–1800, became a colonel in the Austrian service. Also in the eighteenth century Fiachra MacBrady, the 'Bard of Stradone', Phelim Brady (subject of the famous ballad 'The Bold Phelim Brady, the Bard of Armagh') and the Revd Philip MacBrady were noted Gaelic poets. There were three MacBrady Bishops of Kilmore and one of Ardagh. The Cavan Crozier, staff of the early MacBrady bishops, is one of the few Irish croziers to have survived the Reformation and is now in the National Museum in Dublin.

BRANNIGAN

This name is slightly more popular in Ulster than in Leinster but outside of these it is rare in Ireland. The homeland of the sept was in Oriel, which straddled the border between the two provinces.

The Ó Branagáins were a sept of the Cenél Eoghain who made their way into counties Armagh, Monaghan and Louth in the sixteenth and seventeenth centuries. The Brannigans are still most common there. Their name derives from the Gaelic personal name Bran, meaning 'raven'. It is thought that the Fermanagh sept name Ó Branáin is simply a contraction of Ó Branagáin (*see* Brennan).

The Co. Down placename Tullybranigan means 'hill of Brannigan'. Around 1900 the name was used synonymously with Brankin in the Crumlin area of Co. Antrim.

BREEN (*also* MacBrien)

Breens are originally either O'Breen or MacBreen, from the Gaelic names Ó Braoin and Mac Braoin respectively. Some in Ulster may descend from the powerful sept of O'Breen of Brawney, who ruled a territory in counties Offaly and Westmeath. Others may descend from the Donegal sept of O'Breens, who were based in Clonleigh parish in the barony of Raphoe and were erenaghs of the Cistercian grange of Kilfore at Ballymonaster. But most are probably MacBriens or MacBreens of the Fermanagh sept. These are related to the Maguires and the MacManuses, having descended from Brian, a grandson of the original Mánus. The family centred on Mulla-mackervey townland in Aghalurcher, Co. Fermanagh. Their first chief, An Giolla Dubh – the Black Servant – was inaugurated as 'The MacBrian' in 1488 and ruled until 1506. The family multiplied greatly after the Plantation and many became Protestants. A survey of 1962 showed that Breen, together with MacBrien, constituted the seventeenth most numerous name in Fermanagh and found the strongest concentration of the name to be at Ardees in the parish of Inishmacsaint.

BRENNAN

This name is among the thirty most common in Ireland but is much less numerous in Ulster than in the other three provinces. There were several unrelated septs of Ó Braonáin and Mac Branáin in Ireland, most notably in Ossory, east Galway, Kerry, Westmeath and Roscommon.

In Ulster Brennan is most popular in Co. Fermanagh, and in Co. Monaghan (where it was found to rank twenty-third in 1970). Most of these will descend from the Cenél Eoghain sept of Ó Branáin. It is thought that this name is simply a contraction of the Cenél Eoghain sept name Ó Branagáin, both of which derive from the personal name Bran, meaning 'raven' (*see* Brannigan).

The name was also anglicised Brannan. (There is a Ballybranan in Co. Armagh.) Around 1900 Brennan was noted as synonymous with Brannie in the Greyabbey district of the Ards peninsula in Co. Down.

BRESLIN

This Co. Donegal name is properly O'Breslin from the Gaelic Ó Breasláin, the Cenél Énda sept who early ruled a territory around Inniskeel on the Fanad peninsula. The name is still most common in that area, which is remarkable since it is recorded in the Annals of the Four Masters that the O'Breslins were driven out of their territory by the MacSweeneys in 1261, and migrated to Co. Fermanagh just as the Maguire ascendancy began. It is plain that the ordinary members of the sept remained in their homeland. It is thought that the Cannon sept migrated from Donegal with them.

The Breslins were one of the most famous brehon families of Ireland. The leading families who migrated to Co. Fermanagh settled in the parish of Derryvullan and became brehons to the Maguires. Despite this early prominence there are few Breslins remaining in Fermanagh. Some of the Donegal Breslins anglicised their name further to Brice or Bryce and Bryson (which is also an anglicisation of Ó Muirgheasáin – *see* Morrison).

BROWN (*also* Browne)

This is one of the commonest names on these islands. It is among the forty most common in Ireland as a whole and among the ten most popular in Ulster. Its main centres in the province are Co. Derry (where it is one of the five most popular), Co. Down (where it is one of the first ten) and Co. Antrim (one of the first fifteen). Browne with an 'e' is more common in the south of Ireland.

The great majority of the Ulster Browns are of English and Scottish descent. The English name derives from the Old English personal name Brūn, or as a nickname from Old English *brūn*, meaning 'brown of hair or complexion', or from the Norman name Le Brun, 'the Brown'. Many of the Brownes of Ireland descend from a branch of the Norman Le Bruns who came over to Ireland in the twelfth century and became one of the 'Tribes of Galway'.

The Scottish Browns can derive their name from the same sources but most, particularly in the north and west, have a Gaelic origin. The Scots Gaelic name Mac a' Bhriuthainn, 'son of the brehon (judge)' was widely anglicised as Brown, as was the name Mac Ghille Dhuinn, 'son of the brown lad'. Brown was also one of the colour names assumed by the Lamonts after they were 'broken' and forbidden to use their own (*see* Lamont). It is also recognised as a sept name by Clan Macmillan.

John Brown of Georgiemill, near Edinburgh, was one of the fifty Scottish undertakers of the Ulster Plantation and in 1612 was granted 1000 acres around the townland of Corradownan near Killeshandra, Co. Cavan.

In the nineteenth century the greatest Co. Antrim concentration of the name was in the area south of Larne, and in Co. Down in the parish of Moira.

Andrew Brown, 1744–97, was born in Ulster and led a very colourful life. He served in the British army but later fought against them at Lexington and Bunker Hill during the American War of Independence. He then founded the *Philadelphia Gazette* and was the first man to report the debates in the new congress.

Frances Brown, 1816–79, was born in Co. Donegal and though blind, she educated herself by listening to others at their lessons and went on to become a successful poet and novelist.

BROWNE *see* Brown

BUCHANAN (*also* Mawhinney)

Buchanan is of Scottish origin but the Scottish family themselves claim to descend ultimately from a member of one of the great north Ulster septs, the O'Cahans (*see* Kane).

The name itself is territorial, after the district of Buchanan in Stirlingshire, from the Gaelic *both chanain,* meaning 'house of the canon'. But the original name of the Buchanans was MacAuslan, in Gaelic Mac Ausaláin. The name was changed to Buchanan by Gilbrid MacAuslan in the thirteenth century. The clan claims that it was founded in the eleventh century by Ausalan Buoy O'Kayn, a chief of a branch of the O'Kanes of Derry (*see* MacCausland). The MacAldonichs, Gaelic Mac Mhaoldomhnaich, were a sept of Clan Buchanan who later assumed the clan name. There was also a Buchanan sept of Glendaruel in Cowal in Argyllshire who were followers of Clan Campbell. These had no connection whatever with the Clan Buchanan of Loch Lomondside.

In Ulster the name is most common in Co. Tyrone, whence stemmed the ancestors of James Buchanan, 1791–1868, the fifteenth president of the USA. Strangely, some Buchanans in Co. Antrim are Mawhinneys by origin. Mawhinney in the Lisburn area became Mawhannon, which in turn, in south Antrim, became Bohannon before becoming Buchanan. As late as 1900 the two names were still being used interchangeably in the area around Doagh.

The Co. Antrim name Mawhinney, however, is properly MacWhinney, said to be an anglicisation of Mac Shuibhne, a variant of Mac Suibhne (MacSweeney). But most of the Ulster Mawhinneys are of Scottish origin and there it is from MacWhinnie, a Galloway form of MacKenzie.

(MacKenzie is from the Gaelic Mac Coinnich, 'son of Coinneach', a personal name from the root word *can,* meaning 'fair' or 'bright'.) In Galloway MacWhinnie is still pronounced M'Whunye.

BURNS (*also* MacBurney)

Burns is one of the seventy most common names in Ireland and among the thirty most common in Ulster (which claims two-thirds of the Irish total). The name is most common in counties Antrim, Down and Armagh. Though it is originally of Clan Campbell, several Scottish and Irish septs adopted it as an anglicisation.

The Dumfriesshire sept name MacBurney is well known in counties Down and Antrim. It was in Gaelic Mac Biorna from the Norse personal name Bjarnie, which in turn was taken from the Norse word *björn,* meaning 'bear'. This makes it parallel in meaning to the Irish MacMahon, 'son of the bear'. Many of the Dumfriesshire MacBurneys anglicised their name to Burns.

Some of the Leinster O'Byrnes, who came to Ulster at the beginning of the seventeenth century, anglicised their name to Burns, as did many of the Co. Down sept MacBrin (*see* Byrne).

The principal Scottish name Burns, that of the Clan Campbell sept, is of local origin, probably from Burnhouse in Taynuilt, Argyllshire. The fore-fathers of poet Robert Burns migrated from there to Forfarshire where they were known as the Campbells of Burnhouse and later, just as Burness. All Scottish records of the name are in this or similar forms (for example, Bernes, Bernys and so on) and these were pronounced Bur'ness not Burness' until the end of the eighteenth century. It was Robert Burns and his brother Gilbert who, in April 1786, decided to change their name to Burns, which was closer to the local pronunciation of Burness in Ayrshire where they were then living. Robbie's subsequent fame inspired very many others to make the same change.

BYRNE

Byrne is among the ten most common names in Ireland and, it has been estimated, is borne by about one per cent of the population of the Republic of Ireland. Almost four-fifths of this number are from Leinster.

The Byrnes are properly O'Byrne, Gaelic Ó Broin, from the word *bran,* meaning 'raven'. The progenitor of this great sept was Bran, son of Maol-mórda, King of Leinster in the early eleventh century. Driven out of Co. Kildare by the Normans, the O'Byrnes fought the English continuously for three hundred years from their strongholds in the Wicklow mountains.

Their most famous victory came when Fiach MacHugh O'Byrne defeated Lord Grey at Glenmalure in 1580, the engagement immortalised in the song 'Follow me up to Carlow'. However, Fiach MacHugh was captured and beheaded in 1597 and in 1628 his son Phelim was deprived of his inheritance. The Byrnes continued to resist the English, members of the family taking part in the 1641 rising, the Williamite war and the 1798 rebellion.

In Ulster the name is most common in Co. Donegal and in south Monaghan. The Co. Down sept name MacBrin, Gaelic Mac Broin, has the same derivation (from *bran*) and many of this sept changed their name to Byrne, particularly in the Kilkeel and Moira districts. Some Byrnes and MacBrins also changed their name to Burns (*see* Burns).

CAIRNS

This name, in Ulster most common in counties Antrim, Down and Armagh, is Scottish in origin. It is a toponymic taken from the lands of Cairns in the parish of Mid-Calder in Midlothian. The Ulster Cairnses came mainly from Galloway where the first on record was Alexander de Carnys, provost of Lincluden in 1408. His nephew John was the founder of the Galloway branch. Cairnses were among the earliest Ulster settlers at the time of the Plantation. Alexander Cairnes, formerly of Cults in Wigtownshire, came to Donegal around 1610 as general agent to the undertakers in the baronies of Boylagh and Banagh. David Cairns, 1645–1722, was born in Derry and was one of its most prominent defenders during the siege in 1689. Hugh McCalmont Cairns, 1819–85, 1st Earl Cairns, was born at Cultra, Co. Down, and became Lord Chancellor of England.

Some of the name are Irish by origin, the name having been adapted from Kearns, an anglicisation of Ó Ciaráin. Kearns is a common name around Clones in Co. Monaghan (*see* Kearney).

CALDWELL

Ulster Caldwells can be of English, Scottish or Irish descent. The name itself is territorial in origin: if Scottish, from the lands of the name in Renfrewshire; if English, from any one of a number of places so called. It means 'cold spring or 'cold stream', from the Old English *ceald wielle*. The name was common in Edinburgh in the seventeenth century.

But Caldwell was also used as an anglicisation for Ulster Gaelic names. The Horish or Houriskey family of Tyrone, Gaelic Ó hUaruisce, anglicised their name to Caldwell in the mistaken notion that the Gaelic word for 'water', *uisce,* was part of the name (*see* Watters). The Colavins and Cullivans of Co. Cavan, Gaelic Mac Conluain, also adopted the name Caldwell.

Castle Caldwell, the home of the Caldwells of Fermanagh, was purchased from the Blennerhassets in 1670 by Sir James Caldwell, son of the Enniskillen merchant John Caldwell (originally of Ayrshire). The family took a prominent part in the Williamite defence of Erne and Donegal in 1689 and 1690.

The name is most common in counties Antrim, Derry and Tyrone.

CALLAGHAN

Callaghan is among the forty most common names in Ireland, the majority from the Cork area, the homeland of the great Ó Ceallacháin sept. The ancestor from whom these take their name was Ceallachán, King of Munster, died 952. It is thought that the derivation is most probably from the Gaelic *ceallach,* meaning 'strife'. Some of the Ulster Callaghans will be of this connection.

But most descend from a completely different sept, once powerful in Oriel, called Ó Céileacháin, who originally anglicised their name to (O')Kelaghan, Kealaghan and (O')Keelan. It is common in the history of surnames to find that a lesser name soon becomes lost in a more common name of similar sound. These Kelaghans had a stronghold at Liscallaghan, near Fivemiletown in Co. Tyrone. Their name derives from the Gaelic *céile,* meaning 'companion'.

Callaghan is one of the Irish names that has enjoyed a marked resumption of the O' prefix.

CAMERON

In Ireland this name is found almost exclusively in Ulster, where the majority hail from Co. Antrim and most of the rest from Co. Derry.

In the Lowlands of Scotland the name is territorial in origin, mainly from Cameron, previously Camberone, a parish in Fife; otherwise from Cameron near Edinburgh and Cameron in Lennox, Stirlingshire. But in the Highlands it was the name of one of the great clans loyal to the Stuart cause throughout the seventeenth-century civil wars and the 1715 and 1745 rebellions. In this case the name, like Campbell, derives from a distinctive facial characteristic, Gaelic *cam-shrón,* meaning 'wry nose' or 'crooked nose'.

The progenitor of the clan was Domhnull Dubh, Black Donald, who led the clan on the side of the Lord of the Isles at the Battle of Harlaw in 1411 and the hereditary patronymic of the chiefs of the clan, Cameron of

27

Locheil, Inverness-shire, is still Mac Dhomhnuill Duibh. The three main branches of the clan were the MacSorleys of Glen Nevis, Inverness-shire, the MacGillonies of Strone, Argyllshire, and the MacMartins of Letterfinlay, Inverness-shire (*see* Martin). The MacMartins almost all anglicised their name to Cameron.

CAMPBELL

Campbell is an extremely popular and widespread name in Ulster. Nothing can illustrate this better than the report of the Irish registrar general for the year 1890. In that one year there were 349 Campbells born in Ireland and 279 of these were born in Ulster. Campbell was then the thirty-first most common name in Ireland and fifth in Ulster, third in Down, fourth in Armagh, seventh in each of counties Tyrone, Antrim and Derry and thirteenth in Donegal. Not all these Campbells were of Scottish descent and of those who are, not all are Protestant Planters by origin.

The name itself is from the Scots Gaelic Caimbeul, meaning 'wry mouth' or 'crooked mouth', from Gaelic *cam* and *beul*, and was, presumably, a description of the first bearer. The Campbells are actually one of the families of Scotland which used the O' prefix. There is still no Gaelic equivalent for Clan Campbell, it is always Clann O'Duibhne. They descend from a certain Diarmid O'Duine of Lochow and clan tradition claims he was descended from the legendary Diarmuid Ó Duibhne, hero of the Fenian cycle. However, the first to assume the name Campbell was the thirteenth-century clan chief, Gillespic or Archibald O'Duibhne (*see* Gillespie) for whom we have a record as Gillespic Cambel in 1263.

The chiefly house, the Campbells of Argyll, despite leading the covenanters against Charles 1, despite their support for Cromwell (which cost the 8th Earl, later 1st Marquis, of Argyll his head at the Restoration) and despite coming out for the Monmouth rebellion (which cost the 9th Earl his head), grew in power throughout the seventeenth century at the expense of the MacDonalds, Lords of the Isles. The 10th Earl was created 1st Duke in 1701 and his titles give the best illustration of the extent of clan territory at this point: Duke of Argyll, Marquis of Kintyre and Lorn, Earl Campbell and Cowal, Viscount Lochow and Glenlya, Lord Inverary, Mull, Morvern and Tiree. From that point they were avid supporters of the English Crown and led the government forces against the Jacobites in the 1715 and 1745 rebellions. Under government orders, Robert Campbell of Glenlyon in Perthshire, a cadet of the house of Argyll, carried out the massacre of the Clan Iain Abrach MacDonalds of Glencoe in Argyllshire which gave rise to the famous feud.

There is no doubt that most of the Ulster Campbells are of this connection or descend from a branch of the clan, the Galloway MacCampbells, some of whom settled in Co. Down. However, many of the Donegal Campbells descend from the Clan Campbell Mac Ailín galloglass family brought to Tirconnell in the fifteenth century (*see* MacCallion). Further, many of the Tyrone Campbells are really members of the Tyrone sept Mac Cathmhaoil, a name which was subjected to an incredible number of different anglicisations (*see* MacCawell). For instance, two Belfast brothers, Joseph Campbell, 1878–1944, and John P. Campbell, pioneers of the Gaelic revival in Ulster, did a lot of their work under the names Seosamh and Seaghan Mac Cathmhaoil respectively. Joseph was a noted poet, perhaps most famous for penning the lyrics of 'My Lagan love'. John was an illustrator.

The Revd Alexander Campbell, 1786–1866, was born near Ballymena, Co. Antrim, and emigrated to the USA in 1809. He formed his own sect, the Disciples of Christ, who were more commonly known as the 'Campbellites' and, by the time of his death, numbered close on half a million.

CANNING (*also* Cannon)

These two northwest Ulster names have often been confused but are in reality of quite distinct origins, respectively English and Irish.

The Cannings are most numerous in Co. Derry, where most descend from a seventeenth-century English Planter family. George Canning, agent for one of the London guilds, the Ironmongers, came to Ulster from Warwickshire in 1615. He founded the town of Garvagh in Co. Derry. The Cannings of Garvagh had many famous sons. One of these, another George Canning, the poet, 1736–71, was something of a black sheep and died in poverty in London. His son, also George, 1770–1827, was taken back into the family in infancy. He was a brilliant academic and later became British foreign secretary and, for the last few months of his life, prime minister. His son, Charles John, 1812–62, 1st Earl Canning, became governor general of India and then was made first viceroy. The nephew of George Canning, prime minister, also called George, 1778–1840, was created 1st Baron Garvagh in 1818.

Cannon can be an English ecclesiastical name from the Old French *chanoine*, meaning a 'clergyman living with others in a clergy house', and indeed some Cannons in Ulster are descendants of French Huguenot immigrants. But more usually in Ulster the name is an anglicisation of one of two Gaelic sept names. The Oriel sept of MacCannon or MacConnon was originally from the Clones district in Co. Monaghan but in the eleventh century it migrated to the south Monaghan—north Louth area. Its name was anglicised to Cannon, though some later took the names MacConnell or MacCann. However, most of the Ulster Cannons are from Co. Donegal and there the name is an anglicisation of the Gaelic Ó Canann, earlier Ó Canannáin, an important sept of old Tirconnell. The name Kenny is used in that area as a synonym of Cannon and Letterkenny originally meant 'hillside of the O'Cannons'. A branch of these Cannons migrated to Fermanagh with the Breslins.

In Scotland the names Cannan and Cannon were common in Kirkcudbrightshire and Dumfriesshire (where they derive from the Irish Gaelic Ó Canann) and some in Ulster may be of that origin.

CANNON *see* Canning

CARLETON

Carleton is less common than most of the names in this book but has an interesting history in Scotland and England and is connected with the Irish names O'Carolan and O'Carlin. It is most common in Co. Antrim and has two original homelands. The most famous was on the English side of the Scottish Borders. In the east it was made Charlton and this was the name of one of the great riding clans of that area, based in Tynedale. In the west it was Carleton, a common name in Cumbria and Northumbria. The surname derives from the place of the name which is from Old English *ceorla tún*, meaning 'churl's dwelling' or 'serf's dwelling'. Many members of the riding clans came to Ulster at the time of James VI's 'pacification' of the Borders, 1603—13.

However, Carleton is also common in Galloway in Scotland. There it too is a toponymic, from places called Carlton in Kirkcudbrightshire, Wigtownshire and Ayrshire. This placename was originally rendered Cairiltoun (dwelling of the Cairils) in the Whithorn Priory Rentals. The Cairils referred to here were the MacKerrals (Irish Gaelic Mac Fhearghail, 'son of Fearghal'), an Irish family said to have come from Antrim to Carrick in Ayrshire in the eleventh century. Since in Ulster most Carletons are in Co. Antrim it is likely that it is from the Galloway connection that they stem.

General Guy Carleton, Lord Dorchester, 1724—1808, became governor of Quebec. He was born in Strabane, Co. Tyrone. Carleton was also used as an anglicisation of sept names from counties Cavan and Tyrone—Derry (*see* Carlin). William Carleton, the novelist, 1794—1869, was of the latter connection and was born at Prillisk, near Clogher, Co. Tyrone. He is most famous for his *Traits and Stories of the Irish Peasantry*.

CARLIN (*also* Carolan)

Though these surnames were originally in English rendered O'Carolan, the name O'Carolan itself was an anglicisation of two entirely distinct Gaelic names. Carlin is the more usual form in counties Tyrone and Derry, where it derives from Ó Cairealláin, the leading sept of Clann Diarmada. In Co. Donegal the sept were erenaghs of the church lands of Clonleigh in the barony of Raphoe.

In Co. Cavan Carolan is more popular, from the Ó Cearbhalláin sept who early migrated across the provincial border into Co. Meath. Turlough O'Carolan, 1670–1738, the famous blind harper and composer, was of this sept.

Both these sept names were also anglicised as Carleton (*see* Carleton).

CARLISLE

In Ireland Carlisle is an almost exclusively Ulster name and there three-quarters are in Co. Antrim and most of the rest in Co. Down. The name is originally a toponymic from Carlisle in Cumberland but was established in Scotland as early as 1200. The Carlisles were one of the lesser of the riding clans of the Scottish Borders and lived on the Scottish side of the West March. Though the Carlisles mainly arrived in Ulster from the Plantation on, the name was recorded in Co. Antrim as early as 1588. At the beginning of the twentieth century the name was being used interchangeably with Carley in parts of the Belfast area.

CAROLAN *see* Carlin

CARR

This is an English name, meaning 'dweller by the marsh', from the Middle English *kerr*, Old Norse *kjarr*, meaning 'wet ground'. However, most of the Ulster Carrs are of Irish or Scottish descent.

Carr is used as a synonym of the Scottish name Kerr in Ulster and indeed in Scotland itself (*see* Kerr). But most families of the name descend from one of the Ulster septs who so anglicised their names. In Mayo and the counties adjacent to it, Kerrane, in Gaelic Ó Cearáin, was made Carr, as were, in Donegal, Kilcarr, MacElhar and MacIlhair, themselves anglicisations of Mac Giolla Chathair, 'son of the devotee of (St) Cathair'. In Co. Armagh the distinct Oriel septs of Ó Cairre and Mac Cairre were anglicised as Carry, MacCarry and (O')Carr. The Ó Cairre sept was particularly famous in early medieval times when its chief was recorded in the Annals of Loch Cé as 'steward of Cenél Aengusa and royal heir of Oilech'.

Many of the Carrs and Kerrs of Co. Monaghan were originally Mac Giolla Cheara, 'son of the devotee of (St) Ceara (of Killahear)'.

CARROLL (*also* MacCarroll)

Carroll is among the twenty-five most common names in Ireland. It is found in every county of Leinster, Munster and Connacht and, by comparison with these, is relatively uncommon in Ulster.

There were several distinct septs of O'Carroll and MacCarroll in Ireland, all descending from different eponymous ancestors named Cearbhall. The largest and most important of these septs was known as the 'Ely O'Carrolls' of Uíbh Fhailí, modern Co. Offaly. Another Ó Cearbhaill sept were princes of Oriel up until the time of the Norman invasion when their power was destroyed by John de Courcy. Ulster Carrolls will descend mainly from these and from the indigenous Mac Cearbhaill sept, which survives in its homeland of Co. Derry as Carroll and MacCarroll. Cardwells of the Dromore area in Co. Down may well have been Carrolls originally.

The O' prefix has been resumed in many cases during the twentieth century, including those where Mac- would be more accurate.

CARSON

This name, made famous in Ulster history by Edward Carson, 1854–1935, the Dublin barrister who led the struggle against Home Rule, is most common in counties Antrim, Down and Tyrone.

The name was originally spelt Ap'Corsan, and the family was very prominent in the Scottish province of Galloway, particularly in Kirkcudbrightshire and Dumfriesshire (where Corsans were provosts of Dumfries for several generations).

The Carsons arrived in Ulster during the Plantation, mostly in Co. Tyrone, although by the 1660s, the Hearth Money Rolls found them also in counties Antrim and Derry. John Carson, ancestor of the Carsons of Shanroe in Co. Monaghan, was found there in 1667 and had probably moved there recently from some other part of Ulster. Carson was found to be the fifty-third most numerous name in Co. Fermanagh in a survey of 1962.

CASSIDY

In a survey of 1962 Cassidy was found to be the thirteenth most common name in Co. Fermanagh and to be the fifth most common of the native Gaelic names. The Cassidys have been in Fermanagh for over a thousand years and up until the time of the Plantation were very prominent in the area in the fields of literature, medicine and religion. In all the many references to the deaths of illustrious members of the family in the annals, only one did not die of natural causes – he was slain by an aggressor.

For several centuries the Ó Caiside sept provided hereditary physicians and ollavs to the Maguires. But even before the Maguires took control of Fermanagh, the Cassidys are recorded as prominent in these fields; the Gaelic poetry of Giolla Mochuda Mór Ó Caiside, died 1143, is preserved to this day. As erenagh of Devenish, their chief resided at Ballycassidy (Baile Uí Chaiside), just north of Enniskillen. From there their fame spread throughout Ireland and, particularly in the north, Cassidys became doctors to many other chiefs. Besides in its homeland the name is common also in counties Donegal, Antrim and Monaghan and indeed, with the exception of Connacht, throughout the whole island. The Donegal O'Cassidys were erenaghs of part of Conwall in the barony of Kilmacrenan.

The Plantation destroyed their influence and thereafter little is recorded about them save that many continued to flourish in the fields of Gaelic scholarship and literature and in medicine right through to the eighteenth century and, in the case of medicine, well beyond. Also, several Cassidys were priests during the Penal period.

CAUGHEY see MacCaughey

CAULFIELD

It is very difficult to unravel the complexities of this surname in Ulster. Besides being the name of a prominent English settler family it has been used as an anglicisation of several Gaelic names and one of these, Mac Cathmhaoil, was also anglicised in a variety of other ways.

Sir Toby Caulfield, who was born Toby Calfehill in Oxford in 1565, came to Ulster in 1607, obtained large grants of land in counties Antrim and Derry and worked for the English Crown collecting rents and fines on the escheated O'Neill estates. He became 1st Baron Charlemont and the family remained active in the English interest throughout the next two centuries. His descendant James Caulfield, 1728–99, was the first president of the Royal Irish Academy and was made 1st Earl Charlemont. Before the Land Acts of the late nineteenth century, the family owned 26,000 acres in counties Armagh and Tyrone. The family built a stronghold at Aconecarry in Tyrone and renamed it Castlecaulfield, the original nucleus of the modern town.

However, present-day Caulfields do not necessarily descend from the English family, as in pre-Plantation days the Charlemont area was part of the homeland of the once numerous Mac Cathmhaoil sept, many members of which adopted Caulfield as their surname (*see* MacCawell).

Further, in the Kilkeel area of Co. Down some members of the Crossmaglen sept Mac Eoghain are thought to have taken the name Caulfield (*see* MacKeown). And elsewhere in south Down and in east Tyrone and Antrim some of the MacCavanas, Gaelic Mac an Mhanaigh, also anglicised to Caulfield (*see* Kavanagh). So too did some members of the Mac Coileáin and possibly the Mac Gafraidh septs of Co. Fermanagh (*see* Collins *and* MacCaffrey respectively).

CHAMBERS

This name, known throughout Ireland but most common in the northeastern counties of Antrim, Down and Armagh, derives from the Old French *de la chámbre,* meaning 'of the chamber'. It originally pertained to a chamber attendant or an official of the Treasury chamber. It is therefore the same in origin as Chamberlain and Chalmers and indeed, it was found to be synonymous with Chalmers in the Garvagh district of Co. Derry as late as 1900.

Though the name was recorded in Ireland as early as the thirteenth century, most today stem from English and Scottish Planter stock. It has been claimed that the name was used as an anglicisation of the name MacCambridge (from the Scots Gaelic Mac Ambróis) in Co. Antrim, but no evidence for this can be found.

CHRISTIE (*also* Christy)

Apart from some Christies in Dublin, this is an almost exclusively Co. Antrim name and is of Scottish origin. In Scotland and in the north of England Christie was a diminutive or pet form of the personal names Christopher and more usually Christian. (It was recorded as being used interchangeably with the surname Christian in the Lisburn area of Co. Antrim as late as 1900.) Christie was a very common name in Fife. Also MacGilchrist, in Gaelic Mac Gille Chríosd, meaning 'son of the servant of Christ', was an Argyllshire name which was anglicised as Christison and Christie.

In the 1850s in Co. Antrim Christie was found almost exclusively in the barony of Upper Dunluce.

CHRISTY *see* Christie

CLARKE (*also* Cleary)

Clarkes in Ulster can be of English, Irish or Scottish origins and without a confirmed family tree it is impossible for individuals to know which. The name is very common throughout these islands – among the twenty most common in Scotland, thirty in England and forty in Ireland. Half of those in Ireland live in Ulster, where it is among the twenty most popular names. It is well distributed throughout the province but particularly common in counties Antrim and Cavan.

In England and the Lowlands of Scotland the name Clarke meant originally a 'clerk' or 'cleric', meaning a man in a religious order and later a scholar. In Ireland and in the Highlands of Scotland the name was borrowed into the Gaelic language and gave rise to Ó Cléirigh (O'Clery) and Mac an Chléirich (MacCleary) respectively (*see* MacCleary for both).

In both Scotland and Ireland these names have been re-anglicised to Clarke in recent centuries. In Scotland there were Clarke septs associated with several clans including Cameron, Clan Chattan, Mackintosh and Macpherson.

Thomas Clarke, 1858–1916, was born on the Isle of Wight of Irish parents. He spent the first ten years of his life in South Africa and the following ten in Dungannon, Co. Tyrone. One of the leaders of the 1916 rising, he was the first to sign the Proclamation of the Republic.

CLEARY *see* Clarke *and* MacCleary

CLEMENTS

This is an English name, from the Christian name Clement, which derives from the Latin *clemens,* meaning 'humane, merciful'. It was the name of several popes including St Clement, who was third Bishop of Rome after St Peter, and the name was very popular in England from the mid-twelfth century.

However, in Ulster, where Clements is most common in Co. Antrim and to a lesser extent in counties Donegal and Derry, it was anglicised from Mac Laghmain, or shortened from MacClement, a form of MacLamond and thus the name of a branch of the Clan Lamont (*see* Lamont). It has been in Co. Antrim since the early seventeenth century and in the late nineteenth century it was still being used interchangeably with McClamon, McClement and M'Lamond in the Coleraine district of Co. Derry.

COCHRANE

This Scottish name is of territorial origin from the lands of Cochrane near Paisley in Renfrewshire. The name of this place was previously spelt

Coueran and the first person of the name on record was Waldeve de Coueran in 1262. The name means 'red brook'. The Cochranes were a sept of Clan Donald who did well for themselves in the mid-seventeenth century. The main line was raised to the peerage in 1647, and in 1669 Sir William, Baron Cochrane, was created 1st Earl of Dundonald (in Scotland). Some of the Highland MacEacherens adopted the name when they migrated to the Lowlands.

In Ulster, where the name became common from the early seventeenth century, it was also adopted as an anglicisation by some of the old Lough Erne ecclesiastical family of Ó Corcráin or Corcoran (from the Gaelic *corcair,* meaning 'crimson') in Co. Fermanagh. The Ulster name Coughran is a synonym of Cochrane, the Ulster -ough replacing the Scottish -och.

Cochrane is common in counties Derry, Down and Tyrone and, in particular, Co. Antrim, where in the mid-nineteenth century it was almost exclusively found in the barony of Lower Dunluce, near the Giant's Causeway, and especially in Loughanlinch.

COLHOUN

This Scottish clan name is most popular in counties Tyrone and Derry. It has been in Ulster since the Plantation. The name is territorial and derives from the barony of Colquhoun in Dumbartonshire (from Gaelic *coill,* a 'wood', and *cumhann,* 'narrow').

The founder of the family was Umfridas de Kilpatrick or Kirkpatrick who obtained a grant of the lands of Colquhoun in or before 1241. The family claim that his son Ingram was the first to take the name of Colquhoun but the first on record was Robert de Colechon, later referred to variously as de Culchon, of Kylekone, and de Colquhoune. The family became a recognised clan and after acquiring the lands of Luss in Dumbartonshire by marriage (to the Fair Maid of Luss) in the fourteenth century they became known as the Colquhouns of Luss.

In 1603, during the chiefship of Alexander, seventeenth chief of the Colquhouns of Luss, they were attacked by the MacGregors. This was the occasion of the Clan Gregor being outlawed and declared a 'broken' clan by James VI. Sir John, the nineteenth clan chief, was the last person to practise witchcraft openly in Scotland. Colquhoun was also the name of a sept of Clan Stewart of Appin in Argyllshire. Many of the Colquhouns in the Lowlands assumed the names Cowan and MacCowan (*see* Cowan).

Early in the Plantation Sir John Colquhoun of Luss bought 1000 acres in the Newtowncunningham district of Co. Donegal from one of the undertakers, Sir Walter Stewart of Minto in Roxburghshire. He brought over several members of the Colquhoun clan and these were the ancestors of most of the present-day Colhouns of that county as well as Co. Tyrone and Co. Derry.

Around 1900 the name was used synonymously with Cahoon (its usual pronunciation) in the Belfast area and with Choun in north Tyrone.

COLL

This Donegal name is from MacColl, Gaelic Mac Colla, the name of a galloglass family introduced there from Argyllshire in the sixteenth century. Colla was a Gaelic personal name and Colla Uais, a semi-legendary Irish king of the fourth century, is claimed as the great ancestor of the MacDonalds. The MacCalls or MacColls, long settled in Argyllshire, were of the race of Clan Donald but in practice followed the Stewarts of Appin. Although of no connection with the Ulster MacCalls or MacCauls, there has been some intermingling of the two names (*see* MacCall).

COLLINS

This is among the thirty most popular names in Ireland and is well known in Ulster, particularly in Co. Antrim. The name is most common in Munster where it is an anglicised form of Ó Coileáin (Cullane), from *coileán*, meaning 'whelp'. In the west of Ulster Mac Coileáin was anglicised to Collins as well as Caulfield. Elsewhere in the province Collins is a variation of MacCollin, Gaelic Mac Cuilinn, from *cuileann*, meaning 'holly' (*see* Cullen). At the start of the twentieth century, Collins was still being used interchangeably with Cullen around Randalstown, Co. Antrim, and Tandragee, Co. Armagh, with McCallen in Enniskillen, Co. Fermanagh, and with Quillan in Newtownhamilton, Co. Armagh, and Castleblayney, Co. Monaghan.

Of course, Collins *per se* is an English name from the Christian name Colin. This is a double diminutive or pet form of Nicholas, first shortened to Col and then with -in added. Many of the Ulster Collinses are of English stock. Colin in Scotland is more usually from the Gaelic Cailean, a popular personal name with the Campbells (*see* MacCallion).

William Collins, 1838–90, the poet, perhaps most famous for the poem 'Tyrone among the bushes', was born in Strabane, Co. Tyrone.

CONLAN *see* Conlon

CONLON (*also* Conlan)

This common Irish name is well distributed throughout Ulster and can claim no one county as its home. The name in Ireland derives mainly from three unrelated and distinct septs; Ó Conalláin of counties Roscommon and Galway, Ó Coinghiolláin of Co. Sligo, and Ó Coindealbháin of the midlands and Co. Meath. This last sept also anglicised to Quinlan. The name was also spelt Connellan, and Abraham O'Connellan was Archbishop of Armagh from 1247 to 1260. The Book of the O'Connellans was written in medieval times and details many Donegal genealogies.

Around 1900 Conlon and Conlan were being used interchangeably with Connolly in Cootehill, Co. Cavan, Newry, Co. Down, and Dungannon, Co. Tyrone.

CONNELL (*also* MacConnell)

Connell is among the twenty-five most common names in Ireland but is most popular in Munster. There the O'Connells, Gaelic Ó Conaill, 'descendant of Connell', were driven out of their Kerry homeland by the O'Donoghues in the eleventh century. They settled under the MacCarthy Mór chiefs at Ballycarbery, Co. Kerry. Of this sept was Daniel O'Connell the 'Liberator'. Because of his popularity and succeeding Gaelic revivals very many Connells resumed the O' prefix, and O'Connells now outnumber Connells by more than four to one.

Connells in Ulster can be of this connection. Also, a few of the Oriel sept of MacCannon or MacConnon anglicised to MacConnell (*see* Canning). But most Connells and MacConnells, particularly in counties Antrim, Down and Tyrone, are of Scottish origin, a sept of the MacDonnells, the Glens of Antrim branch of the great Clan Donald. These were the MacConnells. Unlike O'Connell, this did not refer to the personal name Connell but to Donald. The original Gaelic name was Mac Dhomhnaill or Mac Dómhnuill and as the 'h' after the 'D' made it silent, Mac Dhomhnaill sounded as Mac'onnell. In Co. Antrim the MacConnells are most numerous in the baronies of Upper Antrim and Lower Massereene, and in Co. Down, in the barony of Lower Castlereagh.

See also Donaldson, MacDonald *and* MacDonnell.

CONNOLLY

This is a very popular Irish name, among the twenty-five most common, and well distributed throughout the whole island. But the Connollys are nowhere so numerous as in Ulster and there the name is most common in Co. Monaghan (where it ranked third in 1970) and Co. Antrim.

It was traditionally accepted that the Connollys stem from three main septs: the Ó Conghalaigh of Connacht (where the name is spelt Connelly); the Ó Conghallaigh of west Cork; and the Ó Conghaile of Co. Monaghan. The Ó Conghaile sept was supposedly a branch of the southern Uí Néill driven north to Monaghan by the Normans. However, it has been suggested that the Monaghan Connollys descend from Henry Mac Con Uladh Mac Mathúna, that is, Henry the son of Cú Uladh MacMahon. (Cú Uladh means 'hound of Ulster'.) Cú Uladh MacMahon died in 1375 as

Tanist of Oriel. These Connollys would therefore have been MacConnollys originally, the change to O'Connolly coming later. If this is correct they should be more properly Ó Conuladh rather than Ó Conghaile. They did not come to prominence in Monaghan until the late fifteenth century, when they were closely associated with the 'Lucht Tighe MacMahons' and were based in an area between Clones and Monaghan town. Corconnolly in Killeevan, Drumconnolly in Tydavnit and Mullaghconnolly near Roslea are all named after the sept. The Monaghan Connollys played a very important part there in organising the rising of 1641, though one of them, Owen O'Connolly, is more famous for his betrayal of the plans of the rising. James Connolly, 1868–1916, socialist and labour leader, was executed as one of the leaders of the 1916 rising. Though born in Edinburgh, he was of a Monaghan family.

The Connollys of Co. Fermanagh appear in the annals much earlier than those of Monaghan and are a distinct sept, Ó Conghaile, of the Fir Luirg (whose name is preserved in that of the barony of Lurg). They were based at Baile Uí Chonghaile (Connolly's town), east of Pettigo. They gave their name to Derrygonnelly (Doire Ó gConaíle, O'Connolly's oakwood).

In the mid-nineteenth century the Connollys of Co. Antrim were found to be mainly concentrated in the barony of Upper Dunluce. It is likely that these Connollys of the Glens of Antrim were originally MacIlchonnelies of Kintyre (where the name is now anglicised as Conley).

CONNOR

Connor is one of the ten most common names in Ireland and although it is very common in Ulster, it is less so than in the other three provinces. In Ulster it is most common in counties Antrim and Derry.

O'Connor, Gaelic Ó Conchobhair, 'descendant of Conor', is one of the most illustrious of Irish names and is that of several septs. The most famous is O'Conor Don and its branches O'Conor Roe and O'Conor Sligo. These descend from Conchobhar, King of Connacht, died 971, and the last two High Kings of Ireland were of this line.

However, the O'Connors of Ulster, a powerful sept in the Keenaght district of Derry, were entirely distinct from these. They descended from Cian, son of Oilioll Ólum, King of Munster in the third century. From Cian, they were known as the Cianachta and this became Keenaght. The sept was overthrown by the O'Kanes in the twelfth century, though its constituent members remained. The name was also made MacConnor, Gaelic Mac Conchobhair, and the present-day MacNaughers, MacNockers, MacNoghers, MacNohers, Noghers and so on are of this connection.

The Revd Abraham Hume, in his study entitled 'Surnames in the county of Antrim' (1857), found that 'the Connors have for their maximum limits the parishes of Magheragall and Ballinderry, and they exist there in such numbers and proximity that distinctive epithets are necessary in conversational intercourse. . . The name is pronounced Connier or Conyer.'

Around 1900 Connor was still being used interchangeably with Mac-Cottar, M'Cottier, MacNoher, Minogher and Minoher, around Limavady, Co. Derry, with MacNoger, MacNogher and Noghar around Ballymoney, Co. Antrim, and with Nocker in the Armagh city district.

There were two famous Ulster artists of the name. John O'Connor, 1830–89, was born in Co. Derry. He started as a scene painter in a theatre in Dublin and later moved to the leading theatres of London before taking up serious painting. He exhibited at the Royal Academy and specialised in recording ceremonial occasions for royalty. William Conor, 1884–1968, was born on the Old Lodge Road in Belfast. He is best remembered for his hundreds of paintings of Belfast working-class life. He claimed to spell his name with one 'n' because he 'could never make 'n's meet'.

CONWAY

This Welsh name is numerous in every province of Ireland. In Munster it is an anglicisation of the Thomond sept name Conoo, from Mac Connmhaigh. It is most common in Connacht, where in Co. Sligo it anglicises as Conboy, from Ó Conbhuidhe, from *cú*, 'hound', and *buidhe*, 'yellow', and in Co. Mayo (which can claim a quarter of all the Conways) as Kanavaghan, from Ó Connmhacáin.

The name itself is Welsh in origin and derives from the river, originally called Conwy. This became Conway, which also became the name of the town and the castle. Most families took their name from these. The family of the Barons Conway of Lisburn, Co. Antrim, was founded by Sir Fulke Conway, died 1624, who in 1602 received a royal grant of the manors of Killultagh and Derryvolgie (comprising Blaris, Lambeg and Derriaghy). He later bought a huge part of Con O'Neill's lands in Co. Down. He founded the town of Lisnagarvey, now Lisburn.

Most of the name in Ulster, who are not of Welsh or English stock, will stem from the Tyrone–Derry sept of MacConamy, from Mac Conmidhe, 'son of the hound of Meath'. This name was also anglicised as MacConomy, Conamy and Conomy. Conway is most common in Co. Tyrone and at the beginning of the twentieth century it was still used interchangeably with MacConamy and MacConomy around Omagh and Cookstown, Co. Tyrone, and Claudy, Co. Derry (and also with Conmee in the Draperstown district of Derry). Though Mac Conmidhe is also the Irish Gaelic for MacNamee, there is apparently no connection between the two names (*see* MacNamee). The forms MacConway and MacConaway are also found in Co. Donegal.

William Conway, 1913–77, Cardinal Archbishop of Armagh and Primate of All-Ireland, was born in Dover Street, Falls Road, Belfast.

COOKE

This is among the fifty most common names in England and many in Ulster will be of English origin. The name in this case is an occupational one, deriving ultimately from the Latin *cocus,* meaning 'cook'. The name in Leinster is mainly of this origin. In Connacht it is an anglicised form of Mac Dhabhóc, also called Mac Uag, a branch of the Burkes. But since the name is most common in Co. Antrim, most will descend from the MacCooks of Kintyre and Arran in Scotland, Scots Gaelic Mac Cuagh. In the Garvagh district of Co. Derry around 1900 the names Cooke and M'Cooke were still being used interchangeably. The Cookes and MacCooks were a sept of Clan Donald. In Scotland generally, the occupational name Cook(e) has been common since the twelfth century.

Cookstown, Co. Tyrone, was founded in the 1620s by Dr Alan Cooke, an English ecclesiastical lawyer. The Revd Henry Cooke, 1788–1868, champion of orthodox Presbyterianism, was born in Grillagh, Co. Derry. His statue, known locally as the 'Black Man', stands looking down Wellington Place in Belfast.

CORR

Though this name is well known in Dublin, it is much more common in Ulster than elsewhere in Ireland. A Co. Tyrone name, it derives from the Ó Corra sept, originally of Tyrone and Fermanagh. However, some Corrs of Co. Tyrone and of Co. Derry are simply descendants of the Gilla Corr mentioned in the Annals of Ulster in 1186 (*see* Corry).

CORRIGAN

This Co. Fermanagh sept, in Gaelic Ó Corragáin, is of the same stock as the Maguires. It is thought that they descend from one Coirdhecán of the Cenél Eoghain in Dromore, Co. Tyrone. They settled early in Fermanagh and were erenaghs of Magheraveely, a few miles west of Clones. There are many references to ecclesiastics of the name in the annals. They are now concentrated mainly in Cleenish, Co. Fermanagh. Branches of the sept migrated south well before Plantation times and settled in counties Louth, Offaly, Tipperary and Monaghan and are now found in most of the counties of Ireland outside Munster. The name was found to be the twenty-fifth most common in Fermanagh in 1962. It is also common in Monaghan, where it is concentrated mainly in Farney.

The most famous of the name in the twentieth century is Mairead Corrigan, one of the founders of the Peace People, awarded, with Betty Williams, the Nobel Peace Prize in 1976.

CORRY (*also* MacCorry)

There are several origins, both Irish and Scottish, for these names. Some of the Tyrone–Fermanagh sept Ó Corra (*see* Corr) anglicised to Corry. Also the Fermanagh sept Mac Gothraidh, 'son of Godfrey', which descends from Gofraidh, son of Donn Mór Maguire, anglicised to MacCorry and Corry (and also Godfrey). This sept spread south and east in medieval times and Corry was already common in Co. Meath in the seventeenth century. The name MacCorry is most common in counties Armagh and Down and many of these will be of the Fermanagh sept (*see* Maguire).

Confusion arises since many Scottish Corrys settled in those parts of the province already inhabited by the Irish Corrys. In Scotland the name is territorial in origin, from the lands of Corrie in Dumfriesshire. (Corrie was originally in Gaelic *coire*, 'cauldron', and later a 'circular glen'.) The surname Corrie has been common in Dumfriesshire since the twelfth century. John Corrie was provost of Dumfries in 1639 and it is thought that it was his son or grandson, also called John, who settled in Belfast before buying Castlecoole in Fermanagh for £860 in 1656. After the Williamite war, he acquired a more considerable estate at the expense of the Maguires. This John was the ancestor of the Earls of Belmore.

The Corrys of Rockcorry and Newry, Co. Down, were a distinguished family. Isaac Corry, 1755–1813, was Chancellor of the Exchequer in Ireland and helped draft the Treaty of Union of 1800 in his house in Newry. He was Henry Grattan's greatest opponent and was wounded in a duel with him.

Lastly, the name Corry is most common in Co. Antrim and some of these may descend from the small Scottish clan of Macquarrie, chiefs of the island of Ulva and part of Mull, some of whom anglicised their name as MacCorry. The names have also often been confused with Curry.

COSGRAVE *see* Cosgrove

COSGROVE (*also* Cosgrave *and* MacCusker)

Cosgrove is the more usual Ulster spelling of this name, which is an anglicisation of several distinct sept names. There were three important septs. The first of these was called Ó Coscraigh and they were chiefs of Feara Ruis in the Carrickmacross area of Co. Monaghan. The second was Mac Coscraigh, a neighbouring but totally distinct family, who were erenaghs of the church lands of Clones, Co. Monaghan. MacCusker, common in Co. Tyrone, is another form of this name. The third was Mac Cosracháin, also anglicised as Cuskery in Co. Armagh. Also, in south Fermanagh, the Mac Giolla Choisgle family, erenaghs of Derrybrusk, anglicised to Cosgrove.

Other origins of the name MacCusker are the Co. Armagh name MacIlcosker, Gaelic Mac Giolla Choscair, and the Fermanagh name Mac Oscair, a branch of the Maguires. Though MacCosker and MacCusker are not unknown in Scotland, they are not common and are there thought to be of Irish origin. The names derive from the Gaelic *coscrach*, meaning 'victorious', and *oscar*, meaning 'champion'.

COULTER

This almost exclusively Ulster name is most common in counties Antrim, Down and Fermanagh. It can be Irish in origin, from the Co. Down sept Ó Coltair, which gave its name to Ballyculter. But it can also be Scottish, a territorial name from the manor of Coulter in Lanarkshire, where it was recorded as a surname from the thirteenth century.

COWAN

In Ireland this is an almost exclusively Ulster name found mainly in counties Antrim, Down and Armagh. It can be of Scottish or Irish origin.

The Scottish name is common throughout the Lowlands, in particular in Ayrshire and Dumfriesshire. There, many of the Colquhouns (pronounced Cahoon) took the name (*see* Colhoun). The Cowans of Corstoun in Fife were the principal family of the name but Cowans were also numerous in Kilchoan (earlier Kill Cowan), Nether Lorn in Argyllshire. The name derives ultimately from St Comgan and in the south Highlands, particularly Argyllshire, it is a shortened form of Mac Gille Chomhgháin, 'son of the servant of (St) Comgan'. There were Cowan and MacCowan septs of clans Dougall, Colquhoun and Donald.

However, Cowan and MacCowan are also the modern forms of the old Co. Armagh name MacCone or MacCoan, Gaelic Mac Comhdháin, and indeed even as late as 1900, Cowan was still used interchangeably with Coan and Cohen in the Banbridge district of Co. Down. The form MacCowan in Armagh was largely absorbed into the more common MacKeown. Cowan has also been used for the Connacht name Coyne, and the Tyrone name MacIlhone (*see* Woods).

COYLE (*also* MacCool)

These two names are often confused. Coyle in Ulster is most common in counties Donegal, Derry, Tyrone and Cavan. The original sept was called

43

Mac Giolla Chomhghaill, 'son of the servant of (St) Comgall' and was based in the parish of Meeragh in the barony of Kilmacrenan in Donegal. The name was first anglicised as MacIlhoyle (which is still extant in its homeland and around Ballymoney, Co. Antrim), then MacCoyle and finally Coyle.

St Comgall was the patron of Galloon parish, which straddles the Fermanagh–Monaghan border, and a family of Mac Giolla Chomhghaill were erenaghs on the Monaghan side. This family anglicised to Coyle and in Monaghan are now numerous in Killeevan and Aghabog. Owing to the mistaken notion that the Gaelic word *coill,* meaning 'wood', was part of this sept's name, it was often anglicised to Woods (*see* Woods).

The homeland of the MacCools is also in Co. Donegal, in Raphoe, and it is most common in that county and in Tyrone. There is confusion over the origins of this name. However, it has been suggested that it too is in Gaelic Mac Giolla Chomhghaill or Mac Comhghaill. In Scotland MacCool is one of the many corrupt forms of MacDougall, Gaelic Mac Dhughaill, and at least some of the MacCools of Ulster will be of this origin. The name has also been made Cole, Cool and MacCole.

CRAIG

Craig is among the fifty most common names in Ulster, where it is mainly found in Co. Antrim and, to a lesser extent, counties Tyrone and Derry. A Scottish name, it appears in the early records in many parts of that country. It meant originally 'crag' or 'rock' and was taken by those who lived near a landmark rock. The name was common in Edinburgh and throughout the Lowlands in the fifteenth and sixteenth centuries.

Sir James Craig of Edinburgh was one of the fifty Scottish undertakers of the Ulster Plantation and in 1610 he was granted 1000 acres in Co. Armagh. He later sold it and bought Alexander Auchmutie's portion of 1000 acres in the barony of Tullyhunco in Co. Cavan and settled many of his kinsmen there.

Another James Craig, born in 1871 in Co. Down, was the son of a self-made whiskey millionaire whose family had come over from Scotland in the seventeenth century. He was the main organiser of the Ulster Volunteer Force in the struggle against Home Rule in the period after 1912 and was the first prime minister of Northern Ireland from its inception in 1921 to his death in 1940. He was created Viscount Craigavon of Stormont in 1927. Craigavon was the name of his father's house in Co. Down. The new town of Craigavon, Co. Armagh, was named after him.

In Co. Antrim in the late nineteenth century the main concentrations of the name were in the baronies of Upper Toome, Lower Toome and Upper

Antrim. It is thought that Craig in north Antrim and on Rathlin Island was originally MacCreig, a name found in Kintyre in Scotland.

CRAMPSEY *see* Bonar

CRAWFORD

Crawford is most common in Co. Antrim, followed by counties Down, Derry, Tyrone and Fermanagh. It is territorial in origin from the barony of the name on the Upper Clyde in Lanarkshire. The craw- element is from Old English *cráwe*, Lowland Scots *craw*, meaning 'crow'. The Crawfords were a sept of Clan Lindsay whose chiefs are the Earls of Crawford.

George Crawford was one of the fifty Scottish undertakers of the Ulster Plantation, and as a son-in-law of one of the chief undertakers, Andrew Stewart, he was granted 1000 acres adjacent to Stewart's portion in Mountjoy, Co. Tyrone. Although he sold the property within ten years, many of the Crawfords he had brought over from Scotland remained.

The name was already very numerous in Co. Antrim by the mid-seventeenth century, and in the mid-nineteenth century the Antrim Crawfords were mainly concentrated in the barony of Upper Glenarm, and had given their name to Crawfordsland in the parish of Kilbride. In mid-nineteenth-century Down the Crawfords were found mainly in the barony of Upper Castlereagh. Crawfordsburn in Co. Down is named after them. One of the Crawford families of Fermanagh came to Ireland, probably from Kilbirnie in Argyllshire, in or about 1630. There it gave its name to Crawford's Hill in the parish of Devenish. In 1962 it was noted as the thirty-sixth most common name in that county.

William Sharman Crawford, 1781–1861, MP and sheriff of Down, was founder of the Ulster Tenant Right Association which became the Tenant League of Ireland. He was born at Crawfordsburn, Co. Down.

CROMIE

In Ireland this name is exclusive to Ulster and there it is almost always found in counties Armagh and Down (Belfast excepted). In Scotland it is spelt Crombie and is a toponymic after the place of that name in the parish of Auchterless in Aberdeenshire. It is most common in that shire and the local pronunciation of both place- and surname omits the 'b'. The placename derives from the Scots Gaelic *crombach*, meaning the 'crooked place'. There were Crombie septs of Clan Donald and Clan Gordon.

In Ulster the Scottish surname Abercrombie has often been shortened to

Crombie and Cromie. Also, in seventeenth-century Co. Armagh there were references to O'Cromys, Irish Gaelic Ó Cromtha (from *crom*, 'bent, crooked') and so some Cromies may have an Irish background. In Co. Down the main concentration of the name is in the Rathfriland district. Crummy is a variant.

CROZIER

In Ireland Crozier is almost exclusive to Ulster. It is an occupational name from the Old French *crosier* or *crosser*, 'bearer of a bishop's crook' or 'of the cross at a monastery'. It can also mean a 'seller of crosses' or 'someone who lived by a cross'.

The Croziers or Crosers were one of the unruly riding clans of the Scottish Borders. They lived mainly on the Scottish side in Upper Liddesdale and Teviotdale, where they were associated in a confederacy with the Armstrongs, Elliots, and Nixons. In 1659 these four names were listed among the 'principal English names' in Co. Fermanagh, with Crozier found particularly around Enniskillen. As such it is likely that these families had come to that county from the Borders (along with the Irvines, Johnstons and so on) who were scattered when James VI 'pacified' the Border region. Though the name is still found in Fermanagh, it is now more common in Co. Armagh.

A distinguished branch of the family lived at Gortraw, near Newtownbutler, Co. Armagh, and was related to the Most Revd John Crozier, 1853–1920, Archbishop of Armagh, who was born at Ballyhaise in Co. Cavan. Captain Francis Rawdon Crozier, *c.* 1796–1848, the Arctic explorer, was born in Banbridge, Co. Down.

CULLEN

This name, which is among the 100 most common in Ireland, is mainly found in Leinster, where it is an anglicisation of Ó Cuilinn, from *cuileann*, 'holly'. This sept took its name from Glencullen in Co. Wicklow where it originated. Some in Ulster may descend from this sept.

In Co. Donegal some members of the Ó Cuileannáin sept anglicised to Cullen instead of Cullinan. The name was common in seventeenth-century Donegal. The name MacCullin was common in sixteenth- and seventeenth-century Co. Monaghan, possibly from the Mac Collúin or Mac Coileáin septs of Co. Fermanagh or from the Mac Ailín galloglasses (*see* Collins, MacCallion *and* MacQuillan).

In 1900 Cullen was being used interchangeably with Collins around Tandragee, Co. Armagh, and Randalstown, Co. Antrim; with Cullion around Derry city; and with Quillan and Quillen in Co. Cavan. Holly has also been recorded as a synonym.

The surname Cullen is found in Scotland, either from the burgh of Cullen in Banffshire, or the Ayrshire and Galloway name which most probably derives from the Irish MacCullen. Some in Ulster may therefore have a Scottish ancestry.

CULLY *see* MacCullough

CUNNINGHAM

This is among the seventy-five most common names in Ireland. Almost half are in Ulster, particularly in counties Antrim and Down. Though a Scottish name, it has also been widely adopted as an anglicisation of several Irish names. In the late nineteenth century there were twenty synonyms recorded for the name in Ireland.

Cunningham is territorial in origin from the place of the name in Ayrshire. It is a hybrid name from Gaelic *cuinneag*, 'milk pail', to which in the twelfth century an English scribe added *-ham*, 'village'. The first to take the name was Robert filius Warnebaldi, who received a grant of the manor and vill of Cunningham, *c.* 1160–80. These Cunninghams migrated to Strathblane in Stirlingshire in the sixteenth century. The main family became Earls of Glencairn in 1488. The name is common throughout Scotland. It was also one of the new names adopted by the MacGregors when their name was proscribed in 1603 (*see* Greer).

No less than five Cunninghams were among the fifty Scottish undertakers of the Ulster Plantation and all were granted lands in Co. Donegal. One, Alexander Cunningham of Sorbie in Wigtownshire, was granted 1000 acres in the baronies of Boylagh and Banagh in Co. Donegal. Although he did not prosper and the lands were taken from him, he and his descendants remained in the area. The remaining four were from Ayrshire – Sir James Cunningham, who was married to the daughter of the Earl of Glencairn, and his relatives Cuthbert, James and John. Between them they were granted 5000 acres in the Portlough district of Raphoe, Co. Donegal. Though all presumably settled some of their kinsmen on their properties, the only one who remained and prospered was John Cunningham of Kilbirnie, Ayrshire, brother of Sir James, whose lands bordered on Lough Swilly. He is remembered in the towns Newtowncunningham and Manorcunningham in Co. Donegal.

However, because of its similarity to several Irish names, Cunningham was adopted as an anglicisation of many Irish septs including the following: around Glenties, Co. Donegal, the MacCunnigans (in Gaelic Mac Cuinneagáin); in Co. Monaghan, the Kennigans (in Gaelic Ó Cuinneagáin) and the Kinahans (in Gaelic Ó Cuinneacháin); around Lisburn, Co. Antrim, and in Co. Derry, the Coonaghans (also in Gaelic Ó Cuinneacháin); in west Derry, east Donegal and in Tyrone, the Conaghans (in Gaelic Ó Connacháin); and in Co. Armagh, the Conagans (in Gaelic Ó Connagáin). Also, in south Down, the MacDonegans changed first to MacConegan and then to Cunningham (though some retain Dunnigan). Most of these names and their variant spellings were still being used interchangeably with Cunningham in the early twentieth century but have now become rare.

CURRAN

This name is common in all the provinces of Ireland but especially Ulster, particularly Co. Donegal. Little is known about the origins of the name.

Generally, it is an anglicisation of Ó Corráin, the name of what are thought to be three unrelated septs in Waterford and Tipperary, Galway and Leitrim, and Kerry. In Donegal, where the name is most common, it is from Ó Corraidhín, giving Curran, Curren and Curreen.

In Scotland the name has been recorded in Ayrshire and Wigtownshire, where it is of Irish origin.

CURRIE (*also* Curry)

These can be of Scottish or Irish origin: the Scottish with the -ie ending and the Irish with the -y ending (about equally divided in Ulster). In practice, however, the two spellings have become confused and are not an accurate guide.

The Irish name derives from Ó Comhraidhe, the name of two unrelated septs, the larger and more famous from Thomond (in Munster), and the other of Co. Westmeath, where they were chiefs of Moygoish.

In Scotland Currie is a variant of Corrie (*see* Corry) but more usually it is from MacVurich, Gaelic Mac Mhuirich, 'son of Murdoch', a name of two distinct origins. The MacVurich sept were hereditary bards to MacDonald of Clanranald and claim descent from the thirteenth-century Irish poet Muireach Albanach. Secondly, the Clan Macpherson are, in Gaelic, Clann Mhuirich after Muiriach or Murdoch, the fourteenth-century progenitor of the clan, and the clan name Mac Mhuirich was anglicised later as Currie and Murdoch (*see* Murdock).

In mid-nineteenth-century Antrim the main concentration of the name was found to be to the north of Ballymoney in the barony of Carey.

Many Curries of Arran, Kintyre and the Isles were originally MacCurdys (*see* MacCurdy).

CURRY *see* Currie

DALY

This is among the twenty-five most common names in Ireland, borne by perhaps 16,000 people. This is remarkable as, unlike most of the great Irish names, it is that of one sept only and, again unlike other common names, there is no suggestion of its having 'absorbed' lesser names along the way.

The Dalys descend from the Ó Dálaigh sept, located originally in the barony of Magheradernon in Co. Westmeath. The derivation is *dálach* from *dáil*, meaning 'assembly'. From the early twelfth century to the late seventeenth century no name was more closely associated with Gaelic literature and no less than thirty O'Dalys were distinguished poets and writers.

The O'Dalys spread from Westmeath and formed sub-septs in counties Clare, Cork, Galway and Cavan, bringing their literary skills with them. In Cavan they became hereditary poets to the O'Reillys of Breffny. The name is still common in that county and in the adjacent Co. Monaghan (where it was found to be the twenty-eighth most numerous in 1970). In Co. Donegal and elsewhere the name is sometimes spelt Dawley which is a closer approximation of the pronunciation of the original Gaelic name.

DAVIDSON (*also* Davison)

In the late nineteenth century the name Davison was most common in Co. Antrim, while Davidson was common in both Antrim and Down. Within Ireland they are almost exclusively Ulster names, stemming almost entirely from the north Scottish Clan Davidson.

Davidson means, obviously enough, 'son of David' (a personal name from the Hebrew Dāwīdh which meant 'beloved one'). Davison means 'son of Davie', the pet form of the name. The Clan Davidson or Clann Dhái descends from David Dhu, fourth son of Muiriach of Kingussie, chief of Clan Chattan. As such they were an important part of the great Clan Chattan federation. It is thought that they were the Clan Kay who fought the Macphersons at the celebrated battle of the North Inch at Perth in 1396. This was a gladiatorial contest of thirty warriors a side to determine who had precedence within Clan Chattan. It was watched by Robert III, his court and a huge crowd. Only one of the Davidsons survived, by climbing the enclosure and swimming the River Tay. They remained at feud with the Macphersons thereafter. The main families were of Cantray in Inverness-shire and of Tulloch in Perthshire. Davison and Davie were septs of Clan Davidson (*see also* Davis, Dawson *and* MacDaid, which were also Davidson septs). The Davidsons or Davisons of Roxburgh in east Teviotdale were a different and much smaller clan known collectively as Clann Dáidh. They were one of the lesser of the riding clans of the Scottish Borders.

Some of the Donegal sept of Mac Daibhéid anglicised to Davison (*see* MacDaid) in that county and also in Tyrone and Derry.

DAVIS

In Ireland this Welsh name, from Dafydd, through Davys, meaning 'son of Davy', is most common in Leinster and Ulster. In the latter it is most common in Co. Antrim. A few may be of Welsh stock but most in the north will be of Scottish origin, a sept of Clan Davidson (*see* Davidson) or descendants of the northwest Ulster sept of Mac Daibhéid (*see* MacDaid). At the beginning of the twentieth century the name was being used interchangeably with MacDaid in the Dungannon district of Co. Tyrone and with Davidson around Coleraine, Co. Derry, and Tandragee, Co. Armagh.

The poet Francis Davis, 'The Belfastman', 1810–85, was actually born in Ballincollig in Co. Cork.

DAVISON *see* Davidson

DAWSON

The personal name Dawe was a diminutive or pet form of David. As such it was quite common in medieval England, and Dawson is an English name. A family of Dawsons who became Earls of Cremorne in Monaghan came to that county from England during the Elizabethan wars of the late sixteenth century. However, it is not thought that many (even of the Monaghan) Dawsons are related to them.

In Scotland the Dawsons were a sept of Clan Davidson (*see* Davidson) numerous in Badenoch in south Inverness-shire. And on the Fermanagh–Donegal border the Irish name Durrian, from Ó Deoráin, has been anglicised Dawson (*see* Doran).

Dawson is most common in Co. Antrim and it may be assumed that these are more likely to be of the Scottish Clan Davidson origin.

DEMPSEY (*also* Dempster)

The name Dempsey is most numerous in Leinster, where it originated in Clanmalier, on the Laois–Offaly border. Ó Díomasaigh, from *díomasach*, meaning 'proud', was the name of this sept, famous for their consistent resistance to English rule from the twelfth-century invasion right through to the Williamite wars of the late seventeenth century. They were subsequently scattered and are now found throughout Ireland. However, since within Ulster they are most common in Co. Antrim, and since in early-twentieth-century Belfast Dempsey was recorded as synonymous with Dempster, also a common name in Antrim, some at least may be of Scottish descent. The name Dempster in Scotland meant a 'judex' or 'judge' in a baronial court.

DEMPSTER *see* Dempsey

DEVINE

This name in Gaelic is Ó Daimhín and the ancestor who gave the sept its name was Daimhín, died 966, the son of Cairbre Dam Argait, King of Oriel. A brother of Daimhín called Cormac was ancestor of the Maguires and the O'Devines, Lords of Tirkennedy. It was a leading Co. Fermanagh sept up until and including the fifteenth century. Later, the power of the leading family was broken by pressure from the O'Neills in the north and the Maguires in the south. However, the name is still known in Fermanagh, although more common in counties Tyrone and Derry. The name stems from the word *damh*, meaning 'ox', and not from *dámh,* meaning 'poet'. The sept gave Clogher in Co. Tyrone its original name, Clochar Mac nDaimhín.

DEVLIN

This important Tyrone sept, in Gaelic Ó Doibhilin, ruled a territory called Muintir Dhoiblin (now Munterdevlin) on the west shore of Lough Neagh in what the English called 'O'Neill's own country'. The sept was of the Cenél Eoghain, descending from one Domailén who gave it its name and was himself a direct descendant of Eoghan (Owen), son of Niall of the Nine Hostages. As such the sept was close kin to the O'Donnellys. The chief of the Muintir Dhoiblin, 'people of Develin', was hereditary sword-bearer to O'Neill and the O'Develins were part of his cavalry.

Devlin is most common in Tyrone (where it is the fifth most numerous name) and in the adjacent counties of Antrim, Derry and Armagh. Over 80 per cent of Irish Devlins are from Ulster. It was estimated in the 1950s that of those living in rural Ulster, 60 per cent still live in the vicinity of their ancestral homeland and at that date a large number of nicknames were used to distinguish between them (Devlin Dhu, Devlin Bán, Devlin Mór, Devlin Culough and so on). An interesting attempt to gentrify the name was recorded around 1900 when it was found that Devlin and D'Evelyn were used interchangeably around Glenavy, Co. Antrim, and in the Poyntzpass district of Co. Armagh.

Joseph Devlin, 1871–1934, born in Belfast, was a journalist for the

Irish News before becoming MP for West Belfast. He re-established the Ancient Order of Hibernians and was president of it for thirty years. He was an MP at Stormont and represented Fermanagh and Tyrone at Westminster.

DICKSON (*also* Dixon)

Generally speaking, the name is spelt Dixon in England and Dickson in Scotland. But on the Scottish Borders, where the name is most common, families have historically used either or both. The Dixons (or Dicksons) were one of the riding clans of the Borders and lived north of Berwick in the East March. Many members of these clans came to Ulster during the Plantation to escape the 'pacification' which James VI imposed on the Borders in the decade after 1603.

In Ireland numbers of the two names are split fairly evenly. But Dickson is more favoured in Ulster, particularly in counties Down and Antrim, and Dixon is most common in counties Dublin and Mayo. (The Mayo Dixons descend from a number of families who migrated there from Co. Donegal.)

Dickson has also been used as an anglicisation of Gaelic Ó Díochon (Deehan or Deighan), in counties Derry and Antrim. Indeed, Dickson was still used interchangeably with both Deehan and Deighan in the Ballymoney district of Co. Antrim at the beginning of the twentieth century.

About the middle of the eighteenth century an Elizabeth Dixon of Ballyshannon, Co. Donegal, moved to England and married a farmer called Wollstonecraft. Their daughter Mary Wollstonecraft, 1759–97, an early feminist, wrote *A Vindication of the Rights of Woman*. Her daughter, famous by her married name, Mary Wollstonecraft Shelley, 1797–1851, was the author of *Frankenstein, or the Modern Prometheus*.

The Revd William Steele Dickson, 1744–1824, United Irishman, was born in Carnmoney, Co. Antrim.

DIVER

This name is virtually exclusive to Co. Donegal. It is in Gaelic Ó Duibhidhir (though sometimes rendered Mac Duibhidhir) and is the name of a sept once well known in medieval Tirconnell. The MacDwyers or MacDyers, another Donegal sept, are distinct and are in Gaelic Mac Duibhir. Both names are based on the Gaelic *dubh*, 'black'. O'Diver was also made Deere, Devers and MacDever.

DIXON *see* Dickson

DOBBIN *see* Roberts

DOHERTY (*also* Dougherty *and* O'Doherty)

Second most popular name in Ulster in 1890 and fifteenth in Ireland, the Dohertys originate from the barony of Raphoe in Co. Donegal and are still most common there and in the adjoining counties. In number the Dohertys in Donegal are second only to the Gallaghers, a very large connection indeed, and Doherty is the single most popular name in Co. Derry.

One of the sons of the fifth-century Niall of the Nine Hostages, founder of the Uí Néill dynasty, was Conall Gulban, who won possession of the area now known as Donegal. From him it took the name Tír Chonaill (Tirconnell). (Another son, Eoghan, conquered and gave his name to what is now Tyrone [Tír Eoghain].) The Dohertys take their name from Dochartach, twelfth in lineal descent from Conall Gulban and were thus in Gaelic Ó Dochartaigh. (The word *dochartach* means 'hurtful'.)

The sept came to prominence in the twelfth century and became kings of Tirconnell. For a short period they lost their power to Norman invaders, but from the departure of the Normans in 1233 to the arrival of the English about 1600 the O'Dohertys ruled Inishowen. In 1608, however, Sir Cahir O'Dougherty rose in rebellion and took Derry city from the English. His defeat and execution marked the end of O'Doherty power and paved the way for the Plantation of Ulster.

In the centuries that followed the name was anglicised with many variant spellings and in almost all cases the O' prefix was dropped. By 1890 only 2 per cent were still using it. However, under the influence of the late-nineteenth-century Gaelic revival, many resumed it and by 1950 half of the Dohertys in Ireland had become O'Doherty again.

After the death of Sir Cahir O'Dougherty in 1608 many of his immediate family followed the path that had been taken a few years earlier in the Flight of the Earls and emigrated to the continent. Since that time the 'clan' has been without a chief. Recently, however, a claimant to the style of 'The O'Doherty' has been traced to Madrid.

DOLAN

The sept of Ó Dobhailén first appears in the records in the twelfth century in Clonmacnowen, Co. Galway, and Athlone, Co. Roscommon, both in the Uí Maine country of Connacht. They are still numerous in those counties but a movement northeastwards has left them common also in counties Leitrim, Fermanagh and Cavan. The name is among the fifteen most common in Co. Cavan. They were erenaghs of Belcoo in Fermanagh and were recorded in that county in the early seventeenth century as the Muintir Uí Dhóláin, 'people of Dolan'. They were then and are still most numerous in Clanawley.

Many of the Dolans of Co. Sligo are originally Devlins (*see* Devlin) and the name Dowling in Fermanagh is a synonym for Dolan.

DONAGHY (*also* Duncan, MacConaghy, MacConkey *and* MacDonagh)

These names all stem from the Scots and Irish Gaelic personal name

Donnchadh, meaning 'brown warrior' (from *donn* and *cath*).This gives the personal names Donagh in Ireland and Duncan in Scotland.

In Ireland the MacDonaghs, Gaelic Mac Donnchadha, are most numerous in Connacht where they are a branch of the MacDermots. A variant of MacDonagh in counties Tyrone and Derry is Mac Donnchaidh, which was anglicised first to MacDonaghy and then Donaghy. In Co. Fermanagh it is thought that most Donaghys descend from Donnchadh Ceallach Maguire, who led the Maguire conquest of Clankelly in the mid-fifteenth century.

However, the Scottish Clan Robertson of Atholl in Perthshire was equally well known as Clan Donnachie, Gaelic Clann Donnchaidh, after its chief Fat Duncan (Donncha Reamhar) de Atholia who lived at the time of Robert the Bruce in the fourteenth century and led the clan at the Battle of Bannockburn in 1314. The MacConachies (also MacConaghy and MacConkey) were a sept of Clan Robertson, their family name in Gaelic being Mac Dhonnchaidh. (The 'h' after the 'D' makes it silent, thus sounding as Mac'onachie.) Also, after the 1745 rebellion, many members of Clan Robertson adopted the name Donachie to conceal their identity.

There were also several MacConochie septs of Clan Campbell, one of which, the MacConachies of Inverawe in Argyllshire, descend from the fourteenth-century Duncan or Donachie Campbell of Lochow. The Clan Gregor MacConachies descend from the three sons of Duncan, seventeenth chief of MacGregor, by his second wife. There was also an old sept of Macconachies on the island of Bute.

In Ulster all this becomes very complicated. As has already been stated, Donaghy is also an Irish name. Duncan, though a Scottish name used as an anglicisation of Donachie and MacConachie, has also in Ulster been used for the Irish Donaghy as well as Donegan and Dinkin. Besides MacDonagh, Donaghy has also been used for Donohoe (*see* Donohoe). MacConaghy has been noted as a synonym for Conaty, MacConaughty, MacConnerty and even Quinn.

Within Ulster MacConaghy and MacConkey are mostly found in Co. Antrim. Donaghy is most common in counties Antrim, Derry and Tyrone and Duncan in counties Antrim and Tyrone. MacDonagh is most numerous in Fermanagh.

See also Roberts.

DONALDSON

This is an anglicisation of MacDonald that has been in use in Scotland, particularly Edinburgh, from the fourteenth century. In Ulster it is most common in Co. Antrim and to a lesser extent Co. Armagh.

Fairly early on the clan name of the great MacDonalds, Lords of the Isles, began to be spelt in a variety of ways, including Donaldson,

Donillson and Donnelson, forms recorded in old charters of the Mac-Donnells of Antrim (from whom the present Earl of Antrim descends). In the 'census' of 1659 Donnellson appears as a 'principal name' in Co. Antrim (*see* Connell, MacDonald *and* MacDonnell).

Around 1900 Donaldson was being used interchangeably with Donnelly (*see* Donnelly) in parts of the Coleraine district of Co. Derry.

DONNELLY

This is one of the seventy most numerous names in Ireland and one of the forty most numerous in Ulster. It is most common in its homeland of Co. Tyrone (where it is fourth most numerous), in Co. Armagh (where it is among the first ten) and in Co. Antrim.

The O'Donnellys, Gaelic Ó Donnghaile, were a Cenél Eoghain sept, who took their name from Donnghaile Ó Néill, died 876, seventeenth in descent from Niall of the Nine Hostages, the founder of the Uí Néill dynasty. (The name comes from *donn*, meaning 'brown [-haired]' and *gal*, meaning 'warrior'.) First based in Donegal, the sept later moved to Tyrone and settled in what became Ballydonnelly, Baile Uí Dhonnghaile (Donnelly's town). Though they were also a bardic family, their chief was hereditary marshall of O'Neill's forces and it is as soldiers that they are most famous. One of the most distinguished was Donnell O'Donnelly who was killed at the Battle of Kinsale in 1602. In the 1641 rising Patrick Modardha O'Donnelly took the castle of Ballydonnelly in Tyrone from Lord Caulfield. When it was retaken it was also renamed as Castle Caulfield. Several of the family fought for the Spanish in the Netherlands in 1652, and others fought for the French in the eighteenth century. In 1689 Patrick Donnelly was a member of the Patriot Parliament for Dungannon, Co. Tyrone, and Daniel O'Donnelly for Strabane, Co. Tyrone.

In the Coleraine district of Co. Derry Donnelly has been used interchangeably with the Scottish name Donaldson (*see* Donaldson).

DONOGHUE *see* Donohoe

DONOHOE (*also* Donoghue)

Donohoe, in Gaelic Ó Donnchadha, like Donaghy and MacDonagh, stems from the personal name Donagh. Common in every province in Ireland, it was the name of several unrelated septs, the most important of which were of counties Cork–Kerry, Galway, Tipperary and Cavan. In Co. Cavan it is among the fifteen most common names. The Co. Cavan sept was based in an area known as Teallach Dhonnchadha (Tullyhunco) which was then ruled by the MacKernans. Donohoe is the more usual spelling in Co. Cavan. Elsewhere the form Donoghue is more usual and there is evidence that the trend is towards the more widespread adoption of this spelling.

Around 1900, on Inishowen in Co. Donegal, Donohoe was being used interchangeably with Donaghy (*see* Donaghy).

DOOGAN (*also* Dougan *and* Dugan)

Generally speaking, Doogan is an Irish name and Dougan and Dugan can be either Scottish or Irish. All ultimately derive from the Gaelic *dubh*, meaning 'black'.

There were several septs of O'Dugan, Gaelic Ó Dubhagáin, in Ireland, the principal four being from Munster and Connacht. What is thought to be the original sept was based around what is now Fermoy in Co. Cork. In the west the name is usually spelt Doogan and this spelling is common in counties Donegal and Fermanagh. These may descend from the O'Doogans, Gaelic Ó Dúgáin, who were erenaghs of Inishkeen in Co. Fermanagh.

In Scotland the names Dugan and Dougan were well known in Wigtownshire. Here these names derive mainly from the Irish Ó Dubhagáin, but they were also anglicised forms of the Scots Gaelic name Dubhagán or Dubucán, meaning 'little black man', which was more usually anglicised as Blackie.

In Ulster Doogan is most common in Co. Donegal, Dougan in counties Antrim and Armagh, and Dugan in counties Antrim, Down and Derry.

DORAN

The O'Dorans, originally Ó Deoráin in Gaelic, were one of the 'Seven Septs of Leix' and were a famous family of brehons and antiquaries. Branches of the sept were early established in Co. Wexford and in counties Armagh–Down and these are the areas were the name is now most common. In mid-nineteenth-century Down the Dorans were almost exclusively found in the Dromara Hills and the Dorrians (a variant of the name) in the parish of Ardkeen on the Ards peninsula. Edmund O'Doran, died 1760, was Bishop of Down and Connor, as was Downpatrick man, the Most Revd Patrick Dorrian, 1814–85.

Doran and Dornan were used interchangeably in the Lisburn, Co. Antrim, district at the start of the twentieth century, but there is no connection between the two. Dornan, in Gaelic Ó Dornáin, is the Antrim and Down form of the Co. Louth name Durnin. This name derives from the Gaelic word *dorn*, meaning 'fist'. Doran, Ó Deoráin, derives from a personal name meaning an 'exiled person'.

DOUGAN *see* Doogan

DOUGHERTY *see* Doherty

DOUGLAS

In Ulster this famous Scottish name is most common in counties Antrim and Derry. The name is territorial in origin, from Douglas in Lanarkshire (from Old Gaelic *dub glas*, meaning 'dark [or black] stream').

The first to take the name was William de Duglas in the twelfth century and from that time on it was one of the most powerful families in Scotland, often viewed by the Stewart kings as their most serious threat (though the two families often intermarried). Their titles will give some idea of the extent of their power. There were Douglas Earls of Morton, Douglas, Annandale, Moray, Ormond, Angus and Forfar, and Dukes of Touraine, Queensbury and Buccleuch, and Hamilton.

The Douglases were one of the riding clans of the Scottish Borders, based in Liddesdale in Dumfriesshire, the most turbulent part of that turbulent region, and some may have come to Ulster at the Plantation when the riding clans were 'broken' by James VI in the decade after 1603.

In Argyllshire Douglas was taken as an anglicisation by the MacLucas family (Gaelic Mac Lúcais, 'son of Lucas').

The Ulster Douglases seem to have preserved the old Dooglas pronunciation. In Scotland the name is now pronounced Duglas.

DOWNEY (*also* MacEldowney)

Downey is found in all the provinces of Ireland. In Ulster it is most common in Co. Antrim, and can be of Scottish or Irish origin.

In Scotland it has two derivations. The first is territorial, from the old barony of Duny or Downie in Angus (where the name is still common). Duny is from the Gaelic *dun*, meaning 'hill'. The first of the name on record is Duncan de Dunny, 1254. The second derivation is as a shortening of MacIldownie, Scots Gaelic Mac Gille Domhnaich, meaning 'son of the lord's gillie (or servant)'.

In Ireland too the name has different origins. Downey is most common in Munster and there it derives from the O'Downeys, Gaelic Ó Dúnadhaigh. In Ulster Downey can be a shortening of Muldowney, in Gaelic Ó Maoldomhnaigh, which in its aspirated form was anglicised as Moloney. Also in Ulster the Irish Gaelic name Mac Giolla Domhnaigh (which has the same meaning as its Scots equivalent) was anglicised, first to MacEldowney, then shortened to MacDowney, then to Downey. MacEldowney is still common in Co. Derry and other forms of it are MacIldowney and MacGildowney.

Pádraig Mac Giolla Domhnaigh did much invaluable work on the origins of Ulster names and his *Some Anglicised Surnames in Ireland* (1923) is an essential reference work on the subject.

DOYLE

This name, which is among the fifteen most numerous in Ireland, is found in nearly every county but is particularly common in Wicklow, Wexford and Carlow, as it was in the fifteenth century. The name was originally in Gaelic Ó Dubhghaill, from *dubh*, 'black', and *gall*, 'foreigner'. *Dubhghall* was used initially to denote a Norseman or Viking. But in Ulster and in Roscommon it is also a form of MacDowell, in Irish Gaelic Mac Dubhghaill, the name of a Clan Dougall sept which came from the Hebrides as gallo-glasses (*see* MacDowell). In mid-nineteenth-century Down the Doyles were mainly found in the parish of Drumgooland.

DUFF

This name, which can be either Scottish or Irish in origin, is found mainly in Leinster and Ulster, and in the latter is most common in Co. Antrim. In both countries the name is mainly of the epithet type, that is, a description of the original bearers; the Gaelic *dubh* means 'black'.

In Ireland it is also a shortening of Duffin, Gaelic Ó Duibhin. In the seventeenth century this name was common in counties Armagh and Monaghan and by the late eighteenth century was common also in Co. Antrim, particularly Ballymena. Another Irish name, Mac Giolla Dhuibh, usually anglicised MacIlduff or MacElduff has become Duff, particularly in Co. Tyrone. Duffy too has been shortened to Duff in many counties (*see* Duffy).

In the Scottish province of Galloway the name MacIlduff, Scots Gaelic Mac Gille Dhuibh, was shortened to Duff. It was also a sept name of Clan MacDuff, Earls of Fife, whose chief had the right of crowning the Pictish Kings of Scotland.

DUFFY

Duffy is among the fifty most common names in both Ireland and Ulster. It is the single most popular name in Co. Monaghan, among the first fifteen in Co. Donegal and among the first twenty in Co. Fermanagh.

Ó Dubhthaigh, 'descendant of Dubhthach (the black one)', was the name of several unrelated Irish septs. Apart from the Connacht O'Duffys who were centred at Lissonuffy, Co. Roscommon, the two most important septs were both of Ulster. The Monaghan O'Duffys ruled the area around Clontibret. The first of the name on record is Patrick O'Duffy, Chief of Teallach Gealacáin, in 1296. (This roughly equates with the modern parish of Clontibret). By 1659 O'Duffy was the third most common surname in that county. They contributed a remarkable number of priests to the Clogher diocese of Co. Tyrone during the Penal period of the eighteenth century. The Fermanagh Duffys are mainly of Monaghan origin but some, particularly around Lower Lough Erne, are of the Uí Briuin Breifne Duffys who originally settled at Ballyduffy near Belleek.

In Co. Donegal the O'Duffys were part of the Clann Conchúir Magh Ithe, a branch of the Cenél Eoghain (*see* Kane). The family were erenaghs of Templecrone in the diocese of Raphoe for eight hundred years. They were kinsmen of the patron of the church, the seventh-century St Dubhthach. The O'Duffys were also erenaghs at Culdaff in the barony of Inishowen. The name is also spelt Doohey and Dowey in Donegal.

James Duffy, 1809–71, the Dublin publisher, was born in Monaghan, as was Sir Charles Gavan Duffy, 1816–1903. In defiance of Daniel O'Connell he founded the Young Irelanders and the newspaper *The Nation* before emigrating to Australia. There he rose to become prime minister of Victoria. His grandson, George Gavan Duffy, 1882–1951, was a signatory of the 1922 Anglo-Irish Treaty and became president of the High Court of Justice in the new southern state. Eoin O'Duffy, 1892–1944, was also a Monaghan man. He fought for the Irish Republican Army during the War of Independence and became the first commissioner of the new Garda Síochána . Dismissed by Eamon de Valera in 1933, he formed the fascist Blueshirts and became the first president of the Fine Gael political party. When he resigned that post he formed an Irish brigade and fought for Franco in the Spanish Civil War.

The Scottish Duffys were a sept of Clan Macfie, earlier MacDuffy, Gaelic Mac Dhuibhshith, meaning 'son of the black (one) of peace', from *dubh,* 'black', and *sith,* 'peace'. The Macfies, a branch of the Clan Alpin, were hereditary keepers of the records of the Lords of the Isles. The home of the clan was the island of Colonsay in the Inner Hebrides, but some followed Cameron of Lochiel, and others the Islay MacDonalds. With the decline of Clan Donald power the Macfies scattered at the beginning of the seventeenth century. Other Macfie sept names well known to Ulster are MacAfee, MacFee, and MacHaffie, now shortened to Mahaffy. All three were particularly well known in Co. Donegal and all are various anglicisations of the original Gaelic name.

DUGAN *see* Doogan

DUNCAN *see* Donaghy

DUNLEAVY (*also* MacAleavey)

Dunleavy is not a very common name in Ulster. MacAleavey is more common and is exclusive to the province. It is most numerous in counties Down and Armagh.

The Irish Dunleavy is more properly MacDunlevy, being in Gaelic Mac Duinnshléibhe, from *donn*, 'brown', and *sliabh*, 'mountain'. The MacDunlevys were a royal family of Ulidia (southeast Ulster), who were driven out by John de Courcy in the twelfth century and migrated to Co. Donegal where they became physicians to the O'Donnells. The sept migrated to Connacht after the Battle of Kinsale in 1602, and Mayo and Sligo are the counties where the name Dunleavy is now most common. The name was also made Donleavy, Leavy, Leevy, MacAleavey, Mac-Aleevy and MacNulty. This last is in Gaelic Mac an Ultaigh, 'son of the Ulidian' (*see* MacNulty).

MacLysaght claims that a branch of the MacDunlevys went to Scotland where the name was made Dunlop and Dunlief. However, Black gives these names quite different origins (*see* Dunlop). Dunleavey is also a Scottish name but is a variant of MacKinley (*see* Finlay).

Brian Donlevy, 1899–1972, was born in Portadown, Co. Armagh. He fought with General John Pershing in Mexico in 1919, then worked in the United States as a model before becoming a leading man in Hollywood.

DUNLOP

This name in Ireland is exclusive to Ulster where two-thirds are in Co. Antrim. It is of Scottish origin.

Dunlop is a common name in Ayrshire, where it derives from the lands of Dunlop in the district of Cunningham. The first of the name on record is Willhelmus de Dunlop in 1260. The placename is from the Scots Gaelic *dùn làpach*, 'muddy hill'. In mid-nineteenth-century Ayrshire the name was pronounced Delap and Dulap and it is interesting to note that around 1900 Dunlop was being used interchangeably with Delap (*see* Lappin) about Ballymena, Co. Antrim, and Enniskillen, Co. Fermanagh.

The name became common in Kintyre after the plantation of Lowlanders there in the seventeenth century. Dunlops from Arran settled in north Antrim in the early seventeenth century. A Bryce or Bryan Dunlop obtained a grant of lands between Ballycastle and Ballintoy from Sir Randall

MacDonnell. He married Christian Stewart, daughter of John Stewart of the island of Bute. In the mid-nineteenth century the greatest concentration of the name in Co. Antrim was found in the barony of Upper Dunluce.

John Dunlap, 1747–1812, was born at Strabane, Co. Tyrone. In Philadelphia he founded the first newspaper in the USA in 1771, the *Pennsylvania Packet*. He also printed the Declaration of Independence and served in Washington's bodyguard.

See also Dunleavy.

DUNN *see* Dunne

DUNNE (*also* Dunn)

Dunne is among the thirty most numerous names in Ireland and, if Irish, was originally O'Dunn, Gaelic Ó Duinn or Ó Doinn, from the personal name Donn, meaning 'brown'. The most famous sept, the O'Doynes, were of Co. Laois and, as Lords of Iregan, were one of the most important families in Leinster. Two-thirds of those of the name are from that province and there it is spelt Dunne. Most of the name who spell it Dunn are from Ulster, in particular the north of Ulster (counties Antrim, Down, Derry and Tyrone). In Ulster the Dunne spelling is common only in Co. Cavan.

Dunne was also the name of one of the lesser of the riding clans of the Scottish Borders who lived on the English side of the East March. Many members of the riding clans came to Ulster when the clans were 'broken' by James VI after 1603.

EAKIN *see* Aiken

EAKINS *see* Aiken

EDGAR *see* Adair

ELLIOTT

Found in every province of Ireland, Elliott is common only in Ulster, which claims 80 per cent of those of the name. It has long been associated with Co. Fermanagh (where it is the fifth most numerous name) and to a lesser extent Co. Cavan. Other Ulster centres are in counties Antrim and Donegal.

There are two possible derivations of the name. In England it was a diminutive or pet form of the personal name Elias (*see* Ellis). But in Scotland it has been noted that an early form of the name was Elwald or Elwold, from the Old English Ælfweald, meaning 'elf-ruler'. The Elliots were one of the great riding clans of the western Scottish Borders, and although there were several branches of the family, the chiefship resided initially with the Elliots of Redheugh in Berwickshire.

After the 'pacification' of the Scottish Borders in the decade following 1603, Elliots, Armstrongs and Johnstons were hanged, outlawed and banished, and many came to Ulster during the 1609 Plantation. They settled particularly in Fermanagh where they seem to have formed a cohesive group, strong enough to ride out the 1641 rising. These three names are now among the first five in the county.

During these upheavals the lands of the Elliots of Redheugh passed to the Eliotts of Stobs in Roxburghshire who took over the chiefship. A third important branch of the family was formed at the end of the seventeenth century by Gilbert Elliot, a descendant of a branch of the Stobs family.

Interestingly, in Scotland there are more than seventy ways to spell the name and all are permissible except Elliott, which for some strange reason the Eliots, Elliots and so on claim to despise. An old rhyme attempts rather unsuccessfully to unravel this:

> The double L and single T
> Descend from Minto and Wolflee.
> The double T and single L
> Mark the old race in Stobs that dwell.
> The single L and single T
> The Eliots of St Germain's be
> But double T and double L
> Who they are, no one can tell.

For double L and double T, the Scots should look across the sea! Of the seventy-six Elliotts born in Ireland in 1890, seventy-one had names spelt with double L and double T.

ELLIS

This English name is numerous only in Dublin and Ulster, where it is particularly common in Co. Antrim. The Hebrew name Elijah was made in Greek Elias and this personal name was very popular in medieval England. It became in Old English Elys or Elis and this came to be the basis of the surname Ellis. It is fairly common in both Scotland and Ireland from about the thirteenth century onwards but most in Ulster arrived in the post-Plantation period.

ENNIS *see* MacGuinness

ERVINE *see* Irvine

ERWIN *see* Irwin

EWING

This Scottish name has been common in Ulster since the seventeenth century and then, as now, it is most numerous in counties Donegal, Derry, Tyrone and Antrim.

In Scotland it is an anglicised form of Ewen or Ewan, Gaelic Eoghan, or, more usually, a shortening of MacEwing, MacEwan, Gaelic Mac Eoghain, a name that also gives MacKeown (*see* MacKeown).

A family of MacEwens in Argyllshire were hereditary senachies and genealogists to the Campbells of Glenorchy and held Barmolloch in Lorne. There were MacEwen septs of Clan Dougall and Clan MacLaren. However, the Clan Ewen which held a large part of the district of Cowal in Argyllshire was, in the fifteenth century, tricked out of its patrimony by the Campbells, and became extinct as a clan. Most of them then became followers of their kinsman MacLachlan of Clan Lachlan. The Ewens, Ewings and MacEwens mostly settled in Lennox, Lochaber and Galloway and are still most numerous there.

The last witch to be put to death in Scotland was Elspeth MacEwan; she was executed in Kirkcudbright in 1698.

FARRELL

This is among the forty most common names in Ireland, and found in every county, though two-thirds are in Leinster alone. The O'Farrells were princes of Annaly, now Co. Longford. Annaly took its name from one Angall, whose great-grandson Feargal, meaning 'man of valour', gave his name to the sept Ó Fearghail. This Feargal was King of Conmacne and was slain at the Battle of Clontarf in 1014. The sept was based at Longford, which was originally called Longphort Uí Fhearghail (O'Farrell's fortress).

Farrell is one of the names influenced by the Gaelic revival, for while those using the O' prefix were outnumbered by fifteen to one in the late nineteenth century, it is now closer to three to one. The name has been noted as a synonym of Farrelly in the Cootehill district of Co. Cavan.

Farrell, Farrelly and Friel are all etymologically the same, that is, from Ó Fearghail, but are not related.

FARRELLY

Co. Cavan has nearly half of all the Irish Farrellys and the name is among the ten most numerous in that county. It is common too in Co. Meath.

The O'Farrellys, Gaelic Ó Fearghaile, 'man of valour', were a Breffny sept whose territory was in the barony of Loughter Lower in north Cavan. There they were erenaghs of the abbey and lands of Drumlane (which became an Augustinian priory). The Gaelic poet Feardorcha O'Farrelly who died in 1746 was from Co. Cavan.

The English name Farley was widely used in the north as a synonym and as late as 1900 the two names were still being used interchangeably in various parts of Co. Cavan. James Lewis Farley, 1832–85, the traveller and writer, was of Cavan parentage and Cardinal John Murphy Fowley Farley, 1842–1918, Archbishop of New York, was born in Co. Armagh.

FAULKNER

This name, common in Co. Antrim, is found in a variety of spellings, but all stem originally from the Old French *fauconnier*, meaning either 'one who hunts with falcons' or a 'keeper and trainer of falcons'. John O'Hart, writing in 1881, claims that the Falkeners of Ireland descend from Nicholas Taylor, grandson of Edward Taylor of Beverley in Yorkshire, who was chief 'Falkiner' to Henry III, c. 1273. In the late nineteenth century Falchenor and Falconer were being used interchangeably in the Strabane district of Co. Tyrone, Falconer and Faulkner around Claudy and Garvagh in Co. Derry, and Falconer and Foulkard around Cookstown, Co. Tyrone.

Brian Faulkner, 1921–77, prime minister of Northern Ireland from 1971 to 1974, was born in Helen's Bay, Co. Down. His father was from Cookstown.

FEE (*also* Foy)

These two names, as well as Fey and Fie, are anglicisations of Ó Fiaich, from *fiach*, meaning 'raven', a sept of the Cenél Eoghain. The original sept were of Co. Fermanagh where the O'Fees, along with the Cosgraves, were erenaghs of Derrybrusk near Enniskillen. The 'census' of 1659 records O'Fee as a principal name in that area.

The name spread to counties Armagh and Cavan. In the latter county particularly it is often spelt Foy and has been confused with the Westmeath and Cavan name Fay, from the Norman de Fae.

The most famous of the name is Tomás Ó Fiaich, Cardinal Archbishop of Armagh and Catholic Primate of All-Ireland, whose family was originally of Co. Louth and later settled in Co. Armagh. The name was also anglicised to Hunt in the mistaken notion that it was from *fiadhach*, meaning 'hunt'.

Fee is also common in Co. Antrim and it is possible that some of these were originally Scottish MacFees (*see* Duffy).

FERGUSON

This is among the fifty most common names of both Scotland and Ulster and in the latter is most numerous in counties Antrim, Down and Derry.

The Scottish Clan Ferguson claims descent from Fergus Mac Erc, descendant of Conn of the Hundred Battles, and prince of the north Antrim kingdom of Dalriada. He, with his two brothers Angus and Lorn, conquered Argyll in 470 and established the Scottish kingdom of Dalriada.

The first settlement of the clan appears to have been at Kintyre. Campbeltown, renamed after the Campbells became its owners, was previously called Kilkerran. The Fergusons of Kilkerran descend from Fergus, son of Fergus, in the time of Robert the Bruce in the fourteenth century and were keepers of the cross of St Ciarán.

The Fergusons of Craigdarroch in Dumfriesshire descend from Fergus, Prince of Galloway, c. 1165, who married a daughter of Henry 1 of England. 'Bonny Annie Laurie', the heroine of the famous song, was the wife of Alexander Ferguson of Craigdarroch. The Fergussons of Atholl in Perthshire descend from Adam, son of Fergus, a descendant of the Lords of Galloway. A branch of these became the Fergusons of Dunfallandy in Perthshire. There were also Ferguson branches in Balquhidder in Perthshire, and in Aberdeenshire.

Since Fergus was a popular personal name in medieval Scotland, both it and MacFergus, Gaelic Mac Fhearghuis, sprang up as surnames in many areas. These names were often anglicised as Ferguson, as was MacKerra, itself a variation of MacFergus (see Ferris).

Most Fergusons in Ulster will probably be of the Galloway connection. In mid-nineteenth-century Antrim the name was mainly concentrated in the barony of Upper Antrim and in Co. Down in the parish of New-townards. The name was found to be the thirty-second most numerous in Co. Fermanagh in 1962 and is particularly common in the Derrygonnelly area.

Sir Samuel Ferguson, 1810–86, poet, antiquary and founder of the Protestant Repeal Association, was born in Belfast. Harry Ferguson, 1884–1960, inventor and engineer, world famous for his revolutionary tractor, was also the first person to fly in Ireland (in a self-made mono-plane in 1910). He was born near Hillsborough, Co. Down.

FERRIS

This Co. Antrim name, previously MacFerries, previously MacFergus, is that of a branch of the Scottish Clan Ferguson (see Ferguson). In Aberdeenshire it was used as a shortening of the name Ferguson itself. In Ulster it can also be an anglicisation of the Connacht name Ó Fearghusa (O'Fergus) or a synonym of the Donegal name Ó Fearadhaigh (O'Ferry – *see* Ferry). In the late nineteenth century the Co. Antrim Ferrises were mainly found in the barony of Upper Massereene around Aghalee.

FERRY

Ferry, also spelt Fairy, is found almost exclusively in Co. Donegal, and is an anglicisation of the old Cenél Conaill sept name Ó Fearadhaigh. This probably derives from the personal name Fearadhach, meaning 'manly'. The name is also well known in Co. Sligo and other parts of Connacht. The O'Ferrys were followers of the MacSweeneys. The name has occasionally been confused with Ferris (*see* Ferris).

FINLAY (*also* MacKinley)

The personal name Finlay is Scottish, from the Gaelic Fionnlagh (from *fionn*, 'fair', and *laoch*, 'hero'). The surname Finlay is an anglicisation of Mac Fhionnlaigh which was also made MacKinlay and MacKinley. (Dunleavey and MacInally are other forms of the name but should not be confused with the indigenous Ulster names Dunleavy and MacAnally.) There were MacKinlay septs of Clans Buchanan, Farquharson, MacFarlane, and Stewart of Appin. The Fin(d)lays and Fin(d)laysons were septs of Clan Farquharson.

In Ulster Finlay is most common in counties Antrim and Down, and MacKinley in counties Antrim and Donegal. However, in Donegal there has been some confusion with the local name MacGinley (*see* MacGinley). Also, in Co. Antrim, the Irish name MacAlee, Gaelic Mac an Leagha, meaning 'son of the physician', was sometimes anglicised as MacKinley.

The main concentration of MacKinleys in mid-nineteenth-century Antrim was in the barony of Carey in the Glens. The MacKinleys of Conagher, near Ballymoney, had three famous sons: Francis MacKinley was hanged for his part in the 1798 rebellion; William McKinley, 1843–1901, twenty-fifth president of the USA, was descended from David MacKinley, born *c.* 1730, and his wife Rachel Stewart; John MacKinley, the early-nineteenth-century poet, was also of this family.

In Co. Down in the late nineteenth century the name Finlay was most common in the area between Bangor and Newtownards. The Jesuit Thomas J. Finlay, 1848–1940, who was of Scottish descent, was born in Co. Cavan. He was president of the Irish Agricultural Organisation Society and campaigned for many years on behalf of the co-operative movement.

FINNEGAN

Finnegan or Finegan is a common name in all the provinces of Ireland. In Ulster it is most numerous in Co. Monaghan (where it is most often spelt

Finegan) and in counties Armagh and Cavan (where it is usually Finnegan).

The original name was Ó Fionnagáin, from the personal name Fionnagán, itself derived from the word *fionn,* meaning 'fair-headed'. There were two septs of the name. The first was based on the Galway–Roscommon border and the name is still common in that area.

But most Finnegans in Ulster and in Ireland as a whole descend from a sept which was based on the borders of the ancient kingdoms of Breffny and Oriel in an area where the modern counties of Cavan, Monaghan and Louth meet. In Co. Monaghan it was the eleventh most numerous name in 1659 and the fifteenth most numerous in 1970 and is now particularly common in Farney.

FITZPATRICK

This is among the seventy most common names in Ireland and is found throughout the island. Within Ulster it is among the fifteen most common in Co. Cavan, in the first twenty in Co. Fermanagh and the first forty in Co. Monaghan. It is also popular in counties Antrim and Down.

The prefix Fitz-, from the French *fils,* meaning 'son', generally denotes a Norman name. However, Fitzpatrick is the only Fitz- name in Ireland that is not of Norman origin, having been assumed by the Mac Giolla Phádraig sept in Kilkenny in 1537 when their chief became Lord Baron of Upper Ossory under Henry VIII's 'surrender and regrant' policy. The original name meant 'son of the devotee of (St) Patrick' and was also anglicised as Gilpatrick, Kilpatrick and MacGilpatrick, (but *see* Kilpatrick for details of the Scottish form of the name). Fitzpatrick has also been shortened to Patrick and Patchy in parts of Ulster. It has also, like Fitzsimons, been shortened to Fitch.

It is thought that the Fermanagh Fitzpatricks are not of the Kilkenny sept but are a branch of the Maguires.

FITZSIMONS

Fitzsimons or Fitzsimmons is a Norman name meaning 'son of Simon'. The main Irish family of the name came to Leinster from England in 1323 but Fitzsimonses had already been in Ulster for a century and a half at that time. Normans, they had come to Co. Down in the train of John de Courcy in 1177. They were related to the Savages and were at one time holders of Kilclief Castle, Co. Down.

In mid-nineteenth-century Down Fitzsimons was the single most numerous name in the barony of Lecale, especially in the area south of Strangford. It was also noted at that time that this was the largest concentration of one name in any barony of Down or Antrim. The name is still most common there and on the Upper Ards. In Ulster it has been shortened to Fitch, Simons and Simon (*see* Simpson).

It is thought that in Co. Cavan Fitzsimmons was originally Mac Siomóin, a branch of the O'Reillys.

FLANAGAN

Flanagan is one of the seventy most common names in Ireland, but in Ulster it is numerous only in counties Fermanagh, Cavan and Monaghan. There were several septs of O'Flanagan, Gaelic Ó Flannagáin, from *flann*, meaning 'red, ruddy'. The most important sept outside Ulster were of the same blood as the O'Connors. Their chief held the hereditary post of steward to the O'Connor Kings of Connacht.

However, the Fermanagh O'Flanagans were an important medieval family and a branch of the Cenél Cairbre, that is, the descendants of Cairbre, a son of the fifth-century Niall of the Nine Hostages, founder of the Uí Néill dynasty. The O'Flanagans were the ruling family of the Cenél Cairbre Tuath Ratha and as such they controlled the entire western side of Lower Lough Erne, from Belleek to Belmore mountain. The sept was based at Ballyflanagan in the present townland of Aghamore in Magheraboy and provided many pastors and priors to Devenish Abbey in the medieval period. The name was noted as the twenty-ninth most numerous in Fermanagh in 1962.

In Co. Monaghan another sept of O'Flanagan was of the Clann Ceallaigh under the MacDonnells of Clankelly. These O'Flanagans descend from Flannacán, son of Fogartach, King of Farney, died 886. Their headquarters was probably in the parish of Donaghmoyne.

FLEMING

While this name is common in the other three provinces of Ireland, it is most numerous in Ulster, especially counties Antrim and Derry. Fleming, Norman French le Fleming, Old French Flamanc, means simply a 'native of Flanders'. Many Flemings migrated to Britain in the twelfth century and settled mainly in the Scottish Borders and in Wales.

Several of the name appear in Scottish records in the second half of the twelfth century but no details are known of the relationships, if any, between them. Baldwin the Fleming was sheriff of Lanark. His family held extensive territories in Lanarkshire and was based at Boghall near Biggar. There was also a sept of Clan Murray called Fleming.

Though many Flemings will have come to Ulster since the Plantation, the name has been common in Ireland from the twelfth century. The De Flemmings came to Ireland from Wales with the Normans in the late twelfth century and were quickly established as one of the leading Anglo-Norman families, acquiring considerable estates in counties Louth and Meath. They took King James's part in the Williamite wars of the late seventeenth century and were consequently ruined. A Nicholas Fleming was Archbishop of Armagh from 1404 to 1416.

FLYNN (*also* Lynn)

Flynn is among the fifty most common names in Ireland but is less numerous in Ulster than in the other provinces. The northern form of the name is Lynn and this is mainly found in Ulster, particularly in Co. Antrim.

Flynn is from the Gaelic Ó Floinn, 'descendant of Flann', meaning 'red, ruddy'. As such the name sprang up in many different localities. There were O'Flynn septs in counties Clare and Kerry, two in Co. Cork and two in north Connacht. In Ulster Flynn is found mainly in Co. Cavan and in the Clones–Roslea district of Monaghan–Fermanagh.

The northern sept of the name spelt it Ó Fhloinn. The 'h' here makes the 'F' silent and the name became O'Lynn, Gaelic Ó Loinn. This sept was once powerful in the Clandeboy O'Neill country of Co. Antrim. Based in the Crumlin–Antrim district, they ruled a territory stretching from Lough Neagh to the sea. They were the senior branch of Clan Rury of Ulidia. Their name was anglicised as Lind, Linn, Lynd, Lynn and even Lindsay (*see* Lindsay).

In Scotland there were also families of Lin or Lynn in both Ayrshire and Wigtownshire. Many of the Plantation settlers hailed from these shires and so it is possible that a few Ulster Lynns are of Scottish stock. The name in this case was taken from that of a waterfall in the parish of Dalry in Ayrshire near the ancient Castle of Lin.

FORD *see* Forde

FORDE (*also* Ford)

This name is common in Ireland as a whole but less so in Ulster. Counties Galway, Cork, Mayo and Dublin, taken together, claim two-thirds of the Irish total. In England and Scotland the name sprang up independently in very many places and was used to denote someone who lived by a ford.

Englishmen of the name appear early in Irish records. One particular family came from Devonshire in the fourteenth century and became land-owners in Co. Meath. Some in Ulster may descend from families such as these or from later, post-Plantation settlers. However, Forde and Ford have been widely used in Ireland as anglicisations of several native Irish names.

In Co. Cork the Forans, Gaelic Ó Fuartháin, widely anglicised their name to Forde, as did the Breffny sept of MacKinnawe, Gaelic Mac Conshnámha. These latter were chiefs of Muintir Cionaoith or Munter Kenny in Co. Leitrim from at least the thirteenth century. Some of the Fordes of south Ulster may descend from these. Others who became Fords were originally called Mac Giolla na Naomh, meaning 'son of the devotee of the saints'. The largest sept of this name was of Connacht but in Tyrone this name became Agnew, Ford, Gildernew and MacAneave.

The Fordes who gave their name to Seaforde, Co. Down, are originally of a Co. Wexford family which claims Welsh extraction.

FORSYTHE

This Scottish name is, in Ireland, almost exclusive to Ulster and there it is found mainly in Co. Antrim and Co. Down. There are two derivations of the name.

The first is that it was taken from some place of the name, now forgotten. We know this because the first on record was Robert de Fauside who signed the Ragman Roll in 1296 and because all the early references in the fourteenth and fifteenth centuries were prefixed by 'de', meaning 'of (the place called)'. Secondly, Forsythe was used as an anglicisation of the Gaelic personal name Fearsíthe, meaning 'man of peace'.

The Forsythe chiefs were members of the royal Stewart household at Falkland. The clan was without a chief or formal recognition from the Lord Lyon King of Arms until 1980 when Alistair William Forsythe, who descends from a Falkland laird living in 1607, was recognised.

In mid-nineteenth-century Antrim the Forsythes were found almost exclusively in the barony of Kilconway and particularly in the parish of Dunaghy, townland of Rosedernott, where there lived thirty Forsythe families.

Interestingly, the name was corrupted to Foursides in the Poyntzpass district of Co. Armagh.

FOSTER

In Ireland this name is common only in Dublin and in Ulster, where it is mainly found in Co. Antrim. It was originally an English name but was common too in Scotland.

In England it has four possible derivations: from the name Forrester or its abbreviation Forster (from the office of 'forest keeper'); from the Old English word forseter, meaning a 'shearer'; a variation of the name Fewster, from the Old French fustrier, meaning a 'saddle-tree maker'; or from 'fosterer' – it was a common practice in early medieval England for a child to be fostered out. As Fostarius (forest keeper) there are several entries of the name in the Domesday Book.

In Scotland it has been found mainly as a contraction of Forrester, the first reference to which was in 1144. A family of the name Forrester was among the burgher nobility in fourteenth-century Edinburgh and the Forresters of Garden were one of Stirlingshire's most powerful families for centuries. The form Fostar first appears in the Scottish records in 1488.

A family of Forsters or Fosters on the Scottish Borders was one of the great riding clans of that district, common all along the English side of the border. Many members of these clans came to Ulster at the time of the Plantation to escape James VI's 'pacification' of the Border country.

Vere Foster, 1819–1900, was born in Copenhagen, the son of a British diplomat of Irish parentage. When he witnessed the effects of the Famine in 1847 he settled in Ireland and devoted his life and his fortune to assisting emigrants, building schools and publishing a range of educational books for the poor. He died poor himself and is buried in Belfast's City Cemetery.

FOX

This English name is found in every county in Ireland, and in Ulster it is most common in Co. Tyrone. Generally in Ulster, as throughout Ireland, the name is of Irish origin. In England it is found mainly in the Midlands and was used in the first instance as a nickname.

In Ireland too it was used as a nickname. Tadhg Ó Catharnaigh, for instance, Chief of Teffia, Co. Meath, who died in 1084, was known as An Sionnach, 'the fox', and his family henceforth took the name Ó Sionnaigh, later Fox (see Kearney).

In south Tyrone and in Co. Armagh the Mac an tSionnaigh sept, 'son of the fox', anglicised their name to MacAshinagh and other branches of this sept used MacAtinney (in north Tyrone and Mayo) and Tinney (in Co. Donegal). All these variants have been further anglicised to Fox. Pádraig Mac Giolla Domhnaigh, in *Some Anglicised Surnames in Ireland* (1923), illustrates this point: 'I know two brothers at Dungannon. One lives in the country and is known by no other name than McAtinny; the other lives in town and is known by the name of Fox.' It has been said that within living memory in the Glens of Antrim Mac an tSionnaigh was anglicised by Protestants of the name to Shannon, while the Catholics became Fox.

By mistranslation the Mac Seanchaidhe septs of north Connacht and Meath–Louth also became Fox. (Their name actually means 'son of the storyteller'.) The Foxes of counties Monaghan and Cavan are of this connection.

Charlotte Milligan Fox, 1864–1916, born in Omagh, Co. Tyrone, founded the Irish Folk Song Society in 1904 and travelled throughout the country collecting songs and airs on a gramophone.

FOY *see* Fee

FRASER *see* Frazer

FRAZER (*also* Fraser *and* Frizell)

There has been some confusion over these surnames. MacLysaght states that Frizell, which has been in Ireland since 1216, is a variant of the Norman name Frisel, meaning a 'Friesian' or 'native of Friesland'. P.H. Reaney claims that the name derives from the Old English *frithu*, meaning 'peace'. Both find 'unaccountable' the connection between Frizell and Frazer in Scotland. And yet Black, the authority on Scottish names, seems quite clear about it.

The original spellings of the name in Scotland, where it first appears in 1160, are de Freselier, de Frisselle and de Fresel and are that of a Norman family that stemmed ultimately from La Fresilière in Anjou in France. Black, in *The Surnames of Scotland: Their Origin, Meaning and History,* states that the name then became Fraissier, meaning 'strawberry bearer', 'probably from the adoption of the flower of the *fraise*, strawberry, as part of the armorial bearings'. This process happened by the first or at most the second generation, for Sir Gilbert of Touch-Fraser in Stirlingshire, died by 1263, was a Frizell. He was the founder of the main line of the Clan Fraser. Fraser, however, continued to be pronounced Frizell or Frisell and indeed to this day in Tweedale and Lothian Frisell is the common pronunciation. Other branches of the family were the Frasers of Durris in Kincardineshire and of Philorth in Aberdeenshire. The main line eventually became known as Clan Fraser of Lovat and their chiefs as Lords Fraser of Lovat. These descend from one Simon, a brother of Sir Alexander Fraser, who fought for Robert the Bruce in the fourteenth century. From this Simon the chiefs of Clan Fraser of Lovat derive their Gaelic name Mac Shimidh, 'son of Simon', pronounced MacKimmie. The septs of Clan Fraser include the Frissells, the Frizells, the MacKimmies, the Simpsons and the Tweedies (*see* Simpson). Fraser is among the twenty most common names in Scotland.

In Ulster Frazer is the more usual spelling and the name is most common in counties Antrim and Down. As in the seventeenth century, Frizell is still most common in Co. Antrim. As late as 1900 Frazer was still being used interchangeably with Frizzle and Frizell in many parts of the province.

FRIEL

This name is almost exclusive to northwest Ulster and north Connacht, being most common in its homeland, Co. Donegal, and to a lesser extent in counties Tyrone and Derry.

It was originally O'Friel, from the Gaelic Ó Firghil, which, like Farrell and Farrelly, means 'man of valour'. The family descends from Eoghan, brother of St Columcille, and many were distinguished ecclesiastics. The sept were co-arbs, or hereditary holders of the office of abbot, of Kilmacrenan and erenaghs of part of Conwall in the parish of Kilmacrenan in Donegal. Florence O'Friel, died 1299, was Bishop of Raphoe. Awley O'Friel became Abbot of Iona in 1203. Cú Chonnacht Ó Firghil was Abbot of Derry in 1539. The chief of the sept had the hereditary right of inaugurating the O'Donnell princes as Lords of Tirconnell.

Brian Friel the playwright was born in Omagh, Co. Tyrone, on 9 or 10 January 1929 (and has two birth certificates to prove it). His greatest success was *Philadelphia Here I Come!*, which ran for a long time on Broadway. He is also one of the founders of the Derry theatre company and publishing house Field Day.

FRIZELL *see* Frazer

FULLERTON (*also* MacCloy)

In Ireland these two Scottish names are almost exclusive to Ulster, and both are most numerous in Co. Antrim, with Fullerton also common in Co. Down.

Fullerton is territorial in origin from the barony of the name in the parish of Dundonald, Ayrshire. The original name was Foulertoune, 'hamlet of the fowler'. The first of the name on record is Alanus de Fowlertoun who founded a convent at Irvine in Ayrshire in the mid-thirteenth century. A branch of the Ayrshire family, the Fullartons of Kinnaber, settled in Angus and in the fourteenth century another branch settled on Arran. The Perthshire Fullertons were originally from Forfar and took their name from a Foulertoun there.

The first of the Fullartons who settled on Arran was called Lewis and from him descend the MacLewis, Gaelic Mac Luaidh, sept. This name became MacCloy and for a very long period MacCloy, MacLewis and Fullarton were used interchangeably. The Fullartons were hereditary coroners of the bailiedom of Arran. One of the family, James, settled in Bute and his descendants were known as MacCamies or Jamiesons (*see* Jamison) or Neilsons (*see* Nelson) and became hereditary coroners of Bute. The Arran Fullartons and their branches were septs of Clan Stuart of Bute.

A James Fullerton was master of the Free School in Dublin in 1588 and was later one of the commissioners of the Ulster Plantation. Nicholas Fullerton acquired a considerable holding during the Plantation, augmented by his nephew Colonel Adam Fullerton, in Co. Derry. In mid-nineteenth-century Antrim the Fullertons were mainly found in the barony of Lower Belfast, particularly near Ballynure.

Livingstone states that the MacCloys of the Clones district of Co. Monaghan are in Gaelic Mac Giolla Eachaidh, more commonly anglicised MacGlaghy. MacCloy in Co. Derry has been made Maloy (*see* Molloy).

FULTON

In Ireland Fulton is found exclusively in Ulster and mainly in Co. Antrim. Most of the early references to the name in Scotland were in Ayrshire and were in the form de Fulton, meaning 'of (the place called) Fulton'. But it has still not been established where this place was. There was a Fulton in the parish of Bedrule in Roxburghshire and some in Scotland may have taken their name from there.

Several Fulton families came to Ulster from Ayrshire in the early years of the Plantation and settled in counties Tyrone, Derry and Antrim. The Lisburn Fultons, in Antrim, for instance, were there in 1611. In mid-nineteenth-century Antrim the name was found mostly in the barony of Lower Belfast, in the Carnmoney district. The Carnmoney Fultons have been there since the early eighteenth century and seem to have had some connection with the Tyrone family.

Robert Fulton, 1765–1815, of Ulster Scots descent, was the first to apply steam to shipping in the USA.

GALBRAITH (*also* MacBratney)

In Ireland these two names are almost exclusive to Ulster where Galbraith, the more numerous, is found mainly in Co. Antrim and MacBratney in both Antrim and Down. They are Scottish in origin.

Galbraith is from the Gaelic for 'foreign or stranger Briton' and originally denoted a Strathclyde Briton settled among the Gaels. The name is also in Gaelic Mac a' Bhreatnaich, 'son of the Briton', and was anglicised as MacBratney. The first Galbraith on record is Gillespick Galbrait who witnessed a charter wherein the Earl of Lennox granted the lands of Colquhoun to Umfridas de Kilpatrick (*see* Colhoun). The same earl granted Gartonbenach (later called Baldernock) in Stirlingshire to Maurice, Gillespick's son, *c.* 1230. These were the ancestors of the Galbraiths of

Baldernock, a sept of Clan MacFarlane and therefore followers of the Earl of Lennox.

At some stage one of these Baldernock Galbraiths quarrelled with Lennox and flex to the island of Gigha, off Kintyre. There his descendants were known as Clann a' Bhreatannaich, 'children of the Britons'. These Galbraiths became a sept of Clan Donald and held Gigha for them until after 1590. The Galbraiths of Kintyre descend from them.

In the Lennox country during the reign of James VI the Galbraiths were commissioned to hunt the Clan Gregor and were then declared 'broken' themselves and outlawed on the advice of the Earl of Argyll. Like the MacGregors, the MacFarlanes and the Lamonts, they were forbidden to use their name.

This happened just prior to the Plantation of Ulster and may well have been an important push factor for the Galbraiths who came to counties Tyrone, Donegal and Fermanagh in the early decades of the Plantation. At the same time it is reasonable to assume that the Galbraiths of Co. Antrim or at least of the north of the county descend from the Gigha–Kintyre connection.

GALLAGHER

In 1890 Gallagher was the fourteenth most common name in Ireland and the third most common in Ulster (after Smith and Doherty). Two-thirds of the Ulster total were in the sept's homeland in Co. Donegal where it was the most numerous name. It was fifth most common in Co. Tyrone and thirteenth in both counties Fermanagh and Derry.

The O'Gallaghers were originally in Gaelic Ó Gallchobhair and descended from one Gallchobhar, meaning 'foreign help'. He was a descendant of Conall Gulban (who gave his name to Tír Chonaill, later Tirconnell), a son of the fifth-century Niall of the Nine Hostages, the founder of the Uí Néill dynasty. As such the Gallaghers claim to be the most royal branch of the Cenél Conaill.

From their bases at Ballybeit and Ballyneglack in Tirconnell they controlled extensive territories in what are now the baronies of Raphoe and Tirhugh and from the fourteenth to the sixteenth centuries they were chief marshalls and commanders of cavalry to the O'Donnell princes of Tirconnell. The Gallaghers were also noted ecclesiastics, providing many bishops to Raphoe and elsewhere in Ireland.

It is thought that the Gallaghers of Fermanagh descend from those who fought for Shane O'Neill against the O'Donnells and settled there after O'Neill's defeat.

GALLIGAN *see* Gillan

GAMBLE

Most of the Gambles in Ireland are in Ulster, where the main centres are in counties Antrim, Down and Derry. Gamble is an English name, found frequently in the Domesday Book, and derives from two personal names, Old Norse Gamall and Old Danish Gamal, meaning 'old'.

In the early seventeenth century families of the name settled in Ulster and in Co. Cork. Since that time the Cork connection has gradually dwindled, while the number of Gambles in Ulster has steadily increased. In the seventeenth century Gambles appear in the Ulster inquisitions, the army lists, Petty's 'census', and the Hearth Money Rolls. A few Gamble families came from Scotland – a father and son, for instance, both called Josias Gamble, settled in Fermanagh about 1670.

GIBB *see* Gibson

GIBSON (*also* Gibb, MacGibbon *and* MacKibbon)

These Scottish names all stem ultimately from the same source, the personal name Gilbert. Gibb was originally a diminutive or pet form of Gilbert and Gibbs and Gibson follow on obviously enough. However, Gibbon, as a personal name, was a further pet form of Gibb, and was popular, especially in Perthshire, from an early date. MacGibbon, which was smoothed in time to Mac'ibbon or MacKibbon, is therefore self-explanatory.

There was a Gibson and MacGibbon sept of Clan Campbell of Argyll in the neighbourhood of Glendaruel. A sept of Clan Buchanan were known as Gibb, Gibson, Gilbertson, MacGibbon and MacGilbert, and descended from the Buchanans of Arduill. There were MacGibbon followers too of Clan Graham of Menteith in Perthshire. A sept of Clan Cameron known as the Clan M'Gillery became Gilbertsons and Gibsons. And in Galloway the name MacGibb or MacGubb became Gibson 'for gentility'.

In Ireland MacGibbon and MacKibbon are almost exclusive to Co. Down (which has two-thirds of the total) and Co. Antrim (which has the rest). A particular concentration has long been in the parish of Annahilt in the barony of Lower Iveagh, Co. Down. According to MacLysaght the Down and Antrim MacKibbons are from Gaelic Mac Fhibín, Fibín being a diminutive of Philip.

The Gibsons are numerous in Ireland and are found in every province, but four-fifths are in Ulster, where again they predominate in counties Antrim and Down. In late-nineteenth-century Antrim they were found concentrated in the hills overlooking Belfast and, in Down, close to the MacKibbons, in the parish of Hillsborough.

A headstone in Bangor Abbey records the death, in 1623, of John Gibson, 'seance Reformacione from Popary the first Dean of Dune [Down] sent by his Maiestie into this Kingdom and receeved by my Lord Clandeboye to be preacher at Bancor'. He had 24 communicants on his arrival and left 1200 at his death.

GILLAN (*also* Galligan, Gillen *and* Gilligan)

These names have been taken together because in different areas of Ulster they have become confused. Gillan and Gillen are most common in counties Antrim, Donegal and Tyrone, and also Sligo. Galligan is almost exclusive to Co. Cavan. Gilligan is less common in Ulster than in Leinster and Connacht but is numerous in Co. Derry.

Galligan is in Gaelic Ó Gealagáin, a sept of Sligo now more numerous in Cavan. It has also been anglicised as White (*see* White), from *geal*, meaning 'white', and also as Gilligan.

However, properly Gilligan is from MacGilligan, in Gaelic Mac Giollagáin, a Co. Derry sept which, in the sixteenth and seventeenth centuries, controlled what was called MacGilligan's Country. Magilligan Strand is named from this sept. In the early seventeenth century it was one of the three chief septs under the O'Cahans.

The key element in the Gaelic forms of Gilligan and Gillan is the word *giolla*, meaning 'lad'. The Gillans, Gaelic Ó Giolláin, were a sept of the Cenél Eoghain. However, Gilligan and Galligan have both been made Gillan or Gillen, as has Gilliland, a variant of MacClelland (*see* MacClelland).

GILLEN *see* Gillan

GILLESPIE (*also* Bishop)

In Gaelic Ulster, Gillespie was originally Mac Giolla Easpuig, and in Scotland, Mac Gill' Easpuig. Both stem from *easpag*, which means 'bishop', and had in turn been borrowed from the Latin *episcopus*. The name therefore meant 'son of the servant of the bishop' and indeed Bishop is one of the anglicisations of the name.

In Ireland nine out of ten Gillespies live in Ulster, particularly in counties Antrim, Donegal, Armagh and Tyrone. This was also reflected in pre-Plantation records where nearly all Gillespies mentioned are Ulstermen. These Irish Gillespies belonged to a sept which originated in Co. Down, a branch of which was early established in Co. Donegal. At the end of the twelfth century Mac Giolla Espcoip was recorded as chief of Aeilabhra in what is now the barony of Iveagh in Co. Down. In the later medieval period the Gillespies of Donegal were erenaghs of Kilrean and of Kilcar in the baronies of Boylagh and Banagh respectively.

Many of the Scottish Gillespies belonged to the Clan Macpherson (itself an ecclesiastical name meaning 'son of the parson') and as such to the great Clan Chattan federation. In the reign of Alexander III in the fourteenth century, Gillies Macpherson, a younger son of Ewan Macpherson, chief of the clan, was first chief of the Macphersons of Invereshie in Inverness-shire. Many of the Macpherson sept names derive from this Gillies including Gillespie, Gillies, Lees, MacLeish and MacLise. Gillespie was most common in Argyllshire and the Isles where it was anglicised much earlier than in Ulster. A John Gilaspison is noted in the records as early as 1376.

In the mid-nineteenth century, concentrations of Gillespies were noted in the Co. Down parishes of Aghaderg and Annahilt though it was not specified whether these were of Scottish or Ulster descent.

Hugh Gillespie of the Clan Macpherson, like many other Jacobites who fought in the 1715 rebellion, was forced to seek refuge in Ulster. His grandson, Major General Sir Robert Rollo Gillespie KCB, 1766–1814, led a colourful career expanding the British Empire in India and the Far East and was killed while leading his troops in an assault on the fortress of Kalunga in Nepal. His statue stands in Comber, Co. Down, the place of his birth.

For some curious reason, never fathomed, the name Archibald was always accepted in both Scotland and Ulster as an anglicisation of Gillespie. The Scot Gillespic O'Duibhne, to take only one instance, famous as the first to take the name Campbell and the progenitor of that great clan, was equally well known as Archibald.

GILLIGAN see Gillan

GILMORE

Though found in every province of Ireland, Gilmore is common only in Ulster and can be of Irish or Scottish origin. In both countries it was originally a Mac- name and meant 'son of the devotee of (the Virgin) Mary', in Gaelic Ulster Mac Giolla Mhuire, and in Scotland Mac Gille Mhóire.

The Ulster sept of the name was once very powerful, controlling a large territory which included the baronies of Antrim, Castlereagh and Lecale. (As such it possessed the Great [Lower] Ards and the name is now sixth most numerous on the Upper Ards.) The sept took its name from a chief of the O'Mornas (thought to be modern Murney) called Mac Giolla Mhuire Ó Morna, died 1276. The power of the sept was early broken by incursions by the Irish O'Neills and MacCartans and the Anglo-Norman Whites and Savages. However, they became followers of the O'Neills of Clandeboy and were prominent in the resistance to the English up to the end of the fifteenth century. Their name was also anglicised as Kilmurry, MacElmurray, MacIlmurry and so on, especially in counties Tyrone and Fermanagh. This was also shortened sometimes to Murray (*see* Murray).

However, the name was also common in Scotland and the Morrisons of Lewis and Harris in the Outer Hebrides (who stemmed originally from Donegal) were known in Gaelic as the Clann Mhic-Gille-Mhóire and Gilmore was the name of one of the leading septs of the clan (*see* Morrison). Some at least of the Gilmores of this origin must go to make up the numbers of the name in Co. Antrim, where the name is most prevalent. The name is also very common in Co. Down and in the mid-nineteenth century it was particularly concentrated in the parish of Garvaghy, barony of Upper Iveagh.

GLASGOW *see* MacCloskey

GORDON

Gordon is one of the more common Scottish names in Ireland, found in Munster, common in Leinster and Connacht, and very common in Ulster (where over half are in Co. Antrim). Though recorded in Ireland as early as the mid-fourteenth century, it became common only after the Ulster Plantation.

The name is territorial in origin, and though it is customary to trace it to places of the name in France, the earliest known home of the Scottish family was Gordon in the Merse in Berwickshire. The first person on record to have taken the name was Richer de Gordun, Lord of Gordon. The family were Anglo-Normans who settled in southern Scotland in the twelfth century. One of them, Adam de Gordon, joined Louis XI of France in the Crusade of 1270. Shortly after that, in the reign of Robert the Bruce, a Sir Adam, Lord of Gordon, was granted the lordship of Strath-bogie in Aberdeenshire. He was slain at the Battle of Halidon Hill in 1333. His great-grandson, also Sir Adam, was slain at the Battle of Homildon in 1402 and left only his daughter Elizabeth as heiress.

Six years later she married Sir Alexander Seton, ancestor of the house of Huntly, and it was he who began the greatest expansion of Gordon power. Though there were many branches of the Gordon family, they alone could not account for the rapid increase in the numbers of those of the name by the end of the fifteenth century. Seton rewarded all those who took the name Gordon and became his vassals with a bowl of meal. This kind of 'adoption' and the giving of symbolic gifts between lord and vassal was very common at the time. Those thus 'adopted' into the family were henceforth known as 'Bow' o' Meal' Gordons. The Gordons subsequently became one of the most powerful clans in Scotland, so strong in the Highlands that their chief was known as the 'Cock of the North'. The name is still among the fifty most numerous in Scotland.

In mid-nineteenth-century Antrim the Gordons were found almost exclusively in the barony of Lower Antrim, particularly in the area between Ballymena and Carnlough and there particularly in Drumleckney. The Irish sept name Mag Mhuirneacháin, usually anglicised as MacGurnaghan, has also been made Gordon in counties Antrim and Down.

GORMAN

This is a common name in all of the provinces of Ireland and in Ulster it is most common in counties Monaghan and Antrim. In Ireland generally it is one of the names that has responded to the Gaelic revivals by resuming the O' prefix. Whereas in 1890 O'Gorman was outnumbered by six to one by Gorman, the name with the prefix is now in the majority. However, in Gaelic Ireland Gorman was a Mac- name, Mac Gormáin (from *gorm*, meaning 'blue'). It is thought the mistake began in the eighteenth century when Chevalier Thomas O'Gorman, 1725–1808, who, as an expert on Irish pedigrees should have known better, assumed the O'.

The original sept was from Slievemargy, near Carlow, but was driven out by the Norman Preston family and settled in counties Clare and Monaghan. The form MacGorman is still found in Co. Monaghan and the importance of the name there is remembered in the placenames Fartagorman near Bellatrain, Killygorman in Killeevan, and Lisdungorman in Clontibret. There is also a Rathgorman in Co. Down. Peadar Livingstone, in *The Fermanagh Story*, claims that the Gormans who were erenaghs of Callowhill in that county were originally Ó Gormáin and so a few at least of the present-day O'Gormans are correctly named. Some Gormans in Ulster were originally Gormleys (*see* Gormley).

GORMLEY

This name is common in Connacht, where it was originally Ó Gormghaile, but in Ulster, where it is most numerous, it is from Ó Goirmleadhaigh. This was the name of the leading sept of the Cenél Moen, so called because it descends from Moen, son of Muireadach, son of Eoghan (who gave his name to Tyrone), son of Niall of the Nine Hostages, the fifth-century founder of the Uí Néill dynasty.

The O'Gormleys originally ruled what is now the barony of Raphoe, Co. Donegal, but were driven out by the O'Donnells in the fourteenth century. They settled to the east and northeast of Strabane, Co. Tyrone, and from there continued to fight the O'Donnells. The Plantation finished their power and little is heard of the sept thereafter, but the name remained, and Gormley is now most common in Co. Tyrone (where it has also often been made Grimes). It is common too in Co. Antrim. In Co. Cavan and elsewhere the name has been changed to Gorman (see Gorman). It has also become Grimley, for instance, in the Keady district of Co. Armagh, and Graham in many areas (see Graham).

GOURLEY

Outside of Dublin this name is found only in Ulster where it is most common in Co. Antrim. It was originally MacGourley, from Mag Thoirdealbhaigh, 'son of Turlough', a Tyrone–Antrim variant of the Armagh–Down name MacTurley. The name, as Gourlay or Gourlie, is also well known in Scotland and there it is territorial in origin, probably from a place of the name in England. Therefore some at least of the Ulster Gourleys may have Scottish roots.

GRAHAM

Graham is among the 100 most numerous names in the whole island, among the twenty most numerous in Ulster, in the first twenty also in Co. Antrim and among the ten most common in counties Down and Fermanagh. It is also very common in counties Tyrone, Armagh and Monaghan. In Scotland, whence it stems, it is among the forty most common.

The name is territorial in origin from Grantham in Lincolnshire, a place noted in the Domesday Book as both Grantham and Graham. The de Grahams were an Anglo-Norman family who settled in Scotland in the early twelfth century. The first of the name on record is William de Graham who witnessed the foundation charter of Holyrood Abbey in 1128. He was later granted the lands of Abercorn and Dalkeith in Midlothian by David 1. From that time the Grahams played a very important part in the affairs of Scotland.

One of these, however, Sir John Graham of Kilbride, near Dunblane, fell out of favour with the Scottish court and migrated with a considerable following to the Debateable Land in the West March of the Scottish Borders. The descendants of these became the Grahams, one of the great riding clans of the Borders. Apart from the Armstrongs they were the most troublesome family on the whole frontier and when James VI of Scotland, James I of England, decided to 'pacify' his 'Middle Shires' the Grahams were particularly savagely treated. Many were hanged or banished and fifty families were transported to Roscommon. Within two years they had scattered. A suggestion that they be rounded up and transported again, to Ulster, was declined by the lord deputy, who preferred to leave well alone.

However, very many Grahams did come to Ulster during the Plantation to escape persecution in the Borders and by 1659 theirs was a 'principal name' in counties Antrim and Fermanagh. Most of the Scottish settlers in Fermanagh were of the Border riding clans, the Armstrongs, Elliotts and Johnstons to name but a few. Although the Grahams remained strong in that county they were unlike the others in that many moved on and the name became widely scattered throughout the province.

In Argyllshire the name MacIlvernock or Warnock, Gaelic Mac Gille Mheárnaig, 'son of the devotee of (St) Ernan', was made Graham as were the Ulster names Grehan and Gormley (see Gormley). The story that some Grahams reversed their name to Maharg to conceal their identity, though attractive, has been discounted. Maharg is a variant of the Scottish MacIlhagga.

GRANT

This Scottish name is common in Leinster, Munster and especially Ulster, where it is most numerous in counties Antrim and Donegal. There are disputes as to the origin of the name.

The Clan Grant is one of the main branches of the Síol Alpine of which Clan Gregor is chief and it is claimed that they descend from Gregor Mór MacGregor who lived in the twelfth century in Strathspey. An extensive moor there called Sliabh-Griantais, 'plain of the sun', is claimed by some to be the origin of the name. However, a Norman family of le Grant, who were neighbours and relations of the Bissetts in Nottinghamshire, came to Scotland with the Bissetts in 1242. The first recorded of the name in Scotland, Sir Lawrence Grant, sheriff of Inverness in 1263, was of this family. From the fourteenth to the sixteenth century the name is invariably preceded by 'le'. This Norman name is descriptive, from the Old French grand or grant, meaning 'great', either in the sense of 'elder' or 'tall'. When the MacGregors' name was proscribed by act of parliament in 1603, Grant was one of the names they assumed (see Greer).

In Ulster most Grants will be of this Scottish origin. MacLysaght claims that a few will be originally Grannys or MacGranns. However, there is evidence that there will be more than a few of that origin. In many parts of

Ulster where the name Mag Raighne, anglicised as Granny, MacGrann, MacGrean and MacGreaney, predominates, Grant is often found overlapping. This is particularly true in south Down, Upper Massereene in Co. Antrim, and in Tyrone, Armagh and Donegal.

General Ulysses Grant, 1822–85, eighteenth president of the USA, was of Tyrone Ulster Scots stock.

GRAY (*also* Grey)

The name Gray in Ulster is mainly Scottish or English though at least some will be of Irish origin. The name is found in every province in Ireland but is common only in Leinster and in Ulster. Ulster claims almost two-thirds of the total and Leinster most of the rest. The name is most common in counties Antrim, Down and Derry.

The name in England is either descriptive (Le Gray), from Old English *grǣg*, meaning 'grey (-haired)', or territorial, from Gray in Normandy (de Gray). In Scotland the first on record was Hugo de Gray in 1248. The Grays became important national figures in Scotland, Lord Gray of Fowlis being Master of the Household of James II in the mid-fifteenth century. A son of one of the Lords Gray had to fly to the north, having killed the constable of Dundee. His descendants became a sept of Clan Sutherland and were based at Skibo in Sutherland.

There were also Grays, a sept of Clan Stewart of Atholl in Perthshire. These were a branch of the Stewarts of Ballechin who, because of a family disagreement, renounced their name and adopted the name MacGlashan, Scots Gaelic Mac Glaisein, from earlier Mac Ghille Ghlais, 'son of the grey lad' (but *see* Green). At some later stage this sept became followers of Clan Donnachie. Many of the MacGlashans, especially those who settled in the Lowlands, anglicised their name to Gray. A family of Grays was one of the lesser of the notorious riding clans of the Scottish Borders and lived south of Berwick on the English side of the East March. Many members of these clans came to Ulster at the time of the Plantation to escape James VI's 'pacification' of the Border region. Mac Giolla Domhnaigh claims that Gray is one of the three colour names adopted by the Lamonts when they were forbidden to use their name. However, it is generally accepted that the three names were Black, Brown and White (*see* Lamont).

In parts of south Ulster, notably Co. Cavan, Mac Cathail Riabhaigh, usually anglicised Culreavy, was made Gray. (The word *riabhach* means 'grey' or 'brindled'.)

The most famous of the name in Ulster is Betsy Grey, 1777–98, of Killinchy, Co. Down, who accompanied her brother and her lover to the Battle of Ballynahinch, carrying a green flag, so the story goes, and with them was slaughtered in the retreat by yeomen.

GREEN (*also* Greene)

This name is very common in all of the provinces of Ireland, mainly because it has been used to anglicise a variety of Irish Gaelic names. However, the name is among the twenty most numerous in England and many in Ulster will be of English descent. In this case the name is locative in origin and denoted a person who lived near a green. It has also been used in Ulster as a shortening of the English name Greenaway, 'dweller by the green way'.

The word *glas* in Gaelic denotes a grey-green colour and where this element appears in Gaelic names the name was often made Green(e). The Derry name MacGlashan, Irish Gaelic Mac Glasáin or Mac Glaisín, was made Green. So too were MacAlesher and MacIllesher, Gaelic Mac Giolla Ghlais. MacLysaght makes no mention of the possibility of a Scottish origin for these names, although Mac Giolla Domhnaigh claims that in Ulster, as in Scotland, these two names are the same, though more often in Scotland made Gray (*see* Gray). The preponderance of the names in counties Derry and Antrim would lend some support to this claim. Further, MacAlesher is a Fermanagh name, and as MacLysaght points out, Peadar Livingstone, in *The Fermanagh Story,* makes the Green(e)s and MacAleshers Mac Giolla Laisir. More work needs to be done on this matter before it can be clarified. The name Greenan, Gaelic Ó Grianáin, found in counties Cavan and Sligo, was anglicised as Green(e). The name in fact is probably from *grian*, meaning 'sun'.

The greatest concentration of the name in mid-nineteenth-century Antrim was in Upper Massereene in the parish of Aghalee, and in Down, in the parish of Hillsborough.

GREENE *see* Green

GREER (*also* Gregg)

These two names are anglicisations of the Scottish MacGregor (itself a rare name in Ulster) and cannot be understood without a more detailed look at the particular history of that clan, a history which has had a profound effect on a wide variety of surnames.

The personal name Gregor is from the Greek for 'watchful' through the Latin *gregorius*. As Gregory it was the name of several of the early popes and became a very popular forename in the Middle Ages. It was early borrowed into Gaelic as Grigour, hence the Gaelic name Mac Griogair, MacGregor. The MacGregors are the senior branch of the Síol Alpine and are traditionally thought to descend from Griogar, third son of Kenneth MacAlpine, the eighth-century King of Scots. However, there is no evidence for this. In historical times, the chiefs of Clan Gregor descend from one Aodh Urchaidh, a native ruler of Glenorchy in Argyllshire. From there they came to control a large territory in Perthshire and Argyllshire including Glenstrae, Glenorchy, Glenlyon and Glengyle.

In the fourteenth century branches of the clan migrated to Dumfriesshire under Gilbrid MacGregor and in later centuries took the names Gregson, Grier and Grierson. In the direct line these became the Griersons or Griers of Lag in the parish of Dunscore. In the late sixteenth or early seventeenth century one of these, James Grierson, removed to Cumberland and changed the name to Greer. His son Henry Greer moved to Northumberland before removing in 1653 to Redford in Co. Tyrone. Henry also used the name Greves, and the names Greer and Greaves have been interlinked ever since. Other Greer descendants of the Griersons of Lag settled at Grange, Rhone-Hill, and Tullylagan in Tyrone and in Lurgan, Co. Armagh. It is interesting that MacGregor was a very popular forename in these families.

To return to the MacGregor story – the clan held their territories only by right of first possession and without title. Their neighbours, the Campbells, acquired Crown charters for the MacGregor lands and the MacGregors were dispossessed, resorted to violence and became notorious raiders. The Colquhouns were given a royal commission to suppress them. They were, however, defeated by the MacGregors at Glenfruin in Dumbartonshire in 1603. This was taken as an act of rebellion and the clan was outlawed, an order was given to disperse them 'by fire and sword', and their name was proscribed. A MacGregor signature was not recognised and no agreement entered into with a MacGregor was legal. It was no crime to kill a man of that name. Many were hunted down and exterminated and the rest sought sanctuary with other clans under a wide variety of aliases.

Like the Lamonts, another 'broken' clan, they adopted colour names, in this case Black, and White or Whyte. They adopted various clan names including Campbell, Dougall, Drummond, Gordon, Graham, Grant, Murray, Ramsay and Stewart. They took their fathers' Christian names and devised new patronymics, MacAdam, MacPeter. They adopted the names of places where they settled, Dochart, Comrie.

But most adopted names as close as possible to their old clan name, Greer, Greg, Gregg, Gregor, Gregorson, Gregory, Gregson, Greir, Grier, Grierson and MacGrier. Apart from a thirty-year period after the Restoration of 1660, the name MacGregor remained proscribed for 170 years, the act not being rescinded until 1775. By this time, several generations later, most of the 'children' of MacGregor had forgotten or preferred to forget and the name was not resumed to any great extent. Many of the diaspora of MacGregors came to Ulster during the Plantation years and after, and the period of proscription remains a great barrier to those seeking to trace their family tree.

In Ireland the name Gregg is almost exclusive to counties Antrim and Down. There are three times as many Greers as Greggs, more than half the Greers are in Co. Antrim and most of the rest are in Armagh and Down.

Samuel McCurdy Greer, 1810–80, a county court judge in counties Cavan and Leitrim, and, with Charles Gavan Duffy, a founder of the Tenant League in 1850, was born in Derry. The feminist Germaine Greer is of a family who emigrated to Australia from Maghera, Co. Derry, in the mid-nineteenth century. John Robert Gregg, 1867–1948, the inventor of Gregg shorthand, was born at Rockcorry, Co. Monaghan. His system is still widely used in North America.

GREGG *see* Greer

GREY *see* Gray

GRIBBEN

In Ireland this name is almost exclusive to counties Armagh, Down and Antrim and has been recorded since medieval times in Down and Armagh as O'Gribben, Gaelic Ó Gribín. It was also recorded in seventeenth-century Co. Armagh as MacGribben. This may be a simple example of the common official confusion between O' and Mac- names or it may have been an anglicisation of Mag Roibín, an Ulster variant of the Connacht name Mac Roibín (Cribben).

Around 1900 the name was being used interchangeably with Griffin, Gaelic Ó Gríobhtha, in the Poyntzpass district of Co. Armagh.

HACKETT *see* MacCaughey

HAGAN *see* O'Hagan

HALL

Hall is a rare name in Connacht, well known in Munster, common in Leinster and very common in Ulster, especially in counties Antrim and Armagh. One of the twenty most numerous names in England and common in Scotland too, it derives from the Old English *heall*, 'hall', and denoted a 'worker at the hall'.

Though it is on record in Munster from as early as the fourteenth century, it did not become common until the Plantation and many of the original Plantation tenants were Englishmen of the name.

The Halls of the Scottish Borders were one of the most notorious of the great riding clans of that turbulent region and the name was widely distributed on both sides of the frontier. They were particularly strong in Liddesdale, the 'cockpit of the Western March', in east Teviotdale and for a long period they also dominated Redesdale. When the Borders were 'pacified' by James VI of Scotland in the decade after 1603 and the power of the riding clans was broken, many members of the clans, including Halls, sought refuge and a new start in Ulster.

In mid-nineteenth-century Antrim the name was found to be particularly concentrated in the Ballinderry district of Upper Massereene.

HAMILL

This popular Ulster name is most common in counties Antrim and Armagh and can be of Irish, Scottish or English origin. In England the name, originally Hamel, derives from the Old English word *hamel*, meaning 'scarred' or 'mutilated'.

In Scotland the name is of Norman territorial origin. The first of the name on record there was William de Hameville in thirteenth-century Annandale in Dumfriesshire. The name is well recorded in Lothian but was most common in Ayrshire and indeed, Hugh Hammill of Roughwood in Ayrshire was one of those who accompanied Montgomery of the Ards to Ulster.

However, already in Ulster at that time, the O'Hamills, Gaelic Ó hAghmaill, were one of the leading septs of the Cenél Binnigh, a branch of the Cenél Eoghain. As such the O'Hamills claim descent from Binneach, son of Eoghan, son of the fifth-century Niall of the Nine Hostages, founder of the Uí Néill dynasty.

The O'Hamills ruled a territory in south Tyrone and Armagh and from the twelfth century were poets and ollavs (learned men) to the powerful O'Hanlons. By the seventeenth century the name was most numerous in Armagh and Monaghan and by 1900 was also common in Louth. The prefix O' is now used only in Co. Derry, and there rarely. The name has also been made Hamilton in that county and elsewhere.

HAMILTON

The Scottish name Hamilton is found in every province of Ireland, but especially in Ulster, where it is among the thirty most common names, among the fifteen most common in counties Down and Tyrone, in the twenty most common in Co. Antrim. It is also well known in most of the other counties, especially Derry and Fermanagh.

In Scotland the original family was Norman, the first on record there being Walter Fitz Gilbert of Hambledone, noted in 1295, and granted the lands of Cadzow by Robert the Bruce in the fourteenth century. Fitz Gilbert's grandson, David de Hamilton, was the first to be styled by the territorial title alone. The name derives not from Hamilton in Lanarkshire but most likely from Hambleton in Yorkshire, a placename derived from the English name Hamel (*see* Hamill). The family became one of the most influential in Scotland and branches included the Dukes of Abercorn and the Earls of Haddington. The name is among the forty most numerous in Scotland.

Though Hamilton was recorded in Ireland before the Plantation, it is with that event that the name is most associated. No less than six of the fifty Scottish undertakers and two of the nine Scottish chief undertakers were Hamiltons. They were granted huge swathes of land in counties Cavan, Armagh, Tyrone and Fermanagh. Further, although not part of the Plantation settlement proper, Sir James Hamilton and Sir Hugh Montgomery between them acquired the O'Neill territory of south Clandeboy, Co. Down (*see* O'Neill). The Hamiltons of Ulster descend from these Hamiltons and from the kinsmen that settled on their estates.

It is not possible here to detail all of the Ulster Hamiltons who distinguished themselves in various fields. Suffice it to say that the name is one of the most important in Ulster's history. Though they are in the minority, there are Catholic branches of the family. Indeed, one of the Hamilton undertakers, Sir George Hamilton, whose estate was at Ardstraw, Co. Tyrone, was a Catholic and settled many Catholics on his lands.

Hamiltons fought on both sides during the Williamite war of the late seventeenth century. Gustavus Hamilton, 1639–1723, born in Fermanagh, organised the defence of Enniskillen, Co. Fermanagh, and Coleraine, Co. Derry, and commanded a regiment at the Battle of the Boyne. He was created Baron Hamilton in 1715 and Viscount Boyne in 1717. Count Anthony Hamilton, *c.* 1645–1720, born in Tyrone, was governor of Limerick and led the retreat of the Irish Horse from the Boyne. He retired with his sister Elizabeth, 'La Belle Hamilton', 1641–1708, to France, where she was much admired for her beauty at the court of Charles II. Anthony wrote the classic *Memoirs of Count Grammont*, for the count, Elizabeth's husband.

The main concentration in late-nineteenth-century Antrim was in the barony of Upper Dunluce, and in Down in the parish of Dromara, though the name was common over almost all of the county. Some of the Co. Derry O'Hamills became Hamiltons (*see* Hamill).

HANLON *see* O'Hanlon

HANNA

This Scottish name is, in Ireland, almost exclusive to Ulster where the great majority are in counties Antrim, Down and Armagh. Hanna is a variant of Hannay which is closer to the original spelling, Ahannay. The origin of this name is not confirmed but it is thought to be from the Gaelic Ó hAnnaidh and as such is interesting as one of the few Scottish names with an O' prefix.

The Hannays stemmed from the ancient province of Galloway. The first on record, Gilbert de Hannethes, signed the Ragman Roll in 1296. The family was associated with the old Celtic lords of Galloway and as such with John Balliol in his struggle with the Norman Bruces for the Scottish throne. But in 1308 they were forced to submit to Edward Bruce when he conquered Galloway.

The main line were the Hannays of Sorbie in Wigtownshire from which branches settled in Ayrshire, Dumfriesshire, Dumbartonshire, Renfrewshire and the Stewartry of Kirkcudbright. The Hannays alternately sided with and feuded against their neighbours the Kennedys, the Dunbars and the Murrays. The last of the feuds, with the Murrays of Broughton in Peebleshire, brought ruin on the family and they were outlawed, the lands of Sorbie in Wigtownshire passing out of their hands in 1640.

Before that, in 1621, Robert Hanna, alias Hana and Hannay, and his brother Patrick received grants of land in Co. Longford. Various other individuals of the name settled in Ulster in the ensuing period with the greatest influx coming between the loss of Sorbie in 1640 and 1690. Many of the name are recorded in the Hearth Money Rolls of several Ulster counties in the 1660s.

James Owen Hannay, 1865–1950, rector of Westport, Co. Mayo, was a successful novelist who wrote under the *nom-de-plume* George Birmingham; he was born in Belfast.

HARE *see* O'Hare

HARKIN

Harkins are found only in Ulster where over half are in Co. Donegal and most of the rest in Co. Derry. The name was originally O'Harkin, Gaelic Ó hEarcáin (from *earc*, meaning 'dark red'). The homeland of the sept was in the barony of Inishowen in Donegal where, with the O'Logherys and the MacLaughlins, they were erenaghs of Cloncha, near Malin Head.

HARPER (*also* Harpur)

Both these names are common in Ulster, Harper especially in Co. Antrim. Though they will have become confused, the -ur ending is still most common in Co. Wexford, where Harpur was the name of an Anglo-Norman family who settled there in the thirteenth century. The name in this case is from the Old French *harpeor*. The English name Harper is from the Old English *hearpere*. Both names originally signified someone who played the harp.

However, most in Ulster will be of Scottish stock and were originally MacChruiters, 'son of the *cruiteir*'. The *cruiteir* or harper was a hereditary office in the households of many of the clan chiefs and great lords. The *cruit* itself was a six-stringed instrument, of which four strings were played by bow and two were plucked with the thumb. The modern form of the name is MacWhirter but most anglicised to Harper and Harperson. (The names Harbison and Harbinson, thought by some to be variants of Harperson, are in fact Scottish forms of Herbertson, and as such have been common in the Glasgow region since the sixteenth century.)

The Harpers and MacChruiters were a sept of Clan Buchanan and the names were most common in Stirlingshire and Argyllshire. Harper was also common in Galloway and Berwickshire.

HARPUR *see* Harper

HARRIS *see* Harrison

HARRISON (*also* Harris)

Both these names are found in every province in Ireland. Harrison is most numerous in Ulster (especially in counties Antrim and Down) but Harris is more common in Leinster and Munster than in Ulster.

Both names of course derive ultimately from Henry, through the intermediate form Hanry, to the popular medieval diminutive or pet form Harry; thus Harry's son becomes Harrison and Harris. Both are among the thirty most common names in England and most in Ulster will be of English stock. But both are well known in Scotland and there was a Harris sept of Clan Campbell.

Harrison was found to be particularly concentrated near Donaghcloney in the parish of Dromore, Co. Down, in the mid-nineteenth century.

HART (*also* Harte)

These names are common throughout Ireland but in Ulster are most numerous in Co. Antrim. They can be of Irish, English or Scottish origin and a verified family tree will be necessary to confirm which.

The Irish name was originally O'Hart, Gaelic Ó hAirt, 'descendant of Art'. The O'Harts were an important sept based originally in Co. Meath. Driven from their homeland by the Anglo-Normans, they settled in Sligo where the name is still most common.

Many in Ulster will be of this stock but many also descend from settlers of the Plantation period and after. The name in Scotland is territorial in origin, a family having migrated there from the manor of Hert in Durham. It became a common name in the Lowlands, particularly Edinburgh. The name in England derives from the Old English word *heorot*, meaning a 'deer'.

At the beginning of the twentieth century the names Hart and Harwood were being used interchangeably in the Waringstown district of Co. Armagh.

Lieutenant General George Vaughan Hart, 1752–1832, was born in Co. Donegal. He had a distinguished career as a soldier, fighting for the British in the American War of Independence and in India. Sir Robert Hart, 1835–1911, inspector-general of customs in China, was one of those besieged in Peking during the Boxer rebellion in 1900. He was described at that time as 'the most powerful European in the East'. He was born at Milltown, Co. Armagh.

HARTE *see* Hart

HARVEY

Outside of Dublin this name in Ireland is found mainly in Ulster, where it is especially common in counties Antrim, Down and Donegal. It is an English name and there and in Scotland it takes the forms Harvey, Harvie, Hervey and Hervie. The name was introduced into Britain by Bretons in the train of William the Conqueror and was originally an Old French name Hervé, from Old Breton Hærviu, meaning 'battle-worthy'. It is early found in Scotland, particularly in the Aberdeen area.

Harrihy, from O'Harrihy, Gaelic Ó hEarchaidh, is a Co. Donegal name which, in Fermanagh, was anglicised as Harvey. It was also noted as a synonym of Harvey in the Strabane district of Co. Tyrone around 1900.

HAUGHEY (*also* Hoey *and* Hoy)

The Ulster name Haughey is rare elsewhere in Ireland. It is properly O'Haughey from the Gaelic Ó hEachaidh, though it was also recorded in Gaelic as a Mac- name, Mac Eachaidh, giving MacGaughey and MacGahey. Around 1900 Haughey was noted as most common in counties Armagh and Donegal. But in both areas the homelands of the septs straddle the border with the Republic (in Donegal–Fermanagh and Armagh–Monaghan) and some changes in the distribution pattern seem to have occurred.

In Co. Armagh, particularly in the Keady district, the name was anglicised to Haffey and Mehaffy, this latter being a variant of the Scottish name MacFie (*see* Duffy).

In Co. Antrim Haughey has become Hoey and Hoy. Hoey can be a native Ulster name of Co. Down, Gaelic Ó hEochaidh; in Co. Monaghan, a variant of Ó hAoidh, Hughes (*see* Hughes); or, when of Planter stock, is thought to be a variant of Hoy.

Hoy is a Scottish name found mainly in Co. Antrim. In Orkney the name is taken from that of the island of Hoy and in the rest of Scotland the name derives from some place no longer identifiable in the Border region. Hoy has also been recorded as a synonym of Hayes (*see* Hayes).

HAWTHORNE

Hawthorne is seldom found in Ireland outside Ulster, where it is concentrated in the eastern counties of Antrim, Down and Armagh. The name derives ultimately from Hawthorn in the parish of Easington in Co. Durham but was early established in the Scottish province of Galloway, where it remains popular. A family of the name were proprietors of Meikle in the parish of Kirkinner in Wigtownshire.

Also the Hawthorns of Kintyre were a sept of Clan Donald. Angus Martin suggests that these were originally Ulster Adrains, Gaelic Ó Dreáin, who acquired the name Hawthorn by pseudo-translation, the word *droighean* in Gaelic meaning 'hawthorn'. The Adrains were a Co. Roscommon sept who were forced out of their homeland by the MacDermots and settled in Ulster. A branch of these did cross to Kintyre where as Drain, MacDrain and O'Drain they became a sept of Clan Donald. The main line of the family were the M'O'Drains, Lairds of Carrin and Drumavoulin of Kintyre.

HAYES

Hayes is an English name, either from Old English *(ge)hæg,* meaning 'dweller by the enclosure', or from Old English *hēah*, meaning 'high' or 'tall'. It is also, both in England and in Ireland, a variant of the Norman name de la Haye. Many of the name in Ulster will be of English stock.

However, Hayes is among the sixty most common names in Ireland and most of those who bear the name will be originally Ó hAodha, 'descendant of Hugh', often anglicised as Hughes. In Ireland there were twelve distinct septs of Ó hAodha, of which three were in Ulster, around Ardstraw in

Co. Tyrone, Ballyshannon in Co. Donegal, and in Farney in Co. Monaghan. Those called Hayes in these areas will most likely be of Ulster Gaelic stock (*see* Hughes). Hayes has also been recorded as a synonym of Hoy (*see* Haughey).

HEANEY (*also* Heeney)

Although found in every province of Ireland, Heaney is nowhere so common as in Ulster, where it is most common in Co. Armagh. (The adjacent county of Louth also has a large concentration.)

Though there were other septs outside Ulster, the largest and most important sept were the O'Heaneys, Gaelic Ó hÉighnigh, of Oriel. In medieval times their sway extended into Fermanagh and Ó hÉighnigh was chief of Fermanagh before the Maguires took over in 1202. Before that they were kings of Fermanagh and of Oriel. It is thought that the O'Heaneys, chiefs of Clan Kearney in Armagh (modern-day Markethill district), were a distinct sept. Another sept of O'Heaney were erenaghs of Banagher in Co. Derry, the church of which was reputedly founded by St Muireadach O'Heaney in 1121. In the seventeenth century the name was recorded as numerous in counties Louth (also a part of Oriel), Armagh and Derry.

The name has been made Bird in the mistaken notion that the Gaelic name incorporated the word *éan*, meaning 'bird' (*see* MacAneny).

The poet Seamus Heaney was born in the townland of Mossbawn in Co. Derry in 1939.

HEENEY *see* Heaney

HEGARTY

Though this name is now most common in Munster, the Hegartys of that province are a branch of an Ulster sept, in Gaelic Ó hÉigceartaigh, from *éigceartach*, 'unjust', whose homeland lay on the borders of counties Derry and Donegal. The O'Hegartys were a sept of the Cenél Eoghain under the O'Neills and in the fourteenth century were based in the Derry barony of Loughinsholin. By the seventeenth century they were most numerous in Tirkeenan in Co. Derry and Inishowen in Co. Donegal and were already well established in Co. Cork. In the USA the name has become Haggerty.

HENDERSON (*also* Hendrie, Hendron, Henry, MacHenry *and* MacKendry)

In Ireland Henderson, Hendrie, Hendron and MacKendry are not common outside Ulster. Henderson (the most numerous) is found mainly in counties Antrim and Tyrone, Hendrie and Hendron are almost exclusive to Co. Armagh and the MacKendrys are nearly all in Co. Antrim. All derive ultimately from the forename Henry, Old French Henri, and all are Scottish in origin. Henry and MacHenry can be variants of the above, but a majority will be of Irish stock. Henry, outside of Dublin and Sligo, is common only in Ulster, particularly in counties Antrim and Tyrone. MacHenry is most common in Munster and Ulster (particularly counties Antrim and Derry).

There are several origins for the Scottish names. Henderson and its synonym Hendron are simply variations of Henryson. There were Hendersons, one of the lesser of the riding clans of the Scottish Borders, who lived in Upper Liddesdale on the Scottish side of the Middle March. The main Lowland family of the name, the Hendersons of Fordell in Fifeshire, descend from the Henrysons of Dumfriesshire. The Hendersons, a sept of Clan Gunn, like some Wilsons and Johnsons, descend from the fifteenth-century George Gunn the Crowner (coroner), in this case through a younger son Henry. This sept was based in the lowlands of Caithness. This brings us to the Hendersons of Glencoe in Argyllshire.

The name Henry was early gaelicised as Eanruig. The Glencoe Hendersons anglicised their name from Mac Eanruig and claim descent from Eanruig Mór Mac Righ Neachtain, 'Big Henry, son of King Nechtan', a semi-legendary Pictish king of the eighth century. The Hendersons held Glencoe for three hundred years before Robert the Bruce. In the fourteenth century the MacDonalds took over the area from the MacDougalls of Lorn in Argyllshire and in 1314 John or Iain MacDonald married the daughter and heiress of Dugald Henderson, Chief of Clann Eanruig. From this union was founded the Clann Iain Abrach, the MacDonalds of Glencoe. The Hendersons remained as hereditary pipers to Mac Iain and the last chief of the name, Big Henderson of the Chanters, was killed by Campbells in the Glencoe massacre of 1692.

The semi-legendary King Nechtan was also the forebear of the MacNaughtons. The names Hendrie, Hendry, MacHendrie, MacHendry, MacKendrick and MacKenrick (all from Gaelic Mac Eanruig) were those of a sept of Clan MacNaughten which descends from one Henry MacNaughton. These names were all anglicised to Henderson, and it is thought that the Henrys of Argyll and Bute were originally MacKendricks.

The Co. Antrim name MacKendry is Scottish in origin but is not known in that form in Scotland. The name represents an Ulster halfway-house between MacKendrick and MacHendry and as such should be included with the Clan MacNaughten sept mentioned above. This would be confirmed by the known MacNaughton presence in north Antrim (see MacKnight). The MacKendrys are most numerous in northeast Antrim and in early times held Kinbaan Castle on the coast north of Ballycastle.

Confusion arises when dealing with the names Henry and MacHenry because of the proximity of Gaelic Irish septs to Scottish Henry–MacHendrie–MacKendrick–MacKendry settlers, particularly in north Antrim and Derry. There, a branch of the O'Kanes, the Mac Éinrí, anglicised to MacHenry. This sept descended from one Dermot O'Cahan, died 1428, chief of the name, through his son Henry. They were known as the MacHenrys of the Loughran, and earlier, the MacHenry O'Cahans. The name was further anglicised to Henry, and even, under the influence of Scottish neighbours, Hendry.

In Co. Tyrone the O'Henerys were a sept based at Cullentra whose territory at one time extended to Glenconkeine in Co. Derry. Their name is in Irish Gaelic Ó hInnéirghe. O'Henery was further anglicised to Henry. (The Mac- equivalent of this Gaelic name gives MacEniry and this form was occasionally adopted in Ulster.) Another Ulster family who anglicised to Henry were the Ó hAiniarraidh, a sept of Oriel in southeast Ulster.

As an indication of the confusion that can arise with these names it should be noted that, around 1900, the name Henry was being used interchangeably with Henery, MacEnery, MacHendrie and MacHenry, all in the Poyntzpass district of Co. Armagh.

Sir James Henderson, 1848–1914, was owner and manager of the *Belfast News-Letter* and was the first Lord Mayor of Greater Belfast. He was born in Belfast. Paul Henry, 1876–1958, one of the greatest Irish painters of the twentieth century, was born in Belfast. In 1912 he holidayed on Achill Island and proceeded to stay there for seven years. From that time on he has been most famous for his landscapes of the west of Ireland.

HENDRIE *see* Henderson

HENDRON *see* Henderson

HENRY *see* Henderson

HERON *see* Herron

HERRON (*also* Heron)

In Ireland the Herrons or Herons are confined mainly to Ulster where most are found equally distributed between counties Antrim, Down and Donegal. The English name Heron was originally a nickname for a thin man with long legs and some in Ulster will be of English stock. Most, however, are of Irish or Scottish descent.

The Donegal name Herron or Harron was originally Ó hEaráin (probably from *earadh,* meaning 'dread'). This was originally an Oriel name common in Co. Armagh where it became Heran. The names MacElheron or MacIlheron can be of both Ulster and Scottish origin and have been known to have been shortened to Heron. The name in Ulster was originally Mac Giolla Chiaráin, meaning 'son of the devotee of (St) Ciaran (of Clonmacnois)' and in the sixteenth century was found mainly in Co. Armagh. It is now most common in counties Antrim and Down, where many will be originally Scottish MacElherans.

MacElheran has the same original meaning but was in Scots Gaelic Mac Gille Chiarain, a name once common in Scotland, especially on the Isle of Bute. The MacElherans were a sept of Clan Donald who took their name from the seventh-century St Ciaran who lived in Kintyre and gave his name to Kilkerran, which was later renamed Campbeltown.

There was also an important family of the name in the Stewartry of Kirkcudbright, the Herons of Kerroughtree. They claim descent from the Herons of Chipchase in Northumberland. The Herons of the Scottish Borders were one of the lesser of the riding clans and lived in the Middle March of the English side of the frontier. Many members of the riding clans came to Ulster after the Borders were 'pacified' by James VI of Scotland in the decade after 1603.

Archie Heron, 1894–1971, socialist, trade-union leader and early associate of James Connolly, was born in Portadown, Co. Armagh.

HEWITT

Virtually all the early references to this name in Ireland, from the late thirteenth century on, place it in Dublin and Munster. The name is still found in these areas but only in Ulster is it common.

There are two derivations of the name. In England it can be either local, from residence in a 'clearing', Old English *hīewett,* or a diminutive of Hugh. In Scotland, where it was common in Berwickshire, it is a pet form of Hugh, from Hew, a Scottish form of the name, with the French diminutive suffix -et.

In Ulster the name is most common in counties Antrim and Armagh.

The poet John Hewitt, 1907–87, was born in Belfast.

HIGGINS

Higgins is among the 100 most common names in Ireland. More than half are in Connacht, and Ulster can claim less than a quarter of the rest. In England a pet form of the name Richard was Hick, which became in spoken form Higg, and Higgin was a pet form of this. Some in Ulster will be of this English origin.

But most will be of Irish stock, Higgins being, as MacLysaght puts it in *Irish Families: Their Names, Arms and Origins*, 'a purely native Irish Gaelic name', originally Ó hUigín (pronounced O'Higgeen). The original Uigín was a grandson of Niall of the Nine Hostages. The name derives from the Gaelic word *uiging*, which approximates to the word 'Viking'. The O'Higginses were originally a sept of the southern Uí Néill, who were based in Leinster but spread westward through Roscommon to Sligo and Mayo. As a bardic family they had a long tradition of noted Gaelic poets. One of these, Tadhg Dall Ó hUiginn, 1550–91, was born either in Co. Sligo or in Fermanagh and was fostered in Donegal. They story is told that he was murdered by six of the O'Haras, who cut out his tongue in response to a severe satire he had written about them. It is possible that Higgins in Fermanagh was originally Ó hEicnigh.

Francis Higgins, 1746–1802, the 'Sham Squire', was born in Downpatrick, Co. Down. A Dublin articled clerk, he acquired the nickname when he married a respectable young lady under the pretence that he was a country gentleman. He was imprisoned for this. Later he owned gaming houses and the *Freeman's Journal*, and is famous for taking £1000 for revealing United Irishman Lord Edward Fitzgerald's hiding place.

In Co. Down at the start of the twentieth century Higgins was being used interchangeably with Hagans and Haggens in the Greyabbey district and with O'Hagan (*see* O'Hagan) around Comber.

HILL

The English name is found in every province of Ireland but two-thirds of those of the name are in Ulster. Petty's 'census' of 1659 found it to be a 'principal name' in Co. Antrim. In the mid-nineteenth century the main concentration of the name was found to be in the north of the Co. Antrim barony of Carey. Next to Antrim the name is most common in Co. Down.

Hill is among the twenty-five most common names in England and there it meant originally 'dweller by or on the hill' from the Old English *hyll*. Less commonly it derives from the personal name Hille, a pet form of Hilary or Hilger.

Moyses Hill, 1555–1630, of an Old Norman Devonshire family, came to Ireland as an officer under the Earl of Essex in 1573 and rose to become Provost Mareschal of Ulster. He married Alice, a sister of Sorley Boy MacDonnell, and built Hill Court (Hillhall) near Lisburn, Co. Antrim. Their son Peter began the building of a fort at Cromlyn and made plans for a village. The job was finished by their second son, Arthur, ancestor of the Marquis of Downshire, who renamed the fort and village Hillsborough.

It has been suggested that in the northwest of the province many of the name Hill may originally have been O'Boyles (*see* Boyle).

The Revd George Hill, 1810–1900, for thirty years librarian of Queen's College Belfast (later Queen's University), was a noted historian. He is most famous for his *The MacDonnells of Antrim* and for editing the *Montgomery Manuscripts*. He was born at Moyarget, Co. Antrim. Sir George Fitzgerald Hill, 1763–1839, a Derry man, became governor of St Vincent and of Trinidad. He is most often remembered for identifying Wolfe Tone, previously his college friend, to the authorities at Lough Swilly, Co. Donegal, in 1798.

HOEY *see* Haughey

HOLMES (*also* MacComb)

The English name Holmes derives from Old Norse *holmr* and denoted 'residence on or near a piece of flat land in a fen', and some in Ireland may be of English origin. But a majority may be of Scottish descent, the name having been anglicised so from a variety of Scots Gaelic names based on the personal name Thomas.

The names MacComas, MacComb, MacCombe, MacCombie, Mac-Combich, MacComie, MacComish, MacCombs, MacThomas and so on are variants of the Gaelic names Mac Thóm, 'son of Tom', Mac Comaidh, a contracted form of Mac Thomaidh, 'son of Tommy' and Mac Tómais and Mac Thómais, 'son of Thomas'. In different combinations, these were septs of Clan Mackintosh, Clan Campbell, Clan MacThomas of Glenshee and Clan MacTavish (itself a form of MacThomas). The Ulster MacCombs are mostly Clan Mackintosh and are most numerous in counties Antrim, Down and Derry. MacComish is found mainly in Down.

Holmes in Scotland can also be from the lands of Holmes, near Dundonald in Ayrshire. The English name Soames is another anglicised form of MacComish. The name Holmes is numerous in all the provinces of Ireland, especially Ulster, where it is most common in Co. Antrim.

See also Thompson.

HOUSTON (*also* Huston, Hutcheson, Hutchinson, MacCutcheon
 and MacQuiston)

These names are interlinked in that they all derive ultimately from the personal name Hugh and were also the names of septs of Clan Donald.

Many, if not a majority, of the Houstons of Ulster are not of this clan, however. The Houstons of Lanarkshire descend from the twelfth-century Hugh de Paduinan (Padinan in the east of the shire). He received a grant of the lands of Kilpeter in the west of the shire. By a century or so later these lands had come to be called Huston (Hugh's place) and the family took the name de Hustone. It is thought that the Houstons of Craigs' Castle in south Antrim and Castlestewart in Co. Tyrone are of this connection and were also forefathers of General Sam Houston, 1793–1863, commander in chief of the Texan forces in the Texan War of Independence (1836). He was also president of Texas and later a US senator.

The names Houston and MacTaghlin are synonymous in Co. Donegal but it is not clear which name is a variant of which, though it is thought most likely that the original name was MacTaghlin, Gaelic Mac Giolla tSeachlainn, 'son of the devotee of (St) Seachlann'.

The French personal name Huchon, a diminutive or pet form of Hugh, was made Hutchin in England and Hutcheon in Scotland. This name in turn was early borrowed into Scots Gaelic as Huisdean or Uisdean. The MacDonalds of Sleat (now Skye) descend from Hugh, a younger son of Alexander MacDonald, Lord of the Isles. This family therefore became known as Clann Uisdeann or Mac Uisdin. By the end of the sixteenth century they were referred to in the Roll of Clans as 'Scheall Hutcheon, that is to say, the offspring of that man callit Hutcheon'. As early as the fifteenth century the name was being anglicised to MacHutchen and Huchonson, hence MacCutcheon and Hutchinson. Mac Uisdein, a variant, was anglicised as MacQuistan, MacQuisten and MacQuiston. Another recorded variant was MacHugh, but most of this name in Ulster will be of Connacht stock. A few Hustons and Hewsons in Donegal and Fermanagh will also be of this stock (*see* MacHugh).

Hutchinson and Hutcheson are most numerous in counties Derry, Antrim and Down. MacCutcheon is most common in counties Tyrone, Antrim and Down, and has been made Kitchen and Kitson in the Newry–Poyntzpass area. Houston and Huston are found mainly in counties Antrim, Derry, Armagh and Down. MacQuiston has also been made MacWhisten and MacQuestion.

Francis Hutcheson, 1694–1746, was probably born at Saintfield, Co. Down. Professor of moral philosophy at Glasgow University, he was an early exponent of utilitarianism and it was he and not Jeremy Bentham who coined the phrase 'the greatest happiness of the greatest number'. Elizabeth Hutchinson from Carrickfergus was the mother of Andrew Jackson, seventh president of the USA (*see* Jackson).

HOY *see* Haughey

HUGHES

Hughes is among the forty most common names in Ireland, among the first fifteen in Ulster, the first five in Co. Armagh, and the first ten in counties Tyrone and Monaghan. Like Hayes (*see* Hayes) it was often used as an anglicisation of the Irish name Ó hAodha, 'descendant of Hugh'.

Hugh, from Old German Hugo, meaning 'heart' or 'mind', through Old French Hue, was a very popular personal name after the Norman Conquest of England and it is the source of at least ninety different modern surnames. Hughes itself was first recorded in the Domesday Book and has now become one of the twenty most common names in England and in Wales. Many in Ulster will be of English or Welsh stock (the name is not common in Scotland), and descend from settlers who arrived first in the 1640s.

The Ulster septs of Ó hAodha who anglicised as Hughes were originally of Ardstraw in north Tyrone (where they were lords of Uí Fiachrach); of the Ballyshannon district of Donegal; of south Down (where in 1160 Ó hAodha was described as King of O'Neach [Iveagh]); of the parish of Tynan, barony of Turanny, Co. Armagh; and of Farney in Co. Monaghan. In Monaghan the variant Ó hAoidh was made Hoey (*see* Haughey).

The Most Revd John Hughes, 1797–1864, was born at Annaloghlan in Co. Tyrone. He was the first Catholic Archbishop of New York and founder of Fordham University.

See also MacHugh.

HUNTER

This name is common only in northeast Ulster, counties Antrim, Derry and Down. Though Hunter is an English name from the Old English word *huntian*, meaning 'to hunt' or 'huntsman', most in Ulster will be of Scottish descent.

The name first came to Scotland from Normandy about 1110 but was early recorded in many different parts of the country, so it is unlikely that the Hunters have one common ancestor. 'Aylmer le Hunter of the County of Are' signed the Ragman Roll in 1296 and it was in Ayrshire that the name became most common. The lands of Hunter were granted to William Hunter by Robert II in 1374 and the Hunters of Hunterston in Ayrshire claim to be the oldest family of the name in Scotland. There were also Hunters, one of the lesser of the riding clans of the Scottish Borders. They lived in the Middle March of the English side of the frontier where they were followers of the Nixons.

Mac Giolla Domhnaigh claims that there were Hunters, a sept of Clan Stuart of Bute, who lived on the Isle of Arran. He also claims that the Tyrone name MacKeighry or MacKeefry, Gaelic Mac Fhiachra, was anglicised as Hunter.

The portrait painter Robert Hunter, 1730–1803, was an Ulsterman. He is most famous for his portrait of John Wesley.

HUSTON *see* Houston

HUTCHESON *see* Houston

HUTCHINSON *see* Houston

IRVINE (*also* Ervine)

The first thing that must be said about these names and Irwin (*see* Irwin) and Erwin is that the two groups are properly distinct but have been widely confused. Even the first of the Irvines of Irvinestown in Fermanagh was known to use the form Irwin and over the rest of the seventeenth century the name of the family appears as 'Erwin of Castle Irwin', Irwin and Irvine.

Though some of the Irvines of Scotland derive their name from Irvine in Ayrshire most were originally Irvings, the name taken from the parish of Irving in Dumfriesshire. The original spelling did survive but most became Irvines, and Urwen was another form. The first on record was Robert de Hirewine in 1226, and in 1324 William de Irwyne, ancestor of the Irvines of Drum, was granted the Forest of Drum in Aberdeenshire by Robert the Bruce.

The Irvines were one of the most famous of the riding clans of the turbulent Scottish Border region and lived in Annandale and Lower Eskdale in the Scottish West March. As George MacDonald Fraser, the historian of the riding clans, puts it, '[the Irvines were] a very tough bunch indeed [and] contributed much to the general disorder'.

Many members of these clans broken by James VI of Scotland came to Ulster during the Plantation to escape persecution. Fermanagh was the main focus of their settlement. By the mid-seventeenth century, these families were well established and had formed a cohesive enough group to ride out the 1641 rebellion which had destroyed the Plantation settlement in the other counties. Irvine was recorded as the eleventh most common name in Fermanagh in 1962.

Lowtherstown in Co. Fermanagh was renamed Irvinestown and from their humble beginnings as Plantation tenants the Irvines rose to become a powerful landlord family, eight Irvines in 1878 owning over 12,000 acres in Fermanagh, over 4000 acres in Tyrone and over 14,000 in Donegal.

William Irvine, 1741–1804, a brigadier general in the American revolutionary army during the War of Independence, and later a prominent politician in Pennsylvania, was born in Fermanagh.

Irvine is most common in Fermanagh and Antrim and Ervine in Antrim and Down.

IRWIN (*also* Erwin)

These names are confused with Irvine (*see* Irvine) in Scotland and in Ulster. Irwin or Erwin derives from the Old English word *eoforwine*, meaning 'boar-friend', and, like the Irvines, the Irwins arrived in seventeenth-century Ulster from Dumfriesshire. A very few of the name in Ulster may be originally O'Hirwen, Gaelic Ó hEireamhóin, a rare Leinster name.

The spelling Irwin is most common in counties Armagh, Antrim, Tyrone and Derry. Erwin is uncommon outside Antrim though strangely the forms Erwin and McErwin were noted as common in the Annahilt district of Co. Down in the mid-nineteenth century.

Thomas Caulfield Irwin, 1823–92, was a widely respected poet in his day. He was born at Warrenpoint, Co. Down.

JACKSON

Jackson is found throughout Ireland, outside Ulster mainly in counties Dublin, Cork and Mayo. In Ulster, where it is most common, it is found mainly in counties Antrim and Armagh.

The name is one of the twenty-five most numerous in England and though it has long been found in Scotland, it was not common there because the personal name Jack was never popular.

It was, however, popular in England, not as in recent times as a diminutive of John, but as a diminutive of James which in Latin is Jacobus, in French Jacques, hence Jack (and Jacobite for the followers of James II and his descendants). Thus the name Jackson meant originally 'son of James'.

One of the earliest people to spot the commercial potential of Belfast was Rowland Jackson, a merchant of Whitehaven in Cumberland, who based himself in the town in 1632. Most of the Jacksons who settled in Armagh and Antrim arrived in the middle of the seventeenth century.

Andrew Jackson, 1767–1845, seventh president of the USA, was born in America two years after his family had emigrated from Ulster. His father, also Andrew, and his mother, Elizabeth *née* Hutchinson, were from the Carrickfergus district. Richard Jackson, 1720–87, 'Omniscient Jackson', was born in Ballycastle, Co. Antrim. A politician who became Lord of the Treasury, he got his nickname because of his extraordinary stores of knowledge.

JAMESON *see* Jamison

JAMIESON *see* Jamison

JAMISON (*also* Jameson *and* Jamieson)

Apart from the Dublin Jamesons, these names are almost exclusive to Ulster, where half are in Co. Antrim and a quarter in Co. Down alone. The names first became common in Ulster in the mid-eighteenth century.

There were Jamesons, the most senior of the septs of Clan Gunn that descend from the fifteenth-century chief, George Gunn the Crowner (coroner), in this case through his eldest son James, who became chief in his time. This family was also known as Mac Shéamuis or MacKeamish.

On the island of Bute the Jamiesons, MacCamies and Neilsons (*see* Nelson) constituted a family which descended from a James Fullarton or MacCloy, one of the Fullartons of Arran (*see* Fullerton.) A sept of Clan Stuart of Bute, they were hereditary coroners of Bute from at least as early as the fourteenth century until the seventeenth century.

There were also Jamiesons, one of the lesser of the riding clans of the Scottish Borders, who lived in the Middle March of the English side of the frontier.

The main concentration of the name in mid-nineteenth-century Antrim was in the barony of Upper Toome.

JENKINS

Jenkins is an English name sometimes also found in Scotland. It is thought to be Flemish in origin and derives from the personal name Jenkin, a diminutive or pet form of Jan, Jen or Jon (John), originally spelt Janekyn. (The name Jennings also derives from a diminutive of these three names, using -in instead of -kin.) In Ireland Jenkins was gaelicised to Sincín or Seincín

In Ulster it is most common in Co. Antrim, in the south of which it has occasionally been made Junkin.

JOHNSON *see* Johnston

JOHNSTON (*also* Johnson)

The main (Scottish) origins of these Ulster names are quite complicated and when one takes into account the large number of Irish and Scottish septs who anglicised their names to Johnston and/or Johnson, there is little room here for more than an outline of the difficulties.

Johnson of course is a simple patronymic but many, especially in Ireland, who should have adopted it, took instead the more common name Johnston. Johnston(e) itself was originally John's Town, pronounced in Scotland John's Toon, and worn down over the years to Johnston. But even on the Scottish Borders, where the name was most common, it was often made Johnson.

Johnson is one of the most common names of the English-speaking world, ranked, for instance, tenth in England and Wales and second in the USA. But it is five times less common than Johnston in Ireland and is over fifteen times less common in Ulster.

Johnston is the tenth most common name in Scotland. At the end of the nineteenth century it was estimated to be the thirty-third most common name in Ireland, fourth in Ulster, second in Antrim, eighth in Armagh and eleventh in Down. In 1962 it was second in Fermanagh. The Johnstone spelling was found at that time to be most common in counties Derry and Cavan.

In Scotland Johnston has a number of origins. The city of Perth was often called Johnston or St Johnston and some families took their name from that. Others took the name from the lands of Jonystoun, now Johnstonburn in East Lothian. But by far the largest and most important (and the source of most of the 'true' Ulster Johnstons) were the Johnstons of Annandale in Dumfriesshire, one of the greatest of the riding clans of the Scottish Borders.

The founder of this family was a powerful landowner who, in about 1174, gave his name to his lands in Annandale. These lands became the parish and barony of Johnstone. His son Gilbert assumed this as his surname instead of the patronymic Johnson. The Johnstones became one of the most powerful and turbulent clans of the West Border. Like the Maxwells they were often wardens of the West March and their feud with the Maxwells was the longest and bloodiest in Border history. It was the ferocity of their feuding that gave them their ironical epithet the 'Gentle Johnstones'. After the 'pacification' of the Borders by James VI of Scotland many members of the riding clans, including the Johnstons, fled to Ulster. They settled principally in Fermanagh and by the mid-seventeenth century the names of the riding clans – Johnston, Armstrong, Elliott, Irvine, Nixon, Crozier and so on – had come to predominate in that county, managing to weather the storm of the 1641 rising which had largely destroyed the Plantation settlement in other counties.

At the beginning of the 1641 rising, there were 260 of the name Johnston alone enlisted under Sir William Cole. Johnston is the second most common name in present-day Fermanagh. No other Plantation county has three settler names (the others are Elliott and Armstrong) in the first five.

Many other Scottish and Irish families anglicised their names to Johnston when Johnson would have been more accurate. And when one considers that Eoin, Owen, Iain, Shane, Seán and so on are all alternative forms of John, the number of possible origins for Johnstons and Johnsons in Ulster multiply. (*See* Jones for the derivation of John.)

John or Iain was the most popular forename in the Scottish Highlands.

The MacIans or Johnsons of Caithness, a sept of Clan Gunn, descend from John, third son of the fifteenth-century George Gunn the Crowner (coroner). A senior branch of the Clan Donald were the MacDonalds (or MacIans) of Ardnamurchan (Argyllshire), descendants of Eóin Sprangach, son of Angus, Lord of the Isles. These were known equally as Johnsons or MacIans, although many, especially those of the island of Coll, anglicised to Johnston. Another senior branch of Clan Donald were the Clann Iain Abrach, the MacDonalds (or MacIans) of Glencoe in Argyllshire, descendants of John Óg, a younger son of Angus, Lord of the Isles. They too anglicised to both Johnson and Johnston and also MacKean, which in counties Derry and Antrim has been made MacKane or MacKain (*see* Kane).

A sept of Glenshee in Perthshire and the island of Bute, originally Mac Gille Sheáin (son of the servant of John), became MacIlcheynes and then MacCheynes. Many of these settled in the Poyntzpass district of Co. Armagh where they became both Johnsons and Johnstons.

In Ireland the name MacKeown and its variants MacCone, MacCune, MacEwen, MacGeown, MacKeon, Magone and so on, have been anglicised as both Johnson and Johnston. The most important of these were the MacKeowns of Co. Antrim, originally Bissetts, who took their name from Eóin Bissett, a Scot who settled in the Glens before the time of the MacDonnells. These, it is thought, more often became Johnstons than Johnsons. Two Co. Armagh septs of MacKeown, Gaelic Mac Eoin and Mac Eoghain, of Creggan and Keady anglicised to both (*see* MacKeown).

Both too have been used as a further anglicisation of MacShan in north Tyrone and MacShane around Armagh city and in the Fews. And the Johnstones of Cavan are often originally MacShanes (*see* MacShane).

Though Johnstons became Johnsons and vice versa and though the 'true' Scottish Johnstons were a very big connection indeed, it is plain that that alone cannot account for the exceptional predominance of Johnston in Ulster and many more families that were properly Johnson became Johnston rather than the other way round.

Francis Johnston, 1760–1829, was born in Armagh city. An architect, he was responsible for designing many of Dublin's famous buildings, including the General Post Office in O'Connell Street.

William Johnston of Ballykilbeg, 1829–1902, a landlord living near Downpatrick, Co. Down, led the campaign against the Party Processions Act of 1850, enacted in response to the Dolly's Brae affair the previous year. The act was strengthened in 1860 and Johnston became involved in 1866. He was jailed for defying the act in 1868 and became an MP in 1869. The act was repealed in 1872.

JONES

Jones comes a close second to Smith in popularity in England and Wales and is a long way in front of Williams, which is third. It is surprising then that it does not fall among even the first 100 in Ireland. None the less, the name is found in nearly every county in Ireland (especially in the larger towns) and is quite common in Ulster.

The Hebrew name Johannon, meaning 'Jehovah has favoured', was latinised Johannes. This was made Johan, Jehan, Jean in France, and became John in England, where, by the fourteenth century, it was nearly as popular a forename as William. Also common was the feminine Joan from Latin Johanna. The surnames Joanes, John, Johns, Jones and so on can derive from any of these names. The extreme popularity of the name Jones in Wales stems from the form Ioan being adopted in the Welsh Authorised Version of the Bible.

Perhaps not surprisingly the Joneses are now found mainly in areas of English settlement at the time of the Plantation, namely counties Antrim and Armagh and in northwest Down.

JORDAN

In England the personal name Jordan became popular in the twelfth century because of the flasks of water from the River Jordan that were brought home by Crusaders for baptismal purposes. Jordan is now a well-known surname in England.

In Ireland Jordans are found in every province and are, in the main, of the family who descend from Jordan d'Exeter who acquired lands in Connacht after the Anglo-Norman invasion of 1172. Like many of these Norman families, the Jordans became 'hibernicised' and they adopted the Gaelic patronymic Mac Siúrtáin. By the sixteenth century they were counted by the English as among the 'wilde Irishe'.

In Ulster the name is most common in counties Antrim and Down. Some of the Down Jordans will descend from the Jordans who came to Ulster in the train of John de Courcy in February 1177 and settled in Lecale. There, by the seventeenth century, they had large possessions in Dunsford, Lismore, Jordan's Crew, Jordan's Acre and so on. Their castle in Ardglass still stands.

Around 1900 Jordan was being used interchangeably with Jardine around Poyntzpass in Co. Armagh and Cootehill in Co. Cavan.

KANE (*also* Keane, MacKane *and* O'Kane)

The O'Kanes, earlier O'Cahans, Gaelic Ó Catháin, were, with the O'Carolans, O'Duffys, and O'Mullans, collectively known as the Clann

Conchúir Magh Ithe, a branch of the Cenél Eoghain. The four septs all descend from Muirceartach Mór Mac Earca, son of Muireadach, son of Eoghan, son of Niall of the Nine Hostages, the fifth-century founder of the Uí Néill dynasty. Magh Ithe was what is now the Laggan district of east Donegal and from there the O'Cahans came in the twelfth century and drove out the O'Connors of Glengiven (now Dungiven, Co. Derry). The O'Cahan was one of the inaugurators of O'Neill and, as Lords of Keenaght and Co. Coleraine (now Co. Derry), they remained a powerful sept until the Plantation.

The last chief, Donnell Ballagh O'Cahan, was inaugurated in 1598 and joined O'Neill against the English in the Nine Years War, 1594–1603. Later he submitted, was granted back a small proportion of his original lands, and was knighted by James 1. None the less, he spent the last twenty years of his life imprisoned without trial in the Tower of London. He died in 1628.

A branch of the O'Cahans in north Antrim was first based at Dunseverick and then, after the 1641 rising, six miles away at Ballinlea. And many of their descendants still inhabit the same region. Some of the MacCaughans (*see* MacCaughey), Gaelic Mac Eacháin, of Antrim and north Derry believe they are originally O'Cahans.

The most common form of the name is Kane but O'Kane is common and increasingly popular. Keane in Ulster is a variant. However, MacKane and MacKain are variants of the Scottish MacKean, itself found in counties Derry and Donegal. MacKean was originally Mac Iain and there were MacIan septs of Clan Gunn, and of the MacDonalds of Ardnamurchan and of Glencoe in Argyllshire (*see* Johnston). The MacKeans of Co. Monaghan are not of this origin but are properly Muckians or Muckeens, Gaelic Ó Mochaidhean, a leading sept in the barony of Cremorne. The MacCloskeys (*see* MacCloskey) of Co. Derry descend from the twelfth-century Bloskey O'Cahan and the MacEvinneys or MacAvinneys from Aibhne Ó Catháin. (MacEvinney in Fermanagh is from Mac Giolla Coimhne, the name of a sept who were erenaghs of Callow Hill.)

Kane is among the seventy-five most common names in Ireland and is most numerous in Ulster. It is among the fifteen most common names in its homeland, Co. Derry, and is also particularly common in Co. Antrim.

Sir Richard Kane, 1666–1736, of the 18th Royal Irish, was born at Duneane, Co. Antrim. He became governor of Gibraltar and of Minorca. Echlin O'Kane, 1720–90, was one of the most famous of the Ulster harpers and performed in several European courts. Sir Robert John Kane, 1809–90, chemist and president of the Royal Irish Academy, was born in Dublin but was of Derry parentage.

KAVANAGH

Kavanagh is among the sixty most common names in Ireland. The great majority of those of the name are from Leinster (where half are in Dublin alone) and less than 10 per cent are from Ulster.

It is one of the very few Irish names that originally had neither a Mac-nor an O' prefix. The name in Gaelic was Caomhánach, meaning 'belonging to Caomhán (Kevin)'. The Kavanaghs are of MacMurrough stock, the first of the name being Domnall (Donal), son of Diarmait Mac Murchada (Dermot MacMurrough), King of Leinster. Dermot is infamous in Irish history for enlisting the help of the English King Henry II and bringing the Anglo-Norman lords to Ireland in 1167. Donal was fostered by one of the successors of St Caomhán and took Caomhánach as his name. When Dermot died in 1171 he was succeeded as King of Leinster by his son-in-law Richard Strongbow. Donal did, however, inherit vast territories in counties Wexford and Carlow and the name prospered throughout the medieval period.

At least some of the Ulster Kavanaghs or Cavanaghs do not descend from the MacMurrough sept. In Co. Antrim and east Tyrone a sept of MacCavanas anglicised to Cavanagh and also Caulfield (*see* Caulfield). Though MacCavana is sometimes erroneously given as Mac Caomhánaigh in Gaelic, it is in fact a form of MacEvanny, Gaelic Mac an Mhanaigh, from *manach*, a 'monk' (*see* Monaghan). Some too of the MacKevenys, Gaelic Mac Géibheannaigh, of the Montiaghs district of Massereene in south Antrim, have anglicised to Kavanagh. Around 1900 Kavanagh was being used interchangeably with Kivnahan on the Inishowen peninsula in Donegal.

The most famous of the Ulster Kavanaghs were both poets. Rose Kavanagh was born in 1859 at Killadry, near Beragh, in Co. Tyrone and Patrick Kavanagh, 1904–67, one of the giants of modern Irish poetry, was born on his father's small farm at Inishkeen in Co. Monaghan.

KEANE *see* Kane

KEARNEY

Kearney is common in every province of Ireland and generally derives either from Ó Catharnaigh, meaning 'warlike', a name also made Fox (*see* Fox), or from Ó Cearnaigh (*cearnach*, 'victorious'). In Ulster it is most often from MacKearney, Gaelic Mac Cearnaigh, a branch of the Cenél Eoghain. They took their name from Cearnach, a brother of Cosgrach, a chief of the O'Hanlons in Armagh.

The 'Kernose', erenaghs of Killaghtee in the Donegal baronies of Boylagh and Banagh, were probably Kearneys. An alternative anglicisation of Mac Cearnaigh, MacCarney, is found in Co. Cavan. The names Carney and Kearney can derive from any of these names.

The village of Kearney on the Upper Ards peninsula in Co. Down probably marks the base of the Kearneys, one of the old pre-Norman families of the area. They are remembered as particularly active in the resistance to the seventeenth-century settlement. Derryharney in Co. Fermanagh was originally Doire Uí Chearnaigh, 'oak wood of O'Kearney'.

In south Down the name has sometimes become confused with Kearns, a variant of the north Connacht sept name (O')Kieran, Gaelic Ó Ciaráin, now numerous in counties Monaghan and Fermanagh. Kearns also became Cairns (*see* Cairns).

KEENAN

Though Keenan is common in Leinster, it is most numerous in Ulster. The O'Keenans, Gaelic Ó Cianáin, were originally a Co. Fermanagh sept, famous as historians to the Maguires, and were based at Cleenish, where they were erenaghs. There are also many medieval references to the name O'Keenan in Co. Derry. The sept early migrated into Co. Monaghan and eastwards to counties Antrim, Down and Louth, and these, with Fermanagh, are where the name is still mainly found.

Keenan is most common in Monaghan and was found to be the eleventh most numerous name there in 1970. The extent of their numbers has given rise to the suggestion that there was a distinct Keenan sept in that county. Tirkeenan near Monaghan town was named after them.

Keenan (of the same Irish origin) was a well-recorded name in the Scottish province of Galloway, whence hailed so many Plantation settlers. It was also noted in Aberdeen.

KELLY

At the beginning of the twentieth century Kelly was found to be second only to Murphy in popularity on the whole island and the sixth most common name in Ulster. It was third most numerous in Co. Derry and in Tyrone, eighth in Co. Donegal, tenth in Co. Monaghan and twelfth in Co. Antrim. Interestingly, the name is common in Scotland and was found to be forty-second most numerous there in 1958.

The name Kelly was originally Ó Ceallaigh, 'descendant of Ceallach', a popular personal name probably meaning 'strife' and the surname came into being in several different areas. There are at least seven and possibly as many as ten distinct septs of O'Kelly in Ireland. Outside Ulster the most important of these were the O'Kellys of Uí Maine who ruled O'Kelly's

Country in Galway and Roscommon. It was a chief of this sept who, in 1351, invited all the poets, musicians and artists of Ireland to a Christmas feast and thus gave rise to the phrase 'O'Kelly's welcome', meaning great hospitality. The sept claims descent from the fourth-century Colla-dá-Críoch, King of Ulster and first King of Oriel, through his son Imchadh.

From another son, Rochadh, descend the O'Kellys of Ulster. This sept, the Cenél Eachach O'Kellys, were based in what is now the barony of Loughinsholin in south Derry. Another branch of the Clann Colla connection were the O'Kellys of Clanbrassil MacCoolechan in north Down. Some Kellys in the west of the province may originally be of the O'Kellys of Ard Ó gCeallaigh in Templeboy, Co. Sligo. The name in Ireland can also derive from MacKelly, Gaelic Mac Ceallaigh.

MacLysaght claims that the preponderance of Kelly in Scotland is due to Irish immigration and this may be partly true. However, Black gives four origins for the name: a variant of the name Kello; territorial from Kelly in Angus or Kelly in Renfrewshire; and in Galloway from MacKelly, Gaelic Mac Ceallaigh. A Dumfriesshire family, MacKellie or MacKaile of Gaitgill, descend from Gilmalgon MacKelli, recorded there in the mid-twelfth century. This name has become Kelly and MacCulloch (but *see* MacCullough) in Wigtownshire. There was a sept of Kellie or Kelly of Clan Donald.

Ned Kelly, the Australian folk hero who was hanged in 1880, was the son of 'Red' John Kelly, a Tipperary man, and Ellen Quinn, whose parents had emigrated from Antrim around 1839.

KENNEDY

Kennedy can be of Irish or Scottish origin. The name is among the twenty most common in Ireland and the fifty most common in Ulster, and, though found in every Irish county, is most numerous in counties Tipperary, Dublin and Antrim.

The name in Ireland was originally O'Kennedy, Gaelic Ó Cinnéide, from *ceann*, meaning 'head', and *éidigh*, meaning 'ugly'. The O'Kennedys descend from Cennedig, a nephew of Brian Boru, who had taken his name from Boru's father. As such they were one of the most important Dalcassian septs and were Lords of Ormonde from the eleventh to the sixteenth century. Originally of east Clare, they settled in north Tipperary and extended their sway as far south as Wexford. (John F. Kennedy, 1917–63, thirty-fifth president of the USA, descended from a Wexford family.) There were three branches of the sept, O'Kennedy Donn (brown), O'Kennedy Fionn (fair) and O'Kennedy Rua (red). A branch of the sept settled in Co. Antrim at the start of the seventeenth century. The name

Kennedy was found to be common in twelve out of the fourteen Co. Antrim baronies in the mid-nineteenth century and it will be very difficult without a verified family tree to know if a family is of this or the Scottish MacKennedy origin.

It is thought that the MacKennedys of Scotland were probably in remote times of Irish O'Kennedy stock. A sept of Clan Cameron, the Kennedys or Mac Ualrigs (MacWalricks) of Lochaber in Inverness-shire, descend from Ualrig Kennedy of Dunure in Ayrshire. The name became very common in Galloway and Ayrshire and the main line became very powerful, first as Lords Kennedy and later as Earls of Cassilis. A seventeenth-century rhyme makes this clear:

> 'Twixt Wigton and the toun of Ayr,
> Portpatrick and the Cruives of Cree,
> No man needs think for to bide there,
> Unless he courts with Kennedie.

The Kennedys of Clogher, Co. Tyrone, descend from one Cornet John Kennedy, c. 1615–80, of the Ayrshire Kennedys, who came there with the Scottish army under Lord Leven in 1641.

Minnagh, from Muimhneach, meaning Munsterman, is a Tyrone name, which in Donegal is occasionally synonymous with Kennedy.

John Pitt Kennedy, 1796–1879, colonial engineer, was born at Carndonagh, Co. Donegal. The great road he built from Simla in India to Tibet still bears his name. Sir Arthur Edward Kennedy, 1810–83, was born at Cultra, Co. Down. He became governor of Gambia, West Australia, Hong Kong and Queensland.

KENNY

Kenny is among the eighty most common names in Ireland but is much less common in Ulster than in the other three provinces, particularly Leinster. The name in Ireland was originally O'Kenny, Gaelic Ó Cionaoith, and was that of several distinct septs, the most important of which were lords of Munter Kenny in Roscommon and descend from the O'Kellys of Uí Maine.

In Ulster the name can be of this or of English origin. But there was also an Ó Cionaoith sept of Co. Tyrone, and the Ó Coinne sept, originally of Uí Eachach in Co. Down, at some time migrated to the Strabane neighbourhood in Co. Tyrone where one of its anglicisations was Kenny. Kennys and MacKennys in Co. Monaghan were originally MacKennas, Gaelic Mac Cionaoith (see MacKenna). In Co. Donegal Kenny is sometimes a synonym for Cannon (see Canning) and has absorbed the more obscure name Keaney.

Around 1900 MacKinney was being used interchangeably with Kenny in the Poyntzpass district of Co. Armagh and with MacKenny near Coleraine, Co. Derry (*see* MacKinney).

KEON *see* MacKeown

KEOWN *see* MacKeown

KERNAGHAN (*also* Kernohan *and* MacKernan)

These names are not common outside Ulster. Kernaghan was in Gaelic Ó Cearnacháin, from *cearnach,* meaning 'victorious'. Although in medieval times noted as a sept of north Donegal, Kernaghan is now most common in Co. Armagh and Kernohan in Co. Antrim.

O'Kernaghans of the Armagh sept became, in south and central Monaghan, MacKernans, a name more usually anglicised from Mac Thighearnáin (MacKiernan), from *tighearna,* a 'lord'. The MacKernans of west Monaghan, of Co. Cavan, and of Co. Fermanagh will be of this origin, descending from either the MacKernans, chiefs of Tullyhunco and a branch of the O'Rourkes, or from the MacKernans, centred at Lisnarick in Fermanagh, kin to the Maguires. Some others may descend from the Roscommon MacKiernans.

Around 1900 Kernaghan was being used interchangeably in the Newry district with the Connemara name Canavan and with the variant Carnahan around Clough in Co. Down.

KERNOHAN *see* Kernaghan

KERR

In its homeland on the Scottish Borders this name was rendered Kerr, Ker, Carr and Carre (it stems from the Middle English *kerr,* Old Norse *kjarr,* and signified a 'dweller by the marsh'). In Ulster it has become confused with the Irish name Carr (*see* Carr) and indeed the two names were still being used synonymously in the Coleraine, Co. Derry, and Lisburn, Co. Antrim, districts at the start of the twentieth century. In Donegal Kerr can also be an anglicised form of MacIlhair or a shortening of Kerin, a variant of Kieran, Gaelic Mac Ciaráin. In Monaghan it is often, like Carr, from Mac Giolla Cheara, a sept which descends from Mahon Mac Giolla Cera, Lord of Cremorne in 1297. Apart from these the majority of the Ulster Kerrs are of Scottish stock.

Kerr is among the forty most common names in Scotland and there, especially on Arran, the name can derive from MacGilker or MacKilgir, Gaelic Mac Gille Chiar, 'son of the dusky lad', from *ciar,* meaning 'dusky'. These were a sept of the Campbells of Glenorchy in Argyllshire.

But the majority will descend from the Kerrs, one of the great riding clans of the Scottish Borders, who settled there in the fourteenth century. They were second only to the Scott family in the Middle March and were strongest in Liddesdale and east Teviotdale. When the riding clans were 'broken' by James VI's 'pacification' of the Borders in the early seventeenth century, many members of the clans came to Ulster to escape persecution. Most settled in, and remained in, Fermanagh and by the mid-seventeenth century Kerrs were well represented there, but unlike the others most did not remain.

Kerr is among the fifty most common names in Ulster and is found in every county. But about half of the Ulster Kerrs are in Co. Antrim, where the name is among the twenty most numerous. It is also very common in counties Down and Tyrone. In the mid-nineteenth century the main Co. Antrim concentration was in the barony of Upper Dunluce, and in Down, in the parish of Dromara.

KEYS *see* MacKay

KIDD

Apart from the Kidds of Dublin this name is almost exclusive to Ulster, where it is most common in counties Antrim and Armagh. In England the name is most often derived from Middle English *kide*, meaning a 'kid', but can also be a form of Kitt, itself a pet form of Christopher. In Scotland the emphasis is the other way round. Kidd is a name of long standing in Angus, especially in Dundee and Arbroath.

George Hugh Kidd, 1824–95, leading obstetrician and president of the Royal College of Surgeons of Ireland, was born in Armagh city.

KILLEN *see* MacCallion

KILPATRICK

Kilpatrick can be in origin Mac Giolla Phádraig, the old form of the Irish name Fitzpatrick (*see* Fitzpatrick). But in Ireland the name is practically exclusive to Ulster (where two-thirds are in Co. Antrim) and the great majority of these are of Scottish stock.

There are different places in Scotland called Kilpatrick, in Gaelic Cill Phadair, 'church of Patrick', and many in Scotland took their name from such places. George Black, in *The Surnames of Scotland*, says, 'Patrick was one of the most popular names in the west of Scotland in pre-Reformation times and in Ireland only became popular after 1600 due probably to its introduction by Scots settlers in Ulster.' Gaelic forms, including Pádruig and Pádair, were also common. The name with the prefix Gille, meaning 'follower', gave Gillepatrick, another common personal name. This gave rise to the surname MacGilpatrick, Gaelic Mac Gille Phadruig, 'son of the follower of (St) Patrick', a name first on record in Moray in 1236. The Gaelic name was anglicised Gilpatrick, Kilpatrick, MacIlpatrick, MacIlfederick and Patterson (*see* Patterson). Patrick as a surname was common in Ayrshire and the Patricks of Dunwinning in Co. Antrim are of this origin.

Kilpatrick has become confused with Kirkpatrick (*see* Kirkpatrick) and both names are generally given as septs of Clan Colquhoun. The Clan Colquhoun Society repudiates this, but it is a fact that the Colquhouns derive their name from Umfridas de Kilpatrick or Kirkpatrick, who was granted the lands of Colquhoun in the early thirteenth century (*see* Colhoun).

In the late nineteenth century the main Co. Antrim concentration of Kilpatrick was in the Ballymoney–Ballymena region, where the name was also used interchangeably with Petherick.

KING

King is found equally in all the provinces of Ireland and is among the ninety most common names on the island. It is among the forty most numerous names in England and many, perhaps a majority, in Ulster will be of this origin. But in Ulster, as throughout Ireland, the name has been used as an anglicisation of several Irish Gaelic names in the mistaken assumption that they contained the element *rí*, meaning 'king'.

In England King, Old English name Cyng, was originally a nickname usually applied to someone of 'kingly' qualities or appearance or was a pageant name for someone who took the role of a king or the 'king of misrule'. In Scotland the name was most common in Berwickshire, Fifeshire and Aberdeenshire. In Perthshire a sept of Clan MacGregor, Mac-an-Righ, meaning 'son of the king', anglicised their name to MacAra, Macaree, MacNee and King. Others of the MacGregors adopted the name King after their name was proscribed (*see* Greer).

MacAree is also an Irish name from Co. Monaghan and it too was anglicised as King, but in this case only because of its similarity in sound to the Irish Gaelic Mac an Ríogh. It is in fact Mac Fhearadhaigh, probably from Fearadhach, meaning 'manly' (*see* MacGarry). The Irish name Mag Fhinn, from *fionn*, meaning 'fair', became MacGinn (*see* MacGinn) in Co. Tyrone and Maginn in counties Antrim and Down. The earlier form MacKinn, Gaelic Mac Fhinn, is now rare, having become King. Gilroy (*see* MacIlroy) was sometimes made King. Other Irish names which were erroneously made King are Conroy, Conry and Cunree.

Besides being found to be synonymous with MacAree and MacKeary near Downpatrick, Co. Down, and in Co. Monaghan, King was also found, around 1900, to be interchangeable with the variant Muckaree and Muckilbuoy in the Banbridge district of Co. Down. Muckilbuoy is presumably from Mac Giolla Bhuidhe (*see* MacEvoy *and* MacKelvey).

William King, 1650–1729, Archbishop of Dublin, was born in Antrim town. A great supporter of the Glorious Revolution and of the Penal Laws against Catholics, he is perhaps most famous for his *State of the Protestants of Ireland under the late King James' Government* (1691).

KIRK

The work 'kirk' for 'church' is common in the north of England and in Scotland, areas where the Danes settled in the tenth century. (The Scandinavians did not use the sound 'ch'.) Kirk is a Scottish name of various local origins, from residence near a church. The Dumfriesshire name Kirkhoe, now rare, also became Kirk.

In Ireland the name is most common in counties Antrim and Louth, though a particular concentration was noted in the parish of Killaney, barony of Upper Castlereagh, Co. Down, in the mid-nineteenth century. In Co. Monaghan the name Kirke is thought to be a variant of Carragher, Gaelic Mac Fhearchair, through the seventeenth-century variants Kearcher and Kirker. Kirk was also noted as synonymous with Kirkpatrick around Coleraine and Limavady in Co. Derry at the start of the twentieth century (*see* Kirkpatrick).

KIRKPATRICK

Kirkpatrick is a name much confused with Kilpatrick (*see* Kilpatrick) and its variants MacIlfederick, MacIlpatrick and so on and with Kirk (*see* Kirk). The name is Scottish, common in Dumfriesshire, where it derives from a chapel dedicated to St Patrick in the parish of Closeburn in that shire. The first on record was the twelfth-century Roger de Kirkpatrick who had a charter from Robert the Bruce for lands in Dumfriesshire near the River Esk. There was a Kirkpatrick sept of Clan Gregor and there may have been one of Clan Colquhoun (*see* Kilpatrick).

In Ireland the name is found almost exclusively in Ulster, where over two-thirds are in Co. Antrim. A survey of 1857 found Kirkpatricks common in thirteen out of the fourteen baronies of that county.

KNOX

Though found in every province of Ireland, the great Scottish name Knox is common only in Ulster and there it is most numerous in Co. Antrim. In late-nineteenth-century Ulster the main concentration of the name was found to be in the barony of Upper Dunluce, especially to the south of Ballymoney, Co. Antrim. However, the most famous of the Knox families which settled in Ireland acquired estates in counties Derry, Mayo, Tipperary and Dublin. All these stemmed originally from Ranfurly in Renfrewshire.

Knox is a Renfrewshire name and the main line of the family descends from one Adam, son of Uchtred, who was granted the lands of Knock by Walter the Steward (ancestor of the Stewarts) in the early thirteenth century. The lands were named after the great crag there called the 'Knock', from Gaelic *cnoc,* meaning a 'hill'.

KYLE

This name is rare in Ireland outside Ulster, where it is most common, now as in the seventeenth century, in counties Antrim and Derry. Most of the name, like the Kyles of Laurel Hill in Co. Derry, stem originally from Ayrshire. The surname Kyle was taken from the district of that name in Ayrshire and was especially common around Irvine in that shire. It has also been suggested that the name is an anglicised form of the Scots Gaelic Mac Suile and indeed Kyle and M'Suile were being used interchangeably in the Ballycastle district of Co. Antrim around 1900 (as were Kyle and Kell around Broughshane in Antrim).

LAFFERTY (*also* Laverty)

Lafferty is an exclusively Ulster name and in 1900 was found only in counties Donegal, Derry and Tyrone. It stems mainly from O'Lafferty or O'Laverty, Gaelic Ó Laithbheartaigh. Both names derive from the Gaelic for 'bright ruler' and are Ulster forms of the Connacht name O'Flaverty or O'Flaherty. (The 'F' in Ulster was often aspirated or silent, thus O'Flynn becomes in Ulster O'Lynn.)

The O'Laffertys were a Donegal sept, the chief of which was Lord of Aileach, famous for the great stone fortress, the Grianán of Aileach, at the head of Lough Swilly. The first to bear the surname was Murchadh Ua Flaithbheartaigh, also known as Murchadh Glúin Ilair, 'of the eagle knee', King of Tyrone, died 972. One of the chiefs, Macraith O'Laverty, died 1197, was described by the Four Masters as the 'Tanist of Tyrone' a short time before the chieftancy of Tyrone passed to the O'Neills. The O'Laffertys were driven from Donegal in the thirteenth century and settled near Ardstraw in Co. Tyrone, their base perhaps marked by the townland of Lislafferty. Monsignor James O'Laverty, 1828–1906, a noted historian and author of the five-volume *Historical Account of the Diocese of Down and Connor,* was of this sept. He was born at Carraban, Co. Down.

Laverty is also an exclusively Ulster name but is found mainly in Co. Antrim. Most of this name will be originally MacLavertys, a sept of Clan Donald, hereditary 'speakers', or heralds, of the Lords of the Isles. The Clan Donald claim that the name was originally Fear Labhairt an Righ, 'the king's speaker' but Black states that the name was actually Mac Fhlaithbheartaich and was thus etymologically similar to the Irish O'Flaverty or O'Lafferty. The MacLavertys claim to be originally a Kintyre branch of the MacDonalds. They were later based on Islay, at the court of the Lord of the Isles. The name became common too on Arran. In the mid-nineteenth century the Antrim Lavertys were found almost exclusively in the barony of Upper Dunluce.

LAMONT

In Ireland Lamont is found mainly in Ulster, where two-thirds of those of the name are in Co. Antrim. Though most of the Lamonts in the USA and some in Ulster believe the name to be French, it is in fact indisputably Scottish, the Clan Lamont or Lamond, Gaelic Mac Laomuinn, at one time being very powerful in south Argyllshire and their chief described as MacLamond of all Cowal.

The family was originally of Ulster Gaelic stock. The Old Norse name Lögmaor, meaning 'lawman' or 'lawyer', was made in Ireland Ladhman, and Ladhman, son of Giolla Colum, son of Fearchar, son of Dúnshléibhe Ó Néill, Prince of Tyrone, was the ancestor of, and gave his name to, the Scottish MacLamonts. (The Scottish MacSweeneys and MacLachlins also descend from Dúnshléibhe.) The MacLamonts were also called MacErchar from Fearchar, the grandfather of Ladhman.

The clan, like most of those in the vicinity of the Campbells, lost most of their lands to them. The feud between the two culminated in the infamous massacre in the late sixteenth century when the Campbells slaughtered all the leading members of the clan. What was left of the Lamonts scattered and were forced to adopt various aliases. These included Black, Brown, Clements, MacSorley, Turner and White (see these names). Many of these, as well as those who retained the name, came to Ulster in the middle to late seventeenth century.

LAPPIN

O'Lappin, Gaelic Ó Lapáin, probably from *lapa*, a 'paw', is one of the oldest hereditary surnames in Ireland (and therefore the world). The Four Masters mention the O'Lappins in the tenth century as erenaghs in Derry.

Lappin is almost exclusively an Ulster name and the O'Lappins were originally one of the leading septs of Tirconnell in Donegal, their chief was the Lord of Cenél Enda. At some unknown date between the eleventh and seventeenth centuries they migrated and settled in Co. Armagh. And it is there and on the adjacent borders of counties Tyrone and Antrim that they are most numerous.

The name was often made Delap, a form of Dunlop (*see* Dunlop), in counties Fermanagh and Derry.

LARKIN

Larkin is from the Gaelic Ó Lorcáin, probably from *lorc*, meaning 'rough' or 'fierce'. The name is common in every province of Ireland and was that of distinct septs in counties Galway, Tipperary, Wexford and Monaghan.

The Monaghan Uí Lorcháin were an important Oriel family, chiefs of Farney and the Uí Breasail of Co. Armagh and it is in Armagh that the name is still most common.

James Larkin, 'Big Jim', 1876–1947, the labour leader, was born in Liverpool of Irish parents but spent his early childhood with his grandparents in Newry, Co. Down.

LARMOUR (*also* Armour)

Both these names are, in Ireland, exclusive to Ulster. Most of the Armours are in Co. Antrim and the Larmours are fairly equally divided between counties Antrim and Down. The names are English occupational names of Norman origin and were originally Anglo-Norman L'Armurer, 'the armourer', from Old French *armurier*. In mid-nineteenth-century Co. Antrim Larmour was found almost exclusively near Ballinderry in the barony of Upper Massereene. It is also found there as Lorimour and Larmer.

The Revd James Brown Armour, 1841–1928, 'Armour of Ballymoney', was a controversial Presbyterian minister who campaigned for Home Rule and the establishment of Catholic universities.

LAUGHLIN *see* MacLaughlin

LAVERTY *see* Lafferty

LAVERY (*also* Lowry)

Lavery is an Irish name found exclusively in Ulster and particularly common in counties Armagh, Antrim and Down. Lowry is well known in every province of Ireland but is most common in Ulster and in particular in counties Antrim and Down. It can be a variant of Lavery and thus Irish, or a Scottish name brought over from Galloway in the post-Plantation period.

The O'Laverys, in Gaelic Ó Labhradha, descend from one Labhradh (whose name meant 'speaker'), the father of Etru, chief of the Monagh, who died in 1056. The sept was based at that time at Magh Rath (now Moira), Co. Down, and it is in that district and the adjoining part of Co. Antrim that the name is still most common. The name was initially anglicised as O'Laviry and O'Lawry and the forms Lavery and Lowry are still found in virtually equal numbers in that area. The two forms, when counted together, constituted the most numerous name in the baronies of Upper and Lower Massereene in Co. Antrim in 1962 and were particularly concentrated in the Montiaghs (in Gaelic *na móinte,* 'the marshes') district to which many Irish moved at the time of the Plantation.

The Laverys were so numerous in these areas that, to distinguish one from the other, there were three branches, Baun-Laverys, Roe-Laverys and Trin-Laverys (*bán,* 'white', *rua,* 'red', *tréan,* 'strong'). Many of the Trin-Laverys of this district took the name Armstrong (*see* Armstrong). Dr John Armstrong, Bishop of Down and Connor from 1727 to 1739, for instance, was born Trenlavery. And the names Lavery and Armstrong were still being used interchangeably in the Lisburn and Crumlin districts of Co. Antrim at the start of the twentieth century. Lavery was also being used interchangeably with Rafferty in Newry, Co. Down, around 1900.

Mac Giolla Domhnaigh claims that the Galloway Lowrys were originally a Gaelic sept called Mac Labharaigh (also giving the rare name Clowery). Black, however, states that Lowrie is a variant of Laurie, itself a diminutive or pet form of Lawrence. Lowrie or Laurie was and remains a common name in Dumfriesshire (whence hailed the famous Annie Laurie) and many of our Ulster Lowrys will be of this stock. The Earls of Belmore in Fermanagh are Lowrys and descend from a Lowry or Laurie of the Lauries of Maxweltown who settled in Tyrone in the first half of the seventeenth century. (Maxweltown is in Kirkcudbrightshire near the town of Dumfries).

Sir John Lavery, 1856–1941, the landscape and portrait painter, was born in Belfast. He designed the first set of Irish banknotes, the head of his wife, Lady Lavery, appearing on the pound note. Cecil Lavery, 1894–1967, Supreme Court judge and senator, was born in Armagh and was one of the founder members of the Irish Volunteers.

LEE

Lee is a common name in all the provinces of Ireland and can be of English, Irish or Scottish origin. In Ulster it is more common in Co. Antrim than elsewhere.

The name in England is local in origin from any one of several places called Lea, Lee, Leigh and so on, and signified a 'dweller by the wood or clearing'. In Scotland it most often takes the form Lee or Ley and is thought to be of English origin. However, it has been suggested that some of the MacLeas or MacLays, a small sept of Clan Stewart of Appin, anglicised to Lee (*see* Livingstone).

Besides those of English or Scottish origin, the name Lee in Ireland is an anglicised form of different Irish names. In Connacht it was originally Ó Laoidhigh, O'Lee, the name of a sept who were physicians to the O'Flahertys. In the north of that province, and also in Laois, it was MacLee, Gaelic Mac Laoidhigh. Both these names derive from *laoidheach*, meaning 'poetic'.

The Gaelic name that was anglicised as Lee in Ulster (and also MacAlea and MacAlee) was Mac an Leagha, 'son of the physician'. In Monaghan it is thought that Lee was originally MacCloy, Gaelic Mac Giolla Eachaidh. For the Scottish MacCloy *see* Fullerton.

LENNON

Though found in every province of Ireland, Lennon is common only in Leinster and Ulster. It is an anglicised form of different Irish surnames and is confused with Leonard (*see* Leonard). Maclennan is a Scottish name (*see* Logan).

There were several distinct septs of O'Lennon, Gaelic Ó Leannáin (either from *leann*, a 'cloak', or from *leannán*, a 'paramour'). The most important of these were erenaghs of Inishmacsaint in Co. Fermanagh and many of the family were priors or canons of Lisgoole, near Enniskillen, in the fourteenth and fifteenth centuries. Also in Fermanagh a sept of Ó Luinigh, Lunny (*see* Lunney), anglicised to Lennon. Both names also became Leonard.

In 1970 the name was found to be the forty-second most common in Co. Monaghan and Livingstone suggests that these are local to that county. The name is one of the most numerous on the Ards peninsula in Co. Down, particularly in the parish of Ardquin. The name is now most common in Co. Armagh.

LEONARD

Leonard is common in every province in Ireland but less so in Ulster than in Leinster and Connacht. Most of the name will be of Irish origin, having been used as an anglicisation of more Irish Gaelic names than almost any other.

Leonard is an English name, deriving from the Old German Leonhard, meaning 'lion-bold'. St Leonard was the patron saint of captives and many churches in England were dedicated to him. Some in Ulster may be of this origin.

The name Mac Giolla Fhinnéin (son of the devotee of [St] Finian), which was anglicised as MacAlinion (and also MacLennan), was made Leonard. (But *see* Logan for the Scottish Maclennan.) This sept were lords of Muintir Pheodacháin in Co. Fermanagh, planted there by the O'Donnells. They drove out the Ó Fuadacháin sept (anglicised as Swift) and became for a time Kings of Fermanagh until their growth was curbed by the rising Maguires. The family descends from Giolla Finnéin O'Muldory, as do the O'Muldorys themselves, once lords of Lough Erne. Leonard was the thirty-fifth most numerous name in Fermanagh in 1962. MacAleenan, a variant of Mac-Alinion, was also anglicised as Lynas and Lyness (*see* Lynas) in south Down.

O'Lennon also became Leonard (*see* Lennon). Gilshenan, Gaelic Mac Giolla Seanáin (son of the devotee of [St] Senan), a sept of Tyrone, anglicised to Leonard, also Nugent (*see* Nugent) and Shannon (*see* Shannon). Lunny (*see* Lunney) also became Leonard, as did the Roscommon name Lenaghan, Gaelic Ó Leannacháin (but *see also* MacClenaghan).

LEVINGSTON *see* Livingston(e)

LINDSAY

This name is not common in Ireland outside of Ulster, where over half of those of the name are in Co. Antrim. Though most will be of Scottish stock some at least will be Irish.

The great Scottish family of Lindsay is counted as one of the Highland clans, because their chief was the first commander of the first Highland regiment, Am Freicedan Dubh – the Black Watch. Their country was the 'Braes of Angus' and the first of the name on record was the twelfth-century Baldric de Lindsay, a Norman. The name is territorial in origin from De Limesay, north of Rouen in France, but it has also been suggested that it derives from Lindsay in Lincolnshire.

From earliest times the Lindsays were powerful in Scotland and in 1180 William de Lindsay was Baron of Luffness and Laird of Crawford. They later became Lords Lindsay and Earls of Balcarres. Sir David Lindsay of the Byres was created Earl of Crawford and his descendants were created Earls of Lindsay. They were known as the 'Lightsome Lindsays'. Many of the MacClintocks (*see* MacClintock) of Dumbartonshire and Argyllshire, anglicised their name to Lindsay. There are apparently over two hundred spellings of the name recorded in Scotland alone.

One of the descendants of the Byres branch of the Lindsays was Thomas Lindesay, of Kingswark in Leith, and two of his sons were among the fifty Scottish undertakers of the Plantation. Bernard had a grant of 1000 acres in the Sperrins and Robert 1000 acres at Tullyhogue in Tyrone, where the O'Neill chiefs had up to that time been inaugurated. Bernard returned to Scotland and his grant was taken over by Robert, who later became high sheriff of Tyrone. He married Janet Acheson, whose father was ancestor of the Earls of Gosford, and they are the ancestors of the present-day Lindsays of Loughry in Co. Tyrone. The Lindsays of Lisnacrieve in Tyrone descend from one James Lindsay, a Presbyterian farmer who left Ayrshire in 1678 to escape religious persecution and settled near Derry. His four sons were numbered among the defenders of Derry in 1689.

But also in Ulster many of the Lynches, Gaelic Ó Loingsigh, Lords of Dalriada in north Antrim, anglicised to Lindsay (see Lynch). In Co. Down this Gaelic name was anglicised Lynchey and the names Lindsay and Lynchey were still being used interchangeably in the Clough area of that county in 1900. A few of the O'Lynns further anglicised their name to Lindsay (see Flynn).

LITTLE (also Lyttle)

These names can be of English, Scottish or Irish origin and are most common in Dublin and in Ulster, especially in counties Antrim and Fermanagh. The name is, of course, English by original derivation and was descriptive of the bearer, from Old English *lytel,* meaning 'small'.

In Scotland, Little was the name of one of the lesser of the riding clans of the Borders. Neighbours of the Beatties, they were based in Eskdale and Ewesdale in Dumfriesshire and were recorded as one of the unruly clans of the West March in 1587. Little can also be a variant of Liddell, a territorial name from Liddel in Roxburghshire, and indeed the two names were recorded as synonymous in the Poyntzpass district of Co. Armagh towards the end of the nineteenth century.

At the same time Little was recorded as a synonym of Beggan in Co. Monaghan. Beggan, Gaelic Ó Beagáin or Ó Beacáin, was the name of a sept of the Clones–Roslea–Donagh area and most of this sept anglicised to Little. However, it is clear that a large number of members of the riding clans of the Scottish Borders settled in Fermanagh at the time of the Plantation and settlers called Little were recorded there in the seventeenth century. It will therefore be difficult, without a confirmed family tree, to determine the origins of any individual.

LIVINGSTON(E) (also Levingston)

In Ireland these names are most common in Ulster, particularly in counties Armagh, Antrim and Down. Livingston is Scottish in origin and was a territorial surname from the lands, now parish, of that name in West

Lothian. A Saxon named Leving or Leuing had a grant of the lands in the early twelfth century and named them Leving'stoun. The family took its name from this. They became prominent in Scottish history from the fourteenth century until the 1715 rebellion, and held the earldoms of Callander in Perthshire, Linlithgow in Linlithgowshire and Newburgh in Fifeshire.

The MacLeas or MacLays, a sept of Clan Stewart of Appin, anglicised their name to Livingstone and Lee (see Lee). It is usually claimed that this name was originally Mac an Leigh, 'son of the physician', and the sept were later taken for MacKinlays (see Finlay). But Black states that the name was Mac Donnshléibhe (see Dunleavy). The African explorer and missionary David Livingstone, 1812–73, was of this sept. There were also Livingstons, hereditary standard-bearers to the MacDougalls of Lorn.

In the mid-nineteenth century in Co. Antrim the name was almost exclusively located in the barony of Upper Toome, and in Down, in the parish of Tullylish, barony of Lower Iveagh. The variants Leviston and Leveson were noted around 1900. The form Levingston has suffered a marked decline in the twentieth century.

LOGAN

Though found in every province of Ireland, this name is common only in Ulster, especially in Co. Antrim. It can be of Scottish, Ulster Gaelic or Ulster Norman origin.

In Ross and Cromarty the Scottish Clan Maclennan or Logan were followers of the MacKenzies of Kintail, Earls of Seaforth, and were standard-bearers to them. They were originally called Logan and descend from one Logan or Loban who came to Kintail in the fourteenth century from Easter Ross. In the fifteenth century they feuded with the Frasers and Gillegorm Logan and most of his followers were slain at Kessock. The Frasers captured Logan's pregnant wife with the intention of killing the child should it be male. A son was born but was so stunted and deformed that he was allowed to live. He became known as 'Crotach' (hump-backed) and when he grew up he took Holy Orders and founded churches in Skye, and in Glenelg in Inverness-shire. Though a priest, he left many children, as was common in medieval times. One of these became a devotee of St Finnan and his progeny were known as Mac Gille Fhinnéin, or Maclennan. The clan retained both names. (See Leonard.) In the Lowlands of Scotland the name Logan was local in origin and most early references were to de Logans, usually of Logan in Ayrshire.

In Ulster, Logan is also the anglicised form of the Irish name Ó Leogháin. Many fifteenth-century clergy in Armagh and Down, for instance, were Logans or O'Louchans. Loggan was listed as a 'principal Irish name' in

Co. Antrim in Petty's 'census' of 1659. However, it is thought that this was a mistake. The name was almost certainly Scottish.

Logan can also be a Norman name and a family of de Logans came to Ulster with Hugelin de Mandeville and were recorded in Carrickfergus, Co. Antrim, as early as 1190. These have now merged with and are indistinguishable from the other Logans of the county. In counties Tyrone and Antrim Logan was often made Lagan.

James Logan, 1674–1751, of Scottish origin, was born in Lurgan, Co. Armagh. A Quaker, he was secretary to William Penn, the founder of Pennsylvania, and held several important offices in the new state. His son and grandson were prominent American politicians.

LOGUE

This name is rare outside Ulster, where over half are in Co. Donegal and most of the rest in Co. Derry. The name was originally in Gaelic Ó Maolmhaodhóg, 'descendant of the devotee of (St) Maodhóg', and became Logue through the anglicised form Mulvogue. Though originally of Co. Galway, the sept early migrated to Donegal–Derry. Around Glenties the name has been confused with Molloy (*see* Molloy).

Cardinal Michael Logue, 1840–1924, Archbishop of Armagh, was born at Carrigart in Co. Donegal. He is perhaps most famous for his denunciation of Charles Stewart Parnell over the O'Shea divorce case.

LONG

This name is common in every province of Ireland, especially Munster, and can be of English, Irish, Scottish or Norman origin. In England and Scotland the name was descriptive of the original bearer. It was noted in Dumfries as early as 1259. The Norman names de Long and le Lung arrived in Ireland with the twelfth-century Anglo-Norman invasion and quickly spread to many parts of the country. The Co. Armagh sept name Ó Longáin, more properly anglicised Longan, was made Long. The name in Ulster is most common in Co. Donegal and was noted as synonymous with Longley in south Down at the start of the twentieth century.

LOUGHLIN *see* MacLaughlin

LOUGHRAN

This old Ulster name is more properly O'Loughran and was originally Ó Luachráin, probably from *luchair,* meaning 'bright'. It was the name of a distinguished ecclesiastical family from west Armagh, a branch of which migrated to Tyrone about 1430. In the seventeenth century, as now, the name was equally common in both counties. It is also common in Co. Antrim.

Thomas O'Loughran, died 1416, was dean of Armagh, and three famous members of the family were martyred for their faith. Fr John O'Loughran was tortured and died in prison in 1576. Fr Patrick O'Loughran was also tortured before being executed with the Bishop of Down and Connor in 1612. And the Franciscan Fr Neilan Loughran was hanged by Cromwellians in 1652. Four different O'Loughrans, all Franciscans, are mentioned in Turlough O'Mellan's account of the 1641–7 war.

The spellings Laugheran and Lochrane are found and the name, mistaken for Loughrey, Gaelic Ó Luaithéirghigh, which means 'descendant of the early riser', was also made Early (but *see* Bell).

LOVE

This name is most numerous in Co. Derry, though a particular concentration of the name was recorded in the Co. Antrim barony of Upper Dunluce in the mid-nineteenth century. These gave their name to the townland of Love's Corkey in the parish of Loughguile. The name can be of English, Scottish or Irish origin.

The name in England derives from Lufu, an Old English female name meaning 'love', or from its male equivalent Lufa. It can also be from the Anglo-French *louve,* the feminine of *loup,* a 'wolf'. The latter of these is thought to be its origin in the Lowlands of Scotland, where it was most common in Paisley and Glasgow. (The diminutive or pet form Lovell is also found there.)

Black claims that MacKinven was the name of a well-known Ayrshire Covenanter family which was given refuge in Kintyre and made its name Love. Angus Martin says there is no evidence for this, and that the name Love derives from the local names MacKinnon or MacKinven. The name of the Clan MacKinnon was originally Mac Fhionnghuin, 'son of Fionngon', a name meaning 'fair-born', and MacKinven was Mac Ionmhuinn, meaning 'beloved son'. In practice in Kintyre the names were interchangeable and both were anglicised as Love. Campbeltown poet Angus Keith MacKinven, who died of wounds received at the Battle of the Somme in 1916, used the pen name A.K. Love.

The Ulster name MacGrath (*see* MacGrath) is pronounced McGraw in parts of the province and so has been made Love by pseudo-translation: *grá* is the Gaelic for 'love'.

LOWRY *see* Lavery

LUNNEY (*also* Lunny)

Lunney is rare outside Ulster and is most common in Co. Fermanagh. The O'Lunneys, Gaelic Ó Luinigh, were an important Co. Donegal sept in the medieval period and were chiefs of Cenél Moen in the barony of Raphoe. But they were forced from there and settled in Tyrone in the barony of Strabane.

A branch of the family then migrated to Fermanagh where they had their headquarters at Ard Uí Luinín on Inishmore Island. Many of the name appear in the Annals as physicians and historians and indeed O'Lunneys worked in the preparation of the Annals of Ulster and the Book of Conquests. The name was also anglicised as Leonard and Lennon (*see* Leonard *and* Lennon).

LUNNY *see* Lunney

LYNAS (*also* Lyness)

In Ireland this name is exclusive to Ulster, particularly counties Antrim and Down. In the seventeenth century it was found mainly in Co. Armagh. It is difficult to be sure about its origins.

MacLysaght claims it is a north of England name and I have found it in both these forms in seventeenth-century burial records of York. English authorities list it in the form Lynes, a variant of Line(s), a pet form of such female names as Avelina and Emalina; or as Lynes and Lines, variants of the Norman name Luynes (the name of the famous French persecutor of the Huguenots); or as Line and Lines, denoting a 'dweller by the line- or lime-tree' (Middle English *line* or *lyne*). However, these names are not listed as northern, nor do any of them offer the specific forms Lynas and Lyness.

The name has occasionally, particularly in south Down, been used for MacAleenan, a variant of MacAlinion (*see* Leonard). Other recorded spellings of the name include Linass, Liness and Lynass.

LYNCH

Lynch is among the twenty most common names in Ireland. Found in every county, it is in Ulster most numerous in Co. Cavan (where it is among the first five) and in Co. Derry. Though it can be of Norman origin, most in the province will be of Ulster Gaelic stock.

The Norman family de Lench, one of the 'Tribes of Galway', were very powerful in Galway city, and provided it with eighty-four mayors between 1484, when Dominick Lynch was given its first charter by Richard III, and 1654, when Catholics were debarred from office.

The name Ó Loingsigh, from *loingseach,* a 'mariner' (giving both Lynch and Lynchey), was the name of several distinct septs. In Ulster one of these was based in central Co. Cavan. The other was based in north

Antrim and Derry and their chief was lord of the ancient kingdom of Dalriada. The verb 'to lynch' derives either from the fifteenth-century mayor of Galway, James Lynch, who hanged his own son for murder or from the American Colonel Charles Lynch, 1736–96, whose father, also Charles, was of the Derry sept.

The Lynches of Donegal are more properly Linchehans, Gaelic Mac Loingseacháin. Lynch, through Lynchey, was also made Lindsay (*see* Lindsay).

LYNESS *see* Lynas

LYNN *see* Flynn

LYONS

Lyons is among the eighty most common names in Ireland but is much less numerous in Ulster than elsewhere. Several Irish names, such as Lyne, Lehane and Lane, were made Lyons, and most in Ireland will be of these origins. In Ulster the name can also be English or Scottish.

The English names Lyon and Lyons derive from 'Lyon', a pronunciation of the personal name Leo or Leon or from a nickname (lion). It can also be a Norman name from the placename Lyons-la-Forêt. In Scotland the form Lyons is not common, but Lyon is recorded there from 1321 and is thought to be of English and ultimately French origin.

The Scottish Lyon has become confused with Lyons in Ulster and, in Co. Donegal, Lyons has been recorded as a synonym of Leehane and Lion.

LYTTLE *see* Little

MACADAM

Apart from the MacAdams of Dublin city, this is an exclusively Ulster name and is most common in Co. Monaghan. It can be of Irish or Scottish origin.

There are two Ulster Gaelic names that anglicised to MacAdam. The Co. Cavan sept name Mac Ádhaimh, 'son of Adam', pronounced and often anglicised MacCaw, was also made MacAdam. Livingstone claims that some at least of this sept became Adamses (*see* Adams). The once influential Co. Armagh erenagh sept of Mac Cadáin anglicised to Mac-Adam, MacCadden and MacCudden.

The Scottish name MacAdam is also found in Ireland, especially in Dublin and Belfast. It was in Scots Gaelic originally Mac Adaim and was first recorded in Scotland in 1160. The most famous family, that of Ayrshire, is a sept of Clan Gregor and descends from Gregor MacGregor, second son of the chief, who took refuge in Galloway when the clan was outlawed (*see* Greer). The famous engineer and road builder John Loudon Macadam, 1756–1836, who was born in Ayr and gave his name to Tarmacadam, was of this sept.

Robert S. MacAdam, 1808–95, was a Gaelic scholar and founder of the *Ulster Journal of Archaeology*. His brother James MacAdam, 1801–61, was a noted geologist. They were both born in Belfast.

MACALEAVEY *see* Dunleavy

MACALINDEN

MacAlinden is an exclusively Ulster name and there two-thirds are in Co. Armagh alone and most of the rest in south Down. The name is in Gaelic Mac Giolla Fhiondáin, which means 'son of the devotee of (St) Fintan (of Clonenagh)'.

The origin of the sept is obscure. MacLysaght claims that it is a branch of the O'Muldorys, descended from Giolla Finden O'Muldory of Armagh. But these, as he points out elsewhere, were the MacAlinions, descendants of Giolla Finian O'Muldory, based in Fermanagh. The two names MacAlinion and MacAlinden are quite distinct and there is no record of one being used as a synonym for the other. Woulfe claims that MacAlinden is of Scottish origin, a variant of MacClinton. MacLysaght agrees that MacClinton means 'son of the devotee of (St) Fintan' but gives the Gaelic as Mac Giolla Fhionntáin, and says it is a west Ulster name.

Around 1900 MacAlinden was being used interchangeably with Linden around Kilkeel, Co. Down, and Poyntzpass, Co. Armagh; with Lundy around Clough in Co. Down; and with both Linden and MacLinden in the Stewartstown district of Co. Tyrone. It has also been made Glendon, Lindie and Lyndon.

MACALLEN *see* Allen *and* MacCallion

MACALLISTER

Apart from a few MacAllisters found in Leinster and Munster, this is a distinctively Ulster name, the great majority, now as in the fourteenth century, being in Co. Antrim.

The personal name Alaxandair, which became Alasdair, is the Gaelic form of Alexander (*see* Alexander). The Clan MacAlister is one of the principal branches of Clan Donald and descends from the thirteenth-century Alexander, brother of Angus Mór and son of Donald, the eponymous ancestor of the MacDonalds. Donald was a grandson of Somerled of Argyll. As such this clan is Irish by origin, Somerled being a descendant of Colla Uais, eldest of the three Collas of Oriel. The clan territory was Kintyre and they were also numerous on Arran and Bute.

From this region the MacAlisters were brought to northeast Ulster by the MacDonnells in the fourteenth century. They are one of the great galloglass families of Ireland. However, they quickly settled and became an Irish sept in their own right and by the mid-seventeenth century the name is recorded in both counties Antrim and Derry as a 'principal Irish name'.

In the mid-nineteenth century the main concentrations of the name in Co. Antrim were in the baronies of Carey and Kilconway. In the latter it was joint most common name with Millar. The variants MacCallister, MacLester and Lester, among others, have been noted. Some MacAllisters, particularly in Co. Fermanagh, will have been originally MacAleshers (*see* Green).

MACANALLY *see* MacNally

MACANENY (*also* MacEneany)

These names are exclusive to Ulster and that part of the ancient kingdom of Oriel that spills into Leinster, namely Louth. Until fairly recently it was accepted as being originally Mac Conaonaigh but this has now been discounted. The original west Monaghan sept was named Mac an Dhéaghanaigh, 'son of the dean'.

The sept were famous ecclesiastics based at Clones, Co. Monaghan, and in the fourteenth century MacAneanys were co-arbs or 'heirs' to St Tighearnach of Clones parish, a position they lost in the fifteenth century to the MacMahons, who in turn lost it to the Maguires. By the seventeenth century they were no longer ecclesiastics but were still numerous in their old lands in Monaghan, Louth, Armagh and Tyrone, the areas in which they are still most common. Since the seventeenth century the name has been more associated with the neighbouring parishes of Roslea, Killeevan and Donaghmoyne than with Clones.

The name holds something of a record in the number of its variant anglicised forms. MacLysaght claims sight of thirty-eight, though he adds that many of these are occasional American mistranscriptions. One particular family can illustrate the potential minefield this represents for those in search of their ancestors. Peter and Mary McEneaney emigrated with their five children from Monaghan to America in 1829. Another child was born in America. Of these eight the graves of six have been located, four in Caledon, Ontario, and two in New York. The six are represented on their headstones as McAneaney, McAneny, McEnaney, McEneaney, McEneany and Bird! Some of the name anglicised to Bird in the mistaken notion that *éan,* the Gaelic for 'bird', was an element in the original name. Indeed, the names MacEneaney and Bird were still being used interchangeably in the Kilmore district of Monaghan around 1900 (*see* Heaney).

Patrick MacEnaney of Co. Monaghan, who died in 1745, became commander-in-chief to the Emperor of Austria. One of his sons became counsellor of state for the empire, and the other, lord lieutenant of Flanders. When they died around 1800, their considerable fortune was left to their relatives in Monaghan.

The MacAneny spelling is more favoured in Tyrone, MacEneany in Monaghan and MacEneaney in Louth.

MACARDLE

This name, which was found to be twelfth most numerous in its homeland of Co. Monaghan in 1970, is almost exclusive to the south of that county, Armagh and Louth. The name in Gaelic was Mac Ardghail, from *ardghal,* meaning 'high valour'.

They are a branch of the MacMahons of Oriel, first noted as Sliocht Ardghail Mhóir Mhic Mathúna, 'the stock of Ardghal Mór MacMahon', who was chief of the MacMahons from 1402 to 1416. They were based originally in the barony of Monaghan and a branch became sub-chiefs in Armagh under the O'Neills of the Fews.

The early-eighteenth-century Gaelic poet James MacArdle was of the Fews district. He was a contemporary of poet Patrick MacAlinden who was married to the poet Siobhán Nic Ardghail (Johanna MacArdle).

MACAREE *see* MacGarry

MACATEER *see* MacIntyre

MACAULEY (*also* MacCauley)

Though found in Leinster and Connacht, these names are most common in Ulster, particularly in counties Antrim and Donegal. They can be of Scottish or Irish origin.

There are two origins for the name in Scotland. The MacAulays of Lewis in the Hebrides, a sept of Clan MacLeod, were in Gaelic Mac Amhlaibh, 'son of Amlaib'. This personal name, pronounced Auley, was the Gaelic form of the Norse Olafr or Olaf. These MacAulays are said to descend from Olave the Black, brother of Magnus, last king of Man and the Isles. (The MacLeods themselves descend from Leod, a son of Olave.)

The MacAulays of Ardincaple in Dumbartonshire are a minor branch of the royal Clan Alpin (of which MacGregor is the most senior). They were in Gaelic Mac Amhalghaidh and this obsolete Irish personal name was also pronounced Auley. A branch of the Dumbartonshire MacAulays came to the Glens of Antrim with the MacDonnells in the early sixteenth century and these are the ancestors of most of our MacAuleys, certainly in Co. Antrim. In the mid-nineteenth century MacAuley was the most common name in the barony of Lower Glenarm and was also very common in Carey.

In Ireland there were also two septs of MacAuley. Coincidentally, they had the same two Gaelic names in origin but were not related, either to each other or to the Scottish families. In counties Offaly and Westmeath lived the important and powerful sept of Mac Amhalghaidh, lords of what the English in Elizabethan times called McGawley's Country. However, in Ulster the name derived from the Mac Amhlaoibh sept whose name, like that of the Lewis MacAulays, derived from the Gaelic form of the Norse name Olaf. These are the descendants of Auley, a son of Donn Carrach Maguire, the first Maguire King of Fermanagh who died in 1302. It is thought that it was this Auley and his sons who first crossed the Erne and won south Fermanagh for the Maguires. The sept gave its name to the barony of Clanawley. The name in Fermanagh is mainly spelt MacCawley or MacCauley.

There are a great number of ways of spelling these names including, as well as those mentioned above, Cauley, Cawley, Gawley, Macauley, MacAwley, MacGawley and Magawley.

MACBRATNEY *see* Galbraith

MACBREARTY *see* MacCurdy

MACBRIDE

MacBride is much more common in Ulster than in the rest of Ireland, though a number can be found in Leinster. The name is most numerous in counties Donegal and Down and is also common in Co. Antrim. It can be of Irish or Scottish origin.

The name in Irish Gaelic is Mac Giolla Bhrighde, 'son of the devotee of (St) Brigid'. (St Brigid was abbess of Kildare and died in 525.) The Gaelic name gave rise to the variants Gilbride, MacGilbride, MacIlvreed, Mucklebreed and so on.

The homeland of the Ulster sept was Co. Donegal where the MacBrides were an important ecclesiastical family in the medieval period. The sept descends from Giolla Bríde Ó Dochartaigh and were erenaghs of

Raymunterdoney (a parish which includes Tory Island). Many of the name were bishops of Raphoe. From the seventeenth century on they were centred at Gweedore.

A branch of the sept early migrated to Co. Down and by the mid-seventeenth century MacBride was noted as a 'principal Irish name' in three baronies of that county. However, by the mid-nineteenth century their greatest concentration in Down was in the barony of Upper Iveagh, in the vicinity of Rathfriland. Livingstone suggests that the Monaghan MacBrides may be descended from a Giolla Bríde MacMahon.

Gilbride, MacBride and MacIlvride were also names of one of the septs of Clan Donald and were common in the Scottish Isles, particularly Arran. These take their name from Gillebride, the father of Somerled of Argyll. In the mid-nineteenth century the main Co. Antrim concentration of the name was found to be in the barony of Lower Dunluce, in an area adjacent to the Giant's Causeway.

One particularly talented Ulster family of the name included the Revd John MacBride, 1650–1715, author, David MacBride, 1726–78, doctor and inventor, and John David MacBride, 1778–1852, head of Magdalen College, Oxford. Co. Monaghan was the birthplace of the miniaturist Alexander MacBride, 1798–1857.

MACBRIEN *see* Breen

MACBURNEY *see* Burns

MACCABE

MacCabe is a common name in Leinster but is nearly twice as common in Ulster, its main centres being Co. Cavan and Co. Monaghan (where it is the sixth most numerous name). The most common Gaelic form of the name is Mac Cába, possibly from *cába*, a 'cape', although its exact derivation is not known.

The MacCabes are thought to have been a branch of the MacLeods of Harris in the Hebrides. They were brought from there in the fourteenth century as galloglasses, initially in the service of the O'Reillys and the O'Rourkes, the two main septs of the kingdom of Breffny. Their main headquarters was at Moyne Hall outside Cavan town. Melaghlin MacCabe, died 1424, was described as the 'Constable of the Two Breffnys'. They seem to have lost all connection with their original Scottish homeland and became a recognised Irish sept in their own right. Indeed the name is not now found in Scotland and the sept is only remembered in connection with their Irish activities.

At the same time as they arrived in Breffny they are first noted in Fermanagh, where they became Maguire's most important galloglasses. By 1580 they are listed among the five most powerful Fermanagh families and MacCabes were still fighting for the Maguires as late as the 1641 rising.

In Monaghan the MacCabes were galloglasses to MacMahon and they became an important family in MacMahon's Country, powerful especially in the baronies of Monaghan, Dartry and Farney. Though the leading families of the name in all these areas lost their estates after the Williamite war of the late seventeenth century, the name remained common in these localities.

The Belfastman William Putnam MacCabe, 1776–1821, a United Irishman, was a romantic figure famed for his disguises and mimicry. When captured by Scottish soldiers in 1798, he convinced them that he too was Scottish and that they had made a mistake. They released him. Cathaoir MacCabe, died 1740, was a bard of Co. Cavan and lifelong friend of Turlough O'Carolan, the famous blind harper and composer. As a practical joke, he hoaxed O'Carolan into believing that he had died, prompting O'Carolan to write a fine elegy about his friend. He himself wrote a famous elegy in Gaelic when O'Carolan died in 1738. The American Protestant bishop Charles Caldwell MacCabe, 1836–1906, was the grandson of a Tyrone man. He is most famous as Chaplain MacCabe of the American Civil War.

MACCAFFERTY

This name is exclusive to Ulster, where over a half are in Co. Donegal, a third in Co. Derry and most of the rest in Co. Antrim. It is in Gaelic Mac Eachmharcaigh, from *each,* 'horse', and *marcach,* 'rider'. The name originates in Co. Donegal, and the family is thought to be a branch of the O'Donnells, among whom the personal name Eachmarcach was popular. The name was also corrupted to MacCaffrey (*see* MacCaffrey) and was anglicised in a variety of forms.

In Co. Mayo it was made MacCafferky and elsewhere Cafferky, Cafferty, MacCagherty, MacCaharty, MacCaherty, MacCaugherty and MacCaverty. It was also corrupted to MacCarthy. At the start of the twentieth century MacCarthy was being used interchangeably with MacCagherty around Dromore, Co. Down, and with MacCaugherty near Greyabbey on the Ards peninsula. MacCaugherty has also been noted as a synonym of MacCartney in the Newtownards district of Co. Down.

MacCarthy, Gaelic Mac Cárthaigh, from *cártach,* 'loving', though the most common Irish Mac- name, is not numerous in Ulster and is found mainly in Belfast and its environs. The MacCarthys were one of the leading septs of Munster, where the vast majority of those of the name now reside.

MACCAFFREY

This name is almost exclusive to Ulster. It is the sixth most numerous name in its homeland, Co. Fermanagh, and is common too in Co. Tyrone and, to a lesser extent, in Co. Monaghan.

The MacCaffreys, Gaelic Mac Gafraidh, are a branch of the Maguires, being descended, like the Fermanagh MacCawleys (see MacAuley), from a son of Donn Carrach Maguire, died 1302, in this case Gafraigh or Godfrey. This is a Norse name which was early gaelicised in both Ireland and Scotland.

The family was originally based in the townland of Ballymacaffrey, parish of Aghavea, near Fivemiletown in Co. Tyrone, but in Fermanagh also it gave its name to Legmacaffry in Galloon and Rossmacaffry in Aghalurcher. By 1580 it was counted among the five most powerful families in Fermanagh. Tadhg MacCaffrey of Lurg led the MacCaffreys in the burning of Lisnarick, the first Fermanagh incident of the 1641 rising. Giolla Pádraig Modartha Mac Gafraidh, chief of the name, was a captain in Maguire's regiment and was killed in the Williamite war of the late seventeenth century.

Some of the name migrated south and in counties Cavan and Meath became Caffreys. (The variants Caffery and Cafferty are also found there.) MacCaffrey is also found in the forms MacCaghery and MacCahery and has been confused with the distinct name MacCafferty (see MacCafferty). Some MacCaffreys in Fermanagh became Beattys and Bettys (see Beattie).

MACCAIG see MacKeag

MACCALL (also MacCaul)

These names are almost exclusive to Ulster, where they are mainly found in the Armagh–Cavan–Monaghan area. They can be of several different origins, both Irish and Scottish.

The once numerous Co. Tyrone sept of Mac Cathmhaoil, pronounced MacCawell (see MacCawell), anglicised their name in a bewildering variety of ways, including MacCaul, MacCall and MacHall. These last two are also anglicised forms of the Donegal and Cavan name MacCahill, Gaelic Mac Cathail. In *The Monaghan Story* Livingstone suggests that most of the Monaghan MacCauls were likely to have been originally

Mac Colla and a branch of the MacMahons, 'Colla being a very common name with the MacMahons'.

In Scotland MacAll, MacCall and MacCaul also derive from the Gaelic Mac Cathail, 'son of Cathal'. The names were common in Ayrshire and the Lowlands. The M'Calls were a family of long standing in Nithsdale in Dumfriesshire but elsewhere in that county the Maccalls, a branch of the MacAulays, were settled from about the end of the fifteenth century. There were MacCalls or MacColls, a branch of Clan Donald, who nevertheless were much more closely associated with the Stewarts of Appin (see Coll). MacCall has been noted as a synonym of Caulfield (see Caulfield).

MACCALLEN see MacCallion

MACCALLION (also Killen, MacAllen, MacCallen and MacKillen)

These names have been brought together here because they represent, in their different forms, descendants of the Campbell galloglasses of Argyll-shire who came to Ulster in the sixteenth century to fight, as mercenaries, for the O'Donnells of Donegal (see Campbell). There remains, however, much work to be done to unravel their respective histories.

Firstly, it must be said that there are no septs of Clan Campbell registered under these names. Further, Gerard Hayes-McCoy, in the definitive account, *Scots Mercenary Forces in Ireland (1565–1603)*, refers to all these galloglasses simply as Campbells. (He makes one passing reference to a Lauchlan MacAllen, a Campbell of Argyll, who was with O'Cahan [see Kane] in the Route in north Antrim in 1567.) MacLysaght and others, for their part, have simply listed the different names under their different Gaelic forms, referring to each as a branch of the Campbells, galloglasses to the O'Donnells.

MacCallion is an exclusively Ulster name found mainly in counties Donegal and Derry. It is rendered in Gaelic Mac Cailín, and Bally-macallion in Co. Derry takes its name from this family. Variants include MacCallan, MacCallen, MacKellian and MacKillion.

MacCallan is the Co. Fermanagh form of MacCallion and was often further anglicised to Collins (see Collins). Peadar Livingstone, author of *The Fermanagh Story,* claims that this is in fact Gaelic Mac Coileáin, from *coileán,* a 'whelp', a name also made MacCullion.

MacAllen, Gaelic Mac Ailín, from *ail,* a 'rock', is another form of the name of this Campbell connection, confused historically with and still noted as a synonym of MacCallion (Mac Cailín). Variants are MacAllion and MacEllen. (But see Allen for other MacAllen origins.)

Killen and MacKillen are names rendered in Gaelic as Mac Coilín. Killen is most common in counties Antrim and Down, and MacKillen is almost exclusive to Co. Antrim. Variants include Collin, Collins, Cullian, MacCullion and so on, and the names have been confused with MacCullen and MacQuillan.

Lastly, it must be said that many Campbells, especially in the northwest, are of this connection and have either retained the name Campbell down through the generations or have reverted to it from one of the above.

George Black, in *The Surnames of Scotland,* states that Cailean or Cailin, usually anglicised as Colin, was 'a personal name more or less peculiar to the Campbells, the chief being always in Gaelic Mac Cailein'. This may go some way to unravelling the Campbell origins of at least MacCallan, MacCallion and MacKillen.

MACCANN

Though most numerous in Ulster, where it is among the fifty most common names, MacCann is also common in Leinster and Connacht. In Ulster it is common in counties Armagh, Antrim and Tyrone. It is among the ten most numerous names in Co. Armagh, its homeland, and has long been associated with the shores of Lough Neagh. The Gaelic form of the name is Mac Cana, but it is disputed whether this was originally Mac Anna, 'son of Annadh', or Mac Cana, from *cano,* a 'wolf cub'.

The MacCanns were Lords of Clanbrassil, a district on the southern shores of Lough Neagh and comprising the present-day baronies of Oneilland East and Oneilland West in Co. Armagh and part of the barony of Middle Dungannon in Tyrone.

This district was previously controlled by the O'Garveys, but it is not known when the MacCanns took over. It was certainly in their possession in 1155 when the Annals of the Four Masters note the death of Amhlaibh Mac Canna and praised the strong drink he had made from the apples of his Armagh orchard. Donnell MacCanna was still styled Chief of Clanbrassil in 1598.

It is interesting, given their connections with Lough Neagh, that Abraham Hume's survey of 1857 found the MacCanns of Co. Antrim 'almost entirely in the barony of Upper Toome', that is, at the north of the lough.

Around 1900 MacCann was being used interchangeably with the Monaghan name Mackin, Gaelic Mac Maicín, in the Newry district of Co. Down. A few of the Oriel sept of MacCannon or MacConnon also anglicised to MacCann (*see* Canning).

MACCARROLL *see* Carroll

MACCARRON

This is an almost exclusively Ulster name, associated mainly with counties Donegal and Derry and with the north of Co. Monaghan.

In the northwest Carron and MacCarron are anglicisations of the Tirconnell name Mac Cearáin, a sept of the Cenél Eoghain. However, all references to the name in the period before 1600 are outside Ulster and are to the MacCarrons, Gaelic Mac Carrghamhna, a sept of the southern Uí Néill based in Co. Westmeath. The head of the sept was referred to as Chief of Maol an tSinna (Chief of the Shannon).

Livingstone suggests that MacCarron could also be originally Mac Cairthinn, the name of a sept who originated along the Foyle in Co. Derry and later moved to the Monaghan district. MacCarn is a variant form there. The MacCarrons of north Monaghan have long been associated with the Ballivikgarran district in Donagh.

MACCARRY *see* MacGarry

MACCARTAN

Apart from a few MacCartans in Dublin and Connacht, this is an exclusively Ulster name, found mainly in its homeland Co. Down and in Co. Armagh.

The name was originally in Gaelic Mac Artáin, 'son of Artán', a diminutive or pet form of Art. The MacCartans take their name from their ancestor Artán, a great-grandson of Mongán MacGuinness of Iveagh in Co. Down. Though normally subordinate to the MacGuinnesses, the MacCartans were, for a short period in the mid-fourteenth century, lords of Iveagh. Generally, however, they were chiefs of Kinelarty, a district, now a barony, in central Down, and were tributaries to the O'Neills.

At the beginning of the twentieth century MacCartney was being used interchangeably with MacCartan in Co. Down, around Newry and Clough, and with MacCarten around Moira (*see* MacCartney).

MACCARTNEY

In Ireland the name MacCartney is almost exclusive to Ulster where two-thirds of those of the name are in Co. Antrim. Though it is thought to be originally an Irish name and it is used as a synonym for current Irish names, most in Ulster will be of Scottish stock.

It is accepted in Scotland that MacCartney, Gaelic Mac Cartáine, is a variant of the Irish name MacCartan, Gaelic Mac Artáin, 'son of Artán', a diminutive of Art (*see* MacCartan). MacLysaght states that the name is that of a sept of Clan Mackintosh. There were MacCardney septs of both Clan Mackintosh and Clan Farquharson but their name was a variant of MacHardy. However, the Mackintosh MacCardney did become MacCartnay in its homeland of Fife, and it is possible that a few of the name in Ulster will be of this origin.

However, most of the Scottish MacCartneys were not from Fife, but from the Stewartry, Ayrshire, Dumfriesshire, Wigtownshire and so on. The name is recorded as common in these areas from the early sixteenth century and its origins before that are obscure. It is presumed from its Gaelic form that the name is Irish. The Macartneys of Auchinleck in Ayrshire are an old family and the MacCartneys of Co. Antrim descend from them.

Captain George Macartney of Auchinleck, 1626–91, came to the Ballymoney district in 1649 and acquired property — it is not known how — at Lissanoure, where he built a castle. He became surveyor general of the province of Ulster and, as captain of his troop, proclaimed King William and Queen Mary at Belfast in 1688. The family prospered and many of his descendants were high sheriffs of Antrim. In 1878 the MacCartneys of Lissanoure Castle owned over 12,000 acres of land in Co. Antrim and the MacArtneys of Tyrone were also substantial landlords. George, 1st Earl Maccartney, 1735–1808, had a distinguished career in the British foreign service, the height of which was his appointment as ambassador to the Emperor of China.

James MacCartney, 1770–1843, born in Ulster, was a famous surgeon in his day and a prominent member of the United Irishmen.

Around 1900 MacCartney was being used interchangeably with MacCartan in Co. Down, in Newry and Clough, with MacCarten in Moira, with MacCaugherty (see MacCafferty) in Newtownards, with MacCarthy near Newry and with Mulhartagh in the Ballyshannon district of Co. Donegal. Mulhartagh is a Tyrone name, in Gaelic Ó Maolfhathartaigh.

MACCAUGHAN *see* MacCaughey

MACCAUGHEY (*also* Caughey, Hackett, MacCaughan, MacGahey *and* MacGaughey)

Caughey, MacCahey, MacCaughey, MacGahey and MacGaughey all derive from the Gaelic Mac Eachaidh. Eachaidh is an old personal name anglicised as Aghy. (Haughey is based on the same personal name.) Aghy is a variant of the older personal name Oghy (Eochaigh). Other variants of the surname are Cahey, MacAghy and MacCaghey. MacCaughan and

MacCahon both derive from a different name, Mac Eacháin, but many of the name have become MacCaugheys.

All these names are virtually exclusive to Ulster but stem from different regions. MacCaughey and MacCahey are Tyrone names also found in Co. Antrim. Caughey is found mainly in Co. Down, where it is most common on the Ards peninsula but also in Co. Antrim. MacGahey is found mainly in counties Monaghan and Antrim and MacGaughey in Armagh and Antrim. MacCaughan and MacCahon are from Co. Antrim and north Co. Derry and some of the name there claim that they were originally O'Cahans of the Route (see Kane).

Sir Samuel McCaughey, 1835–1919, the 'Sheep King', was born near Ballymena, Co. Antrim. He emigrated to Australia, where he rose from being a 'jackeroo', or apprentice on a sheep station, to one of the wealthiest men in the country, his business at one stage sheering one million sheep a year.

Hackett is an English name, in Ulster most common in counties Tyrone and Armagh, where it is used as a synonym of MacCahey and MacGahey.

MACCAUL see MacCall

MACCAULEY see MacAuley

MACCAUSLAND

This Co. Antrim name is in Ireland almost exclusive to Ulster. It is connected with Buchanan.

The Clan Buchanan claims to have been founded in the eleventh century by an Irishman, one Ausalan Buoy O'Kayn (thought to be one of the O'Cahans of the Route – see Kane). However, the first of the name on record is one Absalon, son of Macbethe, who received a charter for the island of Clarines in 1225. This was Clarinch in Loch Lomond, later the gathering place of the Buchanans. MacCausland is taken in Scotland to mean 'son of Absalon'.

Though always associated with Clan Buchanan, the MacAuslans are not counted a sept of that clan, having always maintained a separate clan identity under their own chief, known as the Baron MacAuslan.

The name came to Co. Tyrone in the seventeenth century. The MacCauslands of Dreenagh, Co. Derry, descend from the Macauslans of Dumbartonshire and have had an unbroken connection with Limavady since 1729.

MACCAWELL

This is actually a rare name now, but it is recorded here because it is the closest anglicised form of the Co. Tyrone sept name Mac Cathmhaoil (from *cathmhaol*, meaning 'battle chief') once important and numerous and now disguised under a welter of anglicised forms.

The MacCawells were a sept of the Cenél Eoghain and as such descended ultimately from the fifth-century king, Niall of the Nine Hostages, founder of the Uí Néill dynasty. The first of the name on record (in the Annals of Ulster) was Donnchadh Mac Cathmail, slain in 1180. The MacCawells were also the leading sept of Cenél Fearadaigh, based at Clogher, and at the height of their power in the twelfth century they controlled a large portion of Co. Tyrone and had penetrated deep into Co. Fermanagh. They were one of the seven powerful septs supporting O'Neill. By the mid-fourteenth century their power in Fermanagh had been broken by the Maguires and their influence gradually declined thereafter.

In controlling the seat of power of the Clogher diocese, many were noted as ecclesiastics. From the mid-fourteenth to the mid-sixteenth centuries they provided two bishops to Clogher and numerous abbots, deans, canons and so on, to that diocese as well as to Derry and Armagh. It seems clear that a mass migration of Mac Cathmhaoil occurred in the late sixteenth century, for the name suddenly becomes common in Down and Armagh in the records of that time.

Though the names of the other Cenél Eoghain septs like Devlin, Gormley, Hagan, Quin and so on, all survived, Mac Cathmhaoil, except for a few MacCawells, did not, and the families adopted various anglicisations. These include Campbell, Caulfield and MacCall (*see* each of these names) and Alwell, Alwill, Callwell, Carlos, Cawell, Howell, MacCaul, (Mac)Corless, (Mac)Cowell, (Mac)Cowhill and MacHall.

The Co. Tyrone name MacGirr (*also* MacGerr, MacKerr and Short), originating in the Clogher Valley, represents a branch of Mac Cathmhaoil. They descend from the fourteenth-century Maelechlainn mac an ghirr meic Cathmhaoil, 'Malachy, the son of the short fellow MacCawell'. The form 'Short' is a direct translation.

MACCLEAN (*also* MacLean)

These two names, found in Ulster in virtually equal numbers, are Scottish in origin and represent descendants of Clan Maclean galloglasses who were brought to the province in the late sixteenth century. Though well known in every province of Ireland, they are most common in Ulster where they are found mainly in counties Antrim and Derry.

The name was originally, in Scots Gaelic, Mac Gille Eoin, 'son of the servant of (St) John' and Clan Maclean, or Clan Gillean as they are known, descend from the thirteenth-century Gilleathain na Tuaidh, 'Gillean of the Battle-axe'. His son, who settled in Lorn, signed the Ragman Roll in

1296 as Gillemoir Macilyn. Gillemoir's great-grandson Ian Dhu Maclean settled in Mull. Of his sons, Lachlan Lubanach was progenitor of the Macleans of Duart, chiefly house of Clan Maclean, and Eachin Reganach was progenitor of the Maclaines of Lochbuie.

Initially followers of MacDougall, Lord of Lorn, the two brothers left him and became followers of the MacDonald Lords of the Isles. They were granted a large territory in Mull and by the end of the fifteenth century the Macleans owned most of Mull and Tiree and extensive lands on Islay, Jura and Scarba, and in Knapdale and Morvern in Argyllshire and Lochaber in Inverness-shire. There were then four branches of the clan: Macleans of Duart, Maclaines of Lochbuie and Macleans of Ardgour and of Coll, both cadets of Duart. The chiefs of the clan had their seat at Duart Castle, a massive fortress on Mull.

In the sixteenth century, after the forfeiture of the lordship of the Isles, the various followers of the MacDonalds became independent clans and many hired themselves out as mercenaries. The Macleans who came to Ulster were Macleans of Duart, brought over initially by the O'Donnells, but quickly taken up by the O'Neills. Unlike the earlier galloglasses, they did not settle as one cohesive unit, but enough individuals did settle in Ulster, particularly in Antrim and Derry, to have had an impact on the province's surname structure.

In Scotland at the beginning of the seventeenth century the Macleans were closely allied to the Campbells of Argyll, but by the end of the century, having fought against the Williamite army at the Battle of Killiecrankie in 1689, they were destroyed by, and lost their lands to, the Campbells. The clan scattered and many emigrated to the new world. It can be presumed that some at least came to Ulster. The name is found as MacAlean, MacClane, MacClean, MacLaine, MacLean and so on.

MacLysaght claims that James Maclaine, 1724–50, the 'Gentleman Highwayman', was born in Co. Monaghan. He robbed Lord Eglinton on Hounslow Heath and Horace Walpole in Hyde Park (for which he was executed).

MACCLEARY (also Cleary and MacCleery)

Each of these names can be of Irish or Scottish origin and it will be difficult to distinguish an individual's heritage without a confirmed family tree. The MacClearys and MacCleerys are most common in counties Antrim and Derry and the Clearys and Clerys in Co. Cavan.

To take MacCleary first, the name in this form and in the forms MacChlery and MacClery is common in Scotland where it derives from the

Gaelic Mac an Chleirich, meaning 'son of the clerk', that is, 'cleric'. There were several different families of this name: MacChlry, MacClerie or Maclerie, septs of Clan Mackintosh; MacChlery or Maclerie of Clan Macpherson; MacClery or Maclerie of Clan Cameron; and MacChlery of Clan Campbell. But there was, in Ireland, a sept of MacAlearys, Gaelic Mac Giolla Arraith, a branch of the O'Haras of Sligo, who migrated with them to Co. Antrim and changed their name to MacCleary. Also the Ulster name Mac an Chléirigh, meaning the same as the Scots form, became MacCleary especially in counties Cavan and Monaghan.

The Irish name O'Clery, in Gaelic Ó Cléirigh, also from *cléireach*, meaning a 'clerk' or 'cleric', dates from the middle of the tenth century, and this makes it one of Ireland's oldest hereditary surnames. The name originated in Connacht, where the eponymous ancestor was Cléireach, born *c.* 820, of the line of Guaire the Hospitable, King of Connacht. The O'Clerys were early driven out of their homeland and branches settled in many parts of Ireland, the most important being the great literary sept of the name in Donegal and Derry. A branch also settled in Co. Cavan.

All these names were anglicised most often to Clarke (*see* Clarke). In Scotland they were also made Clarkson and in Ireland, also Clerkin.

Two daughters of an Irish merchant in Marseilles, Julie and Désirée Cleary, became respectively queens of Spain and Sweden under Napoleon.

MACCLEERY *see* MacCleary

MACCLELLAND

Though found in Leinster and Munster, this Scottish Lowland name is common only in Ulster, where it is fairly well distributed, main centres being in counties Antrim, Down, Armagh, Derry and Monaghan.

The name in Scotland was in Gaelic originally Mac Gille Fhaolain, 'son of the devotee of (St) Fillan'. It is recorded as numerous in Galloway (whence hailed so many of our Plantation settlers) from the end of the fourteenth century. Its original anglicised form was Maclellan and the family gave their name to Balmaclellan in the Stewartry.

Sir Robert McClelland of Kirkcudbrightshire was one of the nine Scottish chief undertakers of the Plantation of Ulster. He was initially granted lands in the baronies of Boylagh and Banagh in Donegal but sold his property there to John Murray in 1616. He married a Montgomery and settled in the old O'Neill lands in Down to which he brought many of his MacClelland relatives as tenants. He leased lands in Derry adjoining the portions of the London guilds of Haberdashers and of Clothworkers and administered them from his castle at Ballycastle in Co. Antrim. At the time of Petty's 'census' in 1659 the name MacClelland was most numerous in the baronies of Keenaght and Coleraine in Derry and (as MacClellan) in the Co. Antrim barony of Belfast.

In the mid-nineteenth century the main Co. Antrim concentration of the name was in the barony of Upper Antrim, and in Down in the barony of Upper Iveagh, especially near Banbridge, with Cleland mainly found in the parish of Kilmore in Upper Castlereagh.

The name is also found in the forms MacClellan, MacLellan, MacLelland, Gilliland, and so on.

MACCLENAGHAN (*also* MacLenaghan)

These names, in Ireland found almost exclusively in counties Antrim and Derry, can be of Irish or Scottish origin. It is recorded in the O'Neill Country of sixteenth-century Tyrone as Mac Leanacháin. However, it was once (as MacClannachan, MacClenaghan and so on) a common name in the Scottish province of Galloway, from which so many Plantation settlers stemmed. There it was originally in Scots Gaelic Mac Gille Onchon, 'son of the devotee of (St) Onchú'. It was first recorded in Carrick, Ayrshire in 1513. Both the Irish and Scottish forms of the name have been shortened to Lenaghan, Lenahan and so on, but these can also be from the Roscommon name Ó Leannacháin which has also been anglicised to Leonard (*see* Leonard).

MACCLINTOCK

In Ireland the MacClintocks are found almost exclusively in Ulster and in particular in counties Antrim and Derry. The name was originally in Scots Gaelic Mac Ghille Fhionndaig, 'son of the devotee of (St) Fintan'. The MacClintocks stem from Luss in Dumbartonshire and Lorn in Argyllshire and were first recorded at the beginning of the sixteenth century. As early as 1611 MacClintocks in Scotland began anglicising their name as Lindsay (*see* Lindsay). One at least of the name was in Ulster before the Plantation, a MacClintock of Argyllshire, who was settled in Donegal as early as 1597.

MACCLOSKEY (*also* Glasgow *and* MacCluskey)

MacCluskeys are found in Dublin (of Ulster origin) but apart from these MacCloskey, Glasgow and MacCluskey are found almost exclusively in Ulster. MacCloskey is most common in Co. Derry, where it is among the ten most numerous names, and MacCluskey in Co. Antrim.

The names were originally Mac Bhloscaidh, a branch of the O'Kanes, and descend from one Bloskey O'Cahan recorded in the annals as slayer of Murtagh O'Loughlin and heir to the throne of Ireland in 1196 (*see* Kane). At the time of the first Ordnance Survey in the early nineteenth century the MacCloskeys constituted nearly two-thirds of the population of the parish of Dungiven in Co. Derry, and by-names such as Roe MacCloskey, More MacCloskey and Dimond MacCloskey were needed to distinguish them.

In Ulster and especially Tyrone the Scottish toponymics Glasgow and MacGlasgow have been noted as variants of MacCloskey.

MACCLOY *see* Fullerton

MACCLURE

In Ireland this is a rare name outside Ulster where it is most numerous in counties Antrim and Down. Most in Ulster will be of Scottish origin, but even these may well have been of Irish origin in the more remote past.

There was a small Oriel sept of counties Armagh and Monaghan called in Gaelic Mac Giolla Uidhir. Eugene MacGillaweer, Archbishop of Armagh from 1206 to 1216, was of this sept. The name was anglicised to MacAleer, MacClure, MacLure and, because of its sound, to Weir (*see* Weir).

In Scotland the name MacClure and its variant MacAlear have long been recorded as common in the province of Galloway, home to many Irish names that made their way across the Irish Sea from Down and Antrim. The name was in Scots Gaelic Mac Gille Uidhir, and meant, like its Ulster counterpart, 'son of Odhar's servant'. It seems possible therefore that the Galloway MacClures were originally of Irish stock.

There was also a sept of Clan MacLeod of Harris called MacClure from the Scots Gaelic Mac Gille Leabhair, 'son of the servant of the book'. It has been suggested that some of the MacClures of Co. Derry may be of this origin.

MACCLUSKEY *see* MacCloskey

MACCOMB *see* Holmes *and* Thompson

MACCONAGHY *see* Donaghy

MACCONKEY *see* Donaghy

MACCONNELL *see* Connell

MACCONVILLE

This is an Irish name, in Gaelic Mac Conmhaoil, almost exclusive to Ulster and most common in its homelands of counties Armagh and Down. After the defeat of James II in 1690 six of the name in Co. Down were attainted and lost their lands. In the sixteenth century it was rendered MacConwall and this, along with Conwell (especially in Co. Donegal) and Coville, are forms still found.

Armagh man, the Most Reverend Henry Conwell, 1748–1842, vicar general of Armagh for forty years, was made Bishop of Philadelphia in 1820.

MACCOOL *see* Coyle

MACCORMACK *see* MacCormick

MACCORMICK (*also* MacCormack)

MacCormick, if taken on its own, constitutes one of the fifty most common names in the province. MacCormack is much less numerous but is none the less common. Both names can be of Irish or Scottish origin and the difference in the ending is irrelevant in determining which. Both derive from the Gaelic name Cormac. In Ulster the names are most common in counties Antrim and Down.

In Scotland the name derives from one of the Gaelic forms Mac Cormaic, Mac Cormaig or Mac Chormaig. As a generalisation the -ick spelling was more common in the Highlands, the most famous sept being followers of Maclaine of Lochbuie on the Island of Mull (*see* MacClean) but there were MacCormacks, followers of Clan Buchanan, on Loch Lomondside.

In Ireland the name sprang up independently in a variety of places, adopted by individuals whose father was called Cormac. The only MacCormick connection of any importance was that of Fermanagh. It is thought that these were a branch of the Maguires and were centred at Kilmacormick, 'MacCormick's wood'.

In counties Down and Derry MacCormack is sometimes originally O'Cormack or O'Cormacan. In mid-nineteenth-century Co. Antrim MacCormick was found almost exclusively in the barony of Carey. At the same time in Down it was almost exclusive to the Ards peninsula. (The name was established in Portaferry as early as 1678.)

Dr Robert MacCormack, 1800–90, the Arctic navigator, was of Co. Tyrone parentage.

MACCORRY *see* Corry

MACCOURT

Though found in the other provinces of Ireland, this is an Ulster name and is most common in counties Antrim, Armagh and Monaghan. The name was originally that of an Oriel sept, in Gaelic Mac Cuarta or Mac Cuairt, which was based in southwest Armagh. In the seventeenth-century Hearth Money Rolls of that county it was spelt MacQuorte. The most famous of the name was Séamus Mac Cuarta, 1647–1732, also known as James MacCourt or Courtney, Gaelic poet and friend of Turlough O'Carolan, the famous blind harper and composer. The parish of Cappagh, near Dungannon in Co. Tyrone, was originally Ceapach Mhic Cuarta. The English name Courtney has been recorded as an anglicisation of the name, especially in Co. Monaghan.

MacCourt and the variants MacCord and MacCoard are old names long associated with the parish of Ballintrae in Ayrshire but their origin is not known. Some of our Ulster MacCourts may be of this connection.

MACCOY

MacCoy is a well-known name in Leinster and is found too in Munster and Connacht but it is common only in Ulster, where it is found mainly in counties Antrim, Armagh and Monaghan. It is a variant of the Scottish name MacKay, Gaelic Mac Aoidh, 'son of Hugh' (*see* MacKay).

Most of the name in Ulster descend from the MacKay–MacCoy gallo-glasses brought from Kintyre to fight for the MacDonnells of the Glens of Antrim. The Kintyre MacKays were followers of Clan Donald and it is disputed whether they had any connection with the Clan Mackay of Sutherland.

There will also be some MacCoys, for instance in Fermanagh and Donegal, that were originally Mac Aodha, more usually anglicised MacHugh, a branch of the O'Flahertys in Connemara (*see* MacHugh).

The Ulster Gaelic poet Art MacCoy or MacCooey, *c.* 1715–74, was not of either of these origins, his name in Gaelic being Mac Cubhthaigh.

As late as 1900 the name MacCoy was still being used interchangeably with MacCay near Castlederg, Co. Tyrone, with MacKay around Monaghan town and in Newry, Co. Down, and with MacKie in the Bally-shannon district of Co. Donegal.

MACCRACKEN

In Ireland MacCracken is almost exclusive to Ulster, where half of those of the name are in Co. Antrim and a quarter are in Co. Down. It is a variant of the Argyllshire clan name MacNaughten, Gaelic Mac Neachdainn, 'son of Nechtan' (*see* MacKnight) which was early found in Galloway. From there it came to Ulster in the post-Plantation period.

In the mid-nineteenth century it seems to have been well distributed in Co. Antrim, but in Down it was particularly concentrated in the central Ards peninsula.

Henry Joy McCracken, 1767–98, born in High Street, Belfast, of Huguenot ancestry, commanded the United Irishmen at the Battle of Antrim and for his part in the 1798 rebellion was hanged at Belfast market house.

MACCREA

In Ireland this name is almost exclusive to Ulster, where it is most common in counties Antrim and Tyrone. In the forms MacCrae, MacCrea, MacRee and so on, it is found in Ayrshire and is a variant of the name Macrae, Gaelic Mac-raith. This is one of the very few Gaelic names that is not a patronymic. Like Mac-betha, which means 'son of life', Mac-raith does not refer to a father's name but was a personal name in itself. It means 'son of grace or prosperity' and is thought to have sprung up independently in various parts of Scotland at different times.

However, there is a Clan Macrae who, though recognised as a clan in their own right, were, from the fourteenth century, followers of MacKenzie of Kintail in Wester Ross. They were hereditary bodyguards to the chief of Clan MacKenzie and were known as 'MacKenzie's Shirt of Mail'. The clan name has been variously spelt Macra, Macrach, Macrae, Macraith, Maccraw and so on.

In Ulster, as in Scotland, the name has often been shortened to Rea (*see* Rea).

MACCREADY

Apart from some of the name in Dublin, MacCready is found exclusively in Ulster where it originates. It is most common in counties Down, Derry and Antrim. The name is in Irish Mac Riada and should be properly MacReedy, but the 'c' sound was carried over from the Mac- prefix.

Mac Riada was the name of a Donegal sept who were erenaghs of the church lands of Tulloughobegley in the barony of Kilmacrenan. Of this sept was Donagh MacReidy or MacCready of Coleraine, Dean of Derry, who was martyred for his faith in 1608 by being pulled apart by four horses. The Derry name Mac Conriada, more usually anglicised as Mac-Conready and MacAready, has also been made MacCready.

Some of the name in Ulster will be of Scottish origin, for the form MacRedie is found in Ayrshire, and the forms MacReadie and MacCreadie, are found in Galloway. But in Scotland it is of Irish origin, the first of the name being Andrew Macredie, Provost of Stranrawer (now Stranraer), an Irishman.

MACCREESH *see* MacGuinness

MACCRORY (*also* Rodgers *and* Rogers)

Rodgers and Rogers are English names often found in Scotland and together they constitute one of the most numerous British names in Ireland. Roger was a common personal name in medieval England and Scotland and derives, through the Old French Roger, from the Old German Rodger, meaning 'fame spear'. The surname, with the 's' appended, means simply 'son of Roger'. Rodger as a personal name and Rodgers as a surname are the more common spellings in Scotland. Many of these names in Ulster, most common in counties Down and Antrim, will be of English or Scottish stock.

However, in Ireland the Gaelic name Mac Ruaidhrí, anglicised as MacCrory, MacGrory, MacRory, Magrory and so on, sprang up in many different areas as a simple patronymic, meant to last for one generation — 'Rory's son'. Where the name stuck and was passed on, most at a later stage adopted the name Rogers or Rodgers. Even as late as 1900 Rogers and Rodgers were being used interchangeably with MacGrory, Macrory and Magrory around Cavan town; with MacCrory near Blackwaterstown, Co. Armagh, and Dungannon and Strabane in Co. Tyrone; with MacGrory around Enniskillen, Co. Fermanagh, and Kilkeel, Co. Down; and with MacRory in Dungannon, and in the Draperstown district of Co. Derry. MacCrory in Ireland is virtually exclusive to Ulster, where over half are in Tyrone and a third are in Co. Antrim.

However, there were two MacRory septs in Ulster. One of them, a branch of Clann Colla, was based originally in Tyrone from where a branch early migrated to Co. Derry. There they became erenaghs of the church lands of Ballynascreen in the barony of Loughinsholin. The other sept were erenaghs of Machaire Croise in Fermanagh and were probably a branch of the Maguires.

MacCrory is also a Scottish name, a variant of MacRory, Scots Gaelic Mac Ruairidh. These were an important sept of Clan Donald who also anglicised their name to MacGorry, MacRuer, MacRury and Rorison. Some in Ulster, particularly in Antrim where the MacDonald influence is most felt, will be of this stock. Several MacDonald MacRory families came to Ulster as galloglasses in the early fourteenth century, probably in connection with the invasion of Edward Bruce. It is possible that a few of the name in Ulster descend from these.

MACCULLAGH *see* MacCullough

MACCULLOUGH (*also* Cully, MacCullagh *and* MacCully)

Taken together the origins of these native Ulster and Scottish Planter names are a little complicated. MacCullough and MacCullagh together constitute one of the fifty most common names in Ulster and 80 per cent of those of the name in Ireland are of that province. The names are most numerous in counties Antrim, Tyrone and Down.

The Ulster Gaelic names Mac Cú Uladh or Mac Con Uladh, both meaning 'son of the hound of Ulster', were anglicised as MacCullagh. (The name also gave rise to Coloe, Coloo, MacAnaul, MacAnulla, MacNaul and MacNully, but *see also* MacNally.) In Petty's 'census' of 1659 MacCullough was listed as one of the 'principal Irish names' in the Co. Antrim baronies of Antrim, Belfast, Carrickfergus and Toome and also in the barony of Lower Iveagh in Down. However, many of these must have been Scottish. By the mid-nineteenth century the name in Co. Antrim was concentrated in the east of the barony of Lower Antrim.

Many of the Ulster MacCulloughs stem originally from Scotland, where the name is spelt MacCulloch. These MacCulloughs can be of two origins. MacCulloch is and was common in the province of Galloway, whence stemmed so many of the Ulster settlers. Its origins, however, are totally obscure, and although it has been suggested that it derives from the Scots Gaelic Mac Cullaich, meaning 'son of the boar', it is possible that it too derives from Mac Con Uladh and represents previous Irish settlers in Galloway.

Either way, it is known that it makes its first appearance in the Scottish records in 1296, when Thomas Maculagh del counte de Wiggetone (now Wigtown) rendered homage to Edward I. His family later held castles at Gatehouse of Fleet in Kirkcudbrightshire, and Creetown and Port William in Wigtownshire. It was in Galloway that the softened form MacCully arose, though it is also found in Tyrone as a variant of the Ulster name MacCullagh. (Cully as a native Ulster name can derive from MacCullagh, especially in Tyrone, or from O'Cully, Gaelic Ó Colla, a name from counties Armagh and Antrim.) Also in Wigtownshire, many of the Kellys and MacKellys changed their name to MacCulloch (*see* Kelly).

Yet another connection of MacCulloughs, those of Oban in Argyllshire, belonged to Clan Dougall and were originally called MacLulich. This name, in Gaelic Mac Lulaich, meant 'son of Lulach' (an obsolete personal name derived from the Old Gaelic *lu* and *laogh,* meaning 'little calf'). The progenitor of this family was MacCulloch Lulach, the son of Gillacomgan, Mormaer of Moray. MacCulloch Lulach became King of Scots when (notwithstanding Shakespeare's account) he succeeded MacBeth. Within a matter of months, however, he too was killed and was succeeded by

Malcolm Canmore, *c.* 1157.

James MacCulloch of Wigtownshire was one of the fifty Scottish undertakers of the Ulster Plantation and in 1610 he was granted 1000 acres in Glenties in Donegal. Though he lost his grant four years later, he and his tenants remained.

In Ulster about one-third use the -agh ending and most of the remainder the -ough, although MacCullow and MacCulloch are also found. The -ough spelling is very much more common in counties Antrim and Down, but it must be remembered that the spellings do not necessarily denote the origins of any particular family.

The Co. Donegal name Mac Colla (*see* Coll) has no connection with MacCullough or MacCullagh.

James MacCullagh, 1809–47, a brilliant mathematician and physicist, was born in Upper Badoney, Co. Tyrone. His suicide at the young age of thirty-eight was thought to have been caused by a fit of madness brought on by overwork. John Edward MacCullagh, 1837–85, who became a famous actor in the USA, was born in Coleraine, Co. Derry.

MACCULLY *see* MacCullough

MACCURDY (*also* MacBrearty *and* MacMurtry)

In Ireland, apart from a few MacCurdys in Co. Derry, the name is found exclusively in Co. Antrim, as is MacMurtry. MacBrearty, an exclusively Ulster name, is most common in counties Tyrone and Donegal.

These three names, and also MacMurty, were all originally in Gaelic Mac Muircheartaigh, from Muircheartach or Murtagh, meaning 'sea ruler'. MacCurdy is common on the islands of Arran and Bute, where it is a variant of MacMurtrie, a sept of Clan Stuart of Bute. In the fifteenth century the MacKurerdys, as they were then called, owned most of Bute. MacCurdy and its variants are still found on Bute but have now disappeared from Arran, Kintyre and the Isles, having become Currie (*see* Currie).

Across the North Channel, MacCurdy is a well-known Rathlin name, having been for centuries the most common name on the island. It is common too in the Glens and on the north coast of Antrim, to which it probably came with the Stewarts when they arrived at Ballintoy, having lost their lands in Bute in the mid-sixteenth century.

MacBrearty has the same form in Gaelic but is most likely Irish. MacMurty may have the same Irish origin but has become lost in the Scots MacMurtry.

MACCUSKER *see* Cosgrove

MACCUTCHEON *see* Houston

MACDAID (*also* MacDevitt *and* MacKevitt)

In Ireland MacDaid and MacDevitt are virtually exclusive to Ulster. Over half the MacDaids are in Co. Donegal and most of the rest are divided equally between counties Derry and Tyrone. The variant MacKevitt is exclusive to counties Louth, Monaghan and Down.

The MacDaids, Gaelic Mac Daibhéid, were a Donegal sept, a branch of the O'Dohertys. They take their name from Dáibhidh Ó Dochartaigh, died 1208, a chief of the Cenél Eoghain (*see* Doherty). The name means 'son of David' and was anglicised Davey, Davis, Davison, Davitt, Devitt, MacDaid, MacDavitt and MacDevitt (*see* Davidson *and* Davis). In the kingdom of Oriel the name in Gaelic was Mac Dhaibhéid. The 'h' after the 'D' makes it silent thus making the name sound as Mac'evitt, thus MacKevitt.

The sept were long noted as O'Doherty followers and in 1608 Sir Cahir O'Dougherty's second-in-command at the taking and burning of Derry city was Phelim Reagh MacDavitt, whose family henceforth became known as the 'Burn-Derrys'. There are townlands called Ballydevitt in both Derry and Donegal.

MacDaid is also a Scottish name, one of the many forms of the name of Clann Dhái or Clan Davidson. The name has also been common in the Glasgow area, where it is thought to be of Irish origin. A few in Ulster may be of Scottish origin.

Michael Davitt, 1846–1906, founder of the Land League, was not of this stock but belonged to a branch of the Burkes.

MACDERMOTT

This Connacht name, which is among the 100 most common in Ireland, is in Ulster most common in the west of the province, particularly in counties Donegal and Tyrone.

The name was originally in Gaelic Mac Diarmada and was that of a sept in Co. Roscommon which descends from Tadhg O'Connor, King of Connacht before the Norman invasion. The chiefs of the sept were styled Princes of Coolavin and were based at Moylurg. Another branch of the family in Connacht was known as MacDermott Roe, from *rua*, 'red'.

A number of different synonyms were noted for the name in northwest Ulster at the start of the twentieth century including Deyermott, Diarmid, Diarmod, Diarmond, Diermott and Diurmagh. Also, in Co. Derry at this time, it was found that some families had tried to disguise their name under such gentrifications as De Ermott, Deérmott and De Yermond.

The name, as MacDermid, MacDermott, MacDiarmid, MacDiarmond and so on, is also found in Scotland and represents that of a sept of Clan Campbell of Breadalbane, the MacDiarmids of Glenlyon in Perthshire. These claim descent from Diarmid O'Duine of Lochow, progenitor of the Campbells (*see* Campbell), and are reputed to be the oldest if not the aboriginal race of the district. A few of the name in Ulster may derive from this origin.

MACDEVITT *see* MacDaid

MACDONAGH *see* Donaghy

MACDONALD

This name, one of the 100 most numerous in Ireland, is as common in Leinster as it is in Ulster, and is also found in the other provinces. In Ulster the name is most common in Co. Antrim but the other main centre is in Co. Cavan.

Like many of Ulster's Gaelic septs, the Scottish MacDonalds claim descent from the semi-legendary Irish king, Conn of the Hundred Battles, through Colla Uais, who settled in the Hebrides. From this they are known as Clann Colla, the Children of Coll.

Coming to historic times, the chiefs of Clan Donald descend from the twelfth-century Somhairle or Somerled, Lord of Argyll, who through his marriage to a daughter of Olave the Red of Norway, and through his own conquests, gained control over the western islands and took the title Regulus of the Isles. From his sons descend the MacDougalls of Argyll and Lorn, the Macrorys of Bute, and the MacDonalds of Islay – the Clan Donald.

The name Donald comes from the Gaelic Domnall and meant originally 'world mighty' or 'world wielder'. It is first on record in its Welsh form, Dumnagual, in Roman documents of two thousand years ago. Donald is historically second only to John – Iain as the pre-eminent Highland forename.

The MacDonalds, Gaelic Mac Dhomhnuill, take their name from Donald of Islay, grandson of Somerled. One of Donald's sons, Alexander, the progenitor of the Clan MacAllister, was for a time chief of Clan Donald but was forfeited by Robert the Bruce in the fourteenth century. Some of his sons came to Ireland as galloglasses and his grandson Somhairle MacDonald was the ancestor of the Tyrone sept of MacDonald Gallóglach, the hereditary mercenaries of the O'Neills. This sept settled at Knocknacloy in Co. Tyrone where they rendered services to O'Neill until the end of the sixteenth century.

Donald's other son was Angus Óg who supported Robert the Bruce and in victory was given, by royal grant, the vast territories of his ancestors and the chiefship of Clan Donald. Angus Óg married Áine, a daughter of Cumhaighe Ó Catháin of Derry (O'Cahan – see Kane). The son of this marriage, John of Isla, took the title Dominus Insularum, Lord of the Isles, in 1354.

John's natural (illegitimate) son Iain nan Fraoch was progenitor of the MacIan MacDonalds in Glencoe in Argyllshire. From the sons of John's first marriage (to Amy MacRory) descend the MacDonalds of Clanranald and the MacDonnells of Glengarry. John divorced his wife and married Margaret, the daughter of Robert II. Their eldest son, Donald, succeeded as Lord of the Isles and their second son John Mór, the 'Tanister', founded the MacDonalds of Islay and Kintyre and, by his marriage to Margery Byset (Bissett), heiress to the Glens, he also founded the MacDonnells of Antrim (see MacDonnell). Their third son, Alexander or Alister Carrach, was progenitor of the MacDonalds of Keppoch.

The Clan Donald, through conquests, marriages and the absorption of many small septs and 'broken men', became the most powerful clan in Scotland and at their height controlled the entire western seaboard from the Butt of Lewis in the Outer Hebridies to the south of Kintyre as well as the Isle of Man and part of Antrim. As mentioned above, the MacDonalds are recorded as galloglasses in Ireland from the end of the thirteenth century. Many of them settled and became hereditary galloglass families. As an indication of the scale of MacDonald involvement in the dynastic and anti-English wars of the Irish septs, by the end of the sixteenth century there are MacDonald or MacDonnell galloglasses or descendants of galloglasses recorded in twenty-one Irish counties outside their main concentrations in Antrim and Tyrone.

A feud occurred between the various branches of Clan Donald in the fifteenth century and in 1493 the title of Lord of the Isles was rescinded by the Crown. By the seventeenth century the individual branches had become independent clans in their own right and none of their chiefs laid claim to be the Mac Dhomnuill. Not until 1947 was Alexander MacDonald of MacDonald granted the chiefship of the whole clan.

The decline of the MacDonalds was in effect the decline of the Gaelic way of life in the Highlands and ran parallel with the rise of the Campbells. With the Battle of Culloden in 1746 the clan system was finished and, as a power, so were the MacDonalds. The period that followed, culminating with the Highland Clearances of the nineteenth century, forced many to emigrate to America and the colonies and then, as in previous centuries, many came to Ulster.

From earliest times the history of the MacDonalds was closely bound up with Ireland and in particular with Ulster, and their name, its variants, and those of their dependent septs represent one of the largest family groups in Ulster. From the time of their descent from Conn of the Hundred Battles, through two thousand years of interaction, intermarriage, interalliance and war, they represent, in genealogical terms, an impressive bridge between the peoples of Scotland and Ireland. Anglicised forms of the name include Connell, Donald, Donaldson, Donnellson, Donillson, Kinnell, MacConnell, MacDaniel, MacKinnel, MacWhannel and Whannel. (*See* Connell, Donaldson *and* MacDonnell.)

MACDONNELL

MacDonnell is among the seventy most common names in Ireland and is very numerous in all the provinces. In Ulster it is also well distributed but is most common in counties Antrim and Monaghan. It can be of Irish or Scottish origin.

In Irish Gaelic the name is Mac Domhnaill and outside Ulster the main Irish origin of the name is the MacDonnells, a sept of Thomond in Munster. Most other of the MacDonnells outside Ulster will be descendants of MacDonald galloglasses recorded all over the land from the end of the thirteenth century (*see* MacDonald).

In Ulster, however, there are two origins of the name. In Monaghan, Fermanagh and adjacent areas, most will be descendants of the MacDonnells of Clankelly, Fermanagh's oldest recorded ruling family. When their power was broken by the Maguires they sought refuge in their stronghold of the Connons to the west of Clones and migrated to the MacMahon Country of Co. Monaghan, where, in 1300, MacDonnell of Clankelly was recorded as a sub-chief to MacMahon. The last chief, Giolla na Naemh Mac Domhnaill, was slain in 1501.

For a long time it was thought that the Scottish Clan Donald descended from the Clankelly MacDonnells, but this has now been disproved. (For the Clan Donald origins of the Antrim MacDonnells of the Glens, *see* MacDonald.) The MacDonnells of the Glens, through grants for military service as galloglasses and through the marriage of John Mór MacDonald to Margery Byset (Bissett) of Antrim, carved out an extensive territory and by the mid-sixteenth century had displaced the MacQuillans.

The most famous of this family, Somhairle Buidhe or Sorley Boy MacDonnell, 1505–90, fought successfully for forty years against the O'Kanes, the MacQuillans, the O'Neills and the armies of Queen Elizabeth 1. He annexed the Route and penetrated deep into Derry and Tyrone and as far south as Newry in Co. Down. His son Randal MacSorley MacDonnell was created 1st Earl of Antrim in 1620 and from him the present-day Earl of Antrim descends. (*See* Connell, Donaldson *and* MacDonald.)

Alexander MacDonnell, 1798–1835, who was born in Belfast, was regarded in Europe as one of the great chess masters of his day.

MACDOWELL

This Scottish name is found in Leinster but outside that province is virtually exclusive to the Ulster counties of Antrim and Down. It is occasionally found as a synonym of Doyle (*see* Doyle).

MacDowell is a variant of MacDougal, in Scots Gaelic Mac Dhughaill. The personal name Dughall is from *dubh*, 'black', and *gall*, 'foreigner' or 'stranger', and meant a 'Dane', a 'Viking'. The Scottish Clan Dougall, the MacDougalls of Argyll and Lorn, descend from Dougal, son of Somerled of Argyll (*see* MacDonald). From the mid-fourteenth century MacDougalls or MacDowells are recorded as galloglasses in Ireland, particularly in Roscommon; there they gave their name to Lismacdowell. Some in Ulster may descend from this stock.

But in Scotland the form MacDowell is most common in the province of Galloway, whence stemmed so many of the Plantation settlers. It was first recorded there in the thirteenth century and Sir Dougald MacDowell is recorded as sheriff of Dumfries in 1312. It was in Kirkcudbrightshire that the name came to be pronounced MacDole in common use, but the forms Madole, Madowell, Medole and so on, seem to be exclusive to Ulster.

In mid-nineteenth-century Co. Down the MacDowells were concentrated in the baronies of Lower Castlereagh and Upper and Lower Ards. And in Antrim, in the barony of Lower Belfast, especially to the south of Larne.

The sculptor Patrick MacDowell, 1799–1870, was born in Belfast.

MACELDOWNEY *see* Downey

MACELHINNEY

MacElhinney and MacIlhinney are virtually exclusive to Ulster and there, to counties Donegal, Derry and Tyrone. The name is in Gaelic Mac Giolla Chainnigh, meaning 'son of the devotee of Cainneach (St Canice)', and was that of an obscure sept of the Cenél Eoghain. St Canice was originally from Dromachose in Co. Derry. Another St Canice gave his name to Kilkenny, in Gaelic Cill Chainnigh, 'church of (St) Canice'. Indeed the name Mac Giolla Chainnigh is rendered in Connacht as Kilkenny.

MACELROY *see* MacIlroy

MACELWAIN *see* MacIlwaine

MACELWEE *see* MacKelvey

MACENEANY *see* MacAneny

MACERLAIN (*also* MacErlean)

This Irish name is virtually exclusive to counties Antrim and Derry. It was originally in Gaelic Mac Fhirléighinn. *Fear léighinn* means 'learned man' and, as a title, was applied to the head of a monastic school. The original Irish sept was of north Sligo but early migrated to and settled in Co. Derry. By the seventeenth century it was most common in the Co. Derry parish of Tamlaght O'Crilly.

In the form MacErlane, the name is found in Scotland, though it is accepted there as of Irish origin. It was first recorded in Scotland in 1164 as the name of an official of the monastery on Iona. It later became common in Ayrshire and Dumbartonshire, whence stemmed many of the Plantation settlers and some at least of the Ulster MacErlains and MacErleans will be of this origin.

MACERLEAN *see* MacErlain

MACEVOY

This name is most common in its homeland in Leinster and in Ulster where it is mainly found in Co. Armagh. It is in Gaelic Mac Fhiodhbhuidhe, probably from *fiodhbhadhach*, a 'woodman', and was the name of one of the famous Seven Septs of Leix. They were originally chiefs of Moygoish in Co. Westmeath but early migrated to Co. Laois (then Leix) where they settled in an area comprising the present-day parishes of Mountrath and Raheen.

Some in Ulster will be of this origin but in the case of others their name has become confused with two Ulster Gaelic names. Firstly, the Donegal name MacElwee, Gaelic Mac Giolla Bhuidhe, more commonly anglicised MacKelvey, has been made MacEvoy, particularly in Co. Down. At the start of the twentieth century MacEvoy was being used interchangeably there with Bwee and MacIlbwee near Moira and with MacIlboy around Kilkeel (*see* MacKelvey). Secondly, some MacEvoys, particularly in counties Armagh and Louth, were originally Mac an Bheatha, MacVeigh (*see* MacVeigh).

The name is found as MacEvoy and MacAvoy in the west of Scotland, particularly around Glasgow and in Ayrshire but there it is of Irish origin and dates only from the eighteenth century.

MACFADDEN

In Ireland this name is not common outside Ulster. There it is most numerous in Co. Donegal (where it is among the first ten names) and in counties Antrim and Derry. It can be of Irish or Scottish origin.

MacFadden or MacFadyen has long been associated with west Donegal. In Gaelic it is Mac Pháidín, son of Páidín, a diminutive or pet form of Pádraig (Patrick).

In Scotland MacFadyen, MacFadzean, MacPhadden and so on, are all forms of the name of a sept of Clan Maclaine of Lochbuie (*see* MacClean). Their origins are unclear. It is claimed by some that they were brought by the Maclaines to Mull from Donegal in the fifteenth or sixteenth century. Others claim that the MacFadyens were the original inhabitants of that part of Mull even before the Maclaines. The earliest reference to the name in the Scottish records is in 1304 in Kintyre, but thereafter they are also very common in Galloway. They were known in the Isles as Sliocht nan òr-cheard, the 'race of the goldsmiths'.

The name in Scotland has the same Gaelic form and meaning as in Ireland. The Maclaine MacFadyens also anglicised their name to Paton and Patonson (*see* Patton). MacFadyen in Fermanagh was made Faggy and has been noted as a synonym of Fagan in parts of Donegal.

Canon James McFadden, 1842–1917, the 'fighting priest of Gweedore', was famous for organising Donegal tenants against rack-renting and eviction. He was tried with twelve others for the murder of District Inspector Martin in 1889 but in a deal with the prosecution was released, though his co-defendants received sentences of up to thirty years.

MACFALL

In Ireland this name is virtually exclusive to Ulster, where it is most common in counties Antrim and Derry. It has three distinct Scottish origins but has also been used in Ulster for Mulfoyle.

In Scotland the name is found in the forms MacFail, MacFall, MacFaul and MacPhail. It is in Gaelic Mac Pháil, 'son of Paul'. (Paul is from the Latin *paulus*, meaning 'little'.) There were MacPhail septs of Clan Cameron, Clan Mackay and Clan Mackintosh. Most in Ulster will be of these origins.

However, the north Connacht name Ó Maolfabhail, which means 'descendant of the devotee of (St) Fabhail', more commonly anglicised as Lavelle, was in Donegal made Fall, MacFall, MacPaul and Paul. These MacFalls were based at Carrickbraghy on the Inishowen peninsula. In Ulster the Norman name Melville, found mainly in counties Antrim and Down, was also used as an anglicisation of Ó Maolfabhail.

MACFARLAND (*also* MacFarlane, MacParlan, MacParland, MacPartlan *and* MacPartlin)

These names all derive from the Gaelic forename Parthalán which has long been regarded as the Gaelic equivalent of Bartholomew, but has in fact no etymological connection with it. Parthalán in Irish mythology was the first invader of Ireland to which he came from Sicily 278 years after the Flood. Technically only one of these names, MacFarlane, is Scottish, although it is plain that there has been much confusion in the past between the various forms. Current spellings cannot therefore be treated as a reliable guide to the origins of a particular family.

In Ireland the Gaelic form is Mac Parthaláin, giving MacParland, MacPartlan and so on. The form Mac Pharthaláin gives MacFarland and, in Ireland, MacFarlane. The MacParlans were a sept of the kingdom of Oriel, first on record in the fifteenth century and noted as poets and scribes, the most famous of whom was the fifteenth-century Diarmuid Bacach Mac Parthaláin. The sept was based southeast of present-day Keady in Co. Armagh. The name has also been changed to Bartley and Bartholomew. As MacPartland and MacPartling it is found in the Scottish province of Galloway, where it is of Irish origin.

The Scottish Clan MacFarlane's territory lay between Loch Lomond and Loch Long in Dumbartonshire. They descend from Gilchrist, brother of Maldowen, 3rd Earl of Lennox, through one Parlan or Bartholomew, who lived in the mid-fourteenth century. They were for a time followers of the Lennoxes. By the late sixteenth century, however, they were, like their neighbours the MacGregors, a broken clan. By 1624 they had lost all their lands and many were transported to different parts of the Scottish kingdom. The others scattered, some perhaps attracted by the Plantation settlement in Ulster. Other forms of the clan name in Scotland include MacFarlan, MacFarland, MacParlan and MacParland.

MACFARLANE *see* MacFarland

MACGAHEY *see* MacCaughey

MACGARRY (*also* MacAree, MacCarry *and* MacGeary)

These names are taken together because they all, in their Gaelic forms, derive from the forename Fearadhach, meaning 'manly'. MacGarry is from Mag Fhearadhaigh and is a name as common in Leinster and Connacht as in Ulster. It is that of a sept rélated to the MacHughs of counties Leitrim and Roscommon. In Oriel it was corrupted to O'Garriga.

It was assumed that this name was from *giorraí,* a 'hare', and the name was made Hare (*see* O'Hare). MacGeary or MacGerry are variants found in counties Tyrone and Armagh. (Geary in Ulster may be from this; from the Cork name O'Geary, Ó Gadhra; or from the Roscommon name MacGeary, Mac Gadhra.) The form Megarry was noted as a synonym in the Lisburn area of Co. Antrim at the beginning of the twentieth century.

MacAree, MacCarry and MacKeary are all in Gaelic Mac Fhearadhach. MacAree and MacKeary are most common in Co. Monaghan, where MacAree has occasionally been made King by mistranslation (*see* King). MacCarry is most numerous in Co. Donegal and has been noted as a synonym of MacGarry.

MACGARVEY

MacGarvey is virtually exclusive to Ulster, where the majority are in Co. Donegal and most of the rest in Co. Derry. The name is that of a Donegal sept, in Gaelic Mac Gairbhith, from *garbh,* meaning 'rough'. MacGarvey is not often made Garvey and this in Ulster is usually from the distinct septs of O'Garvey, Gaelic Ó Gairbhith, of Co. Armagh and of Co. Down. MacGarvey and MacGarva are names long recorded in the Scottish province of Galloway, where they are of Irish origin.

MACGAUGHEY *see* MacCaughey

MACGEARY *see* MacGarry

MACGEE *see* Magee

MACGEOWN *see* MacKeown

MACGIBBON *see* Gibson

MACGILL *see* Magill

MACGINLEY

This name is found only in Ulster where 80 per cent of those of the name are in Co. Donegal, making it among the ten most numerous names there. The name is in Gaelic Mag Fhionnghaile, from *fionnghaile,* meaning 'fair valour'. An approximate pronunciation of the Gaelic name would be MacGinnelly and indeed this is recorded as a variant. The MacGinleys were a Donegal sept noted as ecclesiastics and many of the name are recorded as such in the history of the diocese of Raphoe. Peter MacGinley,

1857–1942, one of the organisers of the Gaelic League, was of this sept. He is better known under the pseudonym Cú Uladh.

MacGinley is often confused with the Scottish name MacKinley, Gaelic Mac Fhionnlaigh, particularly because it too is common in Donegal. There is no readily available information as to whether the Donegal MacKinleys are MacGinleys or are of Scottish stock (*see* Finlay).

MacGinley is recorded in Scotland but is neither of Irish origin nor a variant of MacKinley. It was originally in Scots Gaelic Mac Fhionnghal, from Fionnghal, meaning 'fair foreigner or Norseman'.

MACGINN (*also* Maginn)

These names are common only in Ulster, where they are found in most of the nine counties. MacGinn is a form more associated with Co. Tyrone and Maginn with counties Antrim and Down.

The name is in Gaelic Mag Fhinn, from *fionn,* 'fair'. The 'h' after the 'F' makes it silent and so the name is pronounced Mag'inn. MacGinn or MacGinne was listed as a 'principal Irish name' in the barony of Oneilland, Co. Armagh, in Petty's 'census' of 1659.

In counties Mayo and Leitrim the name was made MacGing. An earlier form of the name was Mac Fhinn, initially anglicised as MacKinn. This is now rare, having been made King (*see* King).

MACGOLDRICK

This name, which originates on the Fermanagh–Leitrim border, is most numerous in Ulster, particularly in counties Fermanagh and Tyrone, and in the adjoining part of Connacht, particularly in Co. Sligo. In seventeenth-century Ulster it was most common in Fermanagh, especially at Lurg, and, as MacGolrick and MacGoulrigg, in Co. Donegal.

The sept was a branch of the O'Rourkes, descendants of Uallgharg Ó Ruairc, Ulrick O'Rourke, Lord of Breffny, who died as a pilgrim on his way to the Holy Land in 1231. Uallgharg means 'fierce pride'. The sept's name is in Gaelic Mag Ualghairg.

Recorded anglicisations and variants include Golden, Goulding, Goodwin (*see* MacGuigan) and Magorlick. The name is found in Scotland, as MacGoldrick in the Glasgow district and as MacGorlick in Galloway. In both places it is of Irish origin.

MACGONIGLE

This name and the variant Magonagle are virtually exclusive in Co. Donegal and the adjacent parts of Co. Derry. The name is in Irish Mac

Conghail or Mac Congail and indeed it is also occasionally so spelt in English – MacCongail. The MacGonigles were an ecclesiastical sept found in Donegal from the medieval period. MacLysaght has them as erenaghs of Killaghtee in that county, but in fact the erenaghs there were the Kearneys. The MacGonigles were erenaghs at Killybegs. The sept contributed many priests and two bishops to the diocese of Raphoe. Around 1900 Magon was noted as a synonym in Ballymoney, Co. Antrim.

MACGOVERN (*also* Magauran)

MacGovern is a Co. Cavan name which is well known in Leinster, common in Connacht and very common in Ulster. It is most numerous in Co. Cavan (where it is among the fifteen most common names) and in counties Fermanagh and Leitrim. Other forms of the name are MacGauran, MacGoveran, MacGowran and Magauran.

In Irish the name is Mag Shamhráin and the sept takes its name from one Samhradhán who lived *c.* 1100. He was descended from the eighth-century Eochaidh, one of the O'Rourkes. Eochaidh gave his name to Teallach Eochaid, modern-day Tullyhaw in Cavan. This was long the territory of the MacGoverns. Their strongholds were at Ballymagauran, Bawnboy and Lissanover in Cavan. The sept was one of the most influential in the kingdom of Breffny, and several members of the family were distinguished clerics. The Book of the Magaurans is a famous fourteenth-century manuscript of family poems in Irish. Edmund Magauran, Archbishop of Armagh, was martyred for his faith in 1595.

The name Samhradhán is from *samhradh,* meaning 'summer' and MacGovern has been occasionally further anglicised to Somers and Summers.

MACGOWAN (*also* Magowan)

MacGowan can be an Irish or a Scottish name. In both Ulster and Scotland it meant originally 'son of the smith' and a great many, if not the majority, of the Smiths in Ulster will be originally of this or other Gaelic names. It is important, therefore, that this entry is consulted in conjunction with the entry for Smith.

In Ireland MacGowan and Magowan are largely confined to Ulster and the adjacent parts of Connacht, that is, Leitrim and Sligo. In Ulster MacGowan is most common in Co. Donegal, where it is among the fifteen most numerous names.

The Mac an Ghabhann or Mac Gabhann sept, also known as Muintir Gabhann, from *gabha,* meaning 'smith', originates in central Co. Cavan and in medieval times were one of the principal families of the kingdom of Breffny and were erenaghs of the church lands of Drumully in Dartry, Co. Monaghan. In present-day Co. Cavan MacGowan is no longer as common but its anglicisation, Smith or Smyth, is among the five most numerous names. In the adjacent county of Monaghan Smyth and MacGowan taken together constitute the fifth most common name.

By contrast, in Co. Donegal the original anglicisation MacGowan has survived. There, the MacGowans were erenaghs of Inishmacsaint in the barony of Tirhugh. Another family of MacGowans, in Gaelic Mac In Gabhand, were erenaghs of Ballymagowan at Clogher, Co. Tyrone. Ballygowan in Co. Down is of no connection, being named from one of the septs of O'Gowan (*see* Smith).

In Scotland Mac an Ghobhain or Mac Ghobhainn was anglicised as MacGowan. Mac Gobha, later MacGow, was also made MacGowan. The names all mean 'son of the smith'. As the maker of arms and armour the smith was an important hereditary position in each clan and there were MacGowans found throughout the Highlands. The two most important septs, however, were the MacGowans of Clan Donald and those of Clan Macpherson. There was also a Clan M'Gowan noted in four-teenth-century Nithsdale in Dumfriesshire, and in Stirlingshire there was an old family of MacGowans of uncertain origin.

MACGRATH (*also* Magrath)

MacGrath is among the sixty most common names in Ireland. The name is found in every county but half of those of the name are in Munster, particularly in counties Tipperary, Cork, and Waterford. These descend from the Thomond sept of MacGrath, poets to the O'Briens. However, a quarter of the Irish MacGraths are in Ulster, where the name is most common in Co. Tyrone.

The name has two forms in Irish, Mac Graith and Mag Raith (giving the form Magrath). Confusingly, these names mean 'son of Craith', not Raith. The MacGraths were an important sept of the Donegal–Fermanagh border, based originally at Termonmagrath near Pettigo. There they were lords of Cenél Moen but were driven out of the Ballybofey area by the O'Donnells and settled at Ardstraw in Tyrone. There was also in Fermanagh a family of MacGrath of the Sillees. This was a branch of the Maguires. In Donegal and Derry the name has been made MacGragh and MacGra and in Down, particularly on the Ards peninsula and in Lecale, it has been made MacGraw, Magraw and Megraw.

The most remarkable of the name was the Fermanagh man Miler McGrath, 1523–1622. He was born a Catholic and became a Franciscan friar and later was made Bishop of Down. However, he then became a Protestant, and, while still technically Catholic Bishop of Down, became Protestant Archbishop of Cashel. By 1604 he held four bishoprics and the livings of seventy parishes and had been twice married.

MACGUIGAN

Apart from a few of the name in Connacht, this name in Ireland is exclusively found in Ulster, where it is most common in its homeland of Co. Tyrone. The MacGuigans were a sept of the Cenél Eoghain, erenaghs at Ballinderry on the Derry–Tyrone border.

The name is in Irish Mag Uiginn and is found in a wide variety of anglicised forms, including Fidgeon, Goodfellow, Goodman, Goodwin, MacGoogan, MacGookin, MacGuckan, MacGuckian, MacQuiggan, MacWiggin, Maguigan, Pidgeon and Wigan.

Goodman, Fidgeon and Pidgeon are forms found in Co. Monaghan, Goodfellow in Co. Tyrone and Goodwin in counties Tyrone, Derry and Fermanagh. Goodwin is an English name from Old English *god,* 'good', and *wine,* 'friend'. The forms MacGuckan and MacGuckian can also be from Mag Eochaidhín. MacQuiggan can easily be confused with MacQuiggin, another Ulster name, in Gaelic Mac Guaigín, also anglicised as MacGuiggan.

In the light of these last two Gaelic names it is interesting that the name MacGuigan (*also* as MacGoughan, MacGuckan *and* MacGugan) is found in Scotland, particularly in Argyllshire and Kintyre. There it is from Mac Guagáin, a corrupt form of Mac Eochagáin and is thought to be of Irish origin.

MACGUINNESS (*also* Ennis, MacCreesh, MacNeice, MacNiece, Magennis, Minnis *and* Neeson)

MacGuinness is a well-known name in Connacht and is numerous in Leinster. But the name is most common in Ulster, where it originates. It is in Gaelic either Mag Aonghusa or Mag Aonghuis, both of which mean 'son of Angus'. The name is now found in over twenty different spellings and has further given rise to a variety of other names.

The MacGuinnesses were one of the most important septs of Ulster. They descend from Sárán, a Cruthnic chief in St Patrick's time. Initially the MacGuinnesses were chiefs of Clann Aodha under the O'Haugheys, Chiefs of Iveagh in Co. Down. But by the twelfth century the Mac-Guinnesses were Lords of Iveagh and from their main stronghold in Rathfriland they controlled most of Co. Down for the following four hundred years.

In the sixteenth century, well before the Plantation, many of the MacGuinnesses accepted the Reformation and indeed there were Protestant MacGuinness bishops of Down and of Dromore at that time. The MacGuinness chief of the time was considered by the English Lord Deputy as 'the civillest of all the Irish in these parts'. However, in 1598 his son joined O'Neill and 'returned to the rudeness of the country'. They continued to oppose the English in the wars of the seventeenth century and by its end had been dispossessed of all their lands, members of the ruling family joining the Wild Geese and fighting for France, Spain and Austria.

A branch of the sept in Monaghan became MacCreesh, Gaelic Mac Raois, and around 1900 many families in that county, in Fermanagh and in south Down were still using the name MacGuinness interchangeably with such variants as MacCreesh, MacCreech and Magreece. The name MacNeice or MacNiece is in Gaelic Mac Naois, a variant of MacGuinness. The Antrim name Neeson is in Gaelic Mac Aonghusa, also anglicised as MacNeece. Neeson may also have been an O' name, having been recorded in seventeenth-century Tyrone and Monaghan as O'Neason. Minnis and Mannice are east Ulster variants of MacNeece and MacNish. MacNish and MacNeish can both be variants of MacNeice or can equally represent a sept of the Scottish Clan Gregor.

The Scottish Clan Macinnes, also 'son of Angus', is of obscure origin and little is known of it except that it descends from the original Irish Dalriadic settlement in Scotland. MacCance in northeast Ulster can be a variant of MacInnes or of MacNish.

Ennis presents something of a problem. In Ireland it is in Gaelic Ó hAonghuis, 'descendant of Angus', a variant of O'Hennessy. It is also a Cornish name and in Scotland a variant of Innes, of which clan the Ennises are considered a sept. (The Clan Innes is entirely distinct from Clan Macinnes and the two names bear no relation to each other. Frank Adam claims that the name of the barony of Innes in Moray meant 'greens' and referred to the plain between Innes House and the River Lossie.) However, on the Lower Ards in Co. Down, the names Magennis and Ennis are both common and Ennis here is likely to be a variant of MacGuinness. There were at one time so many Ennises in the Kirkistown area of the Ards that nicknames were used to distinguish different families.

Louis MacNeice, 1907–63, son of a Church of Ireland bishop, was born in Belfast. He is regarded as one of the most important Irish poets of the twentieth century. The brewing family of Guinness are of Co. Down origin but are not direct descendants of the Lords of Iveagh.

MACGUIRE *see* Maguire

MACGURK

MacGurk is most common in Ulster. It is also well known in Leinster, particularly Dublin, where it is spelt MacGuirk. The name is in Gaelic Mag Oirc, not, as previously thought, Mag Cuirc. The MacGurks were a sept of Co. Tyrone and the name is still most common there. Ballygurk near Magherafelt in Co. Derry is in Gaelic Baile Mhic Oirc. The sept belonged to the Cenél Binnigh and as such descended ultimately from Niall of the Nine Hostages, the fifth-century founder of the Uí Néill dynasty. As tenants of the Archbishop of Armagh, they were erenaghs of the church lands of Termonmahuirk in the Omagh barony of Co. Tyrone. For centuries they were joint keepers of St Columcille's Bell.

MACHENRY *see* Henderson

MACHUGH

Though common in Leinster, this name is most numerous in north Connacht and west Ulster and there it is very common. The name is in Gaelic Mac Aodha or Mac Aoidh, 'son of Hugh', and in this Gaelic form has given rise to a wide variety of synonyms (*see* Hughes, MacCoy, MacKay *and* Magee).

A few in Ulster may descend from the Clan Donald sept of MacHugh (*see* Houston) but in west Ulster almost all will be Gaelic Irish. There were two original septs of Mac Aodha, both in Connacht. One was of Co. Galway, based near Tuam, and the other was a branch of the O'Flahertys in Connemara. The name is common in Co. Donegal and, around 1900, was among the ten most numerous in Co. Fermanagh. There, according to Livingstone, they are a branch of the Maguires, descended from Aodh, a grandson of Donn Carrach Maguire. In the past ninety years many of these seem to have reverted to the forms MacGee and Magee.

At the start of the twentieth century MacHugh was being used interchangeably with Hewson around Enniskillen, Co. Fermanagh, with Huston and MacCue around Glenties, Co. Donegal, with MacCue also around Letterkenny, Co. Donegal, and with MacKew near Bailieborough in Co. Cavan.

MACILROY (*also* MacElroy)

Both spellings of this name can be of Ulster Gaelic or Scots Gaelic origin, the former being Mac Giolla Rua and the latter Mac Ghille Ruaidh, both meaning 'son of the red (-haired) youth'. In Ireland the names have also been made Elroy, Gilroy, Ilroy, Kilroy, Roy and so on. The forms MacElroy and MacIlroy are found in various parts of Ireland but are common only in Ulster and in particular in counties Antrim, Down, Fermanagh and Derry.

The MacElroys were an important family in Gaelic Ireland and merit many mentions in the annals. Based originally in Fermanagh, they gave their name to Ballymacelroy on the east side of Lough Erne, Bally-mackilroy in the Clogher barony of Tyrone, and Ballymacilroy in the Upper Toome barony of Antrim. In late-eighteenth-century Fermanagh the name was most common in Magherasteffany and in mid-nineteenth-century Antrim to the west of Ballymena in Lower Toome.

In Scotland there were Gilroy and MacIlroy septs of Clan Grant of Glenmoriston and a MacIlroy sept of Clan MacGillivray. The name was first recorded in Dumfriesshire in 1376 and has long been associated with the parish of Ballantrae in Ayrshire, both of which are in the area whence hailed so many of the Plantation settlers.

MACILVEEN *see* MacIlwaine

MACILWAINE (*also* MacElwain *and* MacIlveen)

In Ireland these names are virtually exclusive to Ulster, where they are most common in counties Antrim and Down. (MacIlwaine is also common in Co. Armagh.) They can be of Scottish or Irish origin.

The Irish name MacIlwaine or MacElwain is in Gaelic Mac Giolla Bháin and means 'son of the white youth'. The sept originated in Co. Sligo but the name there has become Kilbane. In Ulster it became MacIlwaine. The names MacElveen, MacIlveen or MacKilveen are in Irish Gaelic Mac Giolla Mhín, the name of a sept in south Down, meaning 'son of the gentle or mild youth'.

However, it is thought that most of the Ulster MacElwains, MacIlwaines and MacIlvains are of Scottish descent. In Scotland the names MacIlwaine, MacIlvane, MacIlveane and so on, derive from a sept of the Clan MacBean or MacBain and are in fact variants of the clan name, in Scots Gaelic Mac Gille Bheatháin, meaning 'son of the devotee of (St) Beathán'. MacIlvain can also be from Scots Gaelic Mac Ghille Bháin, meaning 'son of the fair youth or servant', a name that was largely anglicised as White (*see* White). The names were common in Dumfriesshire, Ayrshire and Wigtownshire, from whence hailed so many of the Plantation settlers.

MACINTYRE (*also* MacAteer *and* Mateer)

These names mean the same in their original Irish and Scottish forms and in Ulster have often been confused. MacAteer in particular has often become lost in MacIntyre. The name in both Irish and Scots Gaelic is Mac an tSaoir, meaning 'son of the craftsman (carpenter, mason, wright)'. MacIntyre is found in Leinster and Connacht but is most common in Ulster, particularly in counties Derry and Antrim (it is also common in Sligo). MacAteer is virtually exclusive to Ulster, where it is mainly found in counties Antrim, Donegal and Armagh. The MacAteers were a sept of Co. Armagh, possibly based at Ballymacateer near Lurgan. Michael Mac an tSaoir, who was Bishop of Clogher from 1268 to 1287, was of this sept.

In Scotland the MacIntyres, in Gaelic Clan-an-t-Saoir, 'children of the carpenter', were a recognised clan in their own right. They are traditionally thought to have come to Lorn in Argyllshire from the Hebrides and are first recorded in Glen Noe, near Bonawe, Argyll, about 1400. They were hereditary foresters to the Stewarts of Lorn and were later followers of the Stewarts of Appin in Argyllshire and the Campbells of Lorn. The MacIntyres were long famous as pipers. Although most of the name Tyrie derive it from the placename in Perthshire, some will be originally MacIntyres.

Though MacIntyre is a common name in north Derry and north Antrim, it is not common in the Glens of Antrim. However, Wright (*see* Wright) is common there and most of these will be originally MacIntyres from west Argyll. MacAteer was also anglicised, by translation, to Carpenter (especially in south Ulster), and by pseudo-translation to Freeman, *saor* meaning also in Irish Gaelic 'free'.

Other recorded forms of the name are MacEnteer, MacEntyre, MacTeer, MacTier, Mateer, Matier, Tear and Tier.

MACIVOR *see* MacKeever

MACKANE *see* Kane

MACKAY (*also* Keys *and* MacKee)
In Ireland these names are almost exclusive to Ulster, where MacKay is found chiefly in Co. Antrim and MacKee mainly in counties Antrim, Armagh and Down. Both are anglicisations of Mac Aodha or Mac Aoidh, 'son of Hugh', the original name of the Scottish Clan MacKay or Clann Aodh.

The first MacKays in Ireland, also known as MacCoys, are not thought to have had any connection with the Clan Mackay but were Clan Donald galloglasses, followers of the MacDonnells. Some of the present-day MacKays and MacKees may descend from them (*see* MacCoy).

The exact origins of the Clan Mackay are not known beyond the fact that they are early connected with Moray and were probably part of the ancient Clann Morgunn. The clan first came to prominence at the beginning of the thirteenth century in Sutherland and by 1427 the chief, Angus Dow MacKay, could muster four thousand men, which shows how powerful they were at this early stage. The Mackays held Sutherland until as late as the mid-eighteenth century, but as in most parts of the Highlands, were removed during the infamous Clearances.

The MacKays of Inverness-shire, called in Gaelic Clann Ái, were really Clann Dhái or Davidson (see Davidson), a branch of Clan Chattan. The MacKays and MacKees of Galloway and Kintyre were most likely of the Clan Donald as were probably the Mackies of mid-Galloway. These latter were powerful and prominent in the sixteenth and seventeenth centuries, and were enthusiastic supporters of the Covenanters. The MacKays, MacKees and Mackies are probably connected to the MacGees (see Magee), a sept of Clan Donald.

Sir Patrick MacKee of Largs, Ayrshire, was one of the fifty Scottish undertakers of the Plantation of Ulster. He was granted 1000 acres in the Donegal town area but, since he was unable to make progress, the lands eventually passed to John Murray, Earl of Annandale in Dumfriesshire.

MacKee in Ulster can also be from the Irish Mac Aodha or Mac Aoidh (see MacHugh) or from Mac an Chaoich (from caoch, 'blind'), the name of a branch of the O'Reillys of Breffny.

Keys or Keyes is an English name which can be of several origins but most who bear these names in Ulster, particularly in Fermanagh where it is most common, will be originally MacKees.

MACKEAG (also MacCaig, MacKeague, Montague and Teague)

Tadhg was once one of the most common Irish personal names, so common in fact that it gave rise to the derogatory term a 'Taig', meaning a 'Catholic'. None the less, with the exception of Montague, which was itself an anglicisation of MacTague, all these names derive from Tadhg, whether they are of Irish or Scottish origin.

There was a sept of Ó Taidhg based at Termonkenny in Co. Down, with a branch in the barony of Coleraine in Co. Derry and some of the Ulster Teagues descend from these. Most, however, will be originally MacTague, MacTeague, MacTeige and so on, Gaelic Mac Taidhg. This was not a sept as such but was a name which sprang up independently as a patronymic, 'son of Tadhg'. MacTeague is more common in Co. Donegal and MacGague in Co. Cavan. The Norman toponymic Montague (de Montaigue) was taken as further anglicisation of MacTague especially in counties Tyrone and Armagh and most Ulster Montagues will be of this origin.

The name was also found as Mac Thaidhg, also 'son of Tadhg', but in this aspirated form the 'h' after the 'T' makes it silent and the name was pronounced Mac'aig. This was anglicised in Ulster in many different ways including MacAig, MacCague, MacCaig, MacCaigue, MacHaigh, MacKeag, MacKeague and so on. The two most common forms are MacKeag and MacKeague, found in all the nine counties but especially in Down.

In Scots Gaelic the name was Mac Thaoig, from the Irish Gaelic Mac Thaidhg. This was anglicised mainly to MacCaig and MacKaig. These names were most common in Ayrshire and Galloway and, as Maccaig, in Kintyre, Argyll and the Isles. There was a MacCaig sept of Clan Farquharson. The MacCaigs, a sept of Clan MacLeod of Lewis, derive their name from the Gaelic Mac Cuaig, from Scots Gaelic *cuthaig*, 'cuckoo'.

MACKEAGUE *see* MacKeag

MACKEE *see* MacKay

MACKEEVER (*also* MacIvor)

In Ireland these two names are uncommon outside Ulster, where MacIvor is most numerous in counties Tyrone and Derry, and MacKeever in Co. Derry. They can be of both Irish and Scottish origin.

In Monaghan most MacKeevers will be originally Mac Éimhir, 'son of Heber', a favourite forename of the MacMahons, of which they are a branch. But most MacKeevers and MacIvors in Ulster, whether of Irish or Scottish stock, will be originally Mac Íomhair, 'son of Ivar', from the Norse personal name Ivaar.

There were MacIver septs of Clans Campbell, Robertson and MacKenzie. The spelling in Scotland was MacIver until the popularity of Sir Walter Scott's *Waverley*, where the form MacIvor was used. The Scottish names MacUre and Ure derive from the same source.

Around 1900 MacKeever and MacIvor were still being used interchangeably around Dungannon in Co. Tyrone, and Maghera, Garvagh and Moneymore in Co. Derry.

MACKELVEY (*also* MacElwee)

In Ireland these names are exclusive to Ulster. MacKelvey can be of Irish or Scottish origin and is most common in Co. Donegal and adjacent parts of Co. Tyrone. MacElwee is a variant of the Irish MacKelvey and is found mainly in Co. Donegal and the adjacent parts of Co. Derry.

The Scottish name MacKelvey, of Dumfriesshire and Galloway, is in Gaelic Mac Shealbhaigh, 'son of Selbach', an old Gaelic personal name. Most of the name in Ulster, however, will be of Ulster Gaelic stock. The Donegal sept name Mac Giolla Bhuidhe, 'son of the yellow (-haired) youth', was anglicised in many forms in Ulster: MacElwee, MacGilloway, MacGilvie, MacGilway, MacGilwee, MacKelvey, Muckilbuoy; and in Connacht: Calvey, Kilboy, Kilvey, Kilwee, MacCalvey and so on. The Gaelic name Mac Giolla Bhuidhe was also found on the Isle of Man where, however, it was anglicised as Boyd (see Boyd).

As MacIleboy it was noted as a 'principal Irish name' in Upper Iveagh, Co. Down, in the mid-seventeenth century. In that county the name was often made MacEvoy (see MacEvoy) and at the beginning of the twentieth century MacEvoy was still being used interchangeably with Bwee and MacIlbwee around Moira, Co. Down, and with MacIlboy in the Kilkeel district of Co. Down.

MACKENDRY *see* Henderson

MACKENNA

MacKenna, common throughout Ireland, is nowhere so numerous as in Ulster. The name is among the 100 most common names in Ireland, in the first forty in Ulster and the first ten in Co. Tyrone, and it was found in 1970 to be the second most common name in Co. Monaghan.

MacKenna is in Gaelic Mac Cionaoith, the name of a sept of the Cenél Fiachach of Meath, who were introduced as swordsmen into Monaghan by the Fir Leamha of Clogher. The sept settled in and became lords of Truagh in that county. The last chief was Patrick, who died at Tullylough, near Emyvale in Co. Tyrone, in 1616. After the 1606 settlement the MacKennas refused to pay rent for their lands, which were then taken from them. Later in that century a branch settled in the parish of Maghera, Co. Down. The name was so popular in north Monaghan that nicknames had to be used to distinguish familes. Some of these Irish MacKennas became both MacKenny (*see* Kenny) and MacKinney (*see* MacKinney).

Some in Ulster may be of Scottish origin. The Scots Gaelic name Mac Cionaodha (equivalent to the Irish form above), as MacKenna, MacKinney and so on, was common in Galloway, whence hailed so many of the Plantation settlers.

John or Juan MacKenna, 1771–1814, born at Clogher, Co. Tyrone, became a general in Chile and fought with Bernardo O'Higgins in that country's struggle for independence.

MACKEOWN (*also* Keon, Keown *and* MacGeown)

These names derive mainly from the Gaelic name Eoin or Eoghan, 'John'. MacKeown is among the fifty most common names in Ulster and is most numerous in counties Antrim, Down, Armagh and Derry. MacGeown is most numerous in Co. Armagh, and Keown or Keon is mainly found in counties Donegal, Down and Fermanagh. MacKeown can be of Scottish or Irish origin.

The Ulster Gaelic name Mac Eoin or Mac Eoghain, 'son of John', has been anglicised in a wide variety of ways including MacCune, MacEwen, MacGeown, MacKeon, MacKone, MacOwen, Magone, Owens and Owenson. It has also been made Caulfield (*see* Caulfield), has been translated Johnson, and mistranslated Johnston (*see* Johnston). The name MacCowan was also largely absorbed by the more common MacKeown (*see* Cowan).

The main Irish sept of MacKeown or MacKeon was of north Connacht, but there were small septs of MacKeown at Creggan and Derrynoon in Co. Armagh and probably other such small septs in other counties. Keowns and Keons can be originally MacKeowns, but many will be O'Keowns, like those of Fermanagh who were in Gaelic either Ó Ceotháin or – also in Monaghan – Ó hEoghain. Further, like the Keowns, it is thought that some MacKeowns in these areas will be originally O'Keowns.

The great majority of the MacKeowns of Co. Antrim and adjacent areas descend from the Bissetts of the Glens, taking their name from the Scotsman Eoin Bissett, who settled in the Glens in the thirteenth century, well before the MacDonnells. In the mid-nineteenth century MacKeown was found to be common in twelve out of the fourteen Antrim baronies.

MacKeon and MacKeown are also found as variants of the Scottish name MacCune or MacCunn, again Mac Eoghain, an old name in Galloway. A great number of the Plantation settlers came from that province so it is likely that some at least of the MacKeowns and MacCunes of Ulster are of that origin.

MACKERNAN *see* Kernaghan

MACKEVITT *see* MacDaid

MACKIBBON *see* Gibson

MACKILLEN *see* MacCallion

MACKINLEY *see* Finlay

MACKINNEY

In Ireland this name is exclusive to Ulster where it is most common in counties Antrim and Tyrone. It can be of Irish or Scottish origin. It may be assumed that most of those in Tyrone descend from the Mac Coinnigh sept who were based on the Tyrone–Fermanagh border.

The Scottish Clan MacKinnon, Gaelic Mac Fhionnghuin, were also known as MacKinneys and there was a specific MacKinney sept of the clan. Clan MacKinnon was a branch of the Clan Alpin and were followers of the Lords of the Isles. Once powerful, they held lands in the islands of Mull, Skye, Arran, Tiree, Pabay and Scalpa, but by the end of the eighteenth century they were landless. In Galloway MacKinney is a variant of Mac Cionaodha, MacKenna (*see* MacKenna).

Victorian records show that between 1866 and 1890 there was an astounding fourfold increase in the numbers of MacKinneys in Ulster. This was not a result of immigration, but chiefly because of an increasing tendency for MacKenzies in the province to change their name thus. (For MacKenzie *see* Buchanan.) Many MacKennas also adopted MacKinney. Around 1900 MacKinney was being used interchangeably with Kenny in the Poyntzpass district of Armagh and with MacKenny near Coleraine, Co. Derry (*see* Kenny).

MACKNIGHT

A few of this name in Ulster may be of Norman origin. A branch of the Fitzsimonses of Meath took the Gaelic name Mac an Ridire, 'son of the knight', and this was later made MacKnight.

But most, especially in counties Antrim and Down, where the name is most common, are of Scottish origin. The Clan MacNaughten, Gaelic Mac Neachdainn, 'son of Nechtan', claims descent from the eighth-century Pictish king Nechtan. A sept of this clan was called MacKnight, a variant of MacNaughten (which is itself made MacNaughton in Ulster). The MacNaughtens were one of the families brought in by the Mac-Donnells of the Glens of Antrim in the early seventeenth century, Shane Dhu, or Black John MacNaghten, becoming the Earl of Antrim's chief agent. Black John was buried in the family burial ground at Bonamargy Friary near Ballycastle.

The Clan MacNaughten lost all its lands in curious circumstances in 1700 when the last chief, John MacNaughten of Dundarave in Argyllshire, was married, while drunk, to the wrong daughter of Sir James Campbell of Ardkinglas in Argyllshire. The following morning he discovered his mistake and ran off with the right daughter, leaving the wrong one pregnant. The child that was born, a daughter, was drowned by Campbell in a river. The Campbells thus acquired the MacNaughten lands. Shane Dhu had been a brother of the then Laird of Dundarave and in 1818, his descendant, Edward A. MacNaughten of Bushmills, was confirmed by Lyon Court, the supreme heraldic and genealogical arbiter in Scotland, as Chief of the Clan MacNaughten.

The name MacNaught or MacNeight, on record in Dumfriesshire from 1296 and common too in Ayrshire, was made MacKnight in Kirkcudbrightshire and in Galloway generally. MacNaught in Ulster was corrupted to MacNutt.

At the start of the twentieth century MacKnight was being used interchangeably with MacNaghten, MacNeight, Menautt, Minett and Minnitt in various parts of east Ulster. The English name Knight has also been used as an abbreviation. Menaght is a Co. Down variant of MacNaughton and was used interchangeably with Monaghan in the Ards peninsula, Co. Down.

MACLAUGHLIN (*also* Laughlin, Loughlin and MacLoughlin)

Taken together MacLaughlin and MacLoughlin were found, at the start of the twentieth century, to be the twenty-first most common name in Ireland, ninth in Ulster, second in Co. Derry, fifth in Co. Donegal and tenth in Co. Tyrone. Further, MacLoughlin, taken on its own, was twelfth most common in Co. Fermanagh. Three-quarters of those of the MacLaughlin spelling in Ireland were found to be in counties Antrim, Donegal and Derry. Most in Ulster will be of Irish origin, but many will be of Scottish. Laughlin and Loughlin are abbreviated forms. In both Scotland and Ireland the names derive principally from the Norse personal name Lachlann.

Mac Lochlainn was the name of a leading sept of Tirconnell, which was one of the senior branches of the northern Uí Néill, descendants of the fifth-century Niall of the Nine Hostages. Up to the mid-thirteenth century the MacLoughlins were rulers of Ulster. In 1241, however, Dónall Mac Lochlainn was defeated and killed in a battle with Brian Ó Néill and the O'Neill domination of Ulster began. The MacLaughlins were erenaghs of the church lands of Grellagh and of Moville in their homeland, the barony of Inishowen in Co. Donegal, and were also erenaghs of half of all the church lands of Co. Derry. Some at least of the MacLoughlins of Ulster will be originally O'Melaghlins, descendants of Maoilsheachlainn (Malachy II), King of Ireland from 980 to 1002 – when he was dethroned by Brian Boru. By the eighteenth century the name as O'Melaghlin had disappeared, having been replaced by MacLoughlin.

The name, as MacLachlan, MacLauchlan, MacLauchlin and so on, is common in Scotland and is that of the Clan MacLachlan, whose chief seat was in Cowal in Argyll. Their lands there were acquired by Gilleskel Maclachlan in 1292. A branch were hereditary captains of Innischonnel, an island in Loch Awe in Argyllshire, to the Cambells of Argyll.

MACLEAN *see* MacClean

MACLENAGHAN *see* MacClenaghan

MACLOUGHLIN *see* MacLaughlin

MACMAHON

MacMahon is among the seventy most common names in Ireland. It is most numerous in Munster, particularly Limerick and Clare (where it is the most common name). These MacMahons descend ultimately from Mahon O'Brien, grandson of Brian Boru. The name is also common in Leinster, and very common in south Ulster (where it is among the twenty most numerous names in Co. Cavan and is fourth in Co. Monaghan). The name in Gaelic is Mac Mathúna, from *mathghamhan*, a 'bear'.

The MacMahons of Truagh were the leading sept of the kingdom of Oriel and ruled Monaghan from the decline of the O'Carrolls in the early thirteenth century until the end of the sixteenth century. At the beginning of the sixteenth century they had divided themselves into three branches, headed by the three sons of Rory MacMahon – Eoghan in Dartry, Aodh Rua in Farney, and Réamonn around Monaghan town. The descendants of Réamonn became known as the 'Lucht Tighe MacMahons'.

MacMahons were prominent in the wars of the seventeenth century. Heber MacMahon, 1600–50, Bishop of Clogher, commanded the Ulster army of the Confederate Catholics against Charles Coote and died on the scaffold. The last chief of the sept, Hugh MacMahon, was also active in the Confederacy but was betrayed by Owen O'Connolly and was beheaded at Tyburn in London. In the following century there were three other MacMahon Bishops of Clogher, each of whom became Primates of All Ireland. They were Hugh MacMahon, died 1737, and his nephews, two brothers, Bernard, 1680–1747, and Ross Roe, 1698–1748.

Some of the MacMahons in Fermanagh descend from a branch of the Maguires founded by Mahon, a grandson of Donn Carrach Maguire. The name Mahon has been used as a shortening, as has Mohan and Vaughan. However, most Mahons in Ireland are originally Mahans, Gaelic Ó Macháin, or Mohans (*see* Mohan), Gaelic Ó Mócháin, both Connacht names. Many of the name Mathews (*see* Mathews), particularly in south

Ulster, are originally MacMahons. The cognate form of MacMahon in Scotland, in Scots Gaelic Mac Mhathain, became Matheson.

In early-twentieth-century Newtownards, Co. Down, MacMahon was noted as synonymous with MacMechin, a variant of the Antrim and Down name MacMeekin, Gaelic Mac Miadhacháin. The Scottish name Mann has been noted as a variant of Mahon in Belfast (*see* MacManus).

MACMANUS (*also* Mann)

Though numerous in Leinster and Connacht, this name is most common in Ulster. It was found to be the fourth most numerous name in its Ulster homeland, Co. Fermanagh, in 1962. The MacManuses of Connacht, distinct from the Fermanagh sept, descend from Maghnus, died 1181, son of Turlough O'Connor, King of Ireland, and were based in the parish of Kilronan, Co. Roscommon.

The name in Gaelic is Mac Maghnuis, 'son of Manus', the Irish form of the Norse name Magnus. The MacManuses were second only to the Maguires in Fermanagh and descend from Maghnus, a son of Donn Mór Maguire. From their headquarters on the island of Ballymacmanus, modern Belleisle, they had control of the shipping on Lough Erne and were hereditary managers of the fisheries under Maguire. The Annals of Ulster were compiled by Cathal Óg MacManus at Ballymacmanus. Cathal Óg, 1439–98, was chief of the name, vicar general of Clogher and dean of Lough Erne. The sept also gave their name to Knockmacmanus in Aghalurcher. Terence Bellew MacManus, 1823–60, was a Young Irelander who was sentenced to death, had his sentence commuted to transportion, and escaped from Tasmania, making his way to America.

MacManus in Co. Tyrone was made Manasses. In Fermanagh and parts of Tyrone MacManus was made Mayne but most of this name in Ulster will be of Scottish stock, although there they too were originally MacManuses. MacManus is also a Scottish name, the same in Gaelic and of the same meaning as its Ulster counterpart. These MacManuses were a sept of Clan Colquhoun, their name also being made MacMaynes and MacMainess. The Scottish name Mann has been noted in Belfast as a variant of Mahon (*see* MacMahon). Mann is also, like Main, from Magnus and is most common in Co. Antrim. The name Mann is also found in England, where it was originally a personal name from Old English *mann*, 'man', meaning a 'servant'. But most in Ulster will be of Scottish origin.

Ethna Carbery was the pen name of Anna MacManus, *née* Johnston, 1866–1902. A poet and, with Alice Milligan, founder co-editor of *The Northern Patriot* and *Shan Van Vocht*, she did much to stimulate the early Sinn Féin movement. She was born in Ballymena, Co. Antrim. Her husband Seamus MacManus, 1869–1960, poet, historian and novelist, was born near Mountcharles, Co. Donegal.

MACMASTER (*also* Masterson)

MacMaster in Ireland is virtually exclusive to Ulster where most of the name are in counties Antrim and Down. Masterson is most numerous in Leinster, particularly Longford and in the adjacent Ulster county of Cavan. MacMaster is mainly of Scottish and Masterson mainly of Irish origin, though both derive from the same Gaelic name.

In Scotland MacMaster is in Gaelic Mac an Mhaighstir, 'son of the master' ('master' in this sense means a 'cleric'). There were MacMasters, a sept of Clan Buchanan on Loch Lomondside. Also, there were MacMasters in Ardgour in Argyllshire whose chief gave offence to the Lord of the Isles in the fifteenth century. As a result the MacMasters were driven out by the Macleans and settled in Morven in Argyllshire, becoming a sept of Clan Macinnes. The name came to be most common in Dumfriesshire and Wigtownshire.

In Ireland MacMaster is in Gaelic Mac an Mhaighistir, the name of a Breffny sept, a branch of the MacKiernans, which was based on the Longford–Cavan border. Most of this sept had anglicised their name to Masterson by the mid-seventeenth century.

William MacMaster, 1811–87, founded the University of Toronto. He was born in Co. Tyrone. From Co. Down, the Revd Gilbert MacMaster DD, 1778–1854, was a Presbyterian minister in New York. One of his sons, Erasmus, became professor of theology in Chicago and the other, James, became a convert and a leading Catholic journalist. Anew McMaster, 1894–1962, last of the Irish actor–managers, specialised in bringing Shakespeare to more obscure localities around the world. He was born in Co. Monaghan.

MACMENAMIN

In Ireland this name is virtually exclusive to Ulster, where two-thirds of the name are in Co. Donegal and most of the rest in west Tyrone. The name is in Gaelic Mac Meanman, 'son of Meanma', a name which means 'courage' or 'spirit'. The name is first recorded in the Annals of Loch Cé which notes the death of two MacMenamins, nephews of O'Donnell, in 1303. The MacMenamins were a sept of Tirconnell, followers of the O'Donnells, and the name is now concentrated around Letterkenny and Ballybofey in Donegal.

The name is also found in the Scottish province of Galloway where it is of Irish origin.

MACMILLAN (*also* MacMillen, MacMullan *and* MacMullen)

These names are all versions of the name of the Scottish Clan Macmillan. The forms MacMullan and MacMullen, though together four times as common in Ulster as the other two, are not found in Scotland at all. In Ireland all the names are almost exclusive to Ulster and are found mainly in counties Antrim and Down. The name is in Gaelic Mac Mhaoláin or Mac Ghille Mhaoil. This latter form was also anglicised as MacIlveil and MacGilveil, and more commonly Bell (*see* Bell). Indeed, in parts of Argyllshire the Macmillans are known as Na Belich, 'The Bells'.

The Macmillans were a tribe of Moray, originally of the people of Kanteai, one of the subsidiaries of the northern Picts. However, the name was first recorded in Lanarkshire in 1263 when Gilleonan MacMolan appears on an assize. But as a powerful clan it does not appear until 1360, when Malcolm Mór Macmillan received Knapdale in Argyllshire from the Lord of the Isles. A great rock, the Craig Mhic Maolain, at Knap Point, was inscribed (in Gaelic) thus:

> Macmillan's right to Knap shall be
> As long as this rock withstands the sea.

By the early seventeenth century the Macmillans had lost all their lands in Knapdale and the Campbells had disposed of the rock. The Macmillans had by then spread south into Kintyre and to Galloway and Kirkcudbrightshire.

The Buchanans claim that the Macmillans, like themselves, are part of the Síol O'Cain and as such descend from Ausalan Buoy O'Kayn of Derry who settled in Buchanan in the eleventh century. This claim makes the Macmillans a sept of Buchanan. Not surprisingly, the Clan Macmillan dispute this.

Many of the name came to Ulster at the time of the Plantation and settled particularly in north Antrim and in Down. The adoption of the MacMullen or MacMullan form was probably influenced by the preponderance in north Antrim of the Irish name O'Mullan. The names Mullan, Mullen and Mullin can in theory derive from either name and there is evidence that some at least of the O'Mullans adopted the name MacMullan (*see* Mullan).

In mid-nineteenth-century Co. Antrim there was found to be a 'huge concentration' of the name MacMullan in the barony of Carey on the extreme north coast. At the same time in Co. Down the name was most concentrated in the parish of Garvaghy in Upper Iveagh. The name MacMullan is the third most common name on the Upper Ards where it was first recorded before the Plantation.

MACMILLEN *see* MacMillan

MACMULLAN *see* MacMillan

MACMULLEN *see* MacMillan

MACMURRAY *see* Murray

MACMURTRY *see* MacCurdy

MACNALLY (*also* MacAnally)

These names are well known in Leinster, in Connacht (where they are often made Nally), and are most common in Ulster. There they are mainly found in counties Armagh and Monaghan. Taken together they constituted the nineteenth most common name in Monaghan in 1970.

The names can be of two Gaelic origins. Most outside Ulster and many within it will be Mac an Fhailghigh, from *failgheach*, meaning a 'poor man'. But most in Ulster will be Mac Con Uladh. This name is usually translated as 'son of the hound of Ulster', but the Ulster referred to is the old Ulidia, modern southeast Ulster. And in the seventeenth century, as now, this is where the name was most common.

The names are also found as MacAnully, MacEnolly and Knally and around 1900 were found to be synonymous with Manally around Armagh city and with MacAnulla in the Maghera district of Co. Derry (but *see* MacCullough). Historically, the biggest Ulsterman of the name must have been David Rice MacAnally, 1810–95, Methodist minister, teacher and sheriff, who weighed over 26 stone.

MACNAMEE

This name is found in Leinster but is most common in Ulster, especially in counties Derry and Tyrone. The name is in Gaelic Mac Conmidhe, 'son of the hound of Meath', and was that of a sept who were hereditary poets and ollavs to the O'Neills. The two most famous, both Irish Gaelic poets, were the mid-thirteenth-century Giolla Brighde Mac Con Midhe and the late-sixteenth-century Brian Mac Angus MacNamee, chief poet to Turlough Luineach O'Neill. A branch were erenaghs of the church lands of Comber on the River Foyle in Co. Derry. The name is also found as MacConmee and Mee.

The names Conamy, Conomy, MacConamy and MacConomy, also of Derry and Tyrone and also from Mac Conmidhe, are not used as synonyms of MacNamee and have often been made Conway (*see* Conway).

MACNEICE *see* MacGuinness

MACNEILL

Though found in the other provinces of Ireland MacNeill is common only in Ulster, where it is most numerous in counties Derry and Antrim. The name is of Scottish, though ultimately of Irish, origin.

The Scottish Clann Niall or Clan MacNeil claims descent from one Niall, twenty-first in descent from Niall of the Nine Hostages, fifth-century founder of the Uí Néill dynasty. This Niall came to the island of Barra in the Outer Hebrides in 1049 and founded the clan. A descendant of his, Gilleonan Roderick Murchaid MacNeil, received a charter for the island in 1429 from Alexander, Lord of the Isles. A branch was early established on the island of Gigha, north of Kintyre. The MacNeils were celebrated as hereditary poets to the Clan Ranald MacDonalds and as hereditary harpers and pipers to Maclean of Duart on the island of Mull.

After the forfeiture of the lordship of the Isles in 1493 the two branches went their separate ways, those of Barra becoming followers of the Macleans of Duart and those of Gigha, followers of the MacDonalds of Islay and Kintyre. It was the MacNeils of Barra who, with their confederates the Macleans, came to Ireland as galloglasses as early as the mid-fourteenth century. In the late sixteenth century they also came as pirates, often acting in collusion with the famous Gráinne (Grace) O'Malley.

Though they penetrated into Mayo and Leinster, where the name also became MacGreal, most settled in counties Antrim and Derry and in the late fifteenth century the MacNeils, along with the MacQuillans, were lords of Clandeboy. They are recorded in the Annals of the Four Masters as submitting to Con O'Neill in 1471. The MacNeills of north Antrim were followers of the MacDonnells of the Glens brought there in the late sixteenth and early seventeenth centuries, Hugh MacNeill at that time being granted the Ballycastle estate, which he controlled from Dunynie Castle just west of Ballycastle.

Most of the MacNeills of Ulster eventually became Protestant, the most famous being Co. Antrim man Dean Hugh MacNeill, 1795–1879, a vigorous anti-Catholic preacher in England. The MacNeills of the Glens of Antrim mostly remained Catholic and the most famous of these, Eoin MacNeill, 1867–1945, born at Glenarm, was a distinguished historian, co-founder of the Gaelic League, and at one time chief of staff of the Irish Volunteers. James MacNeill, 1869–1938, also born at Glenarm, was a successful administrator in the Indian service before returning to Ireland and joining Sinn Féin. He was governor general of Ireland from 1928 until Eamon de Valera forced the abolition of the office in 1932.

The main Co. Antrim concentration of the name in the mid-nineteenth century was found to be in the barony of Carey, south of Ballycastle.

See also Neill, Nelson *and* O'Neill.

MACNEILLY *see* Neill

MACNICKLE *see* Nicholl

MACNIECE *see* MacGuinness

MACNULTY

This name is not common outside Connacht and Ulster, where it is found mainly in counties Mayo and Donegal respectively. It is originally in Gaelic Mac an Ultaigh, 'son of the Ulsterman', and is also found in the forms MacAnulty and Nulty.

The MacNultys were a sept of south Donegal associated with the O'Donnells and were recorded at different times as followers or as foes of that family. There was also a small sept of MacAnultys in Co. Cavan. The situation as regards Donegal is complicated by the MacDunlevys, a royal family of Ulidia, modern southeast Ulster, who were driven out by John de Courcy in the twelfth century and settled in Donegal. One of the names they assumed there was Mac an Ultaigh, 'son of the Ulidian' (*see* Dunleavy).

Derryman Frank Joseph MacNulty, 1872–1926, became a famous labour leader in the USA.

MACPARLAN *see* MacFarland

MACPARLAND *see* MacFarland

MACPARTLAN *see* MacFarland

MACPARTLIN *see* MacFarland

MACQUADE *see* MacQuaid

MACQUAID (*also* MacQuade *and* Wade)

Though found in Leinster and Connacht, MacQuaid or MacQuade is common only in Ulster. There the name is most common in counties Monaghan and Fermanagh, where it is usually spelt MacQuaid, and in Co. Antrim, where MacQuade is the prevalent spelling.

The name was originally in Gaelic Mac Uaid, 'son of Watt', and was that of a sept of Monaghan centred at Ballyglassloch. The origins of this family are obscure, but they were associated with the church at Donagh.

In 1970 the name was the forty-seventh most common in Co. Monaghan and was found throughout the county except the south.

The name Wade in Ireland has three possible derivations: an English name from the Old English *waddan*, 'to go'; from the Norman French name de la Wade, 'of the ford'; or as a shortening of MacWade, a variant of the above. Most, especially in southeast Ulster, will be of the last derivation. Around 1900 the name MacQuaid was noted as interchangeable with the unusual name MacAragh in the Irvinestown district of Fermanagh.

John Charles McQuaid, 1895–1973, Archbishop of Dublin, was born at Cootehill, Co. Cavan. A vigorously orthodox Catholic, he is perhaps most famous for his opposition to Dr Noel Browne's mother-and-child health scheme of 1951.

MACQUILLAN

MacQuillan is found in Leinster and Connacht but is common only in Ulster, especially in counties Antrim and Monaghan. The Welsh Norman family of de Mandeville came to north Antrim in the late twelfth century and wrested the territory known as the Route and its main stronghold, Dunluce Castle, from the O'Kanes. They rapidly became 'hibernicised' and a recognised Irish sept, prominent in the area until they, in turn, were ousted by the MacDonnells.

The progenitor of the sept was Hugelin de Mandeville and from his name the family took the Gaelic name Mac Uighilín, which was later anglicised as MacQuillan. The de Mandevilles also took the barony of Dufferin in Co. Down and these MacQuillans were for a long time in close alliance with the Savages of the Ards peninsula.

In Co. Monaghan, one of the centres of the name, MacQuillan can be of this de Mandeville origin, but it can equally be an anglicisation of Mac Cuilinn (from *cuileann*, 'holly'), a name also made MacCollin and Mac-Cullen (*see* Collins *and* Cullen). The form Quillan is sometimes used as a synonym of Holly. Lastly, some Monaghan MacQuillans will be originally Campbell galloglasses (*see* MacCallion). MacQuillan has also become confused with MacWilliam and MacWilliams (*see* MacWilliams).

MACQUISTON *see* Houston

MACSHANE

MacShane is common only in Co. Louth and in Ulster, particularly Co. Donegal. In both these counties the MacShanes descend from a branch of the O'Neills. This sept was in Gaelic Mac Seáin, 'son of John', originally of northeast Tyrone.

However, like MacKeag, the name was also widely adopted as a simple patronymic, denoting the son of a particular John rather than a sept as such. From whichever origin, the name was once more common but has been widely anglicised by translation to Johnson and by mistranslation to Johnston (*see* Johnston).

MACSORLEY

In Ireland MacSorley is almost exclusive to Ulster, where it is most common in Co. Tyrone. The name is in Gaelic Mac Somhairle, from a Norse personal name usually anglicised as Somerled.

The name is of Scottish origin. The MacSorleys, one of the three main branches of Clan Cameron, descend from Somerled, armiger to John of Yla, Earl of Ross and Lord of the Isles. There were also MacSorleys, a sept of Clan Lamont, and indeed when the name of that clan was proscribed many took the name MacSorley, holding it for several generations before returning to their original name. Lastly, the progenitor of Clan Donald was Somerled of Argyll and there were MacSorleys, an important sept of that clan.

It was Clan Donald MacSorleys who came to Ulster from the thirteenth through to the late sixteenth centuries as galloglasses. They became very closely associated with the MacDonnells of the Glens of Antrim. Most in Ulster will be of this origin.

MACSWEENEY *see* Sweeney

MACVEAGH *see* MacVeigh

MACVEIGH (*also* MacVeagh)

Though found in Leinster and Connacht these names are common only in Ulster where they are most numerous in counties Antrim and Down. In the seventeenth century they were also common in Co. Donegal. The names are of Scottish origin, Gaelic Mac an Bheatha. This was not a patronymic but was originally a personal name in its own right meaning 'son of life'. The name in Scotland became Beton, MacBeth and MacVeagh.

There were MacBeths of Moray, allies to the MacBains (*see* MacIlwaine) of Clan Chattan, and also MacBeths or Betons of Skye. The main connection, though, were the MacBeths, a sept of Clan Donald, hereditary physicians to the Lords of the Isles. Tradition claims that this sept descends from one Beath who came from Ireland in the train of the widow O'Neill who married Angus Óg of the Isles. MacLysaght also claims they were of O'Neill descent. However, George Hill states that Angus Óg married Áine, a daughter of Cumhaighe Ó Catháin (O'Cahan – *see* Kane) of Derry. Whatever their Irish origin, these MacBeths were based on Islay and a branch settled on Mull and there became physicians to the Macleans of Duart.

MacVeighs of counties Tyrone and Fermanagh can be of this origin but can also be descendants of Scottish galloglass MacEvies, who fought for the O'Neills of Tyrone and the O'Rourkes of Breffny. The north Fermanagh name Eves is of the same origin.

Besides MacVeagh and MacVeigh the name is also found in the form MacVey and has also become confused with MacEvoy (*see* MacEvoy).

MACWILLIAMS

In Ireland MacWilliams is common only in Ulster where it is most numerous in counties Antrim and Derry. The name William, Old German Willihelm, was early introduced to the Highlands of Scotland and quickly gaelicised. The resulting patronymic Mac Uilleim is the origin of the Scottish name MacWilliam, a name more common in Ulster with the 's' appended. Other Scottish forms of the name are MacCullie, MacKillie, MacQuilliam and Williamson (*see* Williamson). There were MacWilliam septs of Clan Gunn and Clan MacFarlane.

In Ulster, particularly Co. Down, the name MacQuillan has become MacWilliam. At the beginning of the twentieth century MacWilliams was still being used interchangeably with MacQuillan near Newry, Co. Down, with MacQuilliams near Magherafelt, Co. Derry, and with MacCollyums in the Toome district of Co. Antrim.

MAGAURAN *see* MacGovern

MAGEE (*also* MacGee)

Taken together these names are among the 100 most common names in Ireland and among the twenty-five most common in Ulster. Magee is found mainly in counties Antrim, Armagh and Down, and MacGee in counties Donegal and Tyrone. The names can be of Scottish or Irish origin. In both countries the Gaelic form is Mag Aoidh, 'son of Hugh'. With names like Magee and Magill the Mag- form is more common in east Ulster and the Mac- form in the west.

Islandmagee on the Antrim coast was once the seat of the Magees, a prominent Irish Gaelic sept. There were also MacGees, recorded as Muintear Mhaoil Ghaoithe, an important ruling sept in medieval Tirconnell. A branch of the Cenél Chonaill, they were erenaghs of Clondahorky in the barony of Kilmacrenan.

Apart from these, the majority of Ulster Magees or MacGees will be of Scottish origin, descendants of settlers who came to the province at the time of the Plantation. The name is found in Scotland as MacGee, MacGhee and MacGhie and was first recorded in Dumfries in 1296. There, and in Ayrshire and Galloway, the name is most common. These were kin to the MacDonald MacHughs or MacKees (*see* MacHugh *and* MacKay).

The name Magee is most concentrated in Antrim around Crumlin, and in Down in Lecale and on the adjacent Upper Ards. MacGees and Magees in Fermanagh are mainly a branch of the Maguires, descendants of Aodh, great-grandson of Donn Carrach Maguire. In Co. Cavan Magee has become Wynne and Wynn because of the -gee ending, which sounds like the Gaelic *gaoithe*, meaning 'of wind'.

The Most Revd William Magee, 1766–1831, Archbishop of Dublin, was also a mathematician. His grandson William Connor Magee, 1821–91, active opponent of Home Rule and rector of Enniskillen, Co. Fermanagh, became Archbishop of York. John Magee, 1750–1809, printer and journalist, was born in Belfast. As proprietor of the *Dublin Evening Post* he was popular for his anti-establishment position, but was several times imprisoned for libel. His son John, 1780–1814, also as proprietor, carried on the tradition, with the same results. Magee College in Derry was founded by Martha Maria Magee, *née* Stewart, *c.* 1755–1846, after a long controversy with the Revd Henry Cooke and the Presbyterian General Assembly.

MAGENNIS *see* MacGuinness

MAGILL (*also* MacGill)

Though found in Leinster and Connacht, these names are common only in Ulster and those parts of Scotland where they originate. As with Magee or MacGee, the Mag- form is more common in east Ulster, especially counties Antrim, Armagh and Down and the Mac- form in west Ulster, especially counties Donegal and Tyrone. Magill is three times more common than MacGill.

The name in Scotland is MacGill, Gaelic Mac an Ghoill, 'son of the Lowlander or stranger (*gall*)'. The name is most numerous in the province of Galloway, whence stemmed so many of the post-Plantation settlers. There were also MacGills on the island of Jura. These were known as the Clann an Ghoill and were recorded as settling in Co. Antrim from the fourteenth century on. MacLysaght claims these were Scottish gallo-glasses but Gerard Hayes-McCoy, in his *Scots Mercenary Forces in*

Ireland (1565–1603), states quite categorically that they 'never appear to have been mentioned as *gallóglaigh'*.

In the mid-seventeenth century MacGill was most common in the Antrim barony of Glenarm. Two hundred years later this was still the case. At this later date a particular concentration of the name was noted in the Co. Down parish of Annahilt. The Co. Armagh name MacGuill is a variant of MacQuill, Gaelic Mac Cuill, not of MacGill. Around 1900 Magill was being used interchangeably with Mackel, Maguil and Mekill in the Poyntzpass district of Co. Armagh.

In Scotland it is thought that MacGill has been used as a shortening of Mac Ghille Mhaoil, a name more usually made Bell and Macmillan (*see* Bell *and* Macmillan). In Ireland it is thought that both MacGill and the shorter form Gill have been used for any one of the wide variety of names that begin Mac Giolla-: MacGilheron, MacGilpatrick and so on.

Patrick MacGill, 1891–1963, was the first of eleven children of a poor farmer in Glenties, Co. Donegal. Initially a navvy, he became a poet and novelist. His most famous works are *Songs of a Navvy, Songs of the Dead End* and the semi-autobiographical novel, *Children of the Dead End*.

MAGINN *see* MacGinn

MAGOWAN *see* MacGowan

MAGRATH *see* MacGrath

MAGUIRE (*also* MacGuire)

Maguire is among the forty most common names in Ireland, among the top twenty-five in Ulster, ten in Co. Cavan, thirty in Co. Monaghan and is the single most common name in Co. Fermanagh. The MacGuire spelling is most favoured in Connacht, particularly in counties Roscommon and Mayo. The name is in Gaelic Mag Uidhir, from the word *odhar*, genitive case *uidhir*, meaning 'dun-coloured'.

Though the name first appears in the annals in 956, the family did not come to prominence until about 1200 when Donn Mór Maguire established the sept in Lisnaskea, Co. Fermanagh. Donn Carrach Maguire, died 1302, was the first Maguire chieftain of all Fermanagh. Between that date and 1600 there were fifteen Maguire rulers of Fermanagh. At the latter date, as Livingstone puts it in *The Fermanagh Story*, 'Fermanagh was simply a Maguire property'. A junior branch was based at Enniskillen and it was these that were most involved in the Nine Years War, 1594–1603, and subsequently it was they who suffered most at the Plantation.

However, the main Lisnaskea line was broken by the Cromwellian and Williamite confiscations. Conor Maguire, 1616–45, Bishop of Clogher, was executed for his part in the 1641 rising. The leading members of the family became prominent among the Wild Geese, particularly in France and Austria. Maguiresbridge in Co. Fermanagh, in Gaelic Droichead Mhig Uidhir, probably derives its name from the Maguires of Derryheely.

As MacGuire, the name is found in Scotland and is that of a sept of the Clan Macquarrie of the island of Ulva. Both the sept name and the clan name derive from the founder of the clan, one Guaire, a brother of Fingon, ancestor of the Mackinnons. The Clan Macquarrie claims that the Fermanagh Maguires descend from Gregor, second son of Cormac Mór Macquarrie, chief of the name. Since Cormac Mór Maguire was active in the mid-thirteenth century, fifty years after Donn Mór Maguire founded the Lisnaskea sept, it is plain that there is no substance to this claim, but none the less some MacGuires in Ulster may be of this Scottish origin.

MALLON

Mallon, and also Mellan and Mellon, are common only in Ulster, particularly in counties Tyrone and Armagh. The names are originally in Gaelic Ó Mealláin, from *meall,* meaning 'pleasant'. The O'Mellans were an important sept who gave their name to the Meallanacht, 'O'Mellan's Country', an area in south Derry and north Tyrone. The name has been much confused with Mullan (*see* Mullan) especially around Cookstown, Co. Tyrone. The O'Mullans were originally located north of the Sperrins and the O'Mellans to the south.

The O'Mellans were a sept of the Cenél Eoghain, descending ultimately from Eoghan (who gave his name to Tyrone), son of Niall of the Nine Hostages, fifth-century founder of the Uí Néill dynasty. With the Mulhollands, the sept were joint keepers of St Patrick's bell, the Bell of the Testament. Their prevalence in present-day Co. Armagh stems from several groups of them being settled on the church lands of the archbishop. Some O'Mellans adopted the Scottish name Munroe.

The Franciscan Turlough O'Mellan's *Ulster War Diary, 1614–17* is an invaluable account of that conflict.

MANN *see* MacManus

MARRON

Although this name is found in Connacht, where it is spelt Marren, it is most common in Ulster. In 1970 it was found to be the twenty-fourth most common name in Co. Monaghan and the third most common name in the south of that county. It is in Gaelic Ó Mearáin, thought to be from *mear*, 'quick, lively'. Historically the name has always been associated with Monaghan, where the sept is thought to have been based in Anna-marron in the barony of Killanny. However, Petty's 'census' of 1659 noted O'Merran as a 'principal Irish name' around Carrickfergus, Co. Antrim. MacLysaght has misread Matheson in saying that Marron and Mearn were used interchangeably in Ballymena in Co. Antrim in 1900. The two names were in fact synonymous in the Portaferry district of Co. Down. The Marrens of Co. Sligo are probably of a distinct sept.

MARSHALL

This name is found in all the provinces of Ireland but is common only in Ulster, where it is strongest in counties Down, Derry and Antrim. It is also well known in Dublin. It has been recorded in Ireland since early medieval times but its current prevalence in Ulster probably stems from post-Plantation Scottish settlers.

The name is Norman, originally le Mareschal. It stems from the Old French *mareschal*, meaning 'horse servant'. (The word survives in modern French as *maréchal*, meaning a 'farrier'.) Although the position of marshall became one of great dignity, it is thought that, in Scotland at least, the majority of Marshalls derive their name from the more humble occupational name. A particular concentration of the name was noted north of Newry in Co. Down in the late nineteenth century.

MARTIN

This name in Ulster can be of Irish, Scottish or English origin. It is among the forty most common names in Ireland and in England and among the top fifty in Scotland. In Ulster it is among the twenty most common names. It is among the first ten in Co. Down and the first twenty in counties Antrim, Monaghan and Cavan.

In Monaghan and Cavan most Martins will be originally MacGilmartins, Gaelic Mac Giolla Mháirtín, meaning 'son of the devotee of (St) Martin'. (This name has also been made Gilmartin and Kilmartin.) The Mac-Gilmartins were a branch of the O'Neills, originally of Tyrone, and still found there and in Fermanagh. Livingstone suggests that many of the Fermanagh Martins are descendants of the Maguires. Also in Tyrone, Martin can be from MacMartin, Gaelic Mac Máirtín, another branch of the O'Neills.

The personal name Martin, a diminutive or pet form of the Latin name Martius, from Mars, god of war, was very popular from an early date and also became a surname in England and Scotland. There are twenty-five places named Saint-Martin in Normandy and de St Martin was a common

Norman name. The de St Martins of East Lothian in Scotland were once a great family who later shortened their name to Martin. Also St Martin of Tours in France was the teacher of St Ninian of Whithorn in Galloway and as such was widely revered in Scotland. This is the origin of the Scots Gaelic name Mac Ghille Mhartainn, 'son of the devotee of (St) Martin', a name shortened to Mac Mhartainn, anglicised to MacMartin and then made Martin. MacMartin was the appellation of the Camerons of Letter-finlay in Inverness-shire, one of the three main branches of the Clan Cameron. Their name was also shortened to Martin. There were also Martins, a sept of Clan Donald, based in Kilmuir in Skye, neighbours of the Macqueens.

In the mid-nineteenth century Martin was found to be common in thirteen of the fourteen Antrim baronies and especially in Lower Antrim and Upper Massereene. At that time Martin was the second most numerous name in Co. Down, especially in Upper and Lower Iveagh, Upper Castle-reagh, Kinelearty, Lecale and Ards, with strong concentrations in the parishes of Loughinisland and Dromore.

Robert Montgomery Martin, 1803–68, from Tyrone, travelled exten-sively and was the author of *The History of the British Colonies*. Henry Newell Martin, 1848–96, was born in Newry, Co. Down, the son of a Congregational minister who emigrated to America. He became a brilliant biologist and was professor in Johns Hopkins University in Baltimore. John Martin, 1812–75, also born in Newry, the son of a Presbyterian minister, became a Young Irelander and was a lifelong friend and brother-in-law to John Mitchel, founder of the newspaper the *United Irishman*. When Mitchel was arrested Martin founded the *Irish Felon,* for which he was tried and transported to Van Dieman's Land (now Tasmania). When he returned to Ireland he was elected MP for Meath. He was known throughout Ireland as 'Honest John Martin'.

MASTERSON *see* MacMaster

MATEER *see* MacIntyre

MATHEWS (*also* Matthews)

In Ireland this name is common only in Ulster, particularly in counties Antrim and Down, and in Dublin and Louth. In Ulster it can be of English, Scottish or Irish origin.

The personal name Matthew is from the Hebrew Mattithyah, meaning 'gift of Yahweh (God)'. It was introduced into England by the Normans and quickly became very popular. The surname Mathews or Matthews was originally Mathewson, 'son of Mathew'.

In Scotland the name MacMath or MacMa, Gaelic Mac Mhatha, meant 'Mathew's son' and was anglicised as Mathewson and also Matheson. MacMath was common in Perthshire, Kintyre, Ayrshire, Galloway and Dumfriesshire. However, the name of the Clan Matheson was originally Mac Mhathain, 'son of the bear', a name cognate with the Irish MacMahon. In Ireland many of the name Mathews, especially in south Ulster, will be originally MacMahons (*see* MacMahon).

MATTHEWS *see* Mathews

MAWHINNEY *see* Buchanan

MAXWELL

Outside of Dublin, Maxwell is common only in Ulster, and there only in counties Antrim and Down. The name is Scottish in origin.

Maccus, son of Undewyn, a Saxon lord in the reign of the Scottish King David I, was granted land on the River Tweed at some time before 1150. His salmon fishery there became known as Maccus's Wiel (from Old English *wael*, a 'pool'). The lands acquired the same name and the Maxwell family took their name from them. It is thought that the place-name and surname Maxton of Roxburghshire derive from the same Maccus. One of the Maxtons of Perthshire penned the famous 'Maxton Litany' which offers an interesting aside on a few Ulster names:

> From the greed of the Campbells,
> From the ire of the Drummonds,
> From the pride of the Grahams,
> From the wind of the Murrays,
> Good Lord, deliver us.

The first on record to use the name Maxwell in its modern form was Sir John Maxwell, chamberlain of Scotland in the thirteenth century. The Maxwells were based in Annandale in Dumfriesshire and became Lords Maxwell and Earls of Nithsdale. They were the strongest of the riding clans of the West March of the Scottish Borders until they were eclipsed by the Johnstones in the sixteenth century. For centuries they were wardens of the West March and stewards of Annandale and Kirkcudbright. Their feud with the Johnstones was perhaps the longest, bloodiest and most famous in Scottish history.

After the riding clans were broken by James VI and their social system eradicated, many Maxwells turned to the Plantation of Ulster to escape persecution. Perhaps not surprisingly they did not follow their neighbours the Johnstones, the Armstrongs, the Irvines and so on, to Co. Fermanagh, preferring to settle in Down and Antrim.

William Hamilton Maxwell, 1792–1850, rector of Balla, Co. Mayo, was a successful novelist. He is best remembered for his *Wild Sports of the West of Ireland*. He was born in Newry, Co. Down.

MEEGAN *see* Meehan

MEEHAN (*also* Meegan)

Meehan is common in every province of Ireland and is found in virtually every county. In Ulster it is most common in Co. Donegal. Meegan is found almost exclusively in Co. Monaghan. Meehan is in Gaelic Ó Miadhacháin and Meegan, Ó Miadhagáin. Both derive from the word *miadhach*, meaning 'honourable'.

There were two septs of O'Meehan. One was of Co. Galway and Co. Clare. The other was a branch of the MacCarthys of Desmond, who migrated in the eleventh century to Co. Leitrim. From there they spread into the adjacent counties of Donegal and Fermanagh. They gave their name to Ballymeehan in the parish of Rossinver in Fermanagh. Successive generations of O'Meehans preserved a manuscript of St Molaise of Devenish for over a thousand years before entrusting it to the National Museum of Ireland in Dublin. Livingstone states that the O'Meehans, erenaghs of Devenish, were in Gaelic Ó Míotháin. The Co. Sligo name Ó Maotháin has also been made Meehan. In Antrim and Down MacMeekin, Gaelic Mac Miadhacháin, has been confused with Meegan and Meighan. Meighan is a variant of Meehan.

At the beginning of the twentieth century Meehan was still being used interchangeably with Mee around Newry in Down, with Meegan around Castleblayney in Monaghan and with Meekin in Belfast.

MERCER

In Ireland Mercer is virtually exclusive to Ulster, where the great majority are in Antrim and Down. The name derives from the French *mercier*, a 'merchant' and, as le Mercier and le Mercer, is fairly common in medieval Irish records. Most in Ulster, however, will be of Scottish origin.

The name in Scotland has the same derivation. The first on record was William le Mercer, who lived at Kelso in Roxburghshire around 1200. The most famous Scottish family of the name were the Mercers of Aldie, who from the mid-fourteenth century were closely associated with the history of Perth. The family at one time exchanged the two 'Inches of Perth' for the right to be buried in St John's Church, Perth. Or as an old rhyme puts it:

Folk say the Mercers tried the town to cheat
When for two Inches they did win six feet.

In the mid-nineteenth century a particular concentration of the name was noted in the parish of Hillsborough in Co. Down. Fifty years later the name was noted as synonymous with Massa in the city of Armagh.

MILLAR (*also* Miller)

The great majority of Millars and Millers in Ireland, outside of Dublin, are in Ulster. Taken together, the names are among the forty most common in Ulster and among the fifteen most common in Co. Antrim. Indeed two-thirds of those of the name are in that county. There are also many in Co. Derry. Millar or Miller was noted as a 'principal name' in Co. Antrim in the mid-seventeenth century. The names are of either English or Scottish origin.

In England Miller was originally Milner. In the south of England this derived from the Middle English *mylne*, a 'mill'. But the name was most common in the northern and eastern counties and there it derived from the Old Norse *mylnari*, a 'miller'.

The spelling Millar is Scottish and as a hereditary surname it did not appear until the fifteenth century. As every burgh had its miller the name sprang up independently all over the country. There were also Millars, a sept of Clan MacFarlane.

In mid-nineteenth-century Co. Antrim the name was found to be, with MacAllister, the most common name in the barony of Kilconway and at the same time a particular concentration was noted on the Ards peninsula in Co. Down. John Millar was an early Plantation tenant in Magheraboy in Fermanagh and the name is still common in that barony.

MILLER *see* Millar

MILLIGAN (*also* Milliken)

In Ireland these names are virtually exclusive to Ulster where half are in Co. Antrim and most of the rest in counties Down and Derry. The names can be of Irish or Scottish origin.

If Irish, the names are in Gaelic Ó Maoileagáin, a form of Ó Maolagáin (*see* Mulligan). Both names are diminutive forms of *maol*, meaning 'bald' or 'tonsured'. In the sixteenth and seventeenth centuries Milligan was most common in northeast Ulster and in Sligo.

However, both Milligan and Milliken are also common across the Irish Sea in Galloway, where they have been recorded since 1296. There they have the same Gaelic derivation and are thought to have been of Irish origin.

Around 1900 Milligan was being used interchangeably with Mulligan about Armagh city, and Moira, Co. Down, and with Mulligan and Mullan around Newry in Co. Down. Alice Milligan, 1865–1953, born in Omagh, Co. Tyrone, was a distinguished poet and organiser for the Gaelic League, whose work did much to influence the early Sinn Féin movement. With Anna MacManus she founded and co-edited *The Northern Patriot* and *Shan Van Vocht*.

MILLIKEN *see* Milligan

MILLS

In Ireland this name is well known in Leinster and Connacht but is most common in Ulster, especially counties Antrim and Down. Not much is known of its history. It is an English name, not particularly common in any area, and may have originally signified a 'dweller by the mills', or it may have derived from 'Miles's son'. In the mid-nineteenth century a particular concentration of the name was noted to the north of Dromore, in the barony of Lower Iveagh in Co. Down.

MINNIS *see* MacGuinness

MITCHELL

Mitchell is common in every province except Munster, and found in nearly every county of Ireland. None the less about half are in Ulster. The name there is mainly of Scottish and English origin, though a few will be Irish.

Mitchell derives from the Hebrew name Michael (which means 'who is like God') through the French form Michel. It was also used as a forename. In England the name can also derive from Middle English *michel*, meaning 'big'. The name is common in England but is among the thirty most numerous in Scotland where it is found in many parts of the country. The Mitchells of the east and northeast are counted as a sept of Clan Innes.

The Co. Roscommon name Ó Maoilmhicil, 'descendant of the devotee of (St) Michael', anglicised as Mulvihil and Melville, was in Ulster, particularly in Co. Donegal, made Mitchell.

John Mitchel, 1815–75, was descended from a Scottish Covenanter who sought refuge in Donegal. The son of a Presbyterian minister in Newry, Co. Down, be became one of the most famous Irish republicans. He founded the newspaper the *United Irishman,* was convicted of treason and transported to Van Dieman's Land (now Tasmania) but escaped to America. His *Jail Journal* is a classic of prison literature.

MOAN *see* Mohan

MOFFATT

In Ireland this name is common only in Co. Sligo and in Ulster, mainly in counties Antrim and Tyrone. It appears in a wide variety of spellings including Maffett, Mefatt, Moffat, Moffet, Moffett, Moffit, Moffitt, and so on. The name first appears in Ireland in the early seventeenth century.

It is of local origin from the town of Moffat in Annandale in Dumfriesshire and was first recorded as a surname in 1232. The Moffats were one of the lesser of the turbulent riding clans of the Scottish Borders, located in the Scottish West March. Many members of the riding clans sought refuge in Ulster when their power and social system were destroyed by James VI.

The Moffetts of Co. Monaghan descend from one James Moffett of Cumberland, who settled there in the early eighteenth century.

MOHAN (*also* Moan)

Apart from a few Mohans and Moans in Connacht, this name is common only in Ulster, where it is most numerous in counties Monaghan and Fermanagh. The name was twenty-seventh most common in Monaghan in 1970.

MacLysaght notes the prevalence of the name in Monaghan but claims that it originates in Connacht as Ó Mócháin, the name of a sept of Co. Galway and another of Co. Roscommon. He states that there are no mentions of Mohan in medieval records in Monaghan.

Livingstone, however, says that the Mohans of Monaghan and Fermanagh were an Uí Chremthainn family based in Clankelly in Fermanagh and descend from one Mocan, brother of Corracan, the progenitor of the Corrigans. Moen, Mone and Mowen are other variants.

The Welsh name Vaughan, which derives from the word *fychan,* meaning 'of small stature', has also been used for Mohan, as has Mahon (*see* MacMahon).

MOLLOY

This name is less common in Ulster than in Leinster and Connacht. The original sept of the name was called Ó Maolmhuaidh and was important in Fercal in Offaly. But Molloy has also been used for several other Irish names. In Ulster these include the Connacht and Donegal name Mulvogue or Logue (*see* Logue) and the Monaghan name Slowey (*see* Sloan). MacCloy in Co. Derry was made Maloy by some families (*see* Fullerton). In Ulster the name is most common in Co. Donegal.

MONAGHAN (*also* Monahan)

These names are common in Ulster, Leinster and Connacht but less so in Munster. In Ulster it is most numerous in Co. Fermanagh. The name is in Gaelic Ó Manacháin, from *manach*, a 'monk'. Indeed some of the family adopted the English name Monks, as did the MacEvannys, Gaelic Mac an Mhanaigh, also from *manach*, 'monk' (*see* Kavanagh).

Most in Ireland descend from the O'Monaghans, lords of the Three Tuaghs (an area between modern Elphin and Jamestown) in Co. Roscommon. The eponymous ancestor of this sept was one Manachán, a ninth-century warrior of Connacht.

However, the O'Monaghans of Fermanagh are a local sept who were based in Lurg and are thought to have descended from the original Fir Manach. The Monaghans of counties Derry and Monaghan are of the same origin. Monaghan was the twenty-fourth most common name in Fermanagh in 1962.

Around 1900 Monaghan was being used interchangeably with Menaght in the Greyabbey district of the Ards peninsula in Co. Down. Menaght is a Co. Down variant of MacNaughton (*see* MacKnight).

MONAHAN *see* Monaghan

MONTAGUE *see* MacKeag

MONTGOMERY

The great majority of Montgomerys in Ireland are in Ulster and more than half are in counties Antrim and Down alone. Although the name is frequently found in Irish records of the thirteenth and fourteenth centuries, particularly in Leinster, most in Ulster descend from the Scottish landlord family so closely connected with the history of Ulster from the time of the Plantation.

The name is Norman in origin, from the castle of Sainte Foi de Montgomery in the diocese of Lisieux in Normandy. Roger de Montgomerie was joint regent of Normandy at the time of the Norman Conquest of England and the family was very powerful in Norman England (Montgomeryshire in Wales is named after it). The first in Scotland was Robert de Mundegumri, died *c.* 1177, who was granted Eaglesham in Renfrewshire. A branch of the Montgomerys of Eaglesham were the Montgomeries of Braidstane in Ayrshire.

It was Sir Hugh Montgomerie of Braidstane, an adviser to James VI, who effected the escape of Conn O'Neill from Carrickfergus in Co. Antrim and had him brought to Braidstane. A deal was struck whereby Montgomery would acquire half of O'Neill's lands in return for Montgomery procuring him a pardon. Sir James Fullarton, a favourite of the king, insisted that the lands be split three ways, among O'Neill, Montgomery and Sir James Hamilton. Fearing to leave O'Neill access to the coast, the king also granted the Ards peninsula (from O'Neill's portion) to Montgomery and Hamilton. In 1622 Sir Hugh was created Viscount Montgomery of the Great Ardes and thereafter assumed the -ery spelling.

Montgomery brought a great number of his kinsmen in from Scotland and cadet branches were founded in Blackstown, Creboy, Ballyhanwood, Ballymagown and Ballynahooe in Co. Down, Ballyhovell in Co. Leitrim, Derrybrusk and Derrygonnelly in Co. Fermanagh, and Ballyleck in Co. Monaghan. The most famous Ulsterman of the name was Field Marshal Viscount Montgomery of Alamein, 1887–1976, who was of a Donegal branch of the family. Leslie A. Montgomery, 1873–1961, who was born in Downpatrick, Co. Down, was, under his pseudonym Lynn C. Doyle (a play on linseed oil), famous for his stories of the fictitious border village Ballygullion.

Around 1900 Montgomery was being used interchangeably with MacGivern about Clough in Co. Down and with the corrupt form Maglammery in Co. Armagh around Poyntzpass and Armagh city.

MOONEY

Mooney is most common in Leinster but is still much more common in Ulster than in Munster and Connacht. The name is in Gaelic Ó Maonaigh, which is either from *moenach*, meaning 'dumb', or from *maonach*, meaning 'wealthy'. There were several unrelated septs of O'Mooneys in Ireland, the most numerous being those of Co. Offaly.

The only known sept of Ulster were the O'Mooneys, erenaghs of the church lands of Shanaghan in the parish of Ardara in Co. Donegal. These descended from one Monach, son of Ailioll Mór. The name has also been made Moany and Money.

A Franciscan, Donagh Mooney, was guardian of the young O'Donnell, Earl of Tirconnell, and the young O'Neill, Earl of Tyrone, at Louvain in Belgium in the early seventeenth century.

MOORE

This name, which can be of English, Irish or Scottish origin, is among the twenty most common in Ireland and has the distinction of being found in every county. A quarter of all the Moores in Ireland are in Co. Antrim alone and the name is common too in counties Derry and Tyrone.

Moore is one of the forty most numerous names in England and can derive from the old personal name More, which is from the Old French name Maur, the Latin name Maurus, meaning a 'Moor' or 'swarthy as a Moor'. It can also derive from residence in or near a moor, from Old English *mor*, meaning 'moor, marsh, fen'.

In Scotland the name is of this latter origin and is rendered Moore, More or, most commonly, Muir. It was first noted, in a variety of places, in the thirteenth century. There were Mores, a sept of Clan Leslie, and Muirs, a sept of Clan Campbell.

In Ireland the name derives from the Gaelic Ó Mórdha, from *mórdha*, meaning 'stately, noble'. This was the name of the leading sept of the Seven Septs of Leix, based at Dunamase, a few miles from Portlaoise, Co. Laois. The O'Mores claim descent from one Mórdha and he, it is claimed, was twenty-first in descent from the legendary Conall Cearnach, hero of the Red Branch Knights of Ulster.

The Co. Antrim name Moorhead is a variant of the Scottish Muirhead, a name first recorded in the fourteenth century and probably taken from Muirhead in the barony of Bothwell in Lanarkshire.

The most famous Ulster Moore in the twentieth century is the novelist Brian Moore who was born in 1921 in Belfast.

MORGAN

Though common in Leinster and well known in Munster and Connacht, this name is most numerous in Ulster, particularly in counties Antrim, Down and Armagh. Morgan is among the fifty most common names in England and Wales. Most in Ulster will very likely be of Welsh origin, deriving from the Old Welsh name Morcant, 'sea-bright'. Variants of this are found in Old British, Old Breton and Cornish as well as Welsh. The Pictish form in Scotland was Morgunn. Historically the name Morgan in Scotland has been found only in Sutherland, the home of the Clann Morgunn, and in Aberdeenshire. It is possible that some in Ulster will be of Scottish origin.

The Morgans of Co. Monaghan are Irish, their name in Gaelic being Ó Murcháin, remembered in the placename Aghamacmoregan.

MORRIS

In Ireland Morris is most common in Leinster, followed by Ulster and Connacht. In Ulster it is most numerous in counties Tyrone and Monaghan. Morris is among the forty most common names in England and Wales but is well known too in Scotland.

The surname Morris derives from the personal name Maurice, a popular name with the Normans and introduced by them into Britain. Maurice is from the Latin name Maurus, meaning 'Moorish' (see Moore).

The Co. Sligo sept of Ó Muirgheasa anglicised their name to Morris, as did the Uí Muireasa of Fermanagh. One of the Norman Tribes of Galway, the de Marries, meaning 'of the marshes', also became Morrises.

MORRISON

Morrison is found in all the provinces of Ireland but is common only in Ulster, particularly in counties Antrim, Down and Fermanagh. It was the twenty-first most common name in Fermanagh in 1962. The name is among the thirty most numerous in Scotland. In Ulster it can be of Scottish or Irish origin although some may be English.

In Co. Donegal the learned sept of Ó Muirgheasáin (from Muirgheas, 'sea valour'), were erenaghs of Clonmany in Inishowen. For generations they were keepers of the Clonmany relic of St Columcille, the 'Miosach'. They anglicised their name to O'Morison, then Morison and Morrison. An earlier anglicisation was O'Mrisane. From this, many took the English name Bryson, especially in Co. Derry. (Bryson, Brice and Bryce were also used in Co. Donegal for Breslin [see Breslin].)

A branch of the Donegal O'Morrisons at some unknown date migrated to Lewis and Harris in the Scottish Isles. Some became bards to the MacLeods of Dunvegan. Their chief had his seat at Habost Ness in Lewis and was hereditary judge of the island. Their name eventually became Morrison and they were known as Clan Morrison, deadly enemies of the Lewis MacAulays. In Gaelic they were known as either Clann-na Breitheamh or as Clann Mhic-Gille-Mhóire. This last-mentioned Gaelic name presents something of a problem, as it is sometimes claimed that the Clan Morrison were originally MacGilmores (see Gilmore).

Elsewhere in Scotland (and also in England) Morrison derives from 'son of Maurice' (see Morris). There were also two septs of Clan Buchanan called MacMaurice, both descending from illegitimate sons, both called Maurice, one of the second Laird of Buchanan and one of the fourth Laird. Both these septs became Morrisons.

MORROW

In Ireland this name is almost exclusive to Ulster where it is most common in counties Antrim, Donegal, Armagh and Down. It is also well known in Co. Fermanagh.

Morrow is an English name and derives either from residence in a row of houses on a moor or from the Old Norse *vrá*, Middle English *wra*, meaning 'nook, corner'. This word also gives the English name Rowe as well as Wray (*see* Rea). Morrow was originally le Murwra in Cumbria.

In Fermanagh Morrow was originally MacMorrow, in Gaelic Mac Muireadhaigh, from Muireadhach, a 'mariner'. This was the name of a sept of Co. Leitrim, based in Loughmoytagh. The name was also anglicised as MacMurry (*see* Murray). Also in Fermanagh some Morrows may be originally Murphys (*see* Murphy), a branch of the Maguires.

In the mid-nineteenth century Morrow was found to be particularly concentrated in the Antrim barony of Lower Glenarm and, in Down, in the parish of Killaney in Upper Castlereagh and in Derryboy near Killyleagh.

MORTON

Apart from a few Mortons in Dublin, this name is virtually exclusive to Ulster, where over half are in Co. Antrim alone. It was first recorded in Ireland in the thirteenth century, but most in Ulster will be of post-Plantation origin.

The name is Scottish and is local in origin, either from Morton in Dumfriesshire, or from the lands of Myrton, a corrupt form of Muirtoun, later Morton, in the parish of Kemback in Fife, from which the most famous family, the Mortons of Cambo, took their name.

MULHOLLAND

Mulholland is almost exclusive to Ulster, where it is most common in counties Antrim, Down and Derry. The name is in Gaelic Ó Maolchalann, 'son of the devotee of (St) Calann'. Although there was a sept of Mulhollands in Co. Donegal, most of the name descend from the Mulhollands of Loughinsholin in Co. Derry. They are famous for having been, with the Mallons, the hereditary keepers of St Patrick's bell, the Bell of the Testament. From the fourteenth century the family spread into the western and southern part of Massereene in Co. Antrim, in which barony the name is seventh most numerous.

MacLysaght states that the Ulster Mulhollands never abbreviated their name to the English name Holland. However, the two names were being used interchangeably around Articlave, near Coleraine, Co. Derry, in 1900. At the same time the variants Mahollum and Maholm were noted in counties Armagh and Down.

Lady Gilbert, 1841–1921, was a novelist who wrote under her maiden name, Rosa Mulholland; she was born in Belfast. Many of her early stories were published in Dickens's *Household Words* and she is best remembered for her novel *A Fair Emigrant*.

MULLAN (*also* Mullen *and* Mullin)

This is a complicated name and can be of various origins. It is among the seventy most numerous names in Ireland and among the first forty in Ulster, where it is most common. It is one of the first ten names in Co. Derry, one of the first five in Co. Tyrone, and is also popular in Co. Antrim. The name is also numerous in both Connacht and Leinster.

The original O'Mullans, in Gaelic Ó Maoláin, from *maol*, meaning 'bald' or 'tonsured', were one of the main septs of the Clann Conchúir Magh Ithe, descendants of the fifth-century king, Niall of the Nine Hostages, founder of the Uí Néill dynasty. Magh Ithe was an area in Co. Donegal which is now known as the Laggan district. From here the Clan Connor invaded and took control of the Keenaght district of northeast Derry, and this was the homeland of the O'Mullans, followers of the O'Cahans (*see* Kane).

Their name was made Mollan, Mullan, Mullane, Mullen, Mullin, and so on, and has become confused with O'Mellon (*see* Mallon). Also the majority of the Scottish Macmillan settlers, both pre- and post-Plantation, adopted the variant MacMullan, and some of these may have shortened their name to Mullan, Mullen and so on. Certainly some who were originally O'Mullans became MacMullans (*see* MacMillan).

In Monaghan a sept of the name Ó Maoláin was based originally at Clones. This was an Oriel family which first anglicised to O'Mollines, later Mollins, Mullan, Mullen and Mullin.

Mullins is different again and is an English name from the Middle English *miln*, a 'mill'. It can also be from the Norman name de Moleyns. Lord Ventry's family in 1841 reverted to their original name de Moleyns from Mullins.

Shane Crossagh O'Mullan became a rapparee in Co. Derry after being evicted in 1729. He was hanged with his two sons at Derry jail after a long, Robin-Hood-like career. Alan Molines or Mullan, died 1690, was born at Ballyculter, Co. Down. An early anatomist, he was the first to describe the vascularity of the lens of the eye, which he discovered after dissecting an elephant that had accidently died in a fire in Dublin in 1681.

MULLEN *see* Mullan

MULLIGAN

Mulligan is equally common in Ulster, Leinster, and Connacht, but rare in Munster. The name originates in Co. Donegal but is now most common in counties Monaghan, Fermanagh and Mayo. It is in Gaelic Ó Maolagáin, which probably derives from the word *maol*, meaning 'bald' or 'tonsured'.

In the medieval period the O'Mulligans were an important sept in Co. Donegal, lords of Tír Mhic Cartháin in the baronies of Boylagh and Raphoe. They were also erenaghs of Tullyfern in Kilmacrenan. They lost their lands during the Plantation and migrated to Fermanagh, Monaghan and Mayo. In Fermanagh they settled in Magherasteffany and Clankelly, and in Monaghan, in the northwest and centre of the county.

Because of the meaning of the Gaelic name some of the sept anglicised to Baldwin. O'Mulligan was also made Molyneux, a Norman name which became 'naturalised' as Irish, being found in England only by emigration from Ireland. A variant of the name is Milligan (*see* Milligan) and around 1900 the two names were being used interchangeably about Armagh city, and in Moira and Newry in Co. Down. Mulligan and Mullan were also being used interchangeably in Newry at that time.

Hercules Mulligan, 1740–1825, was a secret agent for George Washington during the American War of Independence. He was born at Coleraine in Derry. Charles J. Mulligan, 1866–1916, who was born in Tyrone, became a successful sculptor in the USA. The aptly named James Venture Mulligan, 1837–1907, was born at Rathfriland, Co. Down, and became an important explorer in Australia.

MULLIN *see* Mullan

MURDOCH *see* Murdock

MURDOCK (*also* Murdoch *and* Murtagh)

In Ireland Murdock is almost exclusive to Ulster, where it is most common in Co. Antrim. The name is Scottish and derives from two distinct Gaelic origins which have become confused. The spelling Murdock is more common in Ulster but in Scotland is less so.

The Síolachadh Mhuirchaidh were a Clan Donald sept who descended from one Murdoch, an illegitimate son of Angus Mór of Islay, and were based on North Uist. Their name was in Scots Gaelic Mac Mhuirchaidh, from the Irish Gaelic name Murchadh, meaning 'sea warrior', and so is cognate with the Irish name MacMurphy. Mac Mhuirchaidh was anglicised as MacMurchie, MacMurdoch, Murchison, Murdoch, and in Arran, MacMurphy and Murphy (*see* Murphy).

The Clan Macpherson sept of Mac Mhuireadhaigh in Badenoch in Inverness-shire descend from Muiriach or Murdoch, the progenitor of the clan. This name is from Muireach, Irish Muireadhach, a 'mariner', and so is cognate with the Irish MacMorrow or MacMurry (*see* Morrow). The Scottish name was anglicised as Currie, MacCurrach, MacMurdoch,

MacVurich and Murdoch (*see* Curry).

The Irish name Ó Muircheartaigh, from *muircheartach*, a 'navigator', is also common in Ulster as Murtagh. But Murtagh in both Scotland and Ulster can also be originally Murdoch.

The Scotsman William Murdoch, 1754–1839, the inventor of gas lighting, was worshipped as a deity by Nassred-din, the Shah of Persia, who thought him to be a reincarnation of Merodach, 'God of light'.

MURPHY

Murphy is the most numerous name in Ireland, very common in every province and found in every county. In Ulster, where it is among the first fifteen names, it is most common in Co. Armagh, where it is the single most numerous name, and in Co. Fermanagh, where it is ninth and in Co. Monaghan, where it is tenth.

The great majority of those of the name in Ireland are originally O'Murphys, Gaelic Ó Murchadha, 'descendant of Murchadh', a personal name meaning 'sea warrior'. This was the name of three unrelated septs of counties Cork, Wexford and Roscommon. Many in Ulster will descend from one of these.

But the majority of Ulster Murphys will be originally MacMurphys, Gaelic Mac Murchadha. These were originally a Cenél Eoghain sept who controlled the rich lands of Muintir Birn in present-day Tyrone, and were chiefs of Síol Aodha. However, they were driven out of that region by the O'Neills and settled in the highlands of south Armagh under O'Neill of the Fews. There are now fewer Murphys in their homeland of Tyrone than in almost any other Irish county.

Livingstone states that the Murphys of Fermanagh are in Gaelic Mac Murchú, descendants of Murchadh, a brother of Donn Mór Maguire. These MacMurphys were erenaghs of the church lands of Farnamullan and of Tullynagaorthainn, and anglicised their name to both Murphy and Morrow (*see* Morrow).

Finally, the name of the Clan Donald sept of MacMurchie was made MacMurphy and Murphy in Arran and so it is likely that some of the name in Ulster will be of Scottish descent (*see* Murdock).

The Ulsterman Arthur Murphy, 1727–1805, was a respected actor and dramatist. John Murphy, 1812–80, was born at Omagh, Co. Tyrone, and founded the theological publishing house of Murphy and Company in Baltimore. Undoubtedly the largest of the name, and in his day the tallest man in Europe, was Patrick Murphy, 1834–62, who was eight foot one inch tall. He spent most of his short life on exhibition in Britain. His embalmed remains were returned to his native Co. Down.

MURRAY (*also* MacMurray)

Murray is among the twenty most common names in Ireland and is found in every county. It is one of the twenty-five most numerous names in Ulster, among the top ten in Co. Down, the top twenty in Co. Monaghan and is numerous too in Co. Antrim. MacMurray in Ireland is exclusive to Ulster and is most common in counties Antrim, Armagh and Donegal.

Murray is also among the twenty most common names in Scotland and is territorial in origin, from the northern province of Moray. These Murrays descend from Freskin de Moravia of Duffus in Moray, who was granted the lands of Strabrock in West Lothian by David 1. The de Moravias of Duffus were a branch of the royal house of the ancient Pictish 'Mormaers of Moray'. Freskin's grandson William married the heiress of Bothwell and Drumsagard in Lanarkshire and Smailholm in Berwickshire and from him descend the Murrays of Tullibardine in Perthshire, ancestors of the Dukes of Atholl. The name MacMurray is common in the province of Galloway, whence hailed so many of the Plantation settlers. It was first recorded there in 1530 and is of Irish origin.

George Murray of Wigtownshire was one of the fifty Scottish undertakers of the Plantation of Ulster. He was granted 1500 acres in the extreme west of Donegal in 1610. John Murray, Earl of Annandale, eventually took over the 1000 acres near Donegal town that was the portion of Sir Patrick McKee of Largs in Ayrshire and another portion of 1000 acres in the same area, originally that of James McCulloch, also an undertaker.

In Ireland Murray can be used for Ó Muireadhaigh (O'Murry), from Muireadhach, meaning a 'mariner'. Both Murray and MacMurray can be from either Mac Giolla Mhuire, also anglicised as Gilmore, Kilmurray, MacElmurray and MacIlmurray (*see* Gilmore), or from Mac Muireadhaigh, MacMurray, the name of septs in north Co. Down and in Co. Leitrim. Murray is the tenth most common name in Upper Ards in Co. Down. A Cathalan Mac Muiredaig was ruler of the Ards in 1034.

MURTAGH *see* Murdock

NEESON *see* MacGuinness

NEILL (*also* MacNeilly)

Neill is common in Ulster but is even more so in Leinster and Munster. It can be of Irish or Scottish origin. MacNeilly is almost exclusive to Co. Antrim and though the name is indigenous to that county, it has long been common in Galloway and so some in Ulster are likely to have been, in the shorter term, of Scottish origin.

The personal name Neill is from the Gaelic Niall, of which the derivation is uncertain. It may be from *nél*, meaning 'cloud' or from an ancient root word meaning 'passionate, vehement'. The name was early borrowed by the Norsemen and made Njáll and Njal. The Normans, who were originally Norsemen themselves, made the name Nesle and Nêle. In this form it was introduced into England by the Normans. There it was thought to have meant 'black' and was thus latinised Nigellus. By the time the name had travelled full circle to Scotland it had become Nigel.

In Ulster Neill as a surname has several origins. It can be a shortened form of O'Neill (*see* O'Neill), MacNeill (*see* MacNeill) or Neilson (*see* Nelson). In Galloway MacNeillie was shortened to Neil.

MacNeilly is of a different origin. It is in Gaelic Mac an Fhilidh, 'son of the poet', and was the name of an ancient Irish sept of what is now Co. Antrim. *Filidh* in this sense denotes a professional poet, a position of great privilege and with a very well-defined place in Gaelic society. The name was also anglicised MacAnelly, MacAnilly, MacNeely and Neely. These last two can also derive from the Connacht names Conneely and MacNeela.

NELSON

In Ireland this name is common in Dublin, and Ulster where it is most numerous in counties Antrim and Armagh. Nelsons can be of Scottish, English or Manx descent.

Nelson was originally Neilson, 'Neil's son', or was originally 'Nell's son' (in England Nell was a version of the Gaelic Niall). For the origins of the name Niall *see* MacNeill, Neill *and* O'Neill.

On the Isle of Man Nelson was originally MacNeill, anglicised as Neillson, then Nealson, then Neleson, then Nelson. In Scotland, the Neilsons of Craigcaffie in Ayrshire descend from Neil, Earl of Carrick. There were Neilsons, hereditary coroners of Bute, a sept of Clan Stuart of Bute (but *see* Fullerton *and* Jamison). Another family of Neilsons, a sept of Clan Mackay, descend from the fifteenth-century Neil MacNeill Mackay. There were also Nelsons or Neilsons, a sept of Clan Gunn.

In Ulster most Nelsons will be originally of Scottish stock – but not all. The Nelsons of Rory's Glen near Carncastle in Co. Antrim, for example, were English.

Around 1900 Nelson and Neilson were still being used interchangeably about Crumlin and Doagh in south Antrim.

Samuel Neilson, 1761–1803, was born in Ballyroney, Co. Down, the son of a Presbyterian minister. He was one of the founders of the United Irishmen and founded the newspaper *Northern Star* on 4 January 1792.

NESBITT

In Ireland this name is common only in Dublin, and Ulster where it is most numerous in counties Antrim, Armagh and Cavan. It can be of English or Scottish origin.

The name is local in origin. In Scotland it derives from the old parish of Nesbit in Berwickshire and is first on record in the twelfth century. In England it can be of the same origin, or from Nesbitt in Durham or Nesbitt in Northumberland. The placename is from the Old English *nese*, meaning 'nose', and *byht*, meaning a 'bend', and originally described a nose-shaped bend.

The Nesbitts of Cavan are a branch of one of the Nisbet or Nesbitt families who came to the extreme west of Donegal after the Plantation.

NEWELL

Though found in all the provinces this name is common only in Ulster where it is most numerous in counties Down and Antrim. It can be of English or Scottish origin.

Newell can be a variant of either Nevill or Noel. One prominent English family, the Nevilles of Raby, came from Néville in France. Most others took their name from one of the several places in France called Neuville. The name Noel is from the Old French *Noël*, which means 'Christmas', and denoted a person born at that time.

As Neuall, Newall and Newell, the name has long been found in the Scottish province of Galloway, especially in Dumfriesshire, whence hailed so many of the Plantation settlers.

The most famous of the name in Ulster history was Downpatrick man Edward John Newell, 1771–98, a portrait miniaturist. He joined the United Irishmen but was distrusted by the leadership. He became an informer. Rather foolishly he wrote *The Life and Times of Newell, the Informer* which was published privately in Belfast. He was about to leave Ireland on a government passage when he was assassinated.

NICHOLL (*also* MacNickle *and* Nicholson)

In Ireland Nicholl is common only in Ulster, especially in counties Derry and Antrim. Apart from a few MacNickles in Connacht, the name is exclusive to Ulster and in particular Tyrone. Nicholson, however, is found equally in Leinster, Connacht and Ulster (where the main centre is Co. Antrim).

The Latin name Nicolas was borrowed from a Greek name meaning 'conquering people' and was introduced into Britain by the Normans.

Nicholl was a diminutive or pet form of it. The name also derives from de Nicol which actually means 'of Lincoln': the Normans apparently often called Lincoln, Nicol. Nicholson in England can derive from either of these sources.

In Scotland the name was early gaelicised as Mac Neacail and there was once an independent clan in Scotland called MacNicol, based originally in Ross. With the death of its chief in the fourteenth century the family became extinct in the male line. Torquil MacLeod of the Lews (now Lewis) married the heiress and the MacNicols subsequently became a sept of Clan MacLeod of Lewis and were based on Skye. These became both Nicholls and Nicolsons. To confuse the matter there was already existing a sept of Nicolsons recorded in Scorrybreac, Skye, from the eleventh century. The Glenorchy Macnicols in Argyllshire are said to descend from one Nicol MacPhee. Nicholson was also common in Dumfriesshire and around Glasgow.

The Co. Tyrone name MacNicholl or MacNickle is in Gaelic Mac Niocaill. It has occasionally been made Nicholls and Nicholson.

General Sir John Nicholson, 1824–57, was killed in the defence of Delhi during the Indian Mutiny. A statue of him stands in the Market Square of his home town, Lisburn in Co. Antrim.

NICHOLSON see Nicholl

NIXON

Apart from Co. Wicklow, Nixon is common only in Ulster, and there particularly in counties Cavan and Fermanagh. The name meant originally 'son of Nick', a pet form of Nicholas (for derivation of which see Nicholl).

The Nixons were one of the riding clans of the Scottish Borders and were found on both sides of the frontier, in Upper Liddesdale in Roxburghshire and in Bewcastle in England. Important enough to have the Thomsons, Glendennings and Hunters 'under them', they were also part of the powerful Armstrong–Elliot–Nixon–Crozier confederacy. When the power and the social system of the riding clans were destroyed by James VI in the decade after 1603, many members of the clans sought refuge from persecution in Ulster.

Most came to Fermanagh and by the mid-seventeenth century Nixon, along with Armstrong, Elliott, Crozier, Irvine, Johnston and so on, was noted as a 'principal name' in that county. The Nixons of Nixon Hall descend from an Adam Nixon, about whom little is known beyond the fact that he had settled in Fermanagh before 1625. From that county they quickly spread into Cavan.

NOBLE

Outside of Dublin this name is common only in Ulster. It was found to be the eighteenth most numerous name in Fermanagh in 1962 and has been common there since the Plantation. It can be of English or Scottish origin.

The Norman name le Noble, which can mean either 'well known' or 'noble', has been recorded in Ireland since the thirteenth century. In Ross in Scotland the name MacNoble, Gaelic Mac Nobuill, became Noble. Also an English family of the name settled in East Lothian in the twelfth century and the name was also found in Dumbartonshire. The Nobles of Strathnairn, near Inverness, and Strathdearn in Nairnshire were a sept of Clan Mackintosh.

The name is quite common in England and there also means either 'well known' or 'noble'. There were Nobles, one of the riding clans who lived on the English side of the West March of the Scottish Borders. Many members of these clans came to Ulster, particularly to Co. Fermanagh, when their homeland was 'pacified' by James VI in the decade after 1603. Though most in Fermanagh will be of this origin, one prominent family at least claims descent from a settler from Cornwall.

NUGENT

Nugent is common in Leinster and Munster and also in Ulster where it is found mainly in counties Armagh and Tyrone. The name is Norman in origin and was originally de Nogent, 'of Nogent', a common placename in France. The Nugents arrived in Ireland with the twelfth-century Anglo-Norman invasion and were granted lands in Meath and Westmeath. Like several of the Norman families they became 'hibernicised' and their name was made in Gaelic Nuinseann. They became Barons Delvin and Earls of Westmeath.

However, in Co. Tyrone the Gilshenans or Gilsenans, Gaelic Mac Giolla Seanáin, 'son of the devotee of (St) Senan', anglicised to Nugent and also Leonard (see Leonard) and Shannon (see Shannon). Mac Giolla Domhnaigh claims that Nugent was made Mac Uinnseacháin in Armagh.

The Nugents of Portaferry on the Ards peninsula in Co. Down are actually Savages. Andrew Savage, 1770–1846, adopted the name when he inherited a portion of the fortune of his great-uncle, Governor John Nugent of Westmeath. He claimed the title Baron Delvin in 1814.

O'BRIEN

O'Brien is the sixth most common name in Ireland. Three-fifths of the O'Briens are in Mumster, one-fifth in Leinster (mostly Dublin) and the rest divided equally between Ulster and Connacht. This still leaves O'Brien a common name in Ulster, but little is known of its history in the province.

The name is in Gaelic Ó Briain and denotes a descendant of the famous Brian Boru, 941–1014, who became King of Munster and High King of Ireland. The name derives from the word *bran*, meaning a 'raven'. Boru was of the Dalcassian sept of Uí Toirdealbhaigh in Munster, a family that was not of great importance until his rise. It is not true that the use of surnames in Ireland stems from an ordinance of Boru. However, surnames did begin to appear in this period. A descendant of Boru, Domhnall Mór, King of Munster, submitted to Henry II near Cashel in 1172. His son, Donagh Cairbre, 1194–1242, was the first to take the surname O'Brien. There are over three hundred individual O'Briens mentioned in the Annals of the Four Masters. The O'Briens became Earls and Marquises of Thomond, Barons and Earls of Inchiquin and Viscounts Clare.

It is thought that the O'Briens of counties Cavan and Leitrim were a branch of the Thomond family who migrated there in the sixteenth century. However, Livingstone doubts that the O'Briens of Co. Monaghan were connected to the Munster O'Briens, although he offers no clue as to what origin they do have. The same doubt could be expressed about O'Briens in many parts of Ulster.

O'DOHERTY *see* Doherty

O'DONNELL

O'Donnell is one of the fifty most common names in Ireland and one of the forty most common in Ulster. There were three septs of Ó Domhnaill: in Co. Donegal, in Thomond, and in Galway–Roscommon.

The Donegal sept take their name from one Domhnall, died 901, a descendant of Niall of the Nine Hostages, fifth-century founder of the Uí Néill dynasty. The sept was based around Kilmacrenan in Donegal, but from the thirteenth century their influence increased and they became the leading sept of Tirconnell. The family were also erenaghs of Letter and Lisfannon in the parish of Fahan in Inishowen. There are well over three hundred references to individual O'Donnells in the Annals of the Four Masters.

The family is perhaps most famous in Irish history for its part in the Nine Years War. Hugh Roe O'Donnell, 1571–1602, chief of the name, defeated the English in several battles. Rory O'Donnell, 1575–1626, was 1st Earl of Tyrconnell and one of those involved in the famous Flight of the Earls. Many members of the family became outstanding soldiers in the armies of the continent. Hugh O'Donnell, 1739–1814, was the first parish priest of Belfast. The name is one of the few in Ulster to have retained the O' prefix.

O'HAGAN (*also* Hagan)

Apart from Co. Louth this name is common only in Ulster, and in particular in counties Armagh and Down. It is one of the names with which the O' prefix has been increasingly resumed during the twentieth century.

The name is in Gaelic Ó hÁgáin, originally Ó hÓgáin, from óg, 'young'. The O'Hagans and the O'Quins were of the Clann Feargusa, descendants of Fergus, son of Eoghan, son of Niall of the Nine Hostages. The O'Hagans were based at Tullahogue in Co. Tyrone, and there they had the hereditary right of inaugurating O'Neill as King of Ulster. They were also hereditary brehons to O'Neill. Branches settled in and controlled large tracts of land in counties Armagh and Monaghan. The most famous of the Armagh family was Ivor O'Hagan, tutor to St Malachy, *c.* 1100.

Very many of the O'Hagans were with O'Neill at the Battle of Kinsale in 1603 and the family suffered much in the dispossessions that followed. Some of them became rapparees and two were hanged as such at Carrickfergus, Co. Antrim. Mary O'Hagan, 1823–76, who founded the convent of the Poor Clares, was born in Ulster.

The name Ó hAodhagáin, 'descendant of Aodhagán', a pet form of Aodh or Hugh, was also anglicised as O'Hagan. This sept was of Oriel but is now indistinguishable from the Tyrone O'Hagans.

O'Hagan has been made Hagan, Hagans, Haggens, Haghen, Hegan, Higgins (*see* Higgins) and Hoggan, and some may have further anglicised to Aiken (*see* Aiken). The name O'Hogan is of the same derivation but not the same origin as O'Hagan.

O'HANLON (*also* Hanlon)

Less than a quarter of the Hanlons and O'Hanlons of Ireland now live in their homeland of Ulster, the name being most common in Dublin, Kerry, Louth and Wexford. The name is in Gaelic Ó hAnluain, 'descendant of Anluan', a name that probably meant 'outstanding champion'. The name has been subject to a dramatic resumption of the O' prefix during the twentieth century and O'Hanlons now outnumber Hanlons.

The O'Hanlons were one of the most important of the Ulster septs, Lords of Orior and Oneilland in Co. Armagh and, with MacGuinness, controllers of east Ulster. The family was initially conciliatory to the English and managed to retain part of its patrimony at the time of the Plantation, but later in the seventeenth century they fought against the English and were dispossessed. The most famous was 'Count' Redmond O'Hanlon, the outlawed chief who lost his lands in the Cromwellian settlement and began a long and colourful career as a rapparee, during which he kept the counties of Tyrone and Armagh under 'tribute'. After a reward of £200 was offered, he was shot dead in 1681 by his foster brother Arthur O'Hanlon at Eight-Mile-Bridge in Co. Down and his head was spiked over Downpatrick jail.

O'HARA

This name is equally common in Ulster, Leinster and Connacht, its main centres being Dublin, Co. Sligo and Co. Antrim. The name is in Gaelic Ó hEaghra and the family was originally of Co. Sligo, descendants of one Eaghra, pronounced 'ara', a chief of Leyny in that county.

In the fourteenth century a branch migrated to the Glens of Antrim and settled at Crebilly near Ballymena. Here it became an important sept and entered into several marriages and alliances with the great families of Antrim. In the mid-nineteenth century O'Haras were still found concentrated in the barony of Lower Glenarm.

At the beginning of the twentieth century the name was being used interchangeably with Haren in several parts of Co. Fermanagh and so some at least of the O'Haras of that county will be originally O'Harens, Gaelic Ó hÁráin. The O'Harens were erenaghs of Ballymactaggart.

O'HARE (*also* Hare)

Apart from Co. Louth, O'Hare is common in Ulster where three-quarters are in Co. Armagh and most of the rest in Co. Down. The name is among the five most numerous in Co. Armagh.

In Gaelic O'Hare is Ó hIr or Ó hÉir, an Oriel sept, kin to the O'Hanlons, and based in central Armagh. The name was also made Hare and Haire, but is one of the few that had largely retained the O' prefix even before the Gaelic revivals.

Hare is also an English name, taken originally from that of the animal. Also the name MacGarry (*see* MacGarry) was in Oriel corrupted to O'Garriga and then mistranslated as Hare in the assumption that it was based on the word *giorraí*, meaning 'hare'.

In the mid-nineteenth century O'Hare was noted as the most common name in the Co. Down barony of Upper Iveagh, and was particularly concentrated in the parish of Donaghmore.

O'KANE *see* Kane

O'NEILL

There is room here to give no more than a brief outline of the history of this, the most famous family of Ulster, from whose arms the famous Red Hand symbol is taken. The name is one of the very few to have retained not only the O' prefix but also (except for the *fada*s) the Gaelic spelling,

Ó Néill, 'descendant of Niall'. The name is among the ten most numerous in Ireland and the thirty most numerous in Ulster and is among the first ten in counties Antrim, Derry and Tyrone and the first thirty in Co. Monaghan.

The family claims descent from both Conn of the Hundred Battles and Niall of the Nine Hostages, fifth-century founder of the Uí Néill dynasty. Eoghan, son of Niall of the Nine Hostages, gave his name to the Cenél Eoghain, of whom the O'Neills were the chief sept, and to Tír Eoghain, a territory comprising not only Tyrone but most of Derry and part of Donegal. The first to take O'Neill as his surname was one Domhnall, born c. 943. 'Descendant of Niall' in this case refers to his grandfather Niall Glún Dubh, 'Black Knee', High King of Ireland.

The race formed two branches, the southern Uí Néill, based in Meath but extending into Cavan in Ulster, and the northern Uí Néill, based in Tyrone. In the fourteenth century the Tyrone O'Neills formed two branches under Aodh Dubh, 'Black Hugh', King of Ulster, and his brother Niall Ruadh, 'Red Niall', Prince of Tyrone. The latter branch remained the most powerful, the O'Neills of Tyrone. The former branch, under Aodh Buidhe, 'Yellow Hugh', grandson of Aodh Dubh, won large tracts of land in Antrim and Down from the Normans and these became known as the Clann Aodha Bhuidhe or Clandeboy O'Neills. Their principal seat was at Edenduffcarrig, later known as Shane's Castle, northwest of Antrim town. The O'Neills of the Fews in Co. Armagh descend from Aodh, known as Hugh of the Fews, died 1475, second son of Eoghan, chief of the name, who was inaugurated in 1432.

In the sixteenth and seventeenth centuries the struggles to preserve Gaelic Ireland centred around the O'Neills and many of them left an indelible imprint on the history of the province of Ulster. These include Conn Bacach O'Neill, 1484–1559, Shane O'Neill, 1530–67, Hugh O'Neill, 1540–1616, Owen Roe O'Neill, 1590–1649, Sir Phelim O'Neill, 1604–53, and Sir Nial O'Neill, 1658–90. Many others distinguished themselves in the armies of Europe.

In the late eighteenth century the male line of the O'Neills of Shane's Castle ended with Henry O'Neill. His daughter Mary was married to the Revd Arthur Chichester, and their son, the Revd William Chichester, succeeded to the estate and adopted the name O'Neill. His grandson, another Revd William, was in 1868 created Baron O'Neill of Shane's Castle, and from him descends Lord O'Neill of the Maine, better known as Captain Terence O'Neill, prime minister of Northern Ireland from 1963 to 1969. The O'Neills Lords Rathcavan and the O'Neills Baronets of Cleggan are also really Chichesters.

From the twelfth century through to the eighteenth the O'Neills dominated Irish and particularly Ulster history as High Kings of Ireland, Kings of Ulster, Princes of Tyrone, statesmen and soldiers. It was the blind harper Arthur O'Neill, 1737–1816, who coined the saying, 'wherever an O'Neill sits is always the head of the table'. But perhaps the most appropriate quotation pertaining to the family is that of a fourteenth-century poet who said, 'to compare any clan with that of the O'Neills one may as well contend with the ocean'.

See also MacNeill, Neill *and* Nelson.

O'ROURKE *see* Rourke

ORR

In Ireland this name is common only in Ulster, where it is chiefly found in counties Antrim, Down, Derry and Tyrone. MacLysaght states that it derives from the parish of Orr in Kirkcudbrightshire. It is the name of an old Renfrewshire family and is most common in the west of the shire and in particular in the parish of Lochwinnoch.

Mac Giolla Domhnaigh claims that the name was also used as an anglicisation of Scots Gaelic Mac Íomhair, 'son of Ivar', a name also made MacIver, MacIvor, MacUre and Ure (*see* MacKeever). The Ures were a sept of Clan Campbell and this, coupled with the prominence of the name Orr in Kintyre, particularly Campbeltown, lends weight to Mac Giolla Domhnaigh's statement. Some others in Scotland derive the name from the Gaelic *odhar donn, odhar,* meaning 'sallow (of complexion)' and *donn,* meaning 'brown'.

The earliest record of the name in Ireland is that of a settler family already residing in Tyrone in 1655. Within ten years many others are recorded in Derry and adjacent areas. William Orr, 1760–97, was a farmer born at Farranshane in Co. Antrim. A United Irishman, he was arrested on what was popularly thought to be a trumped-up charge of administering a treasonable oath to two soldiers. He was hanged at Carrickfergus in Co. Antrim in 1797 and 'Remember Orr' became a watchword for many years afterwards. James Orr, 1770–1816, also from Co. Antrim, actually took part in the 1798 rebellion but escaped the death penalty.

Orrs of Ulster background became prominent in the USA, and Orrville in South Carolina is named after them. Alexander Ector Orr, 1831–1914, was a pioneer of subways in New York city. He was born at Strabane, Co. Tyrone.

OWENS

This name is common in Leinster, Connacht and Ulster. In Ulster it is most common in Co. Fermanagh, where it was found to be the fourteenth most common name in 1962. It can be of Welsh or Irish origin.

Owen comes from the Old Welsh Ouein, which possibly derives from the Latin Eugenius. Owens means 'son of Owen'. Some at least of this name in Ulster will be of Welsh stock.

The Irish equivalent of Owens is Eoghan and the common Ulster name Mac Eoghain or MacKeown (*see* MacKeown) was also anglicised as MacOwen, Owens and Owenson. The Fermanagh Owenses are in Gaelic Ó hEoghain and were an ecclesiastical family of Co. Sligo, brought to Fermanagh by the Maguires. They were erenaghs of Enniskillen, Pobal and Lisgoole in Fermanagh. Their name was also made Hinds, Hoins, Hoynes, Hynes and Oins.

PARK *see* Parker

PARKER (*also* Park *and* Parks)

In Ireland these names are common only in Ulster, where Park is most common in counties Tyrone and Antrim, Parks in counties Armagh and Antrim and Parker in Antrim. Parker is also numerous in Co. Cork.

Parker is an occupational name from the Old French *parquier*, meaning 'park-keeper', a very important occupation in medieval times. In Scotland it was first recorded in Perthshire in 1296. It is on record in England from much earlier. Though it has been recorded in Ireland since medieval times in each of the four provinces, most in Ulster will be of post-Plantation origin.

Park in England can be from the Old French *parc*, meaning 'park' or 'enclosure', and denoted someone who lived in one. But it is often simply an abbreviation of Parker. In Scotland it can have the same origins, but can also be territorial from the lands of Park in the parish of Erskine in Renfrewshire. The name was common in Glasgow in the sixteenth century. There was also a Clann Mhic Phairc on South Uist which anglicised to Park.

Parks or Parkes is an English name of the same meaning and origin as Park. However, the Breffny name Ó Mochóirghe, 'descendant of the early riser', also anglicised as Early (but *see* Loughran), was in places corrupted to Ó Machaire and this was anglicised as Parkes by mistranslation (*machaire* means a 'field' or 'plain').

PARKS *see* Parker

PATTERSON

This name is among the twenty most common in Scotland. Though found in all the provinces of Ireland, it is common only in Ulster where it is one of the forty most numerous names. It is among the first five in Co. Down and is very common too in counties Antrim, Armagh, Derry and Tyrone. It also takes the forms Paterson and Pattison.

The name is from the Lowlands of Scotland and means 'Patrick's son'. However, a few Highland Gaelic names were also made Patterson. MacFeat, MacPatrick, MacPhadrick, MacPhater and MacPhatrick, were all originally Mac Phadruig, itself a shortening of the earlier Mac Gille Phadruig, meaning 'son of the devotee of (St) Patrick'. All these names were made Paterson or Patterson and also Kilpatrick (*see* Kilpatrick). Also the Galloway name MacFetridge, in Gaelic Mac Phetruis, meaning 'son of Peter' was made Paterson. The Irish name Mac Páidín has been used as a gaelicisation of Patterson. It means 'son of little Pat' and is usually anglicised as MacPadden and Padden.

In the mid-nineteenth century Patterson was found in twelve out of the fourteen baronies of Antrim, and in Down was most common in the barony of Upper Castlereagh. Robert Patterson, 1802–72, the naturalist, was a founder member of the Belfast Natural History Society in 1821 and was its president for many years. He was born in Belfast.

PATTON

In Ireland this name is common only in Co. Mayo and in Ulster, where it is most numerous in counties Antrim, Down and Donegal. It can be of Irish, English or Scottish origin.

In England the name can be either a toponymic from Patten in Salop or Westmoreland, or a diminutive or pet form of Pat. This latter is its most common derivation in Scotland. As Padon, Paton and Patton the name was common in the western counties before the Reformation, when Patrick was a very popular forename. In 1921, according to Black, Paton was found to be the only surname in the fishing village of Usan near Montrose in Forfarshire, the exceptions being 'one or two Perts or Coutts. . . by marriage with Ferryden folks'. MacFadden in Scotland was also made Paton and Patonson (*see* MacFadden).

In Donegal, and in Mayo (where it is spelt Patten), the name is originally Ó Peatáin, from another diminutive of Patrick. This was the name of a sept of Ballybofey in Donegal which first anglicised to O'Pettane and then Patton. The English toponymic Peyton has also been used for this name. However, not all in Donegal are of Irish origin. The Pattons of Springfield in the parish of Clondevaddock descend from one William Patton of Fifeshire who became rector of the parish in 1630. For Padden *see* Patterson.

PHILLIPS

This name is almost equally numerous in Leinster, Connacht and Ulster. In Ulster it is most common in counties Antrim and Monaghan. It can be of English, Scottish or Irish origin.

The personal name Philip derives from a Greek name meaning 'fond of horses' and was very popular in medieval England, giving rise to a wide variety of pet forms. Phillips, which simply means 'son of Philip', is among the fifty most common names in England.

In Scotland it can be of the same derivation or equally can be an anglicisation of MacKillop, Gaelic Mac Fhilip, 'son of Philip'. MacKillop appears in Arran and was also the name of a sept of the MacDonalds of Glencoe in Argyllshire and of a sept of MacDonnell of Keppoch in Inverness-shire. There were also MacKillops, standard-bearers to the Campbells of Dunstaffnage in Argyllshire.

In Connacht Phillips is an anglicisation of Mac Philbín, another diminutive of Philip. In Monaghan, Cavan and Fermanagh, the Phillips and MacPhillips are in Gaelic Mac Pilib, descendants of Phillip MacMahon, died 1486, the co-arb of the church at Clones.

Sir Thomas Phillips was an English soldier serving in Ireland at the end of Elizabeth I's reign. He became the military superintendent of Co. Coleraine (now Co. Derry) and his family has figured large in the history of Limavady since that time. Sir Thomas obtained a licence to make whiskey at Coleraine and in the Route, probably at Bushmills.

POLLOCK

Outside of Dublin this name is found almost exclusively in Ulster, where its main centres are in counties Antrim and Tyrone.

In the late twelfth century 'Peter, son of Fulbert' had a grant of land in Upper Pollock in Renfrewshire and took his name from it. The placename itself means 'little pool'. The name remained popular in Renfrewshire and also spread throughout the Lowlands.

The name first came to Ulster after the Plantation. One family, the Pollocks of Newry, Co. Down, is thought to descend from John Pollock, a lieutenant-of-foot serving in Ireland, son of Robert Pollock of that Ilk, Renfrewshire, in the mid-seventeenth century.

In the late nineteenth century in counties Down, Antrim, Monaghan and Derry, the name Pollock was still being used interchangeably with Poag, Pogue, Poke and Polk, names which appear in the Co. Antrim Hearth Money Rolls of the 1660s. Their origin is not known, nor is it known why they are synonyms of Pollock. The word *póg* (often trans-literated 'pogue') in Gaelic means 'kiss'.

PORTER

Except for some Porters in Dublin this name in Ireland is exclusive to Ulster. It is most common in counties Antrim, Down, Derry and Armagh. It can be of English or Scottish origin.

Porter is an occupational name and though it can derive from the Old French *porteur,* meaning a 'carrier of burdens', its main derivation is from the Old French *portier,* a 'porter' or 'doorkeeper'. In medieval times the office of porter was one of the most important in castle and monastery and came with lands and privileges. The word was in Scotland gaelicised as *portair,* which had the extra meaning of 'ferryman'.

The name is one of the most common in every kind of Irish record since the thirteenth century, but most in Ulster will be of post-Plantation origin. The most famous of the name in Ulster was a Presbyterian minister, the Revd James Porter, 1753–98, of Greyabbey, Co. Down. He was a United Irishman and a series of letters he published under the title *Billy Bluff and Squire Firebrand* drew the attention of the government. He was tried on the false evidence of an informer and hanged at Greyabbey within sight of his home and church.

QUIGG *see* Quigley

QUIGLEY (*also* Quigg)

Quigley is common in all the four provinces of Ireland but is most numerous in Ulster, particularly counties Derry and Donegal. It is in Gaelic Ó Coigligh, which may derive from the word *coigeal,* denoting a 'person with unkempt hair'.

There were O'Quigleys, a sept of the Uí Fiachra of Co. Mayo, and another sept of Inishowen in Donegal. The most common form of the name is now Quigley, but Kegley and Twigley are also found. The name is well known in Fermanagh and Monaghan, a sept of O'Quigley there being erenaghs of Clontivrin in the parish of Clones.

Quigg, an exclusively Ulster name found mainly in Co. Derry but also in Co. Monaghan, can be an abbreviated form of Quigley, but it is also the name of a recognised sept of Co. Derry whose name is in Gaelic Ó Cuaig. Particularly in Co. Down both these names have been made Fivey in the mistaken notion that the Gaelic for 'five', *cúig,* was an element in their construction.

QUIN *see* Quinn

QUINN (*also* Quin)

Quinn is among the twenty most common names in Ireland, found in every county and numerous in every province. It is most common in Ulster where it is among the twenty-five most numerous names. It is the single most common name in Co. Tyrone and one of the first ten in Co. Armagh. Strangely, it was found to be the eleventh most common name in Co. Monaghan in 1890 but by 1970 it had fallen to fifty-second.

The O'Quinns of Tyrone were an important sept of the Cenél Eoghain. With the O'Hagans they were part of the Clann Feargusa, descendants of Fergus, son of Eoghan, son of the fifth-century Niall of the Nine Hostages, founder of the Uí Néill dynasty. Their name is in Gaelic Ó Coinne, taken from Coínne, a grandson of Fergus. Ó Coinne is also anglicised Conney, Cunnea and Quinney. The Clann Feargusa was the fighting vanguard of the O'Neills and within this the O'Quinns acted as quartermasters, responsible for supplies in both peace and war.

There were three other septs of O'Quinn in Ireland, mainly Ó Cuinn, from the personal name Conn, based in north Antrim and in counties Clare and Longford. There has grown up a custom that Catholic families use the spelling Quinn and Protestant ones use Quin. However, there are many exceptions to this rule and in old records there will be many more.

At the start of the twentieth century Quinn was being used interchangeably with Cunnea in Donegal, with MacConaghy (*see* Donaghy) and Queen in Monaghan, with Quenn in Armagh city and with Whin and Whinn in southeast Down.

RAFFERTY

This name is common only in Louth and Ulster, where it is most numerous in Co. Tyrone. The name derives from two distinct Gaelic names which have been treated as one since the fifteenth century.

The first is Ó Raithbheartaigh, from *rath bheartach,* meaning 'prosperity wielder'. This sept originated in counties Donegal and Sligo. In the latter they were one of the Seven Pillars of Innis Screabhainn, a group of prominent families in early Christian times.

The other is Ó Robhartaigh, from *robharta,* meaning 'flood tide'. This is the name of an ecclesiastical sept who were co-arbs to St Columcille on Tory Island off Donegal. This name is properly O'Roarty and the form Roarty is still found in Donegal.

In Newry around 1900 Rafferty was being used interchangeably with Lavery (*see* Lavery).

RAINEY

In Ireland this name is virtually exclusive to Ulster where two-thirds are in Co. Antrim and the great majority of the remainder are in Co. Down. In Ulster the name is mainly Scottish in origin, but some may be from England.

The Old German personal name Raginald, meaning 'counsel-might', was made Reynaud in France. Both were introduced to Britain by the Normans and came to be pronounced Reynold, which became a popular name in its own right. Rainey, Rennie and so on, were diminutive or pet forms of Reynold, which, especially in Scotland, became surnames. The most important family of the name were recorded as Ranys or Rennys in Craig in Angus from the mid-fifteenth century.

In mid-nineteenth-century Antrim the name was particularly concentrated in the barony of Upper Toome.

RAMSAY (also Ramsey)

Apart from a few Ramsays in Dublin this name is in Ireland exclusive to Ulster, where it is most common in Co. Antrim. It can be of Scottish or English origin.

Ramsay is a territorial name from Ramsay in Huntingdonshire or Ramsay in Essex. The Ramsays of Scotland descend from Simund de Ramesie of Ramsay in Huntingdonshire, who was granted lands in Lothian by David I in the twelfth century. A hundred years later the Ramsays were landowners in Angus and by the fourteenth century had divided into several branches.

Ramsay was one of the names adopted by the MacGregors when their name was proscribed (see Greer).

RAMSEY see Ramsay

RANKIN

In Ireland this name is almost exclusive to Ulster, where it is most common in counties Derry and Donegal. Though the name is found in England, most in Ulster will be of Scottish origin.

In England and Lowland Scotland, Rankin was originally a personal name and was a diminutive or pet form of a variety of names that began with Ran-, for example, Randolph, and even names like Reynard or Reginald. In Scotland it was particularly common in Ayrshire, where it was also found as MacRankin.

In the Highlands the name MacRankin was common in the Glencoe district, where it derived from the Gaelic Mac Fhraing, meaning 'son of Francis'. The Rankins and MacRankins of Coll were known as the Clann

Mhic Raing and earlier as the Clann Duille. These were descendants of one Cuduilligh, brought to Argyll with the MacFaddens from Donegal by the Macleans. In Argyllshire the MacRankins were hereditary pipers to the Macleans of Duart and later the Macleans of Coll.

In Derry and adjacent areas the Rankins are thought to be of the Coll MacRankin origin.

REA (*also* Wray)

There are several origins for these names, each of which in Ireland is almost exclusive to Ulster. Three-quarters of all the Ulster Reas are in Co. Antrim and most of the rest in Co. Down. Most of the Wrays are equally distributed between counties Derry and Donegal.

The most obvious and probably the most usual origin for Rea is as a shortening of the Scottish MacCrae, Gaelic Mac-raith (*see* MacCrea). As Rae, Rea and Ree the name is also an old surname in Dumfriesshire, where from the thirteenth to the fifteenth century the name was always spelt Ra or Raa. The name there is thought to be of local origin after some unknown place of the name. A large family of Raes in Dornock in Annandale, Dumfriesshire, was noted as very troublesome in the fifteenth and sixteenth centuries. Rae's Close in Edinburgh was named after a prominent seventeenth-century family of that city.

In England the name Rea has two origins: from Middle English *atte ree,* meaning 'by the stream'; or from Middle English *atte reye,* meaning 'at the island'. Wray can derive from le Wrey, Middle English *wrye,* meaning 'twisted, crooked' or in the north of England from Old Norse *vrá,* meaning 'nook, corner, isolated or remote place'. The name here was first rendered de Wra or in ye Wro and became both Wray and Wroe, later Wrowe and Rowe.

In Ulster the name Reagh, Gaelic Riabhach, meaning 'grey' or 'brindled', was made Rea, as was the Co. Down name of the same derivation, Ó Riabhaigh, more usually anglicised as Reavey. The Co. Antrim name O'Rawe was anglicised Rea and Raw. Its Gaelic origin is unknown. The Wrays of Derry and Donegal descend from a Yorkshire family of the name which settled there in Elizabethan times before the Plantation. However, Wray has been made Raw, Ray and Rea and each of these names has been used interchangeably, as well as for the other names mentioned above.

Rheatown and Rhea County in Tennessee, USA, were named after the Rhea family which stemmed originally from Donegal. John Rea, *c.* 1822–81, was a lawyer and a prominent Young Irelander. He acted for the Catholics in the Dolly's Brae inquiry of 1859 and defended Michael Davitt.

REID

This name is among the 100 most numerous in Ireland and is one of the first forty in Ulster, where it is most common in counties Antrim, Down, Tyrone and Armagh. It can be of several origins, English, Scottish and Irish.

In both England and Scotland Read, Reed and Reid can derive from the word 'red' and denoted a person with red hair or of ruddy complexion, the word 'red' in medieval times being pronounced 'reed'. In England it can also be from a residence in a clearing, Old English *ried*, or can derive from Read in Lancashire, Rede in Suffolk or Reed in Hertfordshire. There were Reads or Reades, one of the lesser of the riding clans of the Scottish Borders. They lived in Redesdale in the West March.

In Scotland the Islay surname MacRory, from Gaelic Mac Ruaraidh, was made Reid. Also the Scots Gaelic name Ruadh, meaning 'red', was nearly always made Reid. The MacInroys, a sept of Clan Donnachie, whose name in Gaelic was Mac Iain Ruaidh, 'son of Red John', was anglicised to both Reid and Roy.

In Ulster the name Ó Maoildeirg (Mulderrig), meaning 'descendant of the red warrior', was made Reid. A sept of O'Muldergs in the Glens of Antrim anglicised to Darragh, MacDarragh and Reid. The Co. Roscommon name Mulready was also occasionally made Reid.

The Revd James Seaton Reid, 1798–1851, was born at Lurgan, Co. Armagh. He was professor of history at Belfast and later at Glasgow, and is most famous for his *History of the Presbyterian Church in Ireland*, a work finished by the Revd William Killen.

REILLY

Reilly is among the first fifteen names in both Ulster and all of Ireland. It is the single most numerous name in its homeland of Co. Cavan and also in Co. Longford, seventh in Co. Fermanagh and thirteenth in Co. Monaghan, and is found in every county in Ireland. It is one of the few names which has been influenced by successive Gaelic revivals to widely resume the O' prefix.

The name is in Gaelic Ó Raghallaigh, 'descendant of Raghallach'. The O'Reillys were for centuries the ruling family of the kingdom of Breffny, and at their height controlled most of Co. Cavan and large parts of Co. Meath. The family was widely involved in trade in medieval Ireland and at one time 'reilly' was a term for Irish money. It has also been suggested that they lived well, as the phrase 'the life of Reilly' indicates. They were also notable as ecclesiastics, the family, since the sixteenth century, providing five Primates of All-Ireland, five bishops of Kilmore, two of Clogher and one of Derry.

Philip MacHugh O'Reilly, died 1657, was a brother-in-law of Owen Roe O'Neill and was responsible for organising the 1641 rising in Co. Cavan. Very many others of the name were distinguished as soldiers on the continent and as writers, journalists, lawyers and scholars in Ireland. Hugh Reilly, a Co. Cavan man, was a master in chancery during the reign of James II and went with him to France. His *Ireland's Case Briefly Stated* (*1695*), which was reprinted several times under various titles, argued strongly in favour of freedom of worship for Catholics. The association of the name with Co. Cavan is remembered in the refrain 'Come back Paddy Reilly to Ballyjamesduff'.

REYNOLDS

Reynolds is more common in Connacht and Leinster than in Ulster. It can be of English origin, but the majority will be of Irish or Scottish stock.

The personal name Reynold derives from the Old French Reynaud and ultimately from the Old German Raginald, both names introduced into England by the Normans. Reynolds means simply 'son of Reynold'.

However, in Ireland and Scotland the Norse personal name Rögnvaldr, which means 'ruler of the gods', was borrowed into Gaelic as Raghnall and this name too was anglicised as Reynolds. Also the MacRanalds or MacRannalls, Scots Gaelic Mac Raonuill, became Crandle, Crangle, Crindle, Cringle, MacReynold and Reynolds.

The Co. Leitrim sept of Mac Raghnaill, the MacRannalls, nearly all anglicised to Reynolds or MacReynolds. Thomas M'Grannell, of the main line, was in the sixteenth century the first to adopt the name Reynolds in obedience to an Elizabethan statute. The sept of Mag Raghainn in counties Armagh and Tyrone, which originally anglicised to Magronan and MacGronan, eventually, some as late as the twentieth century, took the name Reynolds. The Renaghans, in Gaelic Ó Reannacháin, anglicised to Reynolds in the districts around Keady and Crossmaglen in Co. Armagh, and Castleblayney, Co. Monaghan. Around 1900, in the Cootehill district of Co. Cavan, Reynolds was being used interchangeably with Randalson, Reynoldson and Ronaldson.

RICE

This name is common in Leinster and Munster but is most numerous in Ulster, where its main centres are in counties Antrim and Armagh. The name is Welsh in origin and was previously Rhys, which means 'ardour', and many in Ulster will be of Welsh stock. However, the Oriel name Ó Maolchraoibhe (from *craobh,* meaning 'branch') was also for some unknown reason widely anglicised as Rice, as well as, more understandably,

Mulcreevy, Mulgrew and Grew. Most of the Rices of Co. Armagh will be of this origin.

RICHARDSON (*also* Ritchie)

Richardson in Ireland is most common in Dublin and Ulster. In the latter it is most numerous in Co. Antrim. Ritchie is also most common in Co. Antrim and is, in Ireland, exclusive to Ulster.

The personal name Richard derives ultimately from the Old German Ricard, meaning 'powerful-brave', and was one of the most popular names introduced by the Normans into England. There, in the forms Richardson and Richards, it quickly became a surname. Richardson was also common in Scotland. It was first recorded in Lanarkshire *c.* 1315.

One Ulster family of Richardson in Co. Armagh came from Worcestershire in the seventeenth century. John Grubb Richardson, 1813–90, was a liberal linen manufacturer, interested in the welfare of workers. He founded the model village of Bessbrook in Co. Armagh, his work and interest carried on by his son James Nicholson Richardson, 1846–1921, Liberal MP for Co. Armagh. Another family, with estates in counties Tyrone, Monaghan and Cavan, came from Norfolk in the sixteenth century.

In Scotland Richard was often made in pet form Richie, later Ritchie, and as a surname this became common in the Highland Border area. The Ritchies and MacRitchies were a sept of Clan Mackintosh, being a branch of the Mackintoshes of Dalmunzie, among whom Richard was a popular name. MacRitchie was first recorded in Scotland in 1571 in Glenshee in Perthshire. The name was first noted in Ulster in the sixteenth century, in counties Antrim and Down.

William Ritchie, a shipbuilder from Saltcoats in Ayrshire, moved to Belfast in 1791 and opened a shipyard at the Old Lime Kiln dock and played an active role in the growth of the city's shipbuilding industry.

RITCHIE *see* Richardson

ROBB

In Ireland this name is virtually exclusive to Ulster and is most common in Co. Antrim. The name is Scottish and was originally MacRobb, from Robb, a Scottish pet form of Robert. The MacRobbs of Duror in Argyll were a sept of the Stewarts of Appin and descended from an illegitimate son of Robert, son of Dugald, first Chief of Clan Stewart of Appin. The MacRobbs of Callander and Kilmadock in Perthshire descend from Robert, one of the Buchanans of Leny. There was also a MacRobb sept of Clan MacFarlane.

ROBERTS (*also* Dobbin *and* Robertson)

Roberts is twice as common in Ireland, and in Ulster, as Robertson, and is almost as numerous in Leinster and Munster as in Ulster. Half the Robertsons in Ireland are in Ulster. Both names are rare in Connacht.

Robert was a popular Old English personal name and means 'bright fame'. It was the source of many surnames. Roberts and Robertson, though found in England, are more common in Scotland. The most common form in England is Robinson (*see* Robinson). In Scotland the Clan Donnachie was equally well known as Clan Robertson (*see* Donaghy). The forename Robert was early borrowed into Scots Gaelic as Raibert, and this gave the Highland Border name Mac Roibeirt, anglicised as MacRobert. Some of these may have become Roberts or Robertson.

Dob is an Old English diminutive or pet form of Robert and Dobbin therefore represents a double diminutive. The surname Dobbin is common in Co. Antrim, particularly in Carrickfergus. The name first appears as that of the constable of Carrickfergus Castle in 1400. Between 1571 and 1666 seventeen Dobbins were sheriffs and eight were mayors of the town. A branch of the family was established in Co. Armagh in the late seventeenth century. Around 1900 the name was noted as a synonym of Gubby in Blackwaterstown in Co. Armagh. A hotel by the name of the Dobbins Inn is still established in High Street, Carrickfergus.

ROBERTSON *see* Roberts

ROBINSON

This name is found in all the provinces of Ireland, but apart from Dublin it is only really common in Ulster. It is among the eighty most common names in Ireland and among the first twenty in Ulster. It is very common in counties Antrim and Down and is numerous in counties Armagh, Tyrone and Fermanagh.

The name means 'son of Robert', through the diminutive or pet form Robin. It is generally taken to be an English name as opposed to the Scottish Robertson. But although Robinson is among the twenty most common names in England, it was also first recorded in Scotland in 1496 in Irvine in Ayrshire and was common in sixteenth-century Glasgow. Further, there is evidence that common usage in Ulster has blurred the distinction between the two names. It is thought that the Glenarm Robinsons in Co. Antrim may really be Robertsons (*see* Robertson) and the two names were being used interchangeably in Irvinestown, Co. Fermanagh, and Larne, Co. Antrim, around 1900.

RODGERS *see* MacCrory

ROGERS *see* MacCrory

ROLSTON *see* Roulston

ROONEY

Though this name originates in Ulster, it is now almost equally common in Leinster and Connacht. Its greatest concentration in Ulster is in Co. Down.

The O'Rooneys, Gaelic Ó Ruanaidh, were a Co. Down sept who were based in the modern parish of Ballyroney to the north of Rathfriland. The name appears often in the ecclesiastical annals and history of the diocese of Dromore, but it is as a literary family that they are most famous. Ceallach O'Rooney, died 1079, was styled Chief Poet of Ireland. Eoin O'Rooney, died 1376, was chief poet to MacGuinness of Iveagh. William Rooney, 1873–1901, was a noted poet who was involved in the Gaelic revival of the late nineteenth century. At that time the name was found to be synonymous with Rowney around Newry in Co. Down and with Roohan and Runian near Ballyshannon in Co. Donegal.

That Runian was found to be synonymous with Rooney is evidence of the absorption by Rooney of the less common Rooneen or Roonian, Gaelic Ó Rúnaidhin, a name which originated in central Down but which later became associated with south Donegal and north Leitrim.

There are two different origins for Rooney in Co. Fermanagh and adjacent areas. The Ó Maolruanaigh were Kings of Fermanagh before the Maguires. Their name was anglicised as Mulrooney, then Rooney. The distinct sept of Mac Maolruanaigh were lords of part of Clankelly as early as 1296. Their name was anglicised as Macarooney and was still rendered thus in the late nineteenth century. It has now been shortened to Rooney.

ROSS

Though found in Leinster and Munster, Ross is common only in Ulster, where the majority live in counties Antrim, Derry and Down. It has a number of possible origins in both Scotland and England.

In the north of Scotland the Clan Ross derives its name from the district of Ross. The chiefly line, later the Earls of Ross, descends from one Gille Anrias, ancestor of Fercher Ross, also known as Mackinsagart (*see* Taggart). The sept name was originally Ó Beolán. From the same source stemmed the Mac Gille Andrais, anglicised as Anderson, Andrews, Gillanders, MacAndrew, MacGillanders and Ross (*see* Anderson). The parish of Tain in Ross was famous in Victorian times and found its place in encyclopaedias, as the only names there were Ross and Munro, thus necessitating a multitude of nicknames or by-names to distinguish the various families.

In England the name can be originally descriptive from Old French *rous*, 'red (-haired)', but in most cases the name was toponymic in origin. In Bedfordshire and Kent it was from Rots in Normandy but elsewhere it derives from Roose in Lancashire, Ross in either Herefordshire or Northumberland and from Roos in the East Riding of Yorkshire.

The Yorkshire connection is the most pertinent here as the name Ross was first recorded in Scotland in twelfth-century Ayrshire, a large tract of which was then owned by a family of Ross or Ros, originally of Yorkshire. The name became common in Ayrshire and a branch of the Ayrshire de Ros family was one of the more important settler families in seventeenth-century Down.

Amanda McKittrick Ros, 1860–1939, the 'worst novelist in the world', was born in Ballynahinch, Co. Down, as Meg McKittrick. Ross was her married name, from which she dropped an 's' in emulation of the more artistocratic de Ros family name of south Down.

ROULSTON (*also* Rolston)

This name is rare in Ireland outside Ulster, where it is most common in counties Tyrone and Antrim. It is an English toponymic and can derive from several places called Rolleston or Rowlston in Leicestershire, Nottinghamshire, Staffordshire, Wiltshire or Yorkshire. All these placenames were originally spelt Rolvestun, meaning 'Rolf's farm'.

Most in Ulster descend from the Staffordshire Rollestons, R. Rollestone of that shire being one of the English undertakers of the Plantation. He was granted 1000 acres in Teemore in the barony of Oneilland West in Co. Armagh. The name is also found as Rollstone and Rowlston.

ROURKE (*also* O'Rourke)

Rourke is among the 100 most common names in Ireland but is much less numerous in Ulster than in Leinster, where it originates. The name is in Gaelic Ó Ruairc, 'descendant of Ruarc', a Gaelic version of the Norse Hrothrekr, meaning 'honour, praise'.

The O'Rourkes were one of the great princely families of Ireland. The kingdom of Breffny was long disputed between them and the O'Reillys. Indeed the territory was, in the tenth century, divided into Breffny O'Rourke (West Breffny) and Breffny O'Reilly (East Breffny). In 1565 Breffny O'Rourke was made Co. Leitrim by Sir Henry Sidney. However, at their height the O'Rourkes controlled an even larger territory extending from Kells in Co. Meath to Drumcliffe in Co. Sligo. The O'Rourke's main stronghold was at Drumahaire on Lough Gill. In the period after the Cromwellian settlement many became distinguished soldiers in Europe, particularly in Russia and Poland. Joseph O'Rourke, Prince O'Rourke, was general-in-chief of the Russian Empire in 1700.

In Ulster the name is now most common in the south, particularly Co. Cavan. Many of the name have retained the O' prefix and its use is increasing. Other forms of the name include O'Rorke, Rooke and Rorke.

RUSSELL

Though common in Co. Cork and in Leinster, Russell is most numerous in Ulster, especially counties Down and Antrim. It can be of English, Scottish, Norman or Huguenot origin. In all cases it is ultimately a diminutive or pet form of the Old French name Rous, meaning 'red (-haired)'.

The name has long been common in many parts of England and Scotland. There were Russell septs of Clan Buchanan and Clan Cumming. In Ireland Russell has been on record since the Anglo-Norman invasion. In Petty's 'census' of 1659 it was listed as a 'principal name' in counties Antrim, Cork, Dublin, Limerick, Meath and Tipperary. The only Russells of Ireland who can claim and prove descent from the Normans are the Russells of Downpatrick who have been on record there since Osberto Russell accompanied John de Courcy northwards to Ulster in 1177. However, most in Ulster probably descend from settlers who arrived in the post-Plantation period.

Several of the name in Ulster became famous in different fields, including four members of the same family, the Russells of Ballybot, near Newry in Co. Down: the Revd Charles William Russell, 1812–80, president of Maynooth College; his sister Katherine Russell, 1829–98, of the Sisters of Mercy in the USA; his brother the Revd Matthew Russell, 1834–1912, the poet; and his nephew Charles Russell, Lord Russell of Killowen, 1832–1900, the barrister, who is best remembered for his defence of Charles Stewart Parnell. Because Thomas Russell, 1767–1803, was hanged at Downpatrick it is often assumed that he was of the Downpatrick family. In fact he was born in Mallow, Co. Cork. He met Samuel Neilson and Henry Joy McCracken when he was stationed with his regiment at Belfast and joined the United Irishmen. He became the second librarian of Belfast's first library, the Linen Hall, and was executed for his part in Robert Emmet's rebellion of 1803. He was immortalised in Florence M. Wilson's poem, 'The man from God Knows Where'. George William Russell, 1867–1935, the poet and painter, better known as AE, was born in Lurgan, Co. Armagh.

RUTHERFORD

In Ireland this name is virtually exclusive to Ulster, where it is most common in counties Antrim, Derry and Down. The name is territorial in origin from the lands of Rutherford in the parish of Maxton, Roxburghshire, in Scotland. Rutherford is from the Old English *hrýthera ford*, meaning 'ford of the horned cattle'. The name was first recorded there in the twelfth century during the reign of William the Lion and the Rutherfords became one of the powerful riding clans of the Scottish Borders. Many members of these clans came to Ulster to escape persecution when James VI 'pacified' the Borders.

RUTLEDGE

Though found in Leinster and Connacht, this name in Ireland is common only in Ulster, where it is most numerous in counties Tyrone and Fermanagh. The name originates on the Scottish Borders and was long said to derive from Routledge in Cumberland. However, no record of such a place exists there and no one has yet been able to determine where Routledge actually was located.

The Routledges were the most inoffensive of the turbulent riding clans of the Scottish Borders and were long known as 'every man's prey'. They were based in the West March on the English side of the frontier. Very many members of the riding clans came to Ulster to escape James VI's 'pacification' of the Borders. Most appear to have settled in Fermanagh and there is evidence of at least one Rutledge Plantation tenant in that county.

SANDS

This name is not common in Ireland outside Ulster, where the majority are divided equally between counties Armagh and Antrim. In England the name was originally spelt Sandys (though pronounced Sands) and denoted a dweller on sandy soil or near the shore. In Scotland the name is territorial in origin, from the lands of Sands in the parish of Tulliallan in Fife. In 1494 these were owned by Thomas Sands and his mother Isobel Hudson, so he may have been the first to take the name. Sands was noted in the Hearth Money Rolls of counties Antrim and Tyrone in the 1660s.

SAUNDERS *see* Alexander

SAVAGE

Though common in Cork and Dublin this name is most numerous in Ulster, particularly in Co. Down. The name is from the Old French *salvage* or *sauvage* and ultimately from the Latin *silvāticus*, meaning 'savage' or 'wild'.

Le Secur Thomas le Sauvage came to England with William the Conqueror and settled in Derbyshire. A descendant was Sir Geoffrey le Savage of Stainisby. It was his son, William le Savage, born *c.* 1150, who took part in the Anglo-Norman invasion of Ireland and, in 1177, came north to Ulster in the train of John de Courcy. He was granted territory in the Upper Ards in Co. Down and built his stronghold at Ardkeen. He became one of the Ulster palatine barons.

For three hundred years the Savages held their grant only with difficulty against the Gaelic septs of Down, but they gradually became 'hibernicised' and were eventually recorded in the Annals of the Four Masters as Mac an tSábhaisigh. Sir Roland 'Janico' Savage, Lord of Lecale, Co. Down, was in 1482 seneschal of Ulster and was described by the Lord Deputy of Ireland as 'the most famous of the English of the province for his exploits against the Irish'. But by 1515 he was in revolt against the Crown and was noted as 'one of the English great rebels'. By the end of the sixteenth century the then 'Lord Savadge of the Ards' was also an important Ulster rebel.

However, in the next generation Henry Savage of Ardkeen married into the Montgomery family and, though the 1641 rising left the Ards untouched, it was this marriage that is thought to have saved the family from dispossession. The Savages still hold part of the territory originally granted to William le Savage eight hundred years ago.

The Savages of Portaferry have been Nugents since 1814, when Andrew Savage, 1770–1846, high sheriff of Down, adopted the name after inheriting a portion of the fortune of his great-uncle Governor John Nugent of Westmeath (*see* Nugent).

SCOTT

Scott is among the 100 most common names in Ireland and among the first twenty-five in Ulster, where it is most numerous. It is among the top fifteen in Co. Antrim and is common too in counties Down and Derry. Scott is the tenth most common name in Scotland.

The Latin *Scottus* originally meant an 'Irishman' and later, in Scotland, a Gael. The Gaels were the Gaelic Highlanders as opposed to the Gall, the Lowlanders or 'strangers'.

In England, particularly in the border counties, the name came to mean a 'man from Scotland' and not necessarily a 'Gael'. There was also an Old English personal name Scott. The Scotts were one of the most powerful of the riding clans of the Scottish Borders, based in West Teviotdale, Ewesdale and Liddesdale. They descended from the twelfth-century Uchtredus filius Scoti. His son Richard was ancestor of the Scotts of Buccleuch, near Edinburgh, and his other son, Sir Michael, of the Scotts of Balweary in Fife. At their height in the sixteenth century they could field six hundred men in battle. When the power and social system of the riding clans were broken by James VI in the decade after 1603, many came to Ulster to escape persecution. They settled particularly in Co. Fermanagh and Scott was listed as a 'principal name' there in 1659. Others included Armstrong, Elliott, Johnston, Irvine and so on, all names of the riding clans. Scott was also a 'principal name' at that time in Antrim.

The Scottish galloglasses who came to Ulster from the thirteenth to the sixteenth centuries, and in particular the MacDonnells, were sometimes referred to as Albanach, meaning 'Scotsman', and this was later anglicised as Scott.

SHANKS

In Ireland Shanks is exclusive to Ulster, where half are in Co. Antrim and most of the rest in Co. Down. If of English origin, Shanks was a nickname, from Old English *sceanca*, meaning 'shank' or 'leg'. In Ulster most will be of Scottish descent, and the name in this case is territorial in origin, from the lands of that name in Midlothian, and Shank of that Ilk was an ancient family of the region. Most early references to the name, from the fifteenth century, are spelt Shankis.

SHANNON

This name is common in all the provinces of Ireland but is most numerous in Ulster, particularly in Co. Antrim. It can be of Irish or Scottish origin and has nothing to do with the river.

There are several Irish origins for the name. It can be an anglicisation of Ó Seannacháin (Shanahan); of Ó Seanáin (Shinane); of Mac Giolla tSeanáin (Giltenan); of Mac Giolla Seanáin (Gilsenan and Gilshenan); or of Mac an tSionnaigh (MacAtinny, Fox).

The Shannons of the Glens of Antrim are thought to have been Mac an tSionnaigh, 'son of the fox'. It has been said that the Protestants anglicised to Shannon and the Catholics to Fox (*see* Fox *and* Todd).

In Tirkennedy in Fermanagh the sept of Ó Seanáin was prominent before the time of the Maguires. Gilsenan in Tirkennedy was originally Mag Uinseanáin. Both these names became Shannon.

Shannon in Scotland is of Irish origin (Ó Seanáin), but it was often rendered MacShannon. The name is most common in Galloway and in Kintyre, where there was a sept, harpers to the MacDonalds of Kintyre, known variously as Mac O'Shannaig, MacShannachan, O'Shannon, O'Shaig and Shannon.

Cathal O'Shannon, 1889–1969, the Irish trade-union leader, was born in Randalstown, Co. Antrim, and brought up in Derry city.

SHARKEY

Outside of Roscommon, Louth and Dublin this name is most common in Ulster, particularly in its homeland of Tyrone, and in Co. Donegal. The name is in Gaelic Ó Searcaigh and is based on the word *searcach,* which means 'loving'. Very little is known of the history of the name or the sept except that it was originally of Tyrone. Apart from an appearance in the Co. Monaghan Hearth Money Rolls of the 1660s as O'Serky and O'Sharky, it rarely appears in Irish records or annals. It is known that the prefix O' was dropped in the eighteenth century.

SHAW

Though found in the other provinces of Ireland, Shaw is common only in Ulster, particularly in counties Antrim and Down. Though it can be of English origin, from Old English *sceaga,* denoting a 'dweller by the woods', most in Ulster will be of Scottish stock.

In the Lowlands of Scotland the name Shaw is of territorial origin from different places of the name and was most common in Kirkcudbrightshire, Ayrshire, around Greenock in Renfrewshire, and in Stirlingshire. The Highland Shaws are of no connection with these families. They were originally a branch of the Clan Mackintosh and descend from one Sithic, son of Gilchrist, who was grandson of the sixth Chief of Clan Mackintosh. However, they came to be regarded as a clan in their own right. With the Mackintoshes they were a part of the great Clan Chattan federation. Shaw is an anglicised form of Mac Sithich, meaning 'son of the wolf'.

Though the name has been on record in Ulster from the sixteenth century, it only became common after the Plantation. Shaws were among the first settlers brought to the Ards peninsula in Co. Down by Sir Hugh Montgomery but the name is not now found there. In mid-nineteenth-century Antrim the name was most concentrated in the barony of Upper Belfast, and in Down, in the barony of Upper Castlereagh, particularly in the parish of Saintfield. Ballygally Castle, near Larne, Co. Antrim, now a hotel, was built by a Scottish family of Shaws in 1625.

SHEILDS *see* Shields

SHEILS *see* Shields

SHERIDAN

This name is common in Leinster, Connacht and Ulster. It is most common in Co. Cavan, where it is one of the first ten names. In Gaelic it is Ó Sirideáin, a name of uncertain derivation.

The O'Sheridans were originally of Co. Longford and were erenaghs of Granard. However, they later migrated to the adjacent county of Cavan, where they became followers of the O'Reillys.

Many of the Sheridans have become famous. The two most notable are Richard Brinsley Sheridan, 1751–1816, born in Dublin of a Cavan family, who, besides being one of the most well-known dramatists in the English language, was also an MP and held various ministerial posts at Westminster; and Philip Henry Sheridan, 1831–88, who was born at Killinkere in Co. Cavan and was taken to the USA at an early age. He rose to become major general in the American Civil War on the Union side.

SHIELDS (*also* Sheilds, Sheils *and* Shiels)

In Ireland Shields and Sheilds are not common outside Ulster and are most numerous in counties Antrim and Down. Shiels and Sheils are only common in Dublin and Ulster, where they are chiefly found in counties Donegal and Derry. They can be of Irish, Scottish or English origin.

Those of Irish stock are in Gaelic Ó Siadhail, the name of a sept of Inishowen in Donegal, who descended ultimately from the fifth-century Niall of the Nine Hostages, founder of the Uí Néill dynasty. A medical family, they provided physicians to chiefs in various parts of Ireland. In Scotland it was originally a Border surname, deriving from the Middle Englsh *schele*, a word that initially meant a 'shepherd's summer hut' and then a 'small house'. In England it can have the same derivation, but can also derive from Old English *scild*, a 'shield', and denoted a 'shield-maker'. Apart from England, where the forms Shield and Shields are the only ones found, the other spellings listed are common to both Ireland and Scotland, so it will be difficult to determine the origin of a particular family.

James Shields, 1806–79, was born at Altmore, Co. Tyrone, and emigrated to America in 1826. He rose to become a Supreme Court judge, a senator and a brigadier general. George Shiels, 1886–1949, was born at Ballyroney in Co. Antrim. He wrote for the Abbey Theatre in Dublin for over twenty years. His most successful play was *The Rugged Path*.

SHIELS *see* Shields

SIMMS *see* Simpson

SIMPSON (*also* Simms)

In Ireland these two names are common only in Ulster and in particular in Co. Antrim. Simms is also well known in east Donegal. The names can be of Scottish or English origin. Simpson is one of the fifty most common names in Scotland.

The personal name Simon derives from the Old Testament Simeon, which is from the Hebrew Shim'on, a name that might mean 'offspring of hyena and wolf'. Sim was a popular diminutive or pet form of Simon. Simpson and Simms in both Scotland and England can derive from this and both meant 'son of Sim'. Another English derivation of the name Simpson is from one of the three places of that name in Devon, all of which were previously called Siwineston. Simms, too, can be a pet form of Simmond, also from Simon. This name gives the surname Simmonds or Simmons.

The Scottish name MacKimmie is in Gaelic Mac Shimidh, 'son of Simon'. The MacKimmies were a sept of Clan Fraser, among whom the name Simon was popular. Indeed the first chief of Clan Fraser of Lovat was Simon Fraser, and from him each succeeding chief is styled Mac Shimi. MacKimmie was anglicised as Sim, Simson and Simpson.

Both names were recorded in Co. Antrim from the early seventeenth century. In mid-nineteenth-century Antrim, Simpson was most concentrated in the barony of Lower Toome. At the beginning of the twentieth century Simms and Simpson were being used interchangeably in the Newry district of Co. Down.

SINCLAIR

In Ireland this name is common only in Ulster and in particular, in counties Armagh and Derry. The name is that of the Clan Sinclair of Caithness in the far north of Scotland. The Sinclairs were not a clan in the strict sense of the word because they were of Norman origin and their relations with their dependants was feudal in nature. The commonness of the name in Caithness and in Orkney results from tenants taking the name of their lord.

The name was originally St Clare, and derived from the place of that name in Pont d'Évêque in Normandy. A family of the name of St Clare is thought to have come to Scotland with the de Morvilles. Their first Scottish possession was the barony of Roslin, but they rose to control all of Caithness and were Earls of Caithness from the fourteenth to the sixteenth century.

On the west coast of Scotland the name Mac na Cearda, giving MacIncaird, MacNokard and so on, meant 'son of the brassworker' (but *see* Connor for MacNocker, MacNogher and so on). This trade eventually became debased and the word 'tinkler', a Scottish version of 'tinker', was used for it. There were Cairds, a sept of Clan Sinclair, and between this and the appellation Tinkler, the Cairds became Sinclairs. Around 1900 the names Sinclair and Cairdie were still being used interchangeably in Ballycastle, Co. Antrim.

SLOAN (*also* Sloane)

This name is not common in Ireland outside Ulster. Well over half the Sloans are in Co. Antrim and the name is common too in counties Armagh and Down. Though etymologically the name is Irish in origin, Sloans in Ulster can be of Irish or Scottish extraction.

O'Sloan is from the Gaelic Ó Sluagháin, which is ultimately from the word *sluagh*, meaning a 'host' or 'army'. The O'Sloans were a sept of Co. Down and the name, also as Slowan, spread in the seventeenth century into Armagh. The west Ulster name Ó Sluaghadhaigh was important in medieval times. It was anglicised as Slowey and Sloan. The sept of Mac Sluaghaidh was originally of Roslea and Adrumsee in Fermanagh and in Monaghan their name was made Sloane, Slowey, Sloy and Molloy (*see* Molloy).

As Sloan, Sloane and Slowan, the name is common in the Scottish province of Galloway. There it was originally O'Sluaghain, of Irish origin, and was first recorded in 1504.

The most famous of the name was Sir Hans Sloane, 1660–1753, who was born in Killyleagh, Co. Down, of Scottish stock. A physician and naturalist, he bequeathed his massive natural history collection to the state in return for a cash sum to be paid to his family. The collection was the basis of what became the British Museum in London.

SLOANE *see* Sloan

SMALL

Though found in all the provinces of Ireland, Small is numerous only in Ulster, particularly counties Antrim, Armagh and Down. The name in both England and Scotland derives from the Old English *smæl*, meaning 'small, slender, thin'. As Smail, Small and Smeal, it is the name of a sept of Clan Murray. In Ulster it has been used as a synonym of the name Begg, Gaelic *beag*, meaning 'small' (*see* Beggs) or as a synonym of Kielty, the more usual anglicisation of the Gaelic Ó Caoilte. This arose through mistranslation – the Gaelic name was supposed to derive from *caol*, meaning 'slender'. Around 1900 Small was being used interchangeably with Kielty near Cookstown in Co. Tyrone; with Keeltagh and Kieltogh in Clough near Downpatrick in Co. Down; with Kilkey near Derry city; and with Gilkie around Ballykelly, near Limavady, in Co. Derry.

SMITH (*also* Smyth)

The most famous fact about this name is simply its popularity throughout the English-speaking world. It is the most common name in England and Wales, in Scotland and in Ulster, and is fifth in Ireland. It is the single most numerous name in Co. Antrim and is among the first five in counties Down and Cavan, among the first ten in counties Armagh, Derry, Fermanagh and Monaghan and among the first fifteen in Co. Tyrone. It is found in every county of Ireland but is numerically strongest in counties Antrim and Cavan.

Though archetypally the most English of surnames, in Ulster it can be of both Scottish and Irish origin as well as English. Those in Ulster who are of English stock can stem from any part of England, the name having sprung up in a multitude of locations, in fact wherever there was a smith, armourer or farrier.

In Scotland the name MacGow was in Gaelic Mac Gobha, 'son of the smith', and was anglicised as Gow and as Smith. There were Gows or MacGowans, a sept of Clan Macpherson, long known as Sliochd a' Ghobha Chrom, the 'race of the bandy-legged smith', from their ancestor Henry (Gow) of the Wynd. These Smiths became a clan in their own right, one of the seventeen 'tribes' of the great Clan Chattan federation. However, the name Gow was very common all over Scotland up to the nineteenth century and is still common in Inverness-shire and Perthshire. A great many Gows became Smiths.

The same name also became Mac Ghobhainn which was anglicised as MacGowan. Besides the Macpherson MacGowans there was a sept of the name of Clan Donald who were hereditary smiths to the clan. The name is also common in Dumfriesshire. It can be assumed that many of the Scottish MacGowans further anglicised their name to Smith.

The Irish MacGowans, in Gaelic Mac an Ghabhann, also 'son of the smith', from *gabha*, meaning 'smith', were one of the principal septs of Breffny, and in Co. Cavan the great majority anglicised to Smith, as did the Mac In Gabhand sept of Ballymagowan, near Clogher, Co. Tyrone. The Ó Gabhann sept of Drummully in Fermanagh anglicised its name as O'Goan, Goan, Gavin and Smith. The O'Gowans, Gaelic Ó Gabhann, of Co. Down, who gave their name to Ballygowan, also became Smiths. Finally, there were Irish Gows, in Gaelic Gabha, who, mainly in Co. Cavan, anglicised to Smith.

The alternative spellings Smyth and Smythe were adopted at various stages as an affectation of gentility and were both originally Smith.

See also MacGowan.

SMYTH *see* Smith

SOMERVILLE

Most of the Somervilles in Ulster will descend from Scottish settlers who came to the province in the seventeenth century. The name is Norman in origin from the town of the name near Caen in Normandy. It meant 'Sumar's estate'. The first of the name in Scotland was William de Somerville who came in the early twelfth century in the train of David I and was granted lands in Lanarkshire. It has occasionally been used as a synonym of the Sligo name Somahan, Gaelic Ó Somachain. Variants in Ulster include Simvil, Sumeril and Summerly.

SPEERS (*also* Speirs *and* Spiers)

Apart from a few of the name in Dublin, Speers and its variants are common only in Ulster and in particular in Co. Antrim and central Down. It came to Ulster from both England and Scotland in the eighteenth century. In England it derives from the Old English *spere,* a 'spear', and denoted a 'spearman'. In Scotland it is the genitive case of Speir or Spier which is thought to be an official's name, the 'spyer' or 'watchman', from Old French *espier.*

SPEIRS *see* Speers

SPENCE

In Ireland Spence is common only in Ulster. Two-thirds are in Co. Antrim and most of the remainder in Co. Down. The name is common in both Scotland and England, but most in Ulster will probably stem from Scotland.

In both countries the name, as Spence or Spens, denoted the official who was in charge of the larder or provisions room, from Middle English *spense, spence,* from Old French *despense.* The Spences of Wormiston were a sept of Clan MacDuff and were standard-bearers to the clan. They are said to descend from Duncan MacDuff, 4th Earl of Fife.

SPIERS *see* Speers

STEEL *see* Steele

STEELE (*also* Steel)

In Ireland this name is not common outside Ulster. Three-quarters of the Steeles are in Co. Antrim and most of the rest are in Co. Derry. It can be of Scottish or English origin.

In Scotland, where it is also found as Steill, the name is of local origin from one of the places of the name in Ayrshire, Berwickshire or Dumfriesshire. (Ladykirk in Berwickshire was previously called Steill.) In England it was originally a nickname and derives from the Old English *stȳle*, *stēle*, meaning 'steel', and denoted someone who was as hard or reliable as steel.

In mid-nineteenth-century Co. Antrim the name was particularly concentrated in the barony of Lower Dunluce, especially around Ballybogy.

STEEN *see* Stevenson

STEENSON *see* Stevenson

STEPHENSON *see* Stevenson

STEVENSON (*also* Steen, Steenson, Stephenson *and* Stinson)

Though Stevenson and Stephenson are found in the other provinces of Ireland they are common only in Ulster, and particularly in counties Antrim, Armagh and Down. Steenson, Stinson and Steen are exclusive to Ulster and are most numerous in counties Antrim and Armagh.

St Stephen, the first Christian martyr after Christ, is especially revered and the personal name Stephen was a favourite among the Normans, who made it popular in Britain. In Scotland the name was spelt Steven and so, technically at least, Stephenson is more likely to be English and Stevenson Scottish. However, spellings are notoriously unreliable when trying to distinguish the origins of a particular family. Stevenson is much more common in Ulster.

Steen and Stein, as both surname and personal name, are forms of Steven found principally in Ayrshire, Fife, the Lothians and Roxburghshire. Steenson and Stinson in Ulster are variants of Stephenson. Around 1900 Stephenson was being used interchangeably with Steenson about Cootehill in Co. Cavan and Tandragee in Co. Armagh; with Steinson near Ballymena in Co. Antrim; with Stenson around Cootehill; and with Stinson in Blackwaterstown in Armagh and Templepatrick in Antrim. Stevenson has occasionally been used in Ireland as a synonym of the Anglo-Norman name FitzStephen.

STEWART (*also* Stuart)

Stewart is one of the sixty most common names in Ireland. Ninety per cent are in Ulster, making it one of the ten most common names there. It is one of the first five in Co. Antrim and is common too in counties Down, Derry, Donegal and Tyrone. It is one of the most common non-Irish names in Ireland.

The name derives from the Old English *stigweard,* meaning a 'steward', in the sense of a 'keeper of the house', an honourable position. Most of the name in England and in Scotland will descend from this origin. However, the title in Scotland was also applied to the 'Steward' of the royal household, responsible for the collection of taxes, the administration of justice, and in war to assume the first place in the army next to the king.

In early records in Scotland the titles 'dapifer', 'seneschal' and 'steward' were synonymous. The Scottish royal family descends from one Alan Dapifer of Dol in Brittany. Descendants of his, one Walter FitzAlan and his brother Simon, were the first of the family recorded in Scotland. Simon was designated Buidhe, from his yellow hair, as was his son Robert from whom the Boyds descend (*see* Boyd).

In the early twelfth century David I granted Walter lands in Renfrew and in Paisley in Ayrshire and created him High Steward of Scotland. It was this Walter's grandson, also Walter, who was the first to use the surname Stewart. Walter, the sixth steward, married a daughter of Robert the Bruce and their son became King Robert II in 1371, the first of the Stewart dynasty. The Clan Stewart eventually divided into separate clans: the Stewarts of Appin, of Atholl, of Bute and of Galloway. Essentially a Lowland clan, it was referred to by the Gaels as the 'race of kings and tinkers'. The French spelt the name Stuart and through the fame of Mary Queen of Scots, who was brought up in France, this spelling became popular.

The early Stewarts were renowned as a prolific race, but even so this cannot account for the fact that the name is one of the ten most common in Scotland. In fact every bishop or great lord had his steward and the name sprang up in various locations. Stewart was also one of the names adopted by the MacGregors when their own name was proscribed (*see* Greer).

In the mid-fifteenth century Archibald Stewart, Laird of Largyan in Bute, was attainted for taking part in the rebellion of Matthew Stewart, Earl of Lennox, and lost most of his lands. His sons came to north Antrim and were the ancestors of the Stewarts of Ballintoy. Later a great many others of the name came to Ulster at the time of the Plantation.

Andrew Stewart, Lord Ochiltree, of Ayrshire, was one of the nine Scottish chief undertakers of the Plantation and was granted lands at Mountjoy in Tyrone. His grandson, Sir William Stewart, was created Lord Mountjoy in 1682. Stewartstown in Tyrone is named after him. Two other Scottish chief undertakers and six of the fifty Scottish undertakers were Stewarts and were granted lands in Donegal, Cavan, and Tyrone. They stemmed from various Lowland counties.

The most famous of the Ulster Stewarts was Robert Stewart, Viscount Castlereagh, 2nd Marquis of Londonderry, 1769–1822, who was largely responsible for pushing through the Act of Union of 1800. He resigned with William Pitt when George III refused to consent to Catholic emancipation, but later returned to political life and became one of Britain's most famous foreign secretaries. James Stuart, 1764–1842, was the first editor of the *Newry Telegraph* and was later editor of the *Belfast News-Letter*. He is most famous for his account of his native city, *Historical Memoirs of the City of Armagh*.

STINSON *see* Stevenson

STUART *see* Stewart

SWEENEY (*also* MacSweeney)

Sweeney is among the sixty most common names in Ireland. It is more or less equally distributed between Munster, Connacht and Ulster but is less numerous in Leinster.

The name in Gaelic is Mac Suibhne and the family descends from one Suibhne, a Scottish chieftain who flourished around 1200 in Argyll. This chieftain's surname was O'Neill, and at some time an elaborate genealogy was constructed to give the MacSweeneys a descent from the O'Neills. This is not now accepted, though it is plain that the MacSweeneys descend from a mixture of Irish Dalriadic Gaels and Norsemen; in short, they were of the Gall-Gaedhil. His two sons, Dougal and Maolmhuire, were seated at Skipness Castle and Castle Sween respectively, both on Kintyre.

The first on record in Ireland is Murchadh Mear in 1267, son of Maolmhuire. Murchadh's nephew Eoin was the first of the family to settle in Fanad in Tirconnell. The MacSweeneys are one of the most famous of the Scottish galloglass families; they came to Ireland, and more than any other they maintained a distinct organisation. Branches, all descending from Murchadh, settled in various parts of Ireland, with the exception of Leinster, which was the sphere of English influence. Those that concern us most are the MacSweeneys of Fanad, of Banagh, and the

MacSweeneys of the Battleaxes. However, MacSweeney of the Battleaxes is a mistranslation of Mac Suibhne na dTuath, which actually means 'MacSweeney of the Territories' (in Donegal), the word for 'axe' and 'territory' being similar in Gaelic. From the fourteenth to the seventeenth centuries the MacSweeney septs of Tirconnell, chiefly as galloglasses to O'Donnell, played an important part in the military history of Ulster. Together with the native Irish, they suffered after the seventeenth-century wars and many went into exile, becoming distinguished soldiers in the Irish brigades of the continent.

The name is also recorded as MacSwiney and MacSwine and in Gaelic (Mac Suibhne) is the same as that of the Scottish Clan MacQueen to which they are distantly related.

TAGGART

Taggart and its variants are, in Ireland, virtually exclusive to Ulster where they can be of Irish or Scottish origin. The name is most common in Co. Antrim. In both Scotland and Ireland the name is in Gaelic Mac an tSagairt, meaning 'son of the priest'. The word *sagart* was borrowed from the Latin *sacerdos*, a 'priest'. In early medieval times the rule of clerical celibacy was not strictly enforced.

In Scotland the Taggarts and MacTaggarts were a sept of Clan Ross and took their name from Ferchar Mackinsagart, son of the 'Red Priest of Applecross', and first of the Celtic O'Beolan Earls of Ross (*see* Ross). Others may have descended ultimately from less well-known priests, for the name Taggart is common in Dumfriesshire.

In Ulster the Fermanagh sept of Mac an tSagairt was based at Bally-mactaggart in Lurg, where they were erenaghs of the church lands. By the sixteenth and seventeenth centuries the name was common in counties Antrim, Derry, Fermanagh, Donegal, Armagh and Louth.

At the start of the twentieth century Taggart was still being used interchangeably with McAteggart near Stewartstown in Tyrone, and with McTaggart and Teggart near Lisnaskea in Fermanagh. Other variants include Attegart, Haggart, MacEnteggart, Target, Teggart and Teggarty.

TAIT *see* Tate

TATE (*also* Tait)

Though found in Dublin, this name is in Ireland almost exclusive to Ulster. It is most common in counties Antrim and Down, where it is mainly spelt Tate, and in Co. Derry, where Tait is the predominant form. The name can be of either English or Scottish origin and was originally a nickname, from Old Norse *teitr*, meaning 'cheerful, gay'.

The most famous family of the name were the Taits, one of the lesser of the notorious riding clans of the Scottish Borders. They were located in the Middle March on the Scottish side of the frontier and were followers of the Kerrs. In the decade after 1603, James VI's 'pacification' of the Borders encouraged many members of the riding clans to seek refuge in Ulster, where the Plantation was under way. It is likely that some, if not most, of the province's Tates and Taits will be of this origin.

The Revd Faithfull Tate, *fl.* 1620–72, of Co. Cavan, was a noted divine and religious poet. He informed on plans for the rebellion in 1641, for which his house was burned and his children injured. His son, Nahum Tate, 1652–1715, who was born in Dublin, became poet laureate.

TAYLOR

Taylor in Ireland is well known in all the provinces but is common only in Ulster and Dublin. The greatest concentrations are in counties Antrim, Down and Derry. It can be of English or Scottish origin.

Taylor is one of the five most common names in England and derives from the Anglo-French *taillour*, Old French *tailleur*, a 'tailor'. The name can stem from any part of the country. There were Tailors, one of the notorious riding clans of the Scottish Borders, located on the English side of the frontier in the West March. Many members of the riding clans sought refuge in Ulster after James VI's 'pacification' of the Borders in the decade after 1603.

In Lowland Scotland, too, Taylor or Tayleur was a common occupational name in early records and was first noted in 1276 when Alexander le Tayllur was valet to Alexander III. The word in the Highlands was gaelicised *tàillear* and gave rise to the name Mac an Tàilleir, 'son of the tailor', common in Perthshire, which was initially anglicised as MacIntaylor and then Taylor. The Taylors, earlier MacIntaylors, of Cowal in Argyllshire were a sept of Clan Cameron, who descended from an illegitimate son of Ewen Cameron, fourteenth chief of the Camerons of Lochiel. The child was fostered by a tailor's wife and became a famous seventeenth-century warrior, Tàillear dubh na tuaighe, the 'black tailor of the axe'. A rare Galloway surname, MacTaldrach, which became MacTaldridge in Ulster, was also made Taylor.

The name is recorded as le Taylour in medieval Irish records and many in Dublin and the southeast counties will be of this origin. However, those in Ulster will be of Plantation and post-Plantation origin. The name was also recorded in seventeenth-century Co. Antrim as MacTaylor, probably an interim stage between MacIntaylor and Taylor. Jeremy Taylor, 1613–67, Bishop of Down and Connor, was one of the greatest theologians and writers of his age. Though born in Cambridge, he is remembered more for his association with Lisburn, Co. Antrim and Dromore, Co. Down.

TEAGUE *see* MacKeag

THOMPSON (*also* MacComb *and* Thomson)

Thompson is among the fifty most common names in Ireland and among the first ten in Ulster, which claims three-quarters of all those in Ireland. It is the single most numerous name in Co. Down, among the first ten in Co. Antrim, among the first twenty in counties Armagh and Fermanagh, and is also numerous in counties Derry and Longford and in Dublin. Thomson is the prevalent form in Scotland and Thompson is the common spelling in England. However, the great majority in Ireland spell the name Thompson, and many if not most of these will be originally Scottish Thomsons, whose name was altered in Ulster. MacComb in Ireland is exclusive to Ulster, where it is most common in counties Antrim, Down and Derry.

Thomas was a common Anglo-Norman personal name, which derives from the Hebrew *to'ām*, meaning 'twin'. The surname in England means, obviously enough, 'son of Thom', a diminutive or pet form of Thomas. The name Thompson is among the fifteen most common in England and is most numerous around Northampton. Also there were Thomsons, one of the lesser of the riding clans of the Scottish Borders, located in the Middle March on the English side of the frontier. The majority of those members of the riding clans who fled from the 'pacification' by James VI of the Border region in the early seventeenth century settled in Fermanagh. Thomsons were established in many parts of Fermanagh during the Plantation, and these may well have been Border Thomsons.

The name Thomson is among the first five in Scotland and in the Lowlands was of the same derivation as in England – 'son of Thom'. It was first recorded in 1318 when John Thomson, 'a man of low birth, but approved valour', was commander of the men of Carrick (in Ayrshire) in Edward Bruce's invasion of Ireland.

However, the personal name was early borrowed into Scots Gaelic as Tómas and Támhus and gave rise to a variety of Gaelic patronymics. Mac Tómais was the name of a branch of Clan Mackintosh who descended from one Tomhaidh Mór, 'Great Tommy'. By 1587 they appear as a clan in their own right, recorded in the Roll of Clans as Clan M'Thomas in Glenesche (now Glenshee). The name was anglicised as MacTavish, MacThomas, Thompson and Thomson. Iain Mór, seventh chief of Clan MacThomas, joined Montrose at Dundee in 1644 and after his death and their defeat the clan scattered, some perhaps coming to Ulster.

In another spelling of the name, Mac Thómais, the 'h' makes the 'T' silent and so this was anglicised as MacComish and MacCavish. A variant of Mac Tómais was Mac Thomaidh, 'son of Tommy'. This became Mac Comaidh, anglicised initially as Maccomy and then, at the end of the eighteenth century, to MacCombe, MacCombich and MacCombie. In Wigtownshire MacComb and MacCombe derive from the Gaelic name Mac Thóm, 'son of Tom'. A sept of Clan Campbell in Argyll anglicised to MacTavish, Taweson and Thompson. The Macauses or Thomasons were a sept of Clan MacFarlane, descending from one Thomas, a son of the MacFarlane chief in the reign of Robert III. Mac Tómais and its variants have also been anglicised as Holmes (*see* Holmes).

In mid-nineteenth-century Antrim Thompson was found in thirteen of the fourteen baronies and was the most common name in the baronies of Lower Antrim, Lower Massereene and Upper Belfast. In Down Thomson was the most common name in the barony of Kinelarty, especially in the area between Loughinisland and Ballynahinch, but was numerous too in the adjacent baronies. Around 1900 Thompson was still being used interchangeably with MacAvish, MacCavish and MacTavish in north Antrim.

William Thompson, 1805–52, was a naturalist born in Belfast, the son of a linen merchant. His *Natural History of Ireland* became the standard work. William Marcus Thompson, 1857–1907, was born in Derry city of staunch Orange stock. In London he became a barrister, specialising in defending trade unionists, and edited *Reynold's Newspaper,* which regularly attacked the establishment. Hugh Thomson, 1860–1920, was born in Coleraine, Co. Derry. He became a famous illustrator of classic fiction. James Thomson, 1822–92, became a distinguished engineer. He was born in Belfast, as was his brother William, Lord Kelvin, 1824–1907, who became one of the most celebrated scientists and inventors of the Victorian age. He discovered the second law of thermodynamics and broke much new ground in the study of electric currents. He was largely responsible for the laying of the transatlantic telegraph cable. His statue stands in Belfast's Botanic Gardens.

THOMSON *see* Thompson

TODD

In Ireland Todd is almost exclusive to Ulster, where two-thirds are in Co. Antrim and most of the rest in Co. Down. It can be of northern English or Scottish origin. In both countries it was originally a nickname, from Middle England *tod,* a 'fox'. It was first recorded in Scotland *c.* 1270 as

Tod. In the eighteenth century the second 'd' was added, and now the spelling Tod is largely confined to the west coast, while Todd is most common around Edinburgh. There were Todds who were septs of Clan Gordon and Clan MacTavish.

Given its original meaning it is interesting to note that around 1900 Todd was being used interchangeably with Shinnahan near Ballycastle, Co. Antrim. The Gaelic for 'fox' is *sionnach*, which is pronounced 'shinnagh' and a family of Mac an tSionnaigh was once common in that area (*see* Fox *and* Shannon).

TONER

Apart from a few in Dublin, Toners are found almost exclusively in Ulster, particularly in counties Derry and Armagh. A few in Ulster may be English. The name is in Gaelic Ó Tomhrair, from a Norse personal name, Tomar.

However, the family is not of Norse origin, but was a sept of the Cenél Eoghain based originally on the banks of the Foyle, near Lifford in Co. Donegal. They later migrated to Derry and Armagh.

The name is found in England, where it was early imported from Ireland (recorded as Tunere in 1242). It can also be from le Toner, 'dweller by the farm or village', from Old English *tún*.

Variants of the name include Tonner, Tonra and Tonry.

TRAINOR *see* Treanor

TRAYNOR *see* Treanor

TREANOR (*also* Trainor *and* Traynor)

Apart from Dublin city, where Traynor is the usual spelling, this name is common only in Ulster. As Traynor and Treanor it was the seventh most common name in Co. Monaghan in 1970 and was found to be most numerous in the north of the county. It is also, as Trainor and Treanor, numerous in counties Armagh and Tyrone.

The name is in Gaelic Mac Thréinfhir, from *tréan*, 'strong', and *fear*, 'man'. The Gaelic name was pronounced 'MacCrainor' and this, and MacCrennor, are other anglicised forms. The name Armstrong (*see* Armstrong) has also been used by quasi-translation.

Trainor is also an English name, first recorded in Durham and York in the thirteenth and fourteenth centuries, so some in Ulster may be of this origin. The name in this case denoted a 'trapper', from the Middle English verb *trayne*, 'to lay a train (snare)'.

TURNER

In Ireland, outside of Dublin and Cork, this name is most common in Ulster, where it can be of English or Scottish origin. It is most numerous in Co. Antrim.

Turner is an occupational name, from the Old French *tornour*, a 'turner', that is, a lathe-worker. In England it was also, more rarely, recorded as Turnare, 'one who turns a spit' and as Old French *tournoieur*, 'one who takes part in a tournament'. Turner is one of the thirty most common names in England and Wales. In the Lowlands of Scotland the name derives from the 'lathe-worker' origin and was common in Aberdeenshire and Kirkcudbrightshire. According to George MacDonald Fraser, there were also Turners, one of the lesser riding clans of the Scottish Borders, based in Liddesdale, 'the cockpit of the Scottish Middle March'. Many belonging to the riding clans sought refuge in Ulster when James VI 'pacified' the Borders and destroyed the social system there in the decade after 1603.

In the Highlands the name of the trade was borrowed into Gaelic as *tuairnear*, giving rise to the name Mac an Tuairneir, 'son of the turner'. The Macinturners, later MacTourners and Turners, were a sept of Clan Lamont who descended from a fugitive Lamont who settled on Loch Lomondside and became a turner.

Samuel Turner, 1765–1810, was born at Turner's Glen near Newry, Co. Down, and became a barrister. Though he was on the executive committee of the United Irishmen, he was an undercover government informer, receiving a secret pension. In 1798 he 'escaped' to the continent, returning in 1803. His duplicity was discovered only when, on his death, his son applied for a continuance of the pension.

WADE *see* MacQuaid

WALKER

In Ireland, apart from Dublin, this name is common only in Ulster, in particular in counties Antrim, Down and Derry. It can be of Scottish or English origin, being among the twenty most common names in England and Wales and the thirty most common in Scotland.

In medieval times cloth had to be 'fulled', that is, scoured and thickened by being beaten in water. Originally this was done by 'walking', or trampling it in a trough. In the south and east of England this gave rise to the surname Fuller, in the extreme southwest the name Tucker, from the Old English verb *tūcian*, 'to torment', later 'to full', and in the north and west the name Walker.

In the Lowlands of Scotland the name was first recorded in 1324. In the Highlands the Gaelic word for a fuller gave rise to the surname Mac an Fhucadair, 'son of the fuller'. This was anglicised to MacNucator. In its unaspirated form, Mac Fùcadair, it was anglicised as MacFuktor. Both these names were further anglicised to Walker.

The most famous of the name in Ulster history was the Revd George Walker, 1618–90. Born in Co. Tyrone, he became rector of Lissan, Co. Derry, and was governor of Derry during the siege. The truth of his *A True Account of the Siege of Londonderry* was disputed by his chaplain, the Revd John MacKenzie, whose account challenged Walker's self-glorification. Walker was made Bishop of Derry but was killed shortly afterwards at the Battle of the Boyne.

WALLACE

This name is well known in Galway, Cork, Limerick and Dublin but is most common in Ulster where its main centres are in counties Antrim, Down and Derry. It can be of Norman, English or Scottish origin.

The name was common in medieval Ireland as le Waleis, 'the Welshman'. And the name in England is well known as Wallis, meaning 'Welshman' or 'Celt'. In Scotland in the twelfth century the first of the name on record is Richard Wallace or Wallensis, who came to Scotland from Shropshire in the service of Walter FitzAlan, Scottish progenitor of the Stewarts. Shropshire is close to the Welsh border so the name is thought to have meant 'Welshman'.

However, Sir William Wallace, Scotland's national hero, was not a 'Welshman' in this sense. He was the descendant of a Strathclyde Briton and in Scotland generally the Latin name Wallensis meant just that. The name appears in twelfth-century records of Ayrshire and Renfrewshire, parts of the old Strathclyde kingdom. There were Wallaces, followers of the Earls of Crawford, chiefs of Clan Lindsay.

In mid-nineteenth-century Antrim the name was found in twelve out of the fourteen baronies and was the most common name in the barony of Lower Toome. In Co. Down it was most common on the Ards peninsula, particularly between Newtownards and Greyabbey. Wallace has also been used as a synonym of Walsh (*see* Walsh).

Sir Richard Wallace, 1818–90, who gave his name to Wallace Park, Wallace High School and so on, in Lisburn, Co. Antrim, was born in London of uncertain parentage. He was either an illegitimate son of Richard Seymour Conway, 4th Marquis of Hertford, or an illegitimate son of Conway's mother Maria, *née* Fagnani, by an unidentified father. As a youth he was called Richard Jackson. An art collector himself, on the death of his reputed half-brother, Hertford, in 1870, he fell heir to the Conway estate in Lisburn and the finest art collection in private hands in the world.

WALSH (*also* Welsh)

Walsh is quite a common name in Ulster but is more than four times as common in Leinster and Connacht and more than six times as common in Munster. Found in every county, it is among the first five names in Ireland. Welsh is common only in Ulster, where it is most numerous in Co. Antrim.

The name derives from the Middle English *walsche*, Old English *wǣlisc*, meaning a 'foreigner', a 'Welshman', and it is possible that a few in Ulster will be of this English origin. But most in Ulster, as in all of Ireland, will be originally called Breatnach, which is the Gaelic for 'Welshman'. As well as Walsh, this name is also anglicised as Brannagh, Brennagh, Brannick and so on. In Ulster Walsh has also been made Welsh and Welch and occasionally Wallace, which has the same meaning (*see* Wallace).

Henry Walsh, 1784–1844, born in Co. Antrim, was press-ganged in Belfast in 1809 and served six years in the British navy before publishing an account of his adventures. The poet Edward Walsh, 1805–50, was born in Derry. He became something of a *cause célèbre* when he lost his job as a national school teacher for writing for the Fenian newspaper *The Nation*. He then got a job as a teacher in the detention centre on Spike Island, but lost this for waving goodbye to the Fenian John Mitchel as he passed through Cork harbour on a transportation ship. He ended his days teaching in Cork Workhouse.

WARD

Ward is common is every province of Ireland and found in every county, but it is most numerous in Ulster, where it is among the ten most common names in Co. Donegal and among the first twenty in Co. Monaghan. The name is one of the thirty most common in England and Wales, where it is an occupational name, from Old English *weard*, meaning 'watchman, guard'. However, the majority of the Wards in Ulster will be of Irish stock.

Mac an Bhaird, 'son of the bard', was the name of two famous poet septs, one of Co. Galway, poets to the O'Kellys, and the other of Co. Donegal. The latter were professional hereditary bards to the O'Donnells of Tirconnell and were based at Lettermacaward near Glenties. A branch were poets to the O'Neills in Tyrone. The name was first anglicised as Macanward, then MacAward, then MacWard, then Ward. Eight of the

Donegal Macanwards were celebrated as poets in the seventeenth century.

Mac a' Bhaird, the Scottish equivalent, was anglicised as MacWard and does not seem to have been made Ward. Most of the MacWards became absorbed in Baird (which can have the same meaning – *see* Baird). In Co. Down the Wards of Bangor (Viscounts Bangor) and of Castleward are of English origin.

Hugh Boy Macanward, 1580–1635, was born at Lettermacaward in Donegal and became a noted historian. He was the first professor of theology at the Irish College at Louvain in Belgium. John Ward, 1832–1912, was a noted artist and Egyptologist. He was born in Belfast and worked for much of his life in the printing and publishing firm of his father, Marcus Ward.

WATERS *see* Watters

WATERSON *see* Watters

WATSON

In Ireland, apart from some Watsons in Dublin, this name is almost exclusive to Ulster. It is one of the ten most common names in Co. Armagh and is numerous in counties Antrim and Down. It is of Scottish or English origin, being one of the thirty most common names in Scotland and one of the fifty most common in England and Wales.

In England and Lowland Scotland the name derives from Wat or Watt, a diminutive or pet form of Walter (*see* Watt). It is particularly common in the northeastern counties of the Lowlands. MacLysaght claims that in the Highlands the Gaelic name Mac Bhaididh was anglicised as MacQuatt, MacWatt and MacWhatty and then further anglicised as Watson. However, MacWatt and MacWattie can also derive from Walter. A sept of Clan Forbes, the Watts, located in the Aberdeenshire highlands, were also known as MacQuatties, MacWatties, MacWatts, Walters and Watsons. The MacWatties, Watsons and Watts, a sept of Clan Buchanan, descend from Walter, son of Buchanan of Lenny (*see* Beatty). MacWatt, giving Watt and Watson, was also common in Dumfriesshire and Ayrshire.

In mid-nineteenth-century Antrim Watson was most common in the barony of Upper Massereene. In Down it was mainly concentrated in Lower Iveagh, around Moira and between Dromore and Annahilt. It is also very common on the Upper Ards.

WATT

In Ireland Watt is exclusive to Ulster, where it is most common in Co. Antrim. It can be of Scottish or English origin. The Old German personal name Walter was introduced into Britain before the Norman Conquest and after the Conquest became very popular. It was pronounced and often written 'Wauter' hence the abbreviated forms Wat, Watt and Wattie. The name was very common in the Lowlands of Scotland, particularly in Aberdeenshire and Banffshire. In the late nineteenth century a village in Banffshire was found to be inhabited by 300 people, of whom 225 were Watts. Watt also derives from MacWatt and MacWattie (*see* Watson).

WATTERS (*also* Waters *and* Waterson)

Watters in Ireland is common only in Ulster (especially counties Tyrone and Antrim) and in Louth. Waters is found in all the provinces, but is particularly common in Dublin, Sligo, Wexford and Monaghan. Waterson is almost exclusive to Ulster and is most common in Co. Antrim.

Watters and Waters in England and Scotland are forms of Walters, 'son of Walter' (*see* Watt). In Scotland it can also derive from MacWatters. In Ireland Waters, and to a lesser extent Watters, have been used as anglicisations of several Irish names.

The Co. Monaghan sept of Farney called Mac an Uisce (*uisce* means 'water'), followers of the MacMahons, initially anglicised to MacEnuskey and MacEniskey. (MacLysaght claims that this name was Mac Con Uisce.) Virtually all these adopted the name Waters. Mac Uaitéir, also 'son of Walter', was a name that sprang up in several places. It was anglicised as Waters, as was Ó Fuaruisce, also anglicised as Whoriskey. Ó hUaruisce and Ó Tuairisc are variants of Ó Fuaruisce, and are anglicised respectively as Houriskey and Horish, and Toorish, Tourisk or Turish. All these became Waters, and Houriskey also became Caldwell (*see* Caldwell).

Waterson can be a variant of Waters, and indeed the two names were being used interchangeably in Ballyjamesduff in Co. Cavan around 1900. However, it is a Scottish name in origin and was originally Waterstoun, 'Walter's place' (a name early made Waterston and Waterstone), and derives from a few different localities of that name in the Lowlands.

WEIR

In Ireland Weir is virtually exclusive to Ulster, where over half are in Co. Antrim and a quarter in Co. Armagh. It can be of Irish, Scottish or English origin. The name in England derives from the Old English *wer*, meaning a 'weir' or 'fish trap' and denoted a 'dweller by the dam' or 'keeper of the fishing weir'.

In Scotland Weir can be Norman, from one of several places called Vere in Normandy. This placename derives from the Old Norse *ver*, a 'station', as in *fiskiver*, a 'fishing station'. The first of the name recorded in Scotland was the twelfth-century Radolphus de Ver. The Weirs of Blackwood in Lanarkshire claim descent from him. There were Weirs, vassals of the abbots of Kelso, who held extensive lands in Lesmahagow, whose church was one of the most famous sanctuaries in medieval Scotland.

The name MacNair is in Gaelic Mac an Oighre, which means 'son of the heir', and denoted a disinherited senior grandson. It was anglicised as Weir and there were MacNair septs of Clan MacFarlane in Lennox, Dumbartonshire; of Clan MacNaughton in Cowal, Argyllshire; and of Clan MacNab in Perthshire. Also in Dumbartonshire the name Mac a' Mhaoir, 'son of the officer or steward', which is pronounced MacAvweer, was made Weir.

The same Gaelic name appears in Ulster as Mac an Mhaoir, 'son of the steward or keeper', and was that of a Co. Armagh sept who were hereditary keepers of the Book of Armagh at Ballymoyer, Gaelic Baile a' Mhaoir, the 'town of the keeper'. Their name was first anglicised as MacMoyer and then Weir. Many of the Weirs of south Antrim and north Armagh will be of this sept.

The Co. Armagh and Co. Monaghan sept name Mac Giolla Uidhir (*see* MacClure), was initially anglicised as MacGillaweer, which was in turn shortened to Weir. Ó Corra (Corry) was also occasionally made Weir, Wire and Wyre by mistranslation (*corra*, 'edge'). In mid-nineteenth-century Antrim Weir was concentrated in the barony of Upper Toome, and in Down in the barony of Newry.

WELSH *see* Walsh

WHITE

White or Whyte, one of the fifty most common names in Ireland, is well known in Connacht and is very common in Leinster, Munster, and Ulster, where it is most numerous in counties Antrim and Down. It can be of Norman, English, Scottish or Irish origin.

In England the name has three possible origins. The most usual is as a nickname, from Old English *hwit*, meaning 'white', denoting a person of fair hair or complexion. It was common both before and after the Norman Conquest. It can also, from the Old English *wiht*, denote someone who lived by a bend in a river or road. Lastly, it can be based on the Old English *wait*, a 'look-out post'. White is one of the twenty-five most common names in England and Wales.

In Lowland Scotland White is mainly from the Old English *hwit* origin.

In the Highlands, however, the Gaelic name Mac Gille Bháin, 'son of the fair youth or servant', was anglicised as White and Whyte. White and Whyte were also among the colour names adopted by both MacGregors and Lamonts when their own names were proscribed (*see* Greer *and* Lamont). The name is one of the fifty most common in Scotland.

As le White, the name was introduced into Ireland at the time of the Anglo-Norman invasion, and by the fourteenth century it had become numerous in every province. One prominent family of Leixlip in Co. Kildare established themselves in Co. Down in the fourteenth century and became Lords of Dufferin after the rebellion and dispossession of the de Mandevilles (*see* MacQuillan).

White in Ireland was gaelicised as de Faoite. This gave rise to the surname Mac Faoitigh which was in turn re-anglicised as MacWhite, MacWhitty and MacQuitty. Irish names that contain either *bán* or *geal*, which both mean 'white', were also anglicised as White and Whyte. As late as 1900 Bawn was being used interchangeably with White in Banbridge and Dromore in Co. Down, and the Co. Cavan name Galligan, Gaelic Ó Gealagáin, was being used interchangeably with White in Cavan town. The name Bawn in the area around Banbridge and Dromore may have been a shortening of the name of one of the branches of the Laverys, the Baun-Laverys or 'White Laverys' (*see* Lavery).

In mid-nineteenth-century Antrim the main concentration of the name was in the barony of Lower Antrim and in Co. Down, on the Ards peninsula.

Field Marshal Sir George Stuart White, 1835–1912, who was born at Whitehall, Co. Antrim, received the Victoria Cross during the Afghan War, became commander-in-chief in India, and was in command of Natal during the Boer War. He led the forces at Ladysmith throughout the 118-day siege.

WILEY *see* Wylie

WILKINSON

In Ireland Wilkinson is common only in Ulster, particularly in counties Antrim and Armagh. It can be of Scottish or English origin.

Wilkin, like the Scottish Wilkie, is a double diminutive or pet form of William, first shortened to Will, to which -kin was later added. William itself is from the Old German Willihelm, and was for centuries the most popular personal name in England. It gave rise to an enormous number of surnames. Willis for instance, a common name in counties Antrim and Down, stems from both Scotland and England and is a shortened form of 'Willie's son'.

There were Wilkinsons, one of the lesser of the riding clans of the Scottish Borders, based in the Middle March on the English side of the frontier. There were Wilkinsons, Plantation tenants on the church lands of Clankelly in Co. Fermanagh, so it is likely that Wilkinsons fled the persecution of the riding clans by James VI and settled in Ulster, as did so many clan members.

In Kintyre and Islay the name MacQuilken, Scots Gaelic Mac Cuilcein, from the Irish Gaelic Mac Uilcín, 'son of Wilkin', was anglicised as Wilkieson and Wilkinson. Though both MacQuilken and Wilkinson are still found in those areas, Wilkinson is the more common form. Mac-Quilken is a common name on Rathlin Island and these and many of the Antrim Wilkinsons will be of this origin. In north Antrim the two forms are still interchangeable among some families who give their name officially as MacQuilken.

WILLIAMS *see* Williamson

WILLIAMSON (*also* Williams)

In Ireland Williamson is almost exclusive to Ulster and is most common in counties Antrim, Derry, Armagh and Tyrone; most will be of Scottish origin. Williams is less common in Ulster than in Leinster and Munster. It is more common in Co. Antrim than elsewhere and most will be of English or Welsh origin.

The personal name William derives from the Old German Willihelm and when introduced into Britain by the Normans, it became the single most popular personal name in England and remained so until it was superseded by John. It gave rise to a host of surnames including Williamson and Williams but by far the most common was Williams. It is currently the third most numerous name in England, the first being Smith and the second, Jones. In Wales William was made Gwilym, which became the surname Gwilliams and then Williams.

Williams was never common in Scotland which retained the longer Williamson. This was very common in the Lowlands. The Highland name MacWilliam was also anglicised as Williamson (*see* MacWilliams). There were MacWilliams or Williamsons, a sept of Clan Gunn, who descended from a later chief of the clan called William. There were also Williamsons in Caithness, a sept of Clan Mackay.

Charles Williams, 1838–1904, the war correspondent, was born at Coleraine, Co. Derry. As a reporter for the *Evening Standard* and the *Daily Chronicle*, he covered almost every war in Europe and Africa in a thirty-year period, from the Franco-German War in 1870 to the recapture of Khartoum in 1898. He also founded the Press Club.

WILSON

Wilson is one of the most common names in the English-speaking world. It is among the first ten names in the USA and in Scotland and among the first fifteen in England. In Ireland it is one of the thirty most common names and there it is by far the most common purely English name. It is even more common in Ulster; it is among the first five names in Co. Antrim and the first ten in counties Down, Fermanagh and Tyrone and is common too in counties Armagh and Derry. In the province as a whole it is the third most common name.

Wilson is second only to Williams as one of the many surnames that derive from William (*see* Williamson). As such it sprang up in many independent places in England and Scotland. It has been estimated that four-fifths of the Ulster Wilsons are of Scottish ancestry.

The name was very common all over the Lowlands, but from the sixteenth century especially so in Glasgow. In Caithness and Sutherland to the north the Wilsons were a sept of Clan Gunn, descendants of William, one of the sons of the fifteenth-century George Gunn the Crowner (coroner of Caithness). To the east, around Banffshire and Edinburgh, the Wilsons were a sept of Clan Innes.

William Edward Wilson, 1851–1908, was born in Belfast. A self-taught astronomer, he was a pioneer in the study of the sun's temperature and sun spots. It is believed that the ancestors of the twenty-eighth president of the USA, Woodrow Wilson, 1856–1924, were from Co. Down.

WOODS

Though found in all the provinces of Ireland, Woods is most common in Ulster, particularly in counties Antrim, Armagh, Down, Monaghan, Tyrone and Fermanagh. The English name Wood, from the Middle English *atte wode*, 'at the wood', is among the fifteen most common names in England and Wales and is numerous too in Scotland. In Ireland, particularly Ulster, many names have had an 's' added in recent centuries. Woods, which is not common in England or Scotland, is ten times more common than Wood in Ulster.

Many of the name Woods in Ulster will be of Irish stock, Woods having been used as an anglicisation of several Gaelic names on the assumption that the Gaelic word *coill*, meaning 'wood', formed an element in the Gaelic name. Only in the case of MacEnhill was this assumption correct.

MacEnhill is in Gaelic Mac Conchoille, from *cú*, genitive *con*, 'hound' and *coill* 'wood'. The MacEnhills were a sept located near Omagh, Co. Tyrone, who were hereditary keepers of the Bell of Drumragh.

The Donegal and Monaghan name Coyle (*see* Coyle) is in Gaelic Mac

Giolla Chomhghaill, 'son of the devotee of (St) Comgall'. It is also found as MacIlhoyle.

MacQuilly is a Roscommon name, which in Monaghan is made MacGilly and Magilly. In Gaelic it is Mac an Choiligh, 'son of the cock'. It is also anglicised as Cox. (Cox is an English name and derives from the use of 'cock' as an affectionate term for a boy, particularly an apprentice or a servant. This was also added to names as a pet form, for example, Wilcock.)

Quilty or Kielty is a Munster name, in Gaelic Ó Caoilte, which has in Ulster occasionally been made Woods.

The Co. Tyrone name MacIlhone or MacElhone is in Gaelic Mac Giolla Chomhgháin, 'son of the devotee of (St) Comgan'.

Each of these names to a greater or lesser extent was anglicised to Woods. Indeed, as late as 1900, Woods was being used interchangeably with MacElhill (a variant of MacIlhoyle) around Drumquin, near Castlederg, Co. Tyrone; with MacIlhun and MacIlhone around Ballymoney in Antrim; and with MacIlhone near Blackwaterstown in Armagh. It was also being used with Ellwood and Elwood around Moira in Co. Down, and with Smallwoods at Ballykelly, near Limavady, Co. Derry.

WRAY *see* Rea

WRIGHT

In Ireland, outside of Dublin, this name is common only in Ulster, and particularly in counties Antrim, Down and Armagh. It can be of English, Scottish or Irish origin.

In England, where it is one of the twenty most common names, it is more numerous in the north. It derives from the Old English *wyrhta* or *wryhta*, which means a 'worker, chiefly in wood, a carpenter or joiner'. In Lowland Scotland it has the same derivation and was first recorded in the Ragman Rolls of 1296.

In the Highlands, however, the Wrights were a sept of Clan MacIntyre, whose name in Gaelic, Mac an tSaoir, means 'son of the wright'. The Irish Gaelic equivalent gives the name MacAteer. This in Co. Fermanagh was anglicised to Wright, but more generally in Ulster MacAteer was made Carpenter or MacIntyre (*see* MacIntyre).

In mid-nineteenth-century Antrim the greatest concentration of the name was in the barony of Lower Belfast, and in Down, in Lower Iveagh, particularly the parish of Magherally. The name MacIntyre is common in north Antrim and north Derry but not in the Glens of Antrim. It has been suggested that the Wrights of the southern Glens are MacIntyres from west Argyll.

The Revd William Wright, 1837–99, was born at Finard, Co. Down. He was for ten years a missionary in Damascus and became proficient in eastern languages. He wrote largely on biblical subjects but is best remembered for his controversial *The Brontës in Ireland*.

WYLIE (*also* Wiley)

In Ireland this name is virtually exclusive to Ulster and is most common in Co. Antrim. In the mid-nineteenth century it was most common in counties Antrim, Tyrone and Armagh, and in the mid-seventeenth century in counties Antrim, Tyrone and Donegal. Bardsley claims that in England the name derives from the village of Wyly in Wiltshire, but in Scotland, where it is very common, it is accepted as being a variation of Willie, diminutive of William.

Samuel Brown Wylie DD, 1773–1852, was born near Ballymena, Co. Antrim, but emigrated to America in his twenties. He became professor of theology in the Reformed Presbyterian Church and professor of ancient languages in the University of Philadelphia.

YOUNG

This name is common in Leinster and Munster, particularly in Dublin and Cork, but two-thirds of the Youngs in Ireland are in Ulster. It is most numerous in counties Antrim, Tyrone, Down and Derry. It can be of English or Scottish origin. A few in Ulster may be of Irish or Norman stock.

The name in both England and Scotland derives from the Old English *geong*, 'young', and was used to distinguish a father and son of the same Christian name. It is one of the twenty most common names in Scotland where John Yong de Dyngvale was the first on record in 1342. There were also Youngs, one of the lesser of the riding clans of the Scottish Borders, who lived in East Teviotdale in the Scottish Middle March. Many members of the riding clans sought new lives in Ulster when the Borders were 'pacified' by James VI in the decade after 1603.

The Youngs of Culdaff in Donegal claim descent from a settler from Devon. The Young family of Co. Cavan bought Bailieborough Castle from the Baillies. One of them, Sir John Young, became governor of New South Wales and later governor general of Canada. The town of Young in New South Wales is named after him.

The name was actually introduced into Ireland as le Jeune and le Jouen by the Normans in the twelfth century. It is possible that a few in Ulster might be of this origin. The Irish Gaelic epithet óg, 'young', which was often appended to Irish forenames for the same reason as 'young' was in England, occasionally gave rise to the anglicised Young as a surname. So some in Ulster will be of Irish origin.

GLOSSARY

antiquary   a collector or student of antiquities

armiger   a squire carrying the armour of a medieval knight

attaint   to convict of a crime punishable by forfeiture of estate and extinction of civil rights

bawn   a fortified enclosure

brehon   from the Irish Gaelic *breitheamh*, meaning 'judge'. The Gaelic Brehon System of law persisted in many parts of Ireland until the seventeenth century.

by-name   a sobriquet or nickname

Cenél   Irish Gaelic, from *cineál,* meaning 'race' or 'family'. Thus Cenél Eoghain, the 'race of Eoghan'.

clan   from the Gaelic *clann* which means literally 'children'. The anglicised word 'clan' has come to refer to the specifically Scottish form of social organisation in the Highlands in which a common ancestry was not strictly essential. For this reason the word is not generally applied to family groups in Ireland. (*See* sept.)

clearances   the removal of tenants from estates in the Highlands to make way for the more profitable sheep farming; a long process but mainly concentrated in the first half of the nineteenth century

co-arb   from the Irish Gaelic *comharba*, meaning the 'successor to the founder of a church or monastery'. Thus where an abbot was co-arb, he was a descendant of the saint who had founded the monastery and was his 'heir'.

crowner   a coroner. From 1357 until the eighteenth century the Crown appointed coroners in Scotland. They held inquests into murders and had powers of arrest.

Cruthin   the Cruthin or Cruithne were the Pictish people that inhabited Ireland before the arrival of the Gaels

Cymric   relating to the Welsh people and their language

Dalcassian   from the Irish Gaelic *Dál gCais. Dál* means 'tribe' or 'people' and the Dalcassians included all the main septs of Munster.

Dalriadic   from Dál Riada, an ancient kingdom of north Antrim whence in the fifth or sixth century a colony was founded in Kintyre and Argyll, the origin of the Scottish kingdom of Dalriada

diaspora   a dispersion or spreading, as of people originally belonging to one nation or having a common culture

diminutive	strictly, a word formed from another by the use of a suffix expressing smallness; thus Rob-in, meaning 'little Rob'
epithet	descriptive adjective or name
eponymous	name-giving
erenagh	from the Irish Gaelic *airchinneach*, meaning 'hereditary steward of church lands'. A family would hold the ecclesiastical office and the right to the church or monastery lands, the incumbent at any one time being the erenagh.
escheat	the reversion of ownership of property to the Crown, especially subsequent to treason or rebellion
galloglass	from the Irish Gaelic *gallóglach*, a heavily armed mercenary soldier mainly of Scottish origin
Garda Síochána	the police force of the Republic of Ireland; literally, 'guardians of the peace'
genitive	indicating possessive case
Gille	from the Scots Gaelic *gille*, meaning 'lad' or 'youth', 'devotee' or 'servant'
Giolla	from the Irish Gaelic *giolla*, meaning 'lad' or 'youth', 'devotee' or 'servant'
Ilk	'of that Ilk' was a title taken by those whose surname was the same as that of their estate. Thus Johnstone of that Ilk was Johnstone of Johnstone.
laird	a Scottish word which means 'landowner'
local origin	A surname is of local origin when it derives from a specific locality, place or building.
Mac-	from the Gaelic *mac*, meaning 'son'
Mag-	in Gaelic, a form of Mac- often used when the prefix precedes a vowel or silent consonant
matronymic	a name deriving from a mother or other female ancestor
Nic-	from the Gaelic Ní Mhic, and used as the feminine form of Mac-
O'	from the Gaelic Ó, meaning 'grandson', 'grandchild' or 'descendant'; Ní is the feminine form of Ó, meaning 'daughter' or 'descendant'
ollav	from the Irish Gaelic *ollamh*, meaning 'learned man' or 'master'
palatine	(of an individual) possessing royal prerogatives in a territory
Pale (the)	the area, centred on Dublin, under full control of the English Crown. Its size varied greatly throughout the later medieval period.
patronymic	a name deriving from a father or other male ancestor

Pictish	pertaining to the Picts, pre-Celtic people of north Britain, from the Late Latin *Pictī*, meaning 'painted men'
Picto-Cymric	pertaining to the Pictish people of Wales also known as the Prydyn
Plantation (Ulster)	the redistribution of escheated lands after the defeat of the Ulster Gaelic lords and the 'Flight of the Earls' in 1607. Only counties Donegal, Derry, Tyrone, Armagh, Fermanagh and Cavan were actually 'planted', portions of land there being distributed to English and Scottish chief undertakers and undertakers. These were then responsible for settling numbers of English and Scottish families on their lands and for the building of bawns.
Planter	one who acquired lands during the Ulster Plantation Settlement
progenitor	historically, the founder of a particular family
race	a large group of people of common ancestry
rapparee	from the Irish Gaelic *ropaire*, meaning 'highwayman'
reive	to take away by force, particularly livestock
riding clans	the name given to a large group of families on both sides of the English/Scottish Borders. They lived by a particular social system, the economy of which was sustained by the rustling of cattle and livestock. They were thus also known as the reivers, rievers or reavers.
seneschal	steward of a large medieval household
sept	a family group of shared ancestry living in the same locality
servitor	resident English administrative or military official who was granted lands during the Plantation
style	to call or name by a particular title
Tanist	from the Irish Gaelic *tánaiste,* meaning 'heir presumptive to the chiefly title'. In Ireland the Tanist was not necessarily the son of the chief but was elected by the sept.
territorial origin	A surname is of territorial origin when the original bearer took the name from his own lands or the area which he ruled.
toponymic	a surname deriving from a placename
tributary	a sept subject to a larger sept which was required to pay tribute to, and take part in, the wars of that larger sept
Uí	genitive singular and neuter plural of the Gaelic Ó; used in historical sept names

undertakers	powerful English or Scottish landowners who undertook the plantation of British settlers on the lands they were granted
vassal	a feudal tenant, bound to his superior by oath, and responsible for military service on the superior's behalf
vill	a village
Wild Geese	the term for expatriate Irishmen and their descendants who fought, often in Irish Brigades, for the imperial armies of Europe in the seventeenth and eighteenth centuries

SELECT BIBLIOGRAPHY

Adam, Frank *The Clans, Septs and Regiments of the Scottish Highlands* (revised by Sir Thomas Innes of Learney), Edinburgh and London Johnston & Bacon, 1970

Bardsley, Charles Wareing. *Our English Surnames: Their Sources and Significations*, London, Chatto & Windus, 1873

Black, George F. *The Surnames of Scotland: Their Origin, Meaning, and History*, New York, New York Public Library, 1962

Boylan, Henry. *A Dictionary of Irish Biography*, Dublin, Gill & Macmillan, 1978

Byrne, Francis John. *Irish Kings and High-Kings*, London, Batsford, 1973

Crone, John S. *A Concise Dictionary of Irish Biography*, Dublin, Talbot Press, 1937

de Breffny, Brian. *Irish Family Names, Arms, Origins and Locations*, Dublin, Gill & Macmillan, 1982

Fraser, George MacDonald. *The Steel Bonnets; The Story of the Anglo-Scottish Border Reivers*, London, Collins Harvill, 1986

Gillespie, Raymond. *Colonial Ulster, The Settlement of East Ulster*, Cork, Cork University Press, 1985

Greehan, Ida. *Irish Family Names, Highlights of 50 Family Histories*, London, Johnston & Bacon, 1973

Hayes-McCoy, Gerard A. *Scots Mercenary Forces in Ireland (1565–1603)*, Dublin and London, Burns Oates & Washbourne, 1937

Hill, Revd George. *An Historical Account of the MacDonnells of Antrim Including Notices of Some Other Septs, Irish and Scottish*, Belfast, Archer & Sons, 1873

Hill, Revd George. *The Stewarts of Ballintoy with Notices of Other Families of the District*, Coleraine, John McCombie, 1865

Johnston, James B. *Place-Names of Scotland*, London, John Murray, 1934

Livingstone, Peadar. *The Fermanagh Story: A Documented History of the County Fermanagh from the Earliest Times to the Present Day*, Enniskillen, Clogher Historical Society, 1969

Livingstone, Peadar. *The Monaghan Story: A Documented History of the County Monaghan from the Earliest Times to 1976*, Enniskillen, Clogher Historical Society, 1980

Mac Giolla Domhnaigh, Pádraig. *Some Anglicised Surnames in Ireland*, Dublin, Gael Co-operative Society, 1923

McKerral, A. *Kintyre in the Seventeenth Century*, Edinburgh and London, Oliver & Boyd, 1948

MacLysaght, Edward. *Bibliography of Irish Family History*, Dublin, Irish Academic Press, 1982

MacLysaght, Edward. *More Irish Families*, Dublin, Irish Academic Press, 1982

MacLysaght, Edward. *Irish Families: Their Names, Arms and Origins*, Dublin, Irish Academic Press, 1985

MacLysaght, Edward. *The Surnames of Ireland*, Dublin, Irish Academic Press, 1985

Martin, Angus. *Kintyre, The Hidden Past*, Edinburgh, John Donald, 1984

Martine, Roddy. *Scottish Clan and Family Names: Their Arms, Origins and Tartans*, Edinburgh, John Bartholomew, 1987

Matheson, Robert E. *Special Report on Surnames in Ireland*, Dublin, HMSO, 1894

Matheson, Robert E. *Varieties and Synonymes of Surnames and Christian Names in Ireland*, Dublin, HMSO, 1901

Morgan, T.J. and Prys Morgan. *Welsh Surnames*, Cardiff, University of Wales Press, 1985

Mullin, Revd T.H. and Revd J.E. Mullan. *The Ulster Clans: O'Mullan, O'Kane and O'Mellan*, Belfast, privately published, 1966

O'Hart, John. *Irish Pedigrees, or the Origin and Stem of the Irish Nation*, Dublin, M.H. Gill & Son, 1881

Reaney, P.H. *A Dictionary of British Surnames*, London, Routledge & Kegan Paul, 1958

Webb, Alfred. *A Compendium of Irish Biography*, Dublin, M.H. Gill & Son, 1878

Woulfe, Revd Patrick. *Irish Names and Surnames*, Baltimore, Genealogical Publishing Company, 1967

PERIODICALS

Clogher Record
Donegal Annual
Familia
Family Links
The Glynns
Irish Genealogist
Irish Link
Journal of the Upper Ards Historical Society
Seanchas Ardmhacha
The Shakin's of the Bag
Ulster Journal of Archaeology
Ulster Local Studies
Ulster Origins

INDEX OF SURNAMES

de Nicol 205
de Nogent 206
de Paduinan 98
de Ramesie 217
de Ros 224
de St Martin 187–8
de Somerville 234
de Ver 248
de Wra 218
De Yermond 151
Deehan 52
Deere 52
Deérmott 151
Deighan 52
del Bois 18
Delap 60, 118
Dempsey 50–1
Dempster 50–1
D'Evelyn 51
Devers 52
Devine 51
Devitt 151
Devlin 51, 53, 140
d'Exeter 106
Deyermott 151
Diamond MacCloskey 144
Diarmid 151
Diarmod 151
Diarmond 151
Dickson 52
Diermott 151
Dinkin 54
Diurmagh 151
Diver 52
Dixon 52
Dobbin 222
Doherty 52–3, 75
Dolan 53
Donachie 54
Donaghy 53–6, 216, 222
Donald 154
Donaldson 38, 54–5, 154–5
Donegan 54
Donillson 55, 154
Donleavy 60
Donlevy 60
Donnachie 54, 83, 219, 222
Donnellson 55, 154
Donnelly 55
Donnelson 55
Donoghue 55–6
Donohoe 54–6
Doogan 56
Doohey 59
Doran 50, 56–7
Dornan 56
Dorrian 56

Dougall 85
Dougan 56
Dougherty 52
Douglas 12, 57
Dowey 59
Dowling 53
Downey 57–8
Doyle 58, 155
Drain 92
Drummond 85, 189
Dubhagán 56
Dubucán 56
Duff 58
Duffin 58
Duffy 58–9, 64, 86, 92
Dugan 56
Dunbar 89
Duncan 53–4
Dunlap 61
Dunleavey 60, 66
Dunleavy 60, 66, 123, 180
Dunlief 60
Dunlop 60, 118
Dunn 61
Dunne 61
Dunnigan 48
Durrian 50

Eadie 7
Eakin 8
Eakins 8
Early 125, 212
Edgar 6
Edzear 6
Egan 8
Ekin 8
Elchinder 9
Eliott 62
Elliot 11, 46, 61–2, 202
Elliott 11, 61–2, 82, 104, 228
Ellis 61–2
Ellwood 252
Elroy 166
Elshander 9
Elshinder 9
Elwald 61
Elwold 61
Elwood 252
Ennis 163–4
Eoghan 63
Ervine 101
Erwin 101–2
Esnor 9
Eves 183
Ewan 63
Ewen 63
Ewing 63

'MAC' NAMES (ANGLICISED)
('M'', 'MC', 'MAC'
ARE ALL RENDERED 'MAC')

MacAleary 142
MacAleavey 60
MacAlee 66, 120
MacAleenan 121, 126
MacAleer 144
MacAleevy 60
MacAlesher 84, 129
MacAlinden 128, 130
MacAlinion 121, 126, 128
MacAlister 128–9
MacAll 135
MacAllan 9
MacAllen 9–10, 135
MacAllion 135
MacAllister 8–9, 128–9, 152, 191
MacAlpine 84
MacAlshender 9
MacAnally 66, 178
MacAnaul 149
MacAndrew 10, 223
MacAneaney 130
MacAneany 129
MacAneave 8, 70
MacAnelly 203
MacAneny 93, 129–30
MacAnilly 203
MacAnulla 149, 178
MacAnully 178
MacAnulty 180
Macanward 245–6
MacAra 114
MacAragh 181
MacArdle 130
MacAready 147
MacAree 114–15, 158–9
Macaree 114
Macarooney 223
MacArthur 9
MacArtney 138
Macartney 138
MacAshinagh 71
MacAteer 166–7, 252
MacAteggart 238
MacAtinney 71
MacAtinny 71, 228
MacAulay 130–1, 135, 197
MacAuley 130–1, 134
Macauley 131
Macaus 241
MacAuslan 24, 139
Macauslan 139
MacAvinney 107
MacAvish 241
MacAvoy 156
MacAvweer 248
MacAward 245
MacAwley 131

MacBain 166, 182
MacBarron 13–14
MacBaxter 14
MacBean 166
MacBennet 16
MacBennett 16
MacBeth 149, 182–3
Macbethe 139
MacBrady 21
MacBratney 74
MacBrearty 150
MacBreen 22
MacBrian 22
MacBride 131–2
MacBrien 22
MacBrin 25–6
MacBurney 25
MacCabe 132–3
MacCadden 127
MacCafferky 133
MacCafferty 133–4, 138
MacCaffrey 14, 34, 133–4
MacCagherty 133
MacCaghery 134
MacCaghey 138–9
MacCague 169
MacCaharty 133
MacCaherty 133
MacCahery 134
MacCahey 139
MacCahill 134
MacCahon 139
MacCaig 168–9
Maccaig 169
MacCaigue 169
MacCall 37, 134–5, 140
Maccall 135
MacCallan 135–6
MacCallen 37, 135
MacCallion 10, 29, 37, 46, 135–6
MacCallister 129
MacCalvey 170
MacCambridge 34
MacCamie 73, 103
MacCampbell 29
MacCance 164
MacCann 30, 136
MacCannon 29, 38, 136–7
MacCardney 138
MacCarn 137
MacCarney 109
MacCarroll 32, 136
MacCarry 31, 158–9
MacCartan 79, 137–8
MacCarten 137–8
MacCarthy 133–4, 138, 190
MacCarthy Mór 38

MacQuistan 99
MacQuisten 99
MacQuiston 98–9
MacQuitty 249
MacQuorte 146
Macra 147
Macrach 147
Macrae 147
Macraith 147
MacRanalds 220
MacRankin 217–18
MacRannall 220
MacReadie 147
MacRedie 147
Macredie 147
MacRee 147
MacReedy 147
MacReidy 147
MacReynold 220
MacReynolds 220
MacRitchie 221
MacRobb 221
MacRobert 222
MacRory 148, 153, 219
Macrory 148, 152
MacRuer 148
MacRury 148
MacShan 105
MacShane 105, 181
MacShannachan 229
MacShannon 228
MacSorley 28, 117, 182
MacSuile 116
MacSweeney 23, 66, 117, 237–8
MacSwine 238
MacSwiney 238
MacTaggart 238
MacTaghlin 99
MacTague 168
MacTaldrach 239
MacTaldridge 239
MacTavish 98, 240–2
MacTaylor 239
MacTeague 168
MacTeer 167
MacTeigue 168
MacThomas 98, 240
MacTier 167
MacTourner 243
MacTurley 81
Maculagh 149
MacUre 169, 211
MacVeagh 182–3
MacVeigh 156, 182–3
MacVey 183
MacVitty 14
MacVurich 48, 201

MacWade 181
MacWalrick 111
MacWard 13, 245–6
MacWatt 246–7
MacWatters 247
MacWattie 14, 246–7
MacWatty 14
MacWhannel 154
MacWhatty 246
MacWhinney 24
MacWhinnie 24–5
MacWhirter 90
MacWhisten 99
MacWhite 249
MacWhitty 249
MacWiggan 163
MacWilliam 181, 183, 250
MacWilliams 181, 183, 250

Madole 155
Madowell 155
Maffett 193
Mag Aoidh 183
Mag Aonghuis 163
Mag Aonghusa 163
Mag Cuirc 165
Mag Eochaidhín 163
Mag Fhearadhaigh 158
Mag Fhinn 114, 160
Mag Fhionnghaile 159
Mag Mhuirneacháin 80
Mag Oirc 165
Mag Raghainn 220
Mag Raighne 83
Mag Raith 162
Mag Roibín 86
Mag Shamhráin 161
Mag Thoirdealbhaigh 81
Mag Uag 41
Mag Ualghairg 160
Mag Uidhir 185
Mag Uiginn 163
Magauran 161
Magee 165, 183–4
Magennis 7, 163–4
Magill 184–5
Magilly 252
Maginn 114, 160
Maglammery 195
Magon 161
Magonagle 160
Magone 105, 171
Magorlick 160
Magourley 131
Magowan 161
Magrath 162
Magraw 162